Different Roles, Different Voices

HarperCollinsCollegePublishers

Different Roles, Different Voices

Women and Politics in the United States and Europe

Edited by

MARIANNE GITHENS
Goucher College

PIPPA NORRIS
Harvard University and Edinburgh University

JONI LOVENDUSKI
Loughborough University

HarperCollins*CollegePublishers*

Sponsoring Editor: Leo Wiegman
Project Editor: Diane Williams
Design Supervisor: Wendy Fredericks
Cover Design: Kay Cannizzaro
Production Manager: Mike Kemper
Compositor: R. R. Donnelley & Sons Company
Printer, Cover Printer, and Binder: Malloy Lithographing, Inc.

For permission to use copyrighted material, grateful acknowledgment is made to the copyright holders on pp. 275 – 277, which are hereby made part of this copyright page.

Different Roles, Different Voices: Women and Politics in the United States and Europe

Copyright © 1994 by HarperCollins College Publishers

Library of Congress Cataloging-in-Publication Data

Different roles, different voices : women and politics in the United States and
  Europe : revised version / edited by Marianne Githens,
  Pippa Norris, Joni Lovenduski.
    p. cm.
  Includes bibliographical references.
  ISBN 0-06-501306-9
  1. Women in politics—United States. 2. Women in politics-
  -Europe. I. Githens, Marianne. II. Norris, Pippa.
  III. Lovenduski, Joni.
  HQ1391.U5D54 1994
  320'.082—dc20   93-41719
                                                   CIP

93 94 95 96 9 8 7 6 5 4 3 2 1

Contents

CHAPTER 4

Political Recruitment   85
Pippa Norris

CHAPTER 5

Political Issues   122
Marianne Githens

CHAPTER 6

The Women's Movement   172
Marianne Githens

CHAPTER 7

Feminism and Its Political Context   201
Joni Lovenduski

CHAPTER 8

Feminist Political Ideas   229
Joni Lovenduski

CHAPTER 9

Difference and Feminist Politics   250
Joni Lovenduski

Introduction

During the 1970s and 1980s, there was a burgeoning of new publications on women and politics by activists, academics, and journalists. Gender, which had previously been ignored by mainstream political science, increasingly became the focus of analysis. The expansion of primary research questioned established shibboleths and developed new knowledge. While uncovering the clues to some long-standing key questions about women's role in the political arena, investigators discovered new puzzles. In turn, there was a significant growth in the number of university courses in this area. Once peripheral to political science, the subject of women and politics entered the mainstream agenda.

Just as traditional political science was divided into different streams, so was the newer work on women and politics. Three basic approaches, three different emphases or voices, emerged from the study of political behavior, social movements, and political theory, respectively. The first concentrated on women's participation in traditional political activity: voting and electoral behavior; the general characteristics of women active in political affairs, including the significance of social class and professional and occupational backgrounds; patterns of political recruitment; participation in the activities of political parties; the scope and diversity of female office holding at the elective, appointed, and bureaucratic levels; the linkage of women officeholders either to their general constituencies or to women; the existence of a "gender gap"; the circumstances that have stimulated women's increased visibility in politics, particularly those created by the processes of rapid social change; and, given the chronic underrepresentation of women in traditional political activity, the constraints on their participation. The central questions for this approach have been why women were largely absent from political elites; whether they participated in other forms of political activity, such as parties and pressure groups; and whether women's behavior was any different from men's.

Early efforts to explore women's participation in the traditional political arena were basically descriptive or mapping exercises. Later research centered around explanations for why there were so few women. Some studies investigated institutional constraints that might explain the paucity of women in the political elite (in the United States: Kirkpatrick, 1974; Diamond, 1977; Githens, 1977; Welch, 1978; Rule, 1981, 1993; Schramm, 1981; Mandel, 1981; Carroll, 1985; Epstein and Coser, 1981; Baxter and Lansing, 1983; Sapiro, 1983; in Europe: Vallance, 1979, 1986; Randall, 1987; Lovenduski, 1986; Lovenduski and Hill, 1981; Haavio-Mannila, 1985; Hernes and Voje, 1980, Bashevkin, 1985; Norris, 1985, 1987). Others examined the impact of prevailing definitions of women's appropriate role in society, such as the impact of sex roles, the effects of socialization, and the development of political understanding in girls on their subsequent participation (Iglitzin, 1974; Orum et al., 1977; Prestage, 1977; Kelly and Boutilier, 1978). Others focused on the relationship of socialization to political ambition and upward mobility in politics (Perkins and Fowlkes, 1980; Farah, 1976), and still others studied the implications of assigning to women the role of wife and mother as their primary, and perhaps even exclusive, function (Stoper, 1977; Githens and Prestage, 1977).

Research on women in the traditional political arena followed the methods established in the study of mass and elite political behavior, using materials from social surveys and personal interviews. It tended to treat the subject matter with the same methods and rigorous canons of evidence as any other subfield of political science. This tradition, which started with Maurice Duverger's seminal work on *The Political Role of Women* in 1955, took the theoretical parameters of the mainstream discipline for granted. Although inevitably raising some critical questions, this approach regarded traditional forms of political behavior as the norm, and it accepted the notion of woman as the outsider; hence, the central question was why women did not conform to expectations.

Although this approach proved extremely useful in generating information about women and politics, it tended to obfuscate the fact that, contrary to conventional wisdom, women had a long and rich history of political participation. Sometimes their efforts were directed toward the improvement of their own status, as was the case in the nineteenth- and early twentieth-century suffrage movements, or more recently in movements concerned with reproductive rights or equal status; and sometimes toward community-wide concerns, such as peace, the establishment or expansion of social welfare programs, or even participation in the overthrow of a repressive political system (such as the *ancien régime*) or involvement in guerrilla groups (such as the Shining Path in Peru). The lack of congruence between women's actual participation in community affairs and their portrayal as politically passive was based on their limited representation in traditional political institutions. A different approach to the subject of women and politics was essential. Male models for determining participation, leadership, influence, or political effectiveness were derived from formal participation in the public sphere or marketplace, and they simply excluded large categories of women's activities. Some scholars began to alter their definition of politics to embrace a much broader range of activities, including an involvement in social movements and campaigns to change public policy. Hence, the study of social movements, particularly those concerned with changing public policy to accommodate the needs of women, emerged as a second way of looking at women and politics.

The research reflecting this second approach focused mainly on the relationship of women's movements and women's campaigns to the public policy arena, and it covered a wide variety of issues. Several important works dealt with American efforts to enact the Equal Rights Amendment (ERA) (Mansbridge, 1986; Boles, 1979; Hoff-Wilson, 1986). Others concentrated on a broader range of policies concerned with equal status and welfare in the United States (Stetson, 1991; Boneparth and Stoper, 1988; Kendrigan, 1984; Gelb and Palley, 1987; Gordon, 1991; Diamond, 1983; Piven and Fox, 1988; Gelpi et al., 1986; Sidel, 1986). Some of the work, like Gelb and Palley's *Women and Public Policies*, attempted to look beyond the American experience, but the unique character of American politics, especially in terms of the role of pressure groups and the nature of American political parties, often limited the usefulness of public policy models. A considerable body of literature focusing on the women's movement emerged on both sides of the Atlantic and contributed a great deal to an understanding of multiple dimensions of women's political participation (Freeman, 1975; Lovenduski and Outshoorn, 1986; Dahlerup, 1986; Katzenstein and Mueller, 1987; Bystydzienski, 1992; Bashevkin, 1985; Lovenduski, 1986).

Work on social movements drew substantially on the broader literature of political science, history, sociology, and psychology in order to develop its paradigms. By its nature, this approach was less amenable to the canons of political behavior. Hence, rather than surveying evidence, the research concentrated on historical archives, participant observation, reading primary materials, personal interviews with activists, legal studies, and models of the policy-making process. A diversity of methods was imperative for several reasons. Given the mélange of interest groups, campaigns, and women's groups, no one method was capable of dealing satisfactorily with the nuances of the subject matter. This was especially true when cross-cultural research was attempted. Public policy covers a wide range of issues—legislation on equal pay, funding for shelters for battered women, provision of adequate child care for working mothers, battling sexual harassment, banning nuclear missiles, ensuring women reproductive choice. No single approach to investigation is appropriate in all areas. Diverse methods were also needed to understand the rich complexity in each country. Simple policy-making models failed to illuminate a wider comparative context where there were different concerns, issues, strategies, and organizations.

These two approaches, or different voices, generated new knowledge and insights about factors that structured women's lives. In part stimulated by these questions, a third approach drawing on the tradition of political theory and philosophy attempted to move beyond an examination of women as political actors and social movements to explore the implications of the omission and subordination of women in political thought. This approach applied a new critique to the established perspectives on issues such as citizenship, democracy, and equality. It attempted to rethink key concepts central to our understanding of feminism, including the nature of gender and the relationship of feminism with deep-rooted ideological divisions among liberals, socialists, radicals, and conservatives.

One strand in this third approach, particularly strong in America, has been described as the "transforming paradigm" (Ackelsberg and Diamond, 1987). Its premise is that existing paradigms have failed to acknowledge the nature and consequences of structured relationships of domination and subordination. For far too long, women, as an oppressed group, were defined in terms of their oppression, or their deviation from male norms. As a consequence, women's differences, as well as their culture, were ignored. In defining women as "other," as an aberration, political science did not acknowledge women's integrity, values, and contributions. The focus of research must be gender differences not as deficiencies, but as the expression of an authentic voice.

For those who elected this strand, the notion of a woman centered in a different value system created different expectations for men and women. In their view, one consequence was a different ethical and emotional dimension in women. Proponents argued that women operate with a different set of assumptions that result in their having their own worldview, their own interaction patterns, and their own policy agendas (Chodorow, 1978; Gilligan, 1982; Elshtain, 1982; MacKinnon, 1988). Such assertions about gender differences implied that women have a different perception both of politics and their role in it. Traditional conceptions of politics were, to a large extent, irrelevant to women and their needs. Indeed, Gilligan's observations about the differences between girls' and boys' reactions to determining the rules by which they play suggested that women would be, at best, uncomfortable with, and more likely repulsed by, the dynamics of traditional political activity. This strand contended that existing paradigms ignored gender differences. Women must "find their voice." This meant an exploration of the nature, origins, and implications of women's consciousness. In other words, a feminist standpoint must be articulated.

One of the primary vehicles for the articulation of this feminist standpoint was the women's movement, which allowed women to find their own voice, to express a feminist consciousness, and to acknowledge the legitimacy of gender differences. Unlike the treatment of the women's movement in the second approach, which was concerned with policy change, this third approach concentrated on the issue of identity. Traditional political activity, such as participating in the affairs of established political parties, running for public office, seeking political appointment in the executive branch of government, or filling positions in the governmental bureaucracy, interfered with the development of identity of that voice and thwarted the creation of policies in which women were genuinely interested.

Other strands in this third approach focused on women's culture from a different perspective altogether and reached quite different conclusions. These emphasized the issue of citizenship and its implications for women's identity. As time passed, feminists' out-of-hand rejection of traditional political activity gave way to a strategy of restructuring political institutions to make them more "woman-friendly." Feminists addressed the gendered nature of politics and attempted to understand what was "masculine" about political power. This work reflected the range and diversity of political science and feminist scholarship, including theoretical, philosophical, and empirical research. Kathy Jones and Anna Jonasdottir criticized mainstream and feminist treatments of the idea of political interest in their critique of the limitations of the language of political science (Jones and Jonasdottir, 1988). Drawing on the insights of two decades of research on equal opportunity, Cynthia Cockburn (1991) investigated the masculinity of British organizations. Sophie Watson (1990) and others used the insights of discourse analysis to examine the fraternal ethos of Australian state institutions and Susan Moller Okin (1992) offered a reworking of Rawls's theory of justice that accommodated gender equality.

Just as the first approach proved valuable in locating women within traditional politics, so too have the second and third provided important insights into the nature of women's power and their vulnerability by highlighting the diversity and meaning of their roles in society. The essential challenge, and originality, of the study of women and politics is that it forces us to examine its subject matter simultaneously on three levels: political behavior, social movements, and political theory. At the beginning, the research reflected a basic dichotomy not unusual in the discipline of political science: women were studied either in terms of their role as holders of public office—elective, appointive, or administrative—or in the context of the development, processes, and activities of women's movements. Carroll (1985) attempted to weave these two patterns of participation together, but the emphasis was still on the implications of a feminist label for women candidates rather than on a systematic examination of the interaction between women's movements and women officeholders and the implications of this interaction for their public roles.

The collision of these three approaches, which is at the core of the subject of women and politics, may make it prickly and uncomfortable for mainstream political science, but the field is also innovative, exciting, and stimulating for those willing to take a risk. By simultaneously raising questions about the nature of political institutions, the requirements set for any politician entering public life, and feminist concerns about nonhierarchical, collaborative leadership, the study of women and politics provides a fresh perspective on established questions and provides insights about the role of the outsider which may be useful in the broader study of minorities.

This reader is organized around the three different voices characterizing the study of women and politics. Chapter 1 examines some of the challenges mainstream political science has posed and presents contributions of feminist theory to broadening the scope of inquiry about what constitutes political activity. Chapters 2 through 4, concerned with women's political behavior, reflect the first voice. In conformity with the traditional methods used in the study of political behavior, these extracts represent recent research on women's political participation, recruitment, and public opinion. Chapters 5 and 6 exemplify the second voice, including recent work on the women's movement and public policy from a cross-cultural perspective and within specific national settings. Chapters 7 through 9 explore the third voice by focusing on feminist thought as it has affected notions about citizenship, identity, and women's culture.

The entire process of selecting chapter topics and the respective essays for each chapter has been a collaborative effort among the three of us. However, we did assume individual responsibility for writing the chapter opening synthesis and final editing of the essays within the chapter as follows: Marianne Githens prepared chapters 5 and 6; Pippa Norris prepared chapters 2, 3, and 4; and Joni Lovenduski prepared chapters 1, 7, 8, and 9.

Although any book concerned with women and politics should portray the diversity of approaches to the subject matter, it should also recognize the cross-cultural diversity of women's involvement in politics. The extracts included in this reader portray the experiences of women in the United States and western Europe. Too often the American women's movement is treated as the norm rather than as one pattern of women's political involvement. The women's movement in Britain, France, Sweden, Italy, and the Netherlands differs substantially in terms of strategies and tactics, the feminist agenda, and the opportunities for participation.

This book seeks to present this diversity, to articulate once again, and in another sense, different voices. National diversity is a crucial component in any study of women's political involvement. However, it is not possible in a book of this size to include material about all countries in each of the chapters. To have attempted to cover the globe could not have done justice to women's disparate concerns in the countries of central and eastern Europe, in Latin America, in Africa or Asia. Including just a few extracts from these countries would, we believed, represent an inadequate, arbitrary, and unbalanced perspective, so the readings are mainly drawn from a few western European countries and the United States.

This reader has also attempted to address the issue of diversity from the perspective of minority groups within particular countries. This is still another voice, and an important one. Several reading selections touch on the particular needs of minority women and their efforts to cope with their dual status as women and as minorities.

The selection of the extracts for this reader has been difficult. Space limitations always impose tough choices, and there are still regrets about readings which finally had to be omitted. We have sought to make amends for the omissions by including a reading list in each chapter for those who would like to pursue questions further. We hope the reader provides a stimulating and wide-ranging introduction to women and politics and to the different voices it has expressed.

MARIANNE GITHENS
PIPPA NORRIS
JONI LOVENDUSKI

REFERENCES

Ackelsberg, M., and I. Diamond. 1987. "Gender and Political Life: New Directions in Political Science." In B. Hess and M. Farree, *Analyzing Gender: A Handbook of Social Science Research.* Beverly Hills: Sage.

Bashevkin, S. (ed.). 1985. *Women and Politics in Western Europe.* London: Cass.

Baxter, S., and M. Lansing. 1983. *Women and Politics: The Invisible Majority.* Rev. Ed. Ann Arbor: University of Michigan Press.

Boles, J. 1979. *The Politics of the Equal Rights Amendment.* New York: Longman.

Boneparth, E. (ed.). 1982. *Women, Power and Policy.* New York: Pergamon Press.

Bystydzienski, J. (ed.). 1992. *Women Transforming Politics.* Bloomington: Indiana University Press.

Carroll, S. 1985, *Women as Candidates in American Politics.* Bloomington: Indiana University Press.

Chodorow, N. 1978. *The Reproduction of Mothering.* Berkeley: University of California

Press.

Cockburn, C. 1991. *In the Way of Women*. London: Macmillan.

Dahlerup, D. (ed.). 1986. *The New Women's Movement*. Newbury Park, CA: Sage.

Darcy, R., S. Welch, and J. Clark. 1987. *Women, Elections and Representation*. New York: Longman.

Diamond, I. (ed.). 1983. *Families, Politics and Public Policy*. New York: Longman.

———. 1977. *Sex Roles in the State House*. New Haven: Yale University Press.

Duverger, M. 1955. *The Political Role of Women*. Paris: UNESCO.

Eisenstein, Z. (ed.). 1979. *Capitalist Patriarchy and the Case for Socialist Feminism*. New York: Monthly Review Press.

Elshtain, J. 1981. *Public Man, Private Woman*. Princeton: Princeton University Press.

———. 1982. "Feminism, Family and Community." *Dissent* (Fall).

Farah, B. 1976. "Climbing the Political Ladder: The Aspirations and Expectations of Partisan Elites." In D. McGuigan, *New Research on Women and Sex Roles*. Ann Arbor: University of Michigan Press.

Fowlkes, D. 1986. "Concepts of the 'Political': White Activists in Atlanta." In J. Flammang, *Political Women*, pp. 66-86. Newbury Park, CA: Sage, p. 66–86.

Freeman, J. 1975. *The Politics of Women's Liberation*. New York: McKay.

Gelb, J., and M. Palley. 1982. *Women and Public Policies*. Princeton: Princeton University Press.

Gelphi, B. (ed.). 1986. *Women and Poverty*. Chicago: University of Chicago Press.

Gilligan, C. 1982. *In a Different Voice*. Cambridge, MA: Harvard University Press.

Githens, M. 1977. "Spectators, Agitators, or Lawmakers: Women in State Legislatures." In M. Githens and J. Prestage (eds.), *A Portrait of Marginality*. New York: Longman.

Githens, M., and J. Prestage (eds.). 1977. *A Portrait of Marginality*. New York: Longman.

Githens, M., and J. Prestage. 1979. "Styles and Priorities of Marginality." In M. Palley and M. Preston (eds.), *Race, Sex and Social Problems*. Lexington, MA: Lexington Books.

Gordon, L. (ed.). 1990. *Women, the State and Welfare*. Madison: University of Wisconsin Press.

Haavio-Mannila, E., et al. 1983. *Unfinished Democracy: Women in Nordic Politics*. New York: Pergamon Press.

Hoff-Wilson, J. (ed.). 1986. *Rights of Passage: The Past and Future of ERA*. Bloomington: Indiana University Press.

Iglitzin, L. 1974. "The Making of the Apolitical Woman: Femininity and Sex Stereotyping in Girls." In J. Jacquette (ed.), *Women and Politics*, pp. 25-36. New York: Wiley.

Jacquette, J. (ed.). 1974. *Women and Politics*. New York: Wiley.

Jones, K., and A. Jonasdottir. 1988. *The Political Interests of Gender*. London: Sage.

Katzenstein, M. F., and C. Mueller. 1987. *The Women's Movements of the United States and Western Europe*. Philadelphia: Temple University Press.

Kelly, R., and M. Boutilier. 1978. *The Making of the Political Woman: A Study of Socialization and Role Conflict*. Chicago: Nelson-Hall.

Kenrigan, M. L. 1984. *Political Equality in a Democractic Society*. Westport, CT: Greenwood Press.

Kirkpatrick, J. 1974. *Political Woman*. New York: Basic Books.

Lovenduski, J. 1986. *Women and European Politics*. Hempstead: Harvester Wheatsheaf.

Lovenduski, J., and J. Hills. 1981. *The Politics of the Second Electorate: Women and Public Participation*. Boston: Routledge and Kegan Paul.

Lovenduski, J., and J. Outshoorn (eds.). 1986. *The New Politics of Abortion*. London: Sage.

MacKinnon, C. 1989. *Towards a Feminist Theory of the State*. Cambridge: Harvard University Press.

———. 1987. *Feminism Unmodified*. Cambridge: Harvard University Press.

Mandel, R. 1981. *In the Running*. New York: Ticknor & Fields.

Mansbridge, J. 1986. *Why We Lost the ERA*. Chicago: University of Chicago Press.

Norris, P. 1985. "Women in Legislative Elites." *West European Politics* 8(4), October: 90–101.

———. 1987. *Politics and Sexual Equality*. Sussex: Wheatsheaf Books.

Okin, Susan Moller. 1992. *Women in Western Political Thought*. Princeton: Princeton University Press.

Orum, A., R. Cohen, S. Grasmuck, and Amy Orum. 1977. "The Problems of Being a Minority: Sex, Socialization and Politics." In M. Githens and J. Prestage (eds.), *A Portrait of Marginality*, pp. 17–37. New York: Longman.

Pascall, G. 1986. *Social Policy: A Feminist Analysis*. London: Tavistock Press.

Perkins, J., and D. Fowlkes. 1980. "Opinion Representation vs. Social Representation: Or Why Women Can't Run as Women and Win." *American Political Science Review* 74 (September): 92–103.

Piven, F. 1985. "Women and the State: Ideology, Power and the Welfare State." In A. Rossi (ed.), *Life and Gender Course*. Chicago: Aldine.

Piven, F., and H. Cloward. 1988. *Why Americans Don't Vote*. New York: Partheon Books.

Radice, L., E. Vallance, and V. Willis. 1987. *Member of Parliament: The Job of a Backbencher*. New York: St. Martins Press.

Randall, V. 1987. *Women and Politics: An International Perspective*. 2nd ed. Chicago: University of Chicago Press.

Rule, W. and J. Zimmerman. 1993. *United States Electoral Systems: Their Impact on Women and Minorities*. New York: Greenwood Press.

Sapiro, V. 1983. *The Political Integration of Women: Roles, Socialization and Politics*. Urbana: University of Illinois Press.

Schramm, S. 1981. "Women and Representation: Self-government and Role Change." *Western Political Quarterly* 34 (March): 46–59.

Sidel, R. 1987. *Women and Children Last*. New York: Viking Press.

Stoper, E. 1977. "Wife and Politician: Role Strain Among Women in Public Office." In M. Githens and J. Prestage (eds.), *A Portrait of Marginality*. New York: Longman.

Vallance, E. 1979. *Women in the House: A Study of Women Members of Parliament*. London: Athlone Press.

Watson, S. (ed.), 1990. *Playing the State: Australian State Intervensions*. London: Verso.

Welch, S. 1978. "The Recruitment of Women to Public Office." *Western Political Quarterly* September: 372–380.

About the Authors

Marianne Githens, who received her Ph.D. from London School of Economics and is Professor of Politics and Chair of Women's Studies at Goucher College, has been actively involved in research, writing, and teaching in the area of women and politics throughout her professional career. Her scholarly publications in this area are numerous and include among others *A Portrait of Marginality* (Longman, 1977) co-edited with Jewel Prestage and an extended essay on women and politics which appeared in the first edition of Ada Finifter's *Political Science: The State of the Discipline* published by the American Political Science Association. Dr. Githens has received a number of awards and grants including one from the National Endowment for the Humanities for a study of the Women's Peace Movement in America and has served as a consultant to the television docudrama on the suffrage movement in Britain, "Shoulder to Shoulder." In addition to having served as president of the Women's Caucus for Political Science, she has twice held elective office in the Southern Political Science Association. In 1986 she received Goucher's award for being the outstanding teacher in the Division of Social Sciences.

Pippa Norris is Associate Director of the Joan Shorenstein Barone Center on Press, Politics and Public Policy and Lecturer at the Kennedy School of Government, Harvard University. She works on legislative recruitment, comparative electoral behaviour, the politics of the media, and women and politics. Her other books include *Political Representation and Recruitment: Gender, Race and Class in the British Parliament,* co-authored with Joni Lovenduski (1994); *British By-Elections: The Volatile Electorate* (1990); *Politics and Sexual Equality: The Comparative Position of Women in Western Democracies* (1986); and has co-edited *Gender and Party Politics* (1993) and the *British Elections and Parties Yearbook* (annual 1991-1993). She is co-director of the British Candidate Study (funded by the ESRC) and the American Candidate Study (funded by the National Science Foundation). She has taught at Edinburgh, Berkeley, and Harvard Universities.

Joni Lovenduski is Professor of Comparative Politics at Loughborough University in the United Kingdom. She is author of *Women and European Politics* (1986) and co-author of *Political Recruitment and Representation* (1994); *Contemporary Feminist Politics* (1993), *Politics and Society in Eastern Europe* (1987) and co-editor of *Gender and Party Politics* (1993), *The New Politics of Abortion* and *The Politics of the Second Electorate* (1981) as well as numerous articles in scholarly and popular journals on gender and the political process. She is founding convenor of the Standing Group on Women and Politics of the European Consortium for Politics Research and a member of the executive committee of the Political Studies Association of the UK.

CHAPTER
1

Feminist Methodology

The key question in any discussion of feminist methodology is whether feminism implies a distinctive way of learning and knowing things. To answer this question we need to consider the intellectual environment in which it has been explored. Feminism has been part of two important developments. In the social sciences there has for many years been a movement away from universalizing, grand theories and an interest in interdisciplinary research. Feminist scholars share the growing mistrust of large-scale, general world theories and a concomitant preference for explanations that are more local, situated, detailed, and specific. This preference for different kinds of knowledge is a **political** development. Universalizing theories may conceal differences and, as a result, may conceal oppressions. Feminism draws attention to one such concealment when it describes how masculine domination is assumed in so many "neutral" explanations of social phenomena.

The new specificity that feminism prefers has implications for the explainer, as well as for the explanation. More than ever before, and in feminist more than in some other alternative scholarships, the identity and the perspectives of the explainer are regarded as part of the explanation, as something that we need to know if we are to evaluate the knowledge that is offered. The issue of subjectivity is now acknowledged to be important to social science; we recognize that we are not completely or reliably rational beings. Our bodies carry memories, desires, and fears that may operate against our reason. We carry preferences that influence our gaze and scrutiny. All this affects our claims to be knowers and constrains or distorts what we can know. The strategy to accommodate or allow for this in our scholarship is not to seek fruitlessly to excise our unconscious biases, but to be aware of, and to make explicit, those of our characteristics that may affect our account of some event, institution, or relationship. It is not inevitable that women are the ones to see the power embedded in different manifestations of gender relations, but it is more likely.

The idea that knowledge is power is an old one. Philosophers have developed ideas about the power relations that underpin authentic, accepted knowledge in a society, and we know that people who live in different societies often have different understandings of the world. This is true of so-called facts as well as ideas. Indeed, the difference between a fact and an idea is not universally agreed upon. For example, medical professions in different parts of the world recognize different illnesses. It is not simply that diagnosis and treatment are different, but that many diagnoses found in one culture may not exist in another, despite geographic, demographic, and economic similarities. The feminist challenge to political science is similar to our medical example. Feminist ideas about power in gender relations raise questions about experiences that mainstream political science has never included in its definition of politics. New understandings of the significance and means of the male domination of women imply that new definitions of politics are required, and that the agenda of political study should be altered significantly. This has met with some resistance. Political scientists, like other scientists, have questioned their epistemological frameworks only when under unusual political pressure. Feminist scholarship is such a pressure. Feminist theorists and social scientists have brought discourses about knowledge into the social sciences, and male biases in the accepted canon have been made visible and discredited.

Vicky Randall has written an account of the way political science has responded to the challenge of feminist method. She is not convinced about the possibility of a feminist methodology. Moreover, she is skeptical of some of the larger claims made by both camps. But she acknowledges distinctive feminist methods of gathering information, and feminist theory about the nature of knowledge. Randall describes the development of feminist critiques of male knowledge and considers what feminist research should entail. Many feminists stress the need for an equal and reciprocal relationship between the researcher and the subject of her research. They say that the researcher should bring her own experience to the research process, which should reflect the view from below. Randall is sympathetic to such ideas, but she counsels caution in the wholesale adoption of feminist research principles, offering four arguments for proceeding carefully. First, by forming more intimate relationships with the subject, the researcher may well foster different kinds of exploitation rather than remove exploitation from the research process. Second, the feminist belief that the study should be undertaken from below—that is, from the standpoint of the subjected group—implies feminists should undertake only certain kinds of research. This is an unacceptable constraint on what we are allowed to think about. Third, when feminists reject claims that objective research is desirable and possible, they respond in an understandable way to how, in the past, supposed objectivity masked and therefore supported male biases. But the realization that objectivity is not possible does not mean there should not be some detachment if our work is to be convincing. Finally, Randall observes that the scientific method feminism criticizes is too often a caricature, a simplistic and inadequate model that is rarely used. Good political science is modest in its claims, recognizing it cannot be fully objective but attempting to be logical in its way of reasoning. While emphasizing both the political nature and the diversity of the feminist approaches to the study of politics, Randall clearly believes that feminist social science is simply good social science.

Sandra Harding recognizes that the decisions a community makes about what constitutes knowledge are political decisions. The aim of feminism is to change the world, which implies that feminist knowledge is made for a purpose: it is made to solve a problem, to achieve a goal. Implicitly and explicitly, Harding's work is done with a view to the political effects of feminist theorizing. She welcomes the creative tension that results from the absence of ready, reliable, and lasting answers but believes feminist theory discredits male science by exposing its biases as the biases of the dominant group. What are the next steps after this? Harding considers whether feminism should be seeking to construct new, universal forms of science or should be skeptical of such projects. She shows the dangers in both positions but does not choose between them. Rather, she avers that the instabilities generated by unresolved conflict are a productive force in the construction of feminist theory because they are the incentive to intense and continuing debate. Although a convincing feminist methodology has yet to be devised, a distinctive feminist approach to research exists and is used by many social scientists who have constructed a research agenda, and use techniques and approaches, that let women be heard.

JONI LOVENDUSKI

Feminism
and Political Analysis

VICKY RANDALL

What are the implications of feminism for political analysis, more specifically for its methodological and conceptual assumptions?[1] Some feminists believe that these implications are revolutionary and will shake the edifice of traditional political science to its foundations. Some political scientists mistrust feminism as mere ideology, the rationalization of particular interests, and doubt whether it has anything of intellectual importance to contribute. Each of these positions probably exaggerates the coherence and potency both of its own and of the other's perspective; delusions of grandeur go with paranoia. Part of my object is to question the more absurd pretensions of both feminism and political science. Neither offers a monolithic or comprehensive approach to political analysis. It is not a zero-sum confrontation and both can learn from the other.

At the same time one cannot ignore the political context. Feminism does challenge significant aspects of political science as presently constituted. Most directly, of course, feminism presents a political challenge. Given that political science, whatever the disclaimers of its practitioners, remains an innately political activity, it makes a vast difference who the political scientists are, how the profession is structured, how it operates within the institutional matrix of higher education and research and how it is funded. The overwhelming predominance of men in key facilitating roles inevitably influenced previous treatment, or neglect, of women as subject matter, and accounts for much of the resistance to feminist inroads now. By the same token, feminists will probably have more impact on political analysis, when and if their numbers and output in the profession grow, than through the sheer persuasive force of their arguments. This discussion, however, focuses on the intellectual challenge from feminism. Some kinds of feminism call into question the traditional research methods and methodological assumptions of social science. Although many of these criticisms are not new, nor are they always advisable, it is necessary to understand both what they are and *why* they are made. They have also helped to clear a space and create an agenda for a much more important feminist challenge to the conceptualization of politics itself.

DEFINING FEMINISM

In order to assess feminism's implications for political analysis we need to identify what feminism is. This is no easy matter. Feminism as a body of ideas reflects the

4

development of 'second-wave' feminism as a movement from the late 1960s. As such it has from the outset been characterized by diversity and even disagreement, which have if anything intensified over time. The main residue of feminism's first wave could fairly be described as a mixture of equal-rights feminism, that emphasized women's similarity to men and concentrated on issues of women's legal status and employment, and welfare feminism that did not question the primacy of women's domestic role but concentrated instead on their special needs as mothers and wives. The distinctive new ingredient which provided the impetus and agenda for the Women's Liberation Movement of the 1970s came to be known as 'radical feminism'.

Radical feminism originated in the US, particularly amongst younger women who had been involved in student politics and the civil rights movement. This political experience shaped radical feminism in two ways. It contributed ideas about political organization associated with the ideal of participatory democracy and the perception, though this was given a new twist, that 'the personal is political'. But it was the sexist treatment meted out even by black and new left activists that triggered the feminist breakaway and convinced these women that the most fundamental struggle was that between men and women. This conviction has remained the hallmark of radical feminism and its derivatives, though the corollary of insistence on separatism, separation from men, has to varying degrees permeated the rest of the women's movement.

Radical feminism was never a unified tendency. Beyond its insistence on the primacy of the sex war, explanations for women's oppression and strategies to overcome it varied widely. Since these very early days radical feminism, whose history has in any case differed from one country to another, has evolved in a number of ways. One influential variant, particularly in the US, has become known as 'cultural feminism'. Emphasizing the respects in which women are different and superior to men, its extreme separatism is expressed in terms of culture and 'life-style' rather than overt campaigning.

Although radical feminism has dominated in the sense of setting the agenda, it has often been explicitly anti-intellectual. Marxist or socialist feminism, despite incorporating elements of separatism and a series of issues originally raised or highlighted by radical feminism such as abortion, domestic violence and sexual harassment, has persisted in its theoretically very demanding, if not impossible, self-assigned mission of reconciling class analysis with an account of male power. Conflict with radical feminism has at times been bitter, especially over the issue of heterosexuality, but both tendencies have seen themselves as revolutionary in distinction to what they term liberal or reformist feminism. This 'reformist' feminism has also incorporated aspects of radical feminism's analysis and agenda. Previous simplistic understandings of equal rights have been considerably modified to take account of women's different needs, while welfare feminism in its old form has virtually died out, although it is argued that a new revisionist 'conservative' feminism has emerged to occupy much of the same ideological space.[2]

New variants of feminist thinking appeared in the early 1980s, such as anarcho-feminism and eco-feminism. Ideological cohesion has been most severely strained, however, by a growing insistence on the 'politics of identity'; that is, on the differences *between* women. Already implicit in the value placed on individual women's subjective experience in the early consciousness-raising groups, this inevitably became more problematic as feminists began to define specific objectives and to advocate these on behalf of other women. Probably the most difficult challenge, politically and intellectually, for the largely white movement has come from black women.

It would only be a small exaggeration to say that feminism is presently facing a crisis of identity, not only as a movement but in terms of its theoretical relationship to women. Socialist feminists have made strenuous efforts to recognize differences, especially of race and class, amongst women and to incorporate them in their analysis,[3] while radical feminism has tended to deny their importance, either arguing that, whoever they are, all women share a fundamental oppression or, as in the elitist writings of Mary Daly, preferring to concentrate on the true believers, the *real* women as it were.[4] In this context it is necessary to note two further recent developments in feminist theory which can be seen both as a response to this identity crisis in the movement and as a reflection of the growing numbers of feminists in academia and their struggle with the patriarchal understandings of traditional subject disciplines. Feminist standpoint theory, clearly indebted to radical feminism, argues for the possibility of a separate and superior feminist epistemology, grounded in women's distinctive experience.[5] Feminist post-modernism, perhaps taking this position to its logical extreme, denies the validity of any epistemology. Not surprisingly, this has led a number of feminists to question whether post-modernism is in fact compatible with feminism.[6]

The variety of feminist analyses which have had or could have a bearing on political understanding highlights the difficulties in defining feminism. It is hardly possible to specify a core of beliefs that would not be contested by at least some of those who call themselves feminists. Since we nonetheless need some base line for understanding why feminists have been critical of political science and how they want to change it, I suggest that at a minimum feminism involves four assumptions: that women are important; that they have been systematically subordinated to male power and interests (although different brands of feminism would formulate this differently); that this subordination has in some sense been rooted in the sexual division of labour within the family; and that it is unacceptable.

FEMINISM AND METHOD

There is an extensive literature that discusses feminist approaches to social research, though as yet few positive recommendations specifically for feminist political research have emerged.[7] In one of the most helpful expositions, Sandra Harding begins by reminding us of the distinction between research methods, in the sense of techniques for gathering evidence, methodology, or the rationale for how the research is conducted and epistemology or a theory about the nature of knowledge and how it is constituted.[8] In practice of course these are largely interdependent.

Feminist political scientists have extensively criticized their male colleagues' *application* of research methods in the past. They have shown, for instance, how attitude surveys reinforced sex stereotypes by asking leading questions or 'cueing' stereotypal responses and by using inappropriate measures for specific attitudes.[9] They have criticized the selection and mode of employment of particular variables to represent variations in women's status. The arguments against using husband's social class are by now well known but as a recent analysis shows, even level of educational attainment, the central indicator used in one famous study of sex differences in political participation rates, will not have the same socioeconomic status implications for women as for men because to have its full impact it needs to interact with other socioeconomic resources, especially occupation.[10]

But is there a distinctive feminist method? Harding's answer is that in the narrow sense of method, there probably is not. She argues that all social research techniques are some variant of either listening to people and interrogation, observing behaviour or examining historical traces and records, and that feminists use all three and have not come up with anything totally new, although they may go about them in a particular way.[11] Strictly speaking, Harding is obviously right. However, it is still worth paying attention to what a number of feminists say about research methods and what might be called the 'spirit' in which they are applied. For instance several feminist writers have wanted radically to revise the form that interviews take. According to the sociologist Ann Oakley, the 'masculine' interviewing technique requires that the interviewer should only establish sufficient rapport with the interviewee to elicit the needed information and should certainly not directly answer any questions the interviewee might seek to put to them. Oakley objects to this technique's preoccupation with objectivity, hierarchy, and 'science'. She presents as an opposite paradigm her own research with women who were, sometimes literally, in the 'transition to motherhood'. When asked a question like 'Does an epidural ever paralyse women?', she did not, as a standard textbook might prescribe, give a noncommittal reply such as 'I guess I haven't thought enough about it to give a good answer right now' or 'a head-shaking gesture which suggests "that's a hard one"' but did her best to provide a helpful, informative answer. With many of the women she formed lasting friendships. Oakley's approach seems particularly suited to the nature of her research, and more generally to open-ended interviews in situations where the interviewee's trust is essential. However, Oakley goes on to insist that *whenever* a feminist interviews women 'use of prescribed interviewing practice is morally indefensible', though she believes that in any case usually 'the goal of finding out about people through interviewing is best achieved when the relationship of interviewer and interviewee is non-hierarchical and when the interviewer is prepared to invest his or her own personal identity in the relationship'.[12]

Several other feminist social scientists stress the need for an equal and reciprocal relationship between researcher and those researched.[13] (Helen Roberts also discusses the need, in larger research projects, to examine critically the sexual composition, hierarchy and division of labour *within* the research team. In their own research, she and her colleague decided to do the audio-typing themselves because such monotonous work would be soul-destroying for someone else but their own enthusiasm for the project would make it more bearable.[14]) The researcher should use her own experiences as a woman as a source of insight and empathy as well as something to share. Shulamit Reinharz recommends that she keep a personal diary during the research process.[15] Ideally the research project should be worked out together with the women being researched and should help them in some way.[16] Taking this point further, other writers argue that the method should itself involve political struggle because it is through struggle that the true nature of political relations becomes visible.[17]

I do not wish to suggest that there is some kind of feminist consensus on these matters or even that all the views cited here are shared by all the writers. However, taken together they do seem to me to reveal a distinctive approach. I am not thereby arguing that these views are entirely original; on the contrary, their exponents generally acknowledge their debt to radical sociology as it emerged in the 1960s. Nor are these feminist recommendations unproblematic, even in their own terms. As another feminist social researcher, Angela McRobbie, concluded from her own attempts to operationalize these precepts, it is one thing to bring one's personal experience to bear on a project but another to espouse a 'false notion of "oneness"' with all women on the grounds of gender. 'No matter how much our past personal experience figures and feeds into the research programme, we can't possibly assume that it necessarily corresponds in any way to that of the research "subjects"'.[18] She, and more recently Judith Stacey, have also questioned whether it is possible for researcher and research subject to be on equal terms, or whether in fact 'the appearance of greater respect for and equality with research subjects ... masks a deeper, more dangerous form of exploitation'. Women may be persuaded to confide their most intimate secrets to the researcher, who will always determine how these are treated and be able to get away from the research situation when she chooses.[19] Was Oakley in fact exploiting the anxiety of mothers to be, desperate to talk, in unfamiliar hospital surroundings with staff too busy or too clinically aloof to give them reassurance?

Nonetheless, feminist approaches to social research methods do raise important and challenging questions about political and ethical relationships within research projects. They also can be more fully understood in the light of broader methodological questions about 'objectivity' and what research is for.

METHODOLOGICAL ISSUES

The implication of Oakley's views about interviewing is that feminists should only undertake certain kinds of social research. Such a conclusion is more explicitly drawn by Mies and others. Mies maintains that they should seek the 'view from below' rather than the 'view from above', working with women or other oppressed groups. The focus of the research should be upon changing the status quo which requires a process of what Paulo Freire has called 'conscientization'. 'People who before were objects of research become subjects of their own research and action', as they gain awareness of their oppression and take steps to end it.[20] Reinharz does not go so far but requires that the topic of research should be of sincere concern both to the researcher and to her 'subjects' and further be suitable for 'experiential analysis', in which reflection upon their own experience by all involved, including the researcher, can form a central part. This means that it should be a 'what?' question (for instance, what is it like to be a . . . ?) rather than, in the first instance, a 'why?' question.[21]

There may be practical problems about getting institutional sponsorship and funding for this kind of research. Jo Freeman, who as an academic political scientist wrote an excellent account of the early years of the American Women's Liberation Movement, has nonetheless more recently suggested that feminist scholarship is incompatible with academia for this reason.[22] Yet despite its undoubted attractions in some contexts, it does also appear to rule out large areas of inquiry which should be of urgent concern to women. As Carol Smart has pointed out, this participatory model of conducting research will be of little help when studying people more powerful than oneself.[23] In the course of discussing whether *men* can carry out feminist research, Harding suggests that (sympathetic) men could be of particular help in investigating

> some areas of masculine behaviour and thought to which male researchers have easier and perhaps better access than do women researchers: primarily male settings and ones from which women are systematically excluded, such as board rooms, military settings or locker rooms,

a spy in the enemy camp.[24] Of course it would be foolish to reject such assistance if proffered, but is there not a danger of setting up in the area of feminist research a new version of the old familiar sexual division of labour?

More fundamentally still, these prescriptions for a feminist research method imply dissatisfaction with the methodological assumptions of conventional social science. In attacking these assumptions, it must be said that feminists often present a caricature of social science methodology. The social scientist is depicted as firmly believing that through application of scientific method it is possible to pinpoint and 'know' reality. The social scientist, according to this view, maintains that it does not matter how a research topic is decided upon. What is both essential and possible is that the researcher is 'objective', detached in making observations and able to disentangle fact from value. In addition, the social scientist accords undue weight to 'hard' methods seen as approximating those of the natural sciences, especially quantitative analysis.[25]

Why are feminist social researchers frequently so hostile to conventional social science method? There are a number of reasons, some of which are more acceptable than others. In the first place, feminists may claim they are not interested in 'objectivity' in the sense that feminist research has to be *for* women: 'it aims at being instrumental in improving women's lives in one way or another'.[26] To that extent it is partial. This will immediately render it suspect in the eyes of some colleagues who pride themselves on their own professional detachment. Still, as Gloria Bowles reminds us, social science itself originated in a social movement concerned with using a scientific approach for social improvement. Even the later 'behavioural revolution', with its emphasis on empiricism, was partly inspired by a desire to make social science more directly applicable to the solution of social problems, though it may have grown more conservative as it became established and respectable.[27]

Secondly, feminist research tends to accord a great weight to accounts of women's subjective experience. This may partly be a legacy from the movement's early consciousness-raising days but can also be justified on a number of grounds. It was through women feeling able to talk, without being ridiculed or condemned, about such traumatic 'private' experiences as abortion, rape or domestic violence, that feminists grasped their full extent and seriousness. Traditionally, social science tended either to ignore women, include them inappropriately in generalizations purporting to be true for mankind, or make sweeping assertions about women's feelings, experiences or needs. This meant that there was little reliable information already gathered for feminists to work on, let alone to form the bases of testable hypotheses. In this situation some feminist researchers turned to biography and even fiction for insights. Many felt it was essential to allow women to speak for themselves, with as few cues and in an unstructured a way as possible. In a rare example from British political science, Jenny Chapman used open-ended questions in her interviews of women politicians. She writes:

> Although I did not adopt this as a self-consciously 'feminist' technique, my unstated reasoning was that women's experience, the areas of interest to them and the way these are perceived by women are not adequately represented or valued in our mainstream, male-based culture. If we are to get beyond the limitations of that culture, women must be encouraged to speak for themselves. Responses to closed questions inevitably reflect the mind of the researcher (or the constraints of her discipline) far more than open-ended ones.

She found that respondents were often very surprised by her interest in their experiences. Typical comments were "Are you sure you really want to hear about this?" and "My goodness, I don't often get the chance to talk like this".[28] A new impetus for this emphasis on subjective experience may be many feminists' growing interest in understanding the differences *between* women, not putting words into their mouths.

Both of these concerns, with helping women and with listening to women, are laudable, if not always easily realized in practice. As McRobbie and Stacey argue, it may not be possible—indeed the very attempt may be patronizing—to help women involved in the research project itself.[29] One may have to be satisfied with helping women in general and in the much longer term. Letting women speak for themselves is no straightforward undertaking. We noted earlier the danger that in assuming that our own experience as women enables us to understand other women we may project our feelings onto them. We also noted the inherent inequality in the research relationship. These considerations must influence the selection and editing or interpretation of 'subjective' material. Who decides and on what basis which women will speak, on what and what form the eventual record or publications will take? It is still necessary to try.

Where feminist objections to social science method became more worrying is in the rejection of its basic epistemology. In some cases they are simply echoing the long-standing critique of attempts to claim 'scientific' status for the study of society, which has been associated with the 'sociology of knowledge' and its off-shoots. Such feminists rightly argue that it is impossible to be 'objective'. Often, however, they wisely conclude that the feminist social researcher must take her own bias into account when gathering and interpreting information. For Harding this is the hallmark of the best feminist research.[30] Since they argue that social science can never be genuinely objective, such feminist researchers can argue that this makes their work superior to research that does not question its own methodological impartiality. As Roberts points out, taking gender into account in theory and practice should require more rigour, not less.[31]

Frequently, however, the observation that objectivity is impossible goes with rejection of scientific 'rigour' altogether and stems from a rather different critique. A number of 'cultural' feminists have rejected objectivity as an aspect of 'male' rationality. Mary Daly has written about the 'God Method': 'under patriarchy, Method has wiped out women's questions so totally that even women have not been able to hear and formulate our own questions to meet our own experiences'.[32] What is being said here is not simply that because men have been dominant they have used 'Method' in a way that excludes women but that method, or rationality, is innately male and as such a dimension of women's oppression. Catherine MacKinnon, who occupies a rather ambiguous slot between radical and standpoint feminism, expresses this perception well. She says of male dominance: 'It is metaphysically nearly perfect. Its point of view is the standard for point-of-viewlessness, its particularity the meaning of universality'.[33]

For many cultural feminists, the implication drawn has been that women, to discover and free themselves, must abandon the rational mode. In the writings of Susan Griffin, for example, this can reach extraordinarily romantic heights. Women must flee civilization and rediscover their organic, intuitive affinity with nature: 'We are nature seeing nature . . . The red-winged blackbird flies in us, in our inner sight'.[34] There is a parallel here with the argument associated in particular with some French cultural feminists, influenced by the psychoanalytic writings of Lacan, that language itself is masculine, not simply its content at any given time but its inner logic. The implication is that women have to create their own language, in Dale Spender's words 'to re-name the world'.[35] Were such a project really necessary, where would we begin?

·   The position of feminists associated with what has come to be known as standpoint theory clearly owes much to the radical feminist critique of male science. But whereas cultural feminists would not normally concern themselves with the niceties of feminist social research, discounting the whole enterprise as male academicism, standpoint feminists are themselves academics writing for an academic readership. They share the rejection of 'male' objectivity as rooted in exclusive male interests but draw a rather different conclusion. Here they acknowledge a debt to Marx, with his perception that the proletariat, because of its location in the system of production, was 'cognitively privileged' over the bourgeoisie. In different ways, standpoint feminists maintain that women have a distinctive set of experiences which provides them with a privileged vantage-point from which to understand reality. This does not mean that women automatically have this truer understanding. It needs to be developed by reflection upon experience, by consciousness-raising or through political struggle. However, it forms the basis for a feminist epistemology that will be superior to male scientific epistemology.[36]

It is easy enough to point out the problems for feminists to which cultural feminism's Manichean world view gives rise. As Jean Cocks has cogently argued, this brand of feminism tends to accept too uncritically the present male-dominated culture's account of itself and presents an idealized women's culture as its reverse image. Ironically, this means that cultural feminism remains imprisoned in the established way of seeing things, accepting such prevalent oppositions as reason and emotion, mind and body, nature and culture, subject and object. Cocks writes of Griffin:

> No masculinist has been more insistent than she that the development and products of the mind—art, theology, philosophy, mechanical and industrial invention, and above all scientific knowledge—belong to men and that the natural life of the body—fertility, passion, the fulfillment of biological needs, the care of the young, the sick and the dying—belong to women.[37]

Many other feminist theorists have warned against this way of thinking, with its 'essentialist' view of female nature and its acceptance of prevailing dualisms.[38]

Standpoint theory is not so obviously trapped in binary thinking. It aims to arrive at a feminist understanding not through rejection of all that is male but through reflection upon women's experience. In the process, it may well generate valuable new insights and concepts. Nonetheless, the epistemological claims are ambitious to say the least, and extremely problematic. There is first the question of how this crucial experience that all women, directly or indirectly, undergo is to be identified. Hartsock, for instance, suggests that we concentrate on women's activities as contributors to subsistence and as mothers and their relationship to the institutions underpinning and defining these activities.[39] Would examination of this area of experience yield sufficient commonality? Related to this is the issue of the status of this epistemology. If it is superior to men's because, rather as in Hegel's master–slave paradigm, men's privileged situation gives them a distorted and narrow vision of reality, does the same hold, for instance, for the relationship of a black feminist epistemology to a white? Standpoint feminists reject any hint of epistemological relativism but do not adequately resolve this question of the relationship between alternative epistemological standpoints.[40] This may incidentally help to explain the appeal for some feminist academics of post-modernism. It does away with these problems by denying the possibility of any systematic knowledge. However, to feminists seriously committed to exposing and relieving the oppression of women, such a 'solution' is altogether too drastic since it undermines the credibility of feminist claims along with everybody else's.[41]

The cultural and standpoint feminist rejection of 'male' rationality and epistemology and as a consequence of 'scientific method' is understandable but unwise. (This doubtless puts me in Mary Hawkesworth's category of 'empiricist feminist' which, however, she tends to misrepresent.[42]) One is bound to sympathize with the impatience and occasional despair of feminists struggling to cleanse language and theory of their pervasive patriarchal assumptions. The so-called objectivity of masculine science is constantly merging with the normative, even if this is rarely so blatant today as in Carolyn Sherif's example in her own field: 'psychology treated women, blacks and other minorities as well as residents of certain other countries as more "different" than a well-behaved laboratory chimpanzee'.[43] Nonetheless we cannot afford to abandon these essential intellectual tools.

In the first place, if we want feminist research to change things, it has to be convincing. It will hardly convince fellow academics, policy-makers or the media if rigour and method are jettisoned as so much patriarchal baggage.[44] Secondly, in any case feminist objections may be based on a misreading of 'rationality' and 'science'. Rationality 'covers a much smaller area than most people think'.[45] It is rooted in consistency and simply maintains that incompatible statements cannot simultaneously be true. Rationality does not exclude emotion, changing one's mind or being unable to prove something. The criteria for science can be similarly modest. A social science that really did believe that how a research topic emerges is irrelevant, that fact and value can ever be entirely disentangled and which insisted religiously that every piece of social analysis involved identifying a question, generating a hypothesis to answer that question, devising a method of testing the hypothesis and so on, emulating laboratory-style techniques of the natural sciences, would certainly be out of touch with reality. This model of the 'scientific' approach is, one hopes, something of a straw person.

Feminists who criticize scientific method in social science may exaggerate the extent to which, in its narrowest, most easily caricatured sense, it dominates approaches to research. Even in empirical political research there is a 'methodological pluralism', although some methodologies confer higher professional status than others. They may also be taking too literally social science's own more 'scientistic' pretensions, or what could be called the 'ideology' of social science. Good social science at any rate should recognize that it can never be fully 'objective'; it should acknowledge the limited extent to which the so-called 'hard' scientific methods can be usefully applied to the study of human society, but even when they are inapplicable seek to be scientific in the more modest sense of being logical and systematic in its method of reasoning.

A more legitimate target for feminist censure is the way that the use of scientific methods tends to cast an aura of authority over the whole research project, including the importance of the question it is asking and the validity of the conceptual framework it is employing, both of which are in reality subjective or political elements. These are then more likely to become part of the taken-for-granted assumptions of the discipline, more difficult to challenge, or indeed to transcend imaginatively. Since the authors of these projects overwhelmingly have been men, their subjective assumptions, a feminist would argue, have been riddled with sexist or patriarchal understandings. They can also object when the existence of an implicit hierarchy of methods and approaches, in terms of their approximation to the 'rigour' of the natural sciences, leads researchers to make the wrong selection. For instance, they may opt for methods producing data susceptible to quantitative analysis, whose import is trivial or based on simplistic assumptions, when qualitative analysis would have been much more revealing. (It must be admitted that feminist political scientists, particularly in the US, have sometimes fallen into this trap themselves.) Similarly, feminists have questioned the appropriateness of fashionable, seemingly rigorous rational choice theory for explaining or predicting women's political behaviour. They argue from a liberal feminist perspective that its assumption of free moral agency does not take into account the effects of socialization and dependence on the consciousness of the oppressed[46] or, closer to the radical feminist position, that its assumption of individual self-interest does not apply to women with their greater 'sense of connectedness and continuity with other persons and the natural world'.[47]

Feminism, then, has not produced its own, entirely original research method but one can discern a distinctive approach. This is partly a consequence of what it is trying to do: to let women be heard, to use research to help women and not to reproduce and reinforce existing hierarchical relationships in the particular relationship between researcher and researched. While feminist researchers themselves may not be wholly successful in these aims, they do constitute a valid criticism of aspects of traditional research method. The feminist approach also reflects scepticism about the 'scientific' status of social science, which up to a point is well founded and healthy. More worryingly, though, it can stem from wholesale repudiation of 'male' rationality and epistemology. Although any feminist researcher should recognize the kind of exasperation with male-dominated social science expressed in MacKinnon's 'Its point of view is the standard for point-of-viewlessness', and although explorations of a feminist epistemology can open up valuable space and generate fruitful new concepts, ultimately this can only be an intellectual cul-de-sac.

All of these issues have a bearing upon political science. Yet it must also be acknowledged that they have not so far been explicitly or widely taken up by feminist *political* scientists who, while highly critical of its application, have tended for the most part to take methodology in this sense for granted. Their more striking contribution has been a criticism, at many points running parallel to feminist arguments about methodology, of the *conceptual* underpinnings of traditional political science and of the agenda of inquiry and explanatory theory to which these give rise.

Notes

1. Without implying that there is or should be a sharp divide between 'empirical' political research and analysis on the one hand and more prescriptive political theory and thought on the other, the emphasis of this article is upon the former.
2. See J. Stacey, 'The new conservative feminism', *Feminist Studies*, 9 (1983).
3. See for instance, M. Barrett and M. McIntosh, 'Ethnocentrism and socialist-feminist theory', *Feminist Review*, 20 (1985), 23–47 and the responses to that article by C. Ramazanoglu, H. Kazi, S. Lees and H. S. Mirza, 'Feedback: feminism and racism', *Feminist Review*, 22 (1986), 82–105.
4. See M. Daly, *Gyn/Ecology (The Metaethics of Radical Feminism)* (London, The Women's Press, 1978).
5. There may be some disagreement as to who the standpoint feminists are but amongst those who have been identified as exponents are Dorothy Smith, Catherine MacKinnon and Nancy Hartsock. See D. Smith, 'Women's perspective as a radical critique of sociology', C. MacKinnon, 'Feminism, Marxism and the state: towards feminist jurisprudence' and N. Hartsock, 'The feminist standpoint: developing the ground for a specifically feminist historical materialism', all reprinted in S. Harding

(ed.), *Feminism and Methodology: Social Science Issues* (Milton Keynes, Open University Press, 1987).

6. For fairly sympathetic accounts of feminist post-modernism, see J. Flax, 'Postmodernism and gender relations in feminist theory', *Signs,* 12 (1987), 4 and M. Hawkesworth, 'Knowers, knowing, known: feminist theory and claims of truth', *Signs,* 14:3 (1989).

7. Collections of essays on feminist social research include H. Roberts (ed.), *Doing Feminist Research* (London, Routledge and Kegan Paul, 1981); G. Bowles and R. Duelli Klein (eds), *Theories of Women's Studies* (London, Routledge and Kegan Paul, 1983); L. Stanley and S. Wise (eds), *Breaking Out: Feminist Consciousness and Feminist Research* (London, Routledge and Kegan Paul, 1983); Harding (ed.) *Feminism and Methodology.* The only collection dealing specifically with political research is K. B. Jones and A. G. Jonasdottir (eds), *The Political Interests of Gender: Developing Theory and Research with a Feminist Face* (London, Sage, 1988) and few of these essays are directly concerned with empirical research methods.

8. See S. Harding, 'Introduction: is there a feminist method?', in S. Harding (ed.), *Feminism and Methodology* (Milton Keynes, Open University Press, 1987).

9. See for instance the critiques by S. Bourque and J. Grossholtz, 'Politics as an unnatural practice: political science looks at female participation', *Politics and Society,* 4:4 (1974); L. Iglitzin, 'The making of the apolitical woman: femininity and sex-stereotyping in girls' in J. Jaquette (ed.), *Women in Politics* (New York, John Wiley, 1974).

10. See J. Chapman, *Politics, Feminism and the Reformation of Gender* (London, Routledge, 1992). She is criticizing the use of education as an indicator in S. Verba, N. Nie and J. Kim, *Participation and Political Equality* (Cambridge, Cambridge University Press, 1978).

11. Harding, 'Introduction'.

12. A. Oakley, 'Interviewing women: a contradiction in terms', in H. Roberts (ed.), *Doing Feminist Research* (London, Routledge and Kegan Paul, 1981).

13. For instance, L. Stanley and S. Wise, '"Back into the personal" or: our attempt to construct "feminist research"', and S. Reinharz, 'Experiential analysis: a contribution to feminist research', both in G. Bowles and R. Duelli Klein (eds), *Theories of Women's Studies* (London, Routledge and Kegan Paul, 1983).

14. See H. Roberts, 'Women and their doctors: power and powerlessness in the research process', in H. Roberts (ed.), *Doing Feminist Research* (London, Routledge and Kegan Paul, 1981), p. 22.

15. Reinharz, 'Experiential analysis'.

16. Reinharz, 'Experiential analysis'.

17. M. Mies, 'Towards a methodology for feminist research', in G. Bowles and R. Duelli Klein (eds), *Theories of Women's Studies* (London, Routledge and Kegan Paul, 1983); N. C. M. Hartsock, 'The feminist standpoint: developing the ground for a specifically feminist historical materialism', in S. Harding (ed.), *Feminism and Methodology* (Milton Keynes, Open University Press, 1987).

18. A. McRobbie, 'The politics of feminist research: between talk, text and action', *Feminist Review,* 12 (1982), 46–57, at p. 52.

19. J. Stacey, 'Can there be a feminist ethnography?', *Women's Studies International Forum,* 11:1 (1988), 21–27, at p. 22.

20. Mies, 'Towards a methodology for feminist research', p. 126.

21. Reinharz, 'Experiential analysis'.

22. J. Freeman, 'The feminist scholar', *Quest,* 5:1 (1979); cited by G. Bowles, 'Is Women's Studies an academic discipline?', in G. Bowles and R. Duelli Klein (eds), *Theories of Women's Studies* (London, Routledge and Kegan Paul, 1983).

23. C. Smart, *The Ties That Bind: Law, Marriage and the Reproduction of Patriarchal Relations* (London, Routledge and Kegan Paul, 1984); cited by D. Currie and H. Kazi, 'Academic feminism and the process of de-radicalization: re-examining the issues', *Feminist Review,* 25 (1987), 77–98.

24. Harding, 'Introduction', pp. 10–11.

25. See, for instance, Reinharz, 'Experiential analysis'; Stanley and Wise, 'Back into the personal'. Quantitative analysis is specifically singled out for criticism in M. Millman and R. Moss Kanter, 'Introduction', in *Another Voice: Feminist Perspectives on Social Life and Social Science* (New York, Doubleday Anchor Books, 1975). This is excerpted in S. Harding (ed.), *Feminism and Methodology* (Milton Keynes, Open University Press, 1987). A not very persuasive defence of

quantitative analysis can be found in T. E. Jayarantne, 'The value of quantitative methodology for feminist research', in G. Bowles and R. Duelli Klein (eds), *Theories of Women's Studies* (London, Routledge and Kegan Paul, 1983).

26. R. Duelli Klein, 'How to do what we want to do: thoughts about feminist methodology', in G. Bowles and R. Duelli Klein (eds), *Theories of Women's Studies* (London, Routledge and Kegan Paul, 1983), p. 90.

27. Bowles, 'Is women's studies an academic discipline?'

28. Personal communication to the author. Chapman is referring to the research which formed the basis for 'Adult socialization and out-group politicization: an empirical study of consciousness-raising', *British Journal of Political Science*, 17 (1987), 315–340.

29. McRobbie, 'The politics of feminist research'; Stacey, 'Can there be a feminist ethnography?'

30. Harding, 'Introduction'.

31. Roberts, 'Women and their doctors: power and powerlessness in the research process'.

32. M. Daly, *Beyond God the Father* (Boston, Beacon Press, 1973), pp. 11–12; cited in Duelli Klein, 'How to do what we want to do'.

33. MacKinnon, 'Feminism, Marxism, method and the state', p. 137.

34. S. Griffin, *Women and Nature* (New York, Harper and Row, 1980), p. 226.

35. This issue is discussed for instance in K. McKluskie, 'Women's language and literature: a problem in women's studies', *Feminist Review*, 14 (1983), 51–61. D. Spender coined her term in *Man Made Language* (London, Routledge and Kegan Paul, 1980).

36. I have suggested that exponents of standpoint feminism include Smith, MacKinnon and Hartsock (see note 5). For a useful discussion, see Hawkesworth, 'Knowers, knowing, known'.

37. J. Cocks, 'Wordless emotions: some critical reflections on radical feminism', *Politics and Society*, 13 (1984), 27–57, at p. 35.

38. The best critical feminist discussion of the essentialism of cultural feminism is H. Eisenstein, *Contemporary Feminist Thought* (London, Unwin, 1984). The dangers of such dualistic thinking are pointed out in B. Thiele, 'Vanishing acts in social and political thought: tricks of the trade', in C. Pateman and E. Gross (eds), *Feminist Challenges: Social and Political Theory* (London, George Allen & Unwin, 1986).

39. Hartsock, 'The feminist standpoint'.

40. Some particularly trenchant arguments on this issue are to be found in M. Halberg, 'Feminist epistemology: an impossible project?', *Radical Philosophy*, 53 (1989), 3–7. The feminist political theorist, Judith Grant, has also discussed the problems associated with using 'experience' as the basis for feminist epistemology; see J. Grant, 'I feel therefore I am: a critique of female experience as the basis for a feminist epistemology', *Women and Politics*, 7:2 (1987), 99–114.

41. Again see Halberg, 'Feminist epistemology'.

42. Hawkesworth, 'Knowers, knowing, known'.

43. C. Sherif, 'Bias in psychology', in S. Harding (ed.), *Feminism and Methodology* (Milton Keynes, Open University Press, 1987), p. 42.

44. McRobbie, 'The politics of feminist research'.

45. J. Richards, *The Sceptical Feminist: A Philosophical Enquiry* (Harmondsworth, Penguin, 1980), p. 37; cited in Currie and Kazi, 'Academic feminism and the process of de-radicalization'.

46. See V. Sapiro, 'Sex and games: on oppression and rationality', *British Journal of Political Science*, 9 (1979), 385–408.

47. See K. Jones, 'Towards the revision of politics', in K. B. Jones and A. G. Jonasdottir (eds), *The Political Interests of Gender* (London, Sage, 1988).

The Instability
of the Analytical Categories
# of Feminist Theory

SANDRA HARDING

Feminist theory began by trying to extend and reinterpret the categories of various theoretical discourses so that women's activities and social relations could become analytically visible within the traditions of intellectual discourse.... If women's natures and activities are as fully social as are men's, then our theoretical discourses should reveal women's lives with just as much clarity and detail as we presume the traditional approaches reveal men's lives. We had thought that we could make the categories and concepts of the traditional approaches objective or Archimedean where they were not already.

As we all have come to understand, these attempts revealed that neither women's activities nor gender relations (both inter- and intra-gender relations) can be added to these theoretical discourses without distorting the discourses and our subject matters. The problem here is not a simple one, because liberal political theory and its empiricist epistemology, Marxism, critical theory, psychoanalysis, functionalism, structuralism, deconstructionism, hermeneutics, and the other theoretical frameworks we have explored both do and do not apply to women and to gender relations. On the one hand, we have been able to use aspects or components of each of these discourses to illuminate our subject matters. We have stretched the intended domains of these theories, reinterpreted their central claims, or borrowed their concepts and categories to make visible women's lives and feminist views of gender relations. After our labors, these theories often do not much resemble what their nonfeminist creators and users had in mind, to put the point mildly. (Think of the many creative uses to which feminists have put Marxist or psychoanalytic concepts and categories; of how subversive these revised theories are of fundamental tendencies in Marxism and Freudianism.) On the other hand, it has never been women's experiences that have provided the grounding for any of the theories from which we borrow. It is not women's experiences that have generated the problems these theories attempt to resolve, nor have women's experiences served as the test of the adequacy of these theories. When we begin inquiries with women's experiences instead of men's, we quickly encounter phenomena (such as emotional labor or the positive aspects of "relational" personality structures) that were made invisible by the concepts and categories of these theories. The recognition of such phenomena undermines the legitimacy of the central analytical structures of these theories, leading us to wonder if we are not continuing to distort women's and men's lives by our extensions and reinterpretations. Moreover, the very fact that we borrow from these theories often has the unfortunate consequence of diverting our energies into endless disputes with the nonfeminist defenders of these theories: we end up speaking not to other women but to patriarchs.

Furthermore, once we understand the destructively mythical character of the essential and universal "man" which was the subject and paradigmatic object of nonfeminist theories, so too do we begin to doubt the usefulness of analysis that has essential, universal woman as its subject or object—as its thinker or the object of its thought. We have come to understand that whatever we have found useful from the perspective of the social experience of Western, bourgeois, heterosexual, white women is especially suspect when we begin our analyses with the social experiences of any other women. The patriarchal theories we try to extend and reinterpret were created to explain not men's experience but only the experience of those men who are Western, bourgeois, white, and heterosexual. Feminist theorists also come primarily from these categories—not through conspiracy but through the historically common pattern that it is people in these categories who have had the time and resources to theorize, and who—among women—can be heard at all. In trying to develop theories that provide the one, true (feminist) story of human experience, feminism risks replicating in theory and public policy the tendency in the patriarchal theories to police thought by assuming that only the problems of *some* women are human problems and that solutions for them are the only reasonable ones. Feminism has played an important role in showing that there are not now and never have been any generic "men" at all—only gendered men and women. Once essential and universal man dissolves, so does his hidden companion, woman. We have, instead, myriads of women living in elaborate historical complexes of class, race, and culture.

I want to talk here about some challenges for theorizing itself at this moment in history, and, in particular, for feminist theorizings. Each has to do with how to use our theories actively to transform ourselves and our social relations, while we and our theories—the agents and visions of reconstruction—are themselves under transformation. Consider, for instance, the way in which we focus on some particular inadequate sexist or earlier feminist analysis and show its shortcomings—often with brilliance and eloquence. In doing so, we speak from the assumptions of some other discourse feminism has adopted or invented. These assumptions always include the belief that we can, in principle, construct or arrive at the perspective from which nature and social life can be seen as they really are. After all, we argue that sexist (or earlier feminist) analyses are wrong, inadequate, or distorting—not that they are equal in scientific or rational grounding to our criticisms.

However, we sometimes claim that theorizing itself is suspiciously patriarchal, for it assumes separations between the knower and the known, subject and object, and the possibility of some powerful transcendental, Archimedean standpoint from which nature and social life fall into what we think is their proper perspective. We fear replicating—to the detriment of women whose experiences have not yet been fully voiced within feminist theory—what we perceive as a patriarchal association between knowledge and power.[1] Our ability to detect androcentrism in traditional analyses has escalated from finding it in the content of knowledge claims to locating it in the forms and goals of traditional knowledge seeking. The voice making *this* proposal is itself super-Archimedean, speaking from some "higher" plane, such that Archimedes' followers in contemporary intellectual life are heard as simply part of the inevitable flux and imperfectly understood flow of human history. (And this is true even when the voice marks its own historical particularity, its femininity.) When it is unreflective, this kind of postmodernism—a kind of absolute relativism—itself takes a definitive stand from yet further outside the political and intellectual needs that guide our day-to-day thinking and social practices. In reaction we wonder how we can not want to say *the way things really are* to "our rulers" as well as to ourselves, in order to voice opposition to the silences and lies emanating from the patriarchal discourses and our own partially brainwashed consciousnesses. On the other hand, there is good reason to agree with a feminist postmodernist suspicion of the relationship between accepted definitions of "reality" and socially legitimated power.

How then are we to construct adequate feminist theory, or even *theories*—whether postmodern or not? Where are we to find the analytical concepts and categories that are free of the patriarchal flaws? What are the analytical categories for the absent, the invisible, the silenced that do not simply replicate in mirror-image fashion the distorting and mystifying categories and projects of the dominant discourses? Again, there are two ways to look at this situation. On the one hand, we can use the liberal powers of reason and the will, shaped by the insights gained through engaging in continuing political struggles, to piece what we see before our eyes in contemporary social life and history into a clear and coherent conceptual form, borrowing from one androcentric discourse here, another one there, patching in between in innovative and often illuminating ways and revising our theoretical frameworks week by week as we continue to detect yet further androcentrisms in the concepts and categories we are using. We can then worry about the instability of the analytical categories and the lack of a persisting framework from which we continue to build our accounts. (After all, there should be some progress toward a "normal" discourse in our explanations if we are to create a coherent guide to understanding and action.) On the other hand, we can learn how to embrace the instability of the analytical categories; to find in the instability itself the desired theoretical reflection of certain aspects of the political reality in which we live and think; to use these instabilities as a resource for our thinking and practices. No "normal science" for us![2] I recommend we take the second course, an uncomfortable goal, for the following reason.

The social life that is our object of study and within which our analytical categories are formed and tested is in exuberant transformation.[3] Reason, will power, reconsidering the material—even political struggle—will not show these changes in ways over which our feminisms should rejoice. It would be a delusion for feminism to arrive at a master theory, at a "normal science" paradigm with conceptual and methodological assumptions that we presume all feminists accept. Feminist analytical categories *should* be unstable—consistent and coherent theories in an unstable and incoherent world are obstacles to both our understanding and our social practices.

· · ·

. . . New understandings of the history of science and sexuality expand our understanding immensely, they do not tell us whether a science apparently so inextricably intertwined with the history of sexual politics can be pried loose to serve more inclusive human ends—or whether it is strategically worthwhile to try to do so. Is history destiny? Would the complete elimination of androcentrisms from science leave no science at all? But isn't it important to try to degender science as much as we can in a world where scientific claims are *the* model of knowledge? How can we afford to choose between redeeming science or dismissing it altogether when neither choice is in our best interest?

· · ·

CULTURE VERSUS NATURE AND GENDER VERSUS SEX

Historians and anthropologists show that the way contemporary Western society draws the borders between culture and nature is clearly both modern and culture bound.[4] The culture versus nature dichotomy reappears in complex and ambiguous ways in a number of other oppositions central to modern, Western thinking: reason versus the passions and emotions; objectivity versus subjectivity; mind versus the body and physical matter; abstract versus concrete; public versus private—to name a few. In our culture, and in science, masculinity is identified with culture and femininity with nature in all of these dichotomies. In each case, the latter is perceived as an immensely powerful threat that will rise up and overwhelm the former unless the former exerts severe controls over the latter.

This series of associated dualisms has been one of the primary targets of feminist criticisms of the conceptual scheme of modern science. It is less often recognized, however, how the dualism reappears in feminist thinking about gender, sex, or the sex/gender system. . . . I have talked about eliminating gender as if the social could be cleanly separated from the biological aspects of our sexual identities, practices, and desires. In feminist discourses, this mode of conceptualizing sexuality is clearly an advance over the biological determinist assumption that gender differences simply follow from sex differences. Since biological determinism is alive and flourishing in sociobiology, endocrinology, ethology, anthropology and, indeed, most nonfeminist discourses, I do not want to devalue the powerful analytical strategy of insisting on a clean separation between the known (and knowable) effects of biology and of culture. Nevertheless, a very different picture of sexual identities, practices, and desires emerges from recent research in biology, history, anthropology, and psychology.[5] Surprisingly, it could also be called biological determinism, though what is determined on this account is the plasticity rather than the rigidity of sexual identity, practice, and desire. Our species is doomed to freedom from biological constraints in these respects, as existentialists would put the issue.

The problem for feminist theory and practice here is twofold. In the first place, we stress that humans are *embodied* creatures—not Cartesian minds that happen to be located in biological matter in motion. Female embodiment is different from male embodiment. Therefore we want to know the implications for social relations and intellectual life of that different embodiment. Menstruation, vaginal penetration, lesbian sexual practices, birthing, nursing, and menopause are bodily experiences men cannot have. Contemporary feminism does not embrace the goal of treating women "just like men" in public policy. So we need to articulate what these differences are. However, we fear that doing so feeds into sexual biological determinism (consider the problems we have had articulating a feminist perspective on premenstrual syndrome and work-related reproductive hazards in ways that do not victimize women). The problem is compounded when it is racial differences between women we want to articulate.[6] How can we choose between maintaining that our biological differences ought to be recognized by public policy and insisting that biology is not destiny for either women or men?

In the second place, we have trouble conceptualizing the fact that the culture versus nature dichotomy and its siblings are not simply figments of thought to be packed up in the attic of outmoded ideas. The tendency toward this kind of dualism is an ideology in the strongest sense of the term, and such tendencies cannot be shucked off by mental hygiene and will power alone. The culture/nature dichotomy structures public policy, institutional and individual social practices, the organization of the disciplines (the social vs. the natural sciences), indeed the very way we see the world around us. Consequently, until our dualistic practices are changed (divisions of social experience into mental vs. manual, into abstract vs. concrete, into emotional vs. emotion denying), we are forced to think and exist within the very dichotomizing we criticize. Perhaps we can shift the assumption that the natural is hard to change and that the cultural is more easily changed, as we see ecological disasters and medical technologies on the one hand, and the history of sexism, classism, and racism on the other.[7] Nonetheless, we should continue insisting on the distinction between culture and nature, between gender and sex (especially in the face of biological determinist backlash), even as we analytically and experientially notice how inextricably they are intertwined in individuals and in cultures. These dichotomies are empirically false, but we cannot afford to dismiss them as irrelevant as long as they structure our lives and our consciousnesses.

SCIENCE AS CRAFT: ANACHRONISM OR RESOURCE?

Traditional philosophies of science assume an anachronistic image of the inquirer as a socially isolated genius, selecting problems to pursue, formulating hypotheses, devising methods to test the hypotheses, gathering observations, and interpreting the results of inquiry. The reality of most scientific research today is quite different, for these craft modes of producing scientific knowledge were replaced by industrialized modes in the nineteenth century for the natural sciences, and by the mid-twentieth century for the vast majority of social science research. Consequently, philosophy of science's rules and norms for individual knowledge seekers are irrelevant to the conduct of, and understanding of, most of contemporary science, as a number of science critics have pointed out.[8]

However, it is precisely in areas of inquiry that remain organized in craft ways where the most interesting feminist research has appeared.[9] Perhaps all of the most revolutionary claims have emerged from research situations where individual feminists (or small groups of them) identify a problematic phenomenon, hypothesize a tentative explanation, design and carry out evidence gathering, and then interpret the results of this research. In contrast, when the conception and execution of research are performed by different social groups of persons, as is the case in the vast majority of mainstream natural science and much social science research, the activity of conceptualizing the research is frequently performed by a privileged group and the activity of executing the research by a subjugated group. This situation insures that the conceptualizers will be able to avoid challenges to the adequacy of their concepts, categories, methods, and interpretations of the results of research.

This kind of analysis reinforces the standpoint theorists' argument that a prescriptive theory of knowledge—an epistemology—should be based on a theory of labor or human activity, not on a theory of innate faculties as empiricist epistemology assumes. In fact, the feminist epistemologies . . . are all grounded in a distinctive theory of human activity, and in one that gains support from an examination of the preconditions for the emergence of modern science in the fifteenth to seventeenth centuries. Feminists point to the unification of mental, manual, and emotional labor in women's work which provides women with a potentially more comprehensive understanding of nature and social life. As women increasingly are drawn into and seek men's work—from law and policy-making to medicine and scientific inquiry—our labor and social experience violate the traditional distinctions between men's and women's work, thus permitting women's ways of understanding reality to begin to shape public understandings. Similarly, it was a violation of the feudal division of labor that made possible the unity of mental and manual labor necessary to create science's new experimental method.[10]

Traditional philosophy of science's prescriptive image of the scientific inquirer, as craftsman, then, is irrelevant as a model for the activity that occupies the vast majority of scientific workers today. This image instead reflects the practices of the very few scientifically trained workers who are engaged in the construction of new research models. However, since the scientific worldview that feminism criticizes was constructed to explain the activity, results, and goals of the *craft labor* that constituted science in an earlier period, and since contemporary feminist craft inquiry has produced some of the most valuable new conceptualizations, it looks like we need to think more carefully about which aspects of the scientific worldview to reject and retain. Perhaps the mainstream enterprise of today is not scientific at all in the original sense of the term! Can it be that feminism and similarly estranged inquiries are the true offspring of Copernicus, Galileo, and Newton? Can this be true while at the same time these offspring undermine the epistemology that Hume, Locke, Descartes, and Kant developed to explain the birth of modern science? Once again, we are led to what I propose should be regarded as fruitful ambivalence toward the science we have. We should cultivate both "separatist" craft-structured inquiry *and* infuse the industrially structured sciences with feminist values and goals.

These are some of the central conceptual instabilities that emerge in considering the feminist criticism of science. Several of them arise in feminist theorizing more generally. I have been arguing that we cannot resolve these dilemmas in the terms in which we have been posing them and that instead we should learn how to regard the instabilities themselves as valuable resources. If we can learn how to use them, we can match Archimedes' greatest achievement—his inventiveness in creating a new kind of theorizing.

Notes

1. See, e.g., Maria C. Lugones and Elizabeth V. Spelman, "Have We Got a Theory for You! Feminist Theory, Cultural Imperialism and the Demand for 'the Women's Voice,'" *Hypatia: A Journal of Feminist Philosophy* (special issue of *Women's Studies International Forum*) 6, no. 6 (1983): 573–82; many of the selections in *New French Feminisms,* ed. Elaine Marks and Isabelle de Courtivron (New York: Schocken Books, 1981); Jane Flax, "Gender as a Social Problem: In and For Feminist Theory," *American Studies/Amerika Studien* (June 1986); Donna Haraway, "A Manifesto for Cyborgs: Science, Technology, and Socialist Feminism in the 1980's," *Socialist Review* 80 (1983): 65–107.
2. See Thomas S. Kuhn, *The Structure of Scientific Revolutions* (Chicago: University of Chicago Press, 1970). "Normal science" was Kuhn's term for a "mature science," one where conceptual and methodological assumptions are shared by the inquirers in a field.
3. Perhaps it has always been. But the emergence of "state patriarchy" from the "husband patriarchy" of the first half of the century, the rising of people of color from colonized subjugations, and the ongoing shifts in international capitalism all insure that this moment, at any rate, is one of exuberant transformation. See Ann Ferguson, "Patriarchy, Sexual Identity, and the Sexual Revolution," *Signs: Journal of Women in Culture and Society* 7, no. 1 (1981): 158–99, for discussion of the shifts in forms of patriarchy.
4. See esp. the responses to Sherry Ortner's "Is Female to Male as Nature Is to Culture?" (in *Woman, Culture and Society,* ed. M. Z. Rosaldo and L. Lamphere [Stanford, Calif.: Stanford University Press, 1974]) in MacCormack and Strathern, eds.
5. See references cited.
6. Inez Smith Reid, "Science, Politics, and Race," *Signs* 1, no. 2 (1975): 397–422.
7. Janice G. Raymond makes this point in "Transsexualism: An Issue of Sex-Role Stereotyping," in Tobach and Rosoff, eds., vol. 2.
8. Jerome Ravetz, *Scientific Knowledge and Its Social Problems* (New York: Oxford University Press, 1971); Rose and Rose, eds. Rita Arditti, Pat Brennan, Steve Cafrak, eds., *Science and Liberation* (Boston: South End Press, 1980).
9. Hilary Rose in particular has pointed this out in "Hand, Brain and Heart," and in "Is a Feminist Science Possible?" Perhaps all new research paradigms must be established through craft activity, as Kuhn argued.
10. Edgar Zilsel, "The Sociological Roots of Science," *American Journal of Sociology* 47, no. 4 (1942): 545–60.

FURTHER READING FOR CHAPTER 1

Bourque, S., and J. Grossholtz. 1974. "Politics as an Unnatural Practice: Political Science Looks at Female Participation." *Politics and Society* 4: 4.

Bowles, G., and R. Duelli Klein (eds.). 1981. *Theories of Women's Studies*. London: Routledge & Kegan Paul.

Eisenstein, H. 1984. *Contemporary Feminist Thought*. London: Allen and Unwin.

Evans, Judith, et al. 1986. *Feminism and Political Theory*. London: Sage.

Flax, J. 1987. "Postmodernism and Gender Relations in Feminist Theory." *Signs* 12: 4.

Harding, S. (ed.). 1987. *Feminism and Methodology: Social Science Issues*. Milton Keynes: Open University Press.

Hawksworth, M. 1989. "Knowers, Knowing, Known: Feminist Theory and Claims of Truth." *Signs* 14: 3.

Jones, K. B., and A. Jonasdottir (eds.). 1988. *The Political Interests of Gender*. London: Sage.

Lovenduski, J. 1981. "Toward the Emasculation of Political Science." In Dale Spender (ed.), *Men's Studies Modified*. London: Pergamon Press.

Roberts, H. (ed.). 1981. *Doing Feminist Research*. London: Routledge.

Thiele, B. 1986. "Vanishing Acts in Social and Political Thought: Tricks of the Trade." In C. Pateman and E. Gross (eds.), *Feminist Challenges: Social and Political Theory*. London: Allen and Unwin.

CHAPTER
2

Political Participation

Political participation is usually understood as citizen activity that aims to influence government—through casting a ballot, campaigning within parties, lobbying an official, or raising money for a candidate. Political participation by citizens is distinct from recruitment into government office, although one may lead to the other.

In recent years questions about the extent and nature of gender differences in political participation have proved controversial. There are three main perspectives. The traditional view, common in the 1950s and 1960s, suggested that women were less involved and less interested than men in most conventional forms of political life, in terms of elected office, party membership, interest group activity, campaign work, and, to a lesser extent, voting.[1] In their classic study *Participation and Political Equality,* Verba, Nie, and Kim compared participation across seven nations in the mid-1960s to early 1970s.[2] Men were found to be more active than women in all countries, with the least difference in the United States and the greatest disparities in India, Nigeria, and Yugoslavia. The gender gap was modest in voting but increased with more difficult forms of political activity. The authors concluded that differences in resources and psychological involvement provide only part of the answer to the puzzle of women's lower participation rate.

The cause of the "participation gap" was not self-evident. Debate revolved around the relative importance of gender differences in structural life-styles (domestic constraints, socioeconomic resources, and organizational affiliations) and/or political attitudes (sex role socialization, political efficacy, and confidence). Today the traditional perspective is subject to considerable criticism,[3] although it continues to receive support from some recent studies.[4]

During the 1970s the standard view came under attack from two quarters. According to the radical perspective, women do not participate less than men; instead, they participate differently. If so, the focus needs to move from conventional electoral politics to a wider range of political arenas and activities, especially more ad hoc and unstructured community associations, voluntary organizations, and protest groups.[5] Often these areas are neglected, compared with voting or party membership, because by its nature unconventional participation is more difficult to study except in an ad hoc fashion.

Finally, the revisionist perspective accepts that women may have been less involved in mass political activity during the 1950s but it suggests that the extent of the participation gap has been exaggerated and that much of the evidence supporting the traditional view is open to criticism. This view holds that over time, the participation gap has closed, because of social trends in women's life-styles in regard to education, employment, and the family.[6] The revisionist camp therefore emphasizes the similarities rather than differences in the mass political behavior of women and men in the 1980s.

Which perspective seems most plausible? Carol Christy compared various forms of participation—voting, party membership, campaign work, media attention, and political discussion—across six countries. She found that gender differences in voting participation had narrowed by the 1980s in the United States, Sweden, Norway, West Germany, Britain, and Canada, although there were differences in the rates of change. The study concluded that in most cases, sex differences had indeed diminished over time, although they had not yet disappeared completely.[7]

We cannot assume that all women have equal opportunities to participate. Jewel Prestage focuses on the involvement of African American political women. Prestage argues that within the context of the civil rights movement, African American women consciously chose to confront the issue of sexism, playing a significant role in local communities, in national organizations, and in mass demonstrations against racism.

PIPPA NORRIS

Notes

1. See L. Milbrath, *Political Participation* (Chicago: Rand McNally, 1968), p. 18; R. E. Lane, *Political Life* (Glencoe, IL: Free Press, 1959), pp. 204–234; Maurice Duverger, *La Participation des Femmes a la view politique* (Paris: UNESCO, 1955), pp. 13–74; G. Almond and S. Verba, *The Civic Culture* (Boston: Little, Brown, 1965), pp. 324–325.
2. Sidney Verba, Norman Nie, and Jae-on Kim, *Participation and Political Equality: A Seven-Nation Comparison* (Cambridge: Cambridge University Press, 1978).
3. Susan Bourque and Jean Grossholtz, "Politics and Unnatural Practice: Political Science Looks at Female Participation," in Janet Siltanen and Michelle Stanworth, *Women and the Public Sphere* (London: Hutchinson, 1984), pp. 103–121; Kathleen Jones, "Towards a Revision of Politics," in Kathleen Jones and Ann Jonasdottir, *The Political Interests of Gender* (London: Sage, 1988), pp. 20–27.
4. See Stephen Earl Bennett, *Apathy in America: Causes and Consequences of Citizen Political Indifference* (Dobbs Ferry, NY: Transnational Publishers, 1986), pp. 72–75.
5. M. Weber, C. C. Odorisio, and G. Zincone, *The Situation of Women in the Political Process in Europe, Part I* (Strasbourg, Council of Europe, 1984), p. 66.
6. Pippa Norris, "Gender Differences in Political Participation in Britain: Traditional, Radical and Revisionist Models," *Government and Opposition* 26(1), Winter 1991, pp. 56–74.
7. For further work see Carol Christy, *Sex Differences in Political Participation: Processes of Change in Fourteen Nations* (New York: Praeger, 1987).

Trends in Sex Differences in Political Participation: A Comparative Perspective

CAROL A. CHRISTY

INTRODUCTION

The United States and Europe have seen some striking changes in gender roles during the twentieth century. Women have flooded into schools and universities, the paid work force, the electorate, and, in some instances, political office. Here we will examine changes in women's representation in such mass-level political activities as voting, participating in election campaigns, and discussing and following politics. Two questions are addressed. First, how much change has occurred? More specifically, do we see any differences in the amount of change across countries or by various types of political participation? Second, what are the reasons for the changes in sex differences in political participation?

Explanations for change generally focus on two types of factors. One is changes in women's interest and general psychological involvement in politics. Traditionally, women were socialized to believe that politics was men's affair, but this belief has weakened due to more egalitarian childhood socialization and adult resocialization. The second is changes in women's opportunities and resources facilitating political participation. Traditional domestic roles, lower education levels, and less contact with politically involved people constrain women's political activity.[1]

This analysis will examine a third set of factors, which can operate independently of changes in gender role attitudes and behavior. Specifically, factors associated with political systems can facilitate or inhibit women's political participation. At elite levels of political activity, political institutions have long been observed to affect women's representation. For example, proportional representation, with candidates nominated and listed by political parties, favors women's representation in legislatures. Therefore, when countries such as France change electoral systems, women's representation may also change.[2]

At the mass level, women's recruitment into political parties and campaign work is also affected by elements of the political system. For example, parties which recruit a high proportion of party members through unions tend to particularly overrepresent men. Thus, because Germany and the United States have different methods of recruitment into parties and campaigns, the two countries differ in trends in party membership.[3] Also, within each country, such factors account for differences in the rates of change between activities conducted through party organizations and those undertaken individually. For instance, following campaigns or politics in the media is generally an act undertaken by isolated individuals and is not easily mobilizable. Trends in these types of activity coincide better with trends in psychological involvement in politics and campaigns.

METHODOLOGY

Reliable data on trends in sex differences in political participation are difficult to obtain. The earliest reports of trends were limited to voter turnout, derived from official election statistics collected in a number of European countries.[4] The United States also saw a number of trend studies based on the presidential election surveys administered since the late 1940s.[5] Although still limited to electoral behavior, these studies did include more kinds of political participation. Only recently are trends other than voting being reported for other countries, such as Canada, France, Germany, Great Britain, and the Netherlands.[6] These new trend data now permit the examination of comparative rates of change in activities other than voting.

This study looks at trends in six countries: Sweden, Norway, West Germany, Great Britain, Canada, and the United States. The best trend data are found for these countries.

The trend data come from four sources. The International Consortium for Political and Social Research (ICPSR) provided the surveys of the United States, Canada, Great Britain, and West Germany. The Swedish and Norwegian Social Science Data Services made available surveys of their countries. Official turnout statistics have been published for Norway, Sweden, and West Germany. And, finally, for West Germany the data published by the Allensbach Institute supplement the ICPSR data.

The trends range from thirty-six years for the United States to twenty years for Canada. . . . These surveys include measures of a wide variety of political activities: voting, party membership, campaign work, campaign meeting attendance, vote solicitation, discussion of politics or campaigns, and following politics or campaigns in newspapers or the electronic media. Also available are measures of psychological involvement in politics (interest in politics or the campaign, concern about the outcome of the election, and partisanship) and two measures of political efficacy (the belief that one can understand and have an effect on politics). Unfortunately, trend data are not yet available for other types of participation receiving attention in recent decades, such as protest and community activity.[7] . . .

Sex differences are measured by gamma, a positive sign indicating that men participate more than women. The higher the number, the greater the male-female difference.[8]

The rates of change in sex differences are summarized by the slopes derived from the least squares method of regression analysis. A positive sign indicates that sex differences have narrowed, and the larger the number, the greater the diminution.[9]

Note that trend data are extremely scarce on the attitudes and behavior underlying these changes in sex differences in political participation. The surveys examined here rarely ask questions about gender roles, such as whether politics is deemed an appropriate activity for women. Thus, explanations for the trends in political activity cannot be fully explored.

COMPARATIVE RATES OF CHANGE

Table 1 displays the average annual change in sex differences, as summarized by the slopes of linear regression equations. In 53 of the 60 cases, sex differences

Table 1   ESTIMATED YEARLY CHANGE IN SEX DIFFERENCES IN PSYCHOLOGICAL INVOLVEMENT AND POLITICAL PARTICIPATION, BY COUNTRY

Country	Sweden	Norway	West Germany	Great Britain	Canada	USA
Political interest	−.009*	−.004	−.010*	−.012	+.001	
Campaign interest					+.004	−.001
Election concern			−.005		−.001	
Partisanship	−.004	+.002	−.004	−.002	−.001	−.003*
Political efficacy			−.011*		.000	−.002*
Intellectual efficacy					−.007	.000
Follow politics		−.009				−.001
Newspaper attention	−.009*	−.010	−.010*	−.002		−.001
Television/radio attention	−.005	−.009*	-.007	−.007		+.001
Political discussion	−.010	−.013	−.008	−.014*		
Political discussion (other)	−.010*			−.014*		
Vote solicitation		−.010			−.009	−.003
Meeting attendance			−.008*	−.013*	−.005	.000
Campaign work				−.012	−.009	−.005
Party activism	−.012					
Party membership	−.002	−.007	−.002	−.009		−.009
Voter turnout	-.008*	-.003*	-.003*	−.011*	-.002	-.006*

Note: The change in sex differences (measured by gamma) is estimated by the least squares method of regression analysis. A negative sign denotes that sex differences have diminished, and an asterisk denotes that the change is significant at the .05 level.

have diminished by this estimation, and in only 4 cases do they appear to be widening. However, the reduction is statistically significant in only 17 instances because of the small number of cases and irregularities in the trends.

The actual trends, presented in Table 4, clearly show these irregularities. A curvilinear pattern, where sex differences diminished more rapidly in the 1950s and early 1960s than later, is discernible for Sweden (for political interest and partisanship) and West Germany (for partisanship, political efficacy, and radio/television attention).[10] However, the many irregularities in all the trends make any assumption about either curvilinearity or linearity fairly tenuous.

Table 1 suggests quite marked variations in the rate of change by nation and by type of participation, the diminution ranging from .001 to .014 (gamma). Three patterns are theoretically relevant.

Cross-national Variations   Sex differences diminished most rapidly in Great Britain (the average rate being .009, gamma), followed by West Germany and Sweden (.008) and then Norway (.007). The United States and Canada averaged a much slower reduction (.0024 and .0031, respectively). In short, sex differences narrowed two to four times faster in Europe than in North America.

There are two types of explanations for these cross-national variations. One is that those aspects of gender roles most relevant to political participation have changed more rapidly in Europe than in North America. Documentation of this explanation is difficult because the relevant measures of gender roles are either poor or unobtainable. Moreover, available data on gender roles can be discrepant with the political participation trends. For example, in West Germany sex differences in work force participation did not decline until recently, yet sex differences in political participation diminished relatively rapidly in comparison to the other countries. In contrast, sex differences in work force participation *have* narrowed in the other five countries.[11] Although employment mildly stimulates women's political participation,[12] its impact is not strong enough to account for the cross-national variations in rates of change.

Equally difficult to document, the second type of explanation for the cross-national variations is changes in the interaction of gender roles with political participation. For example, perhaps traditional gender roles are becoming less of a barrier to political activity in Europe than in North America, due to Europe's greater expansion of the welfare state. With this expansion, the state increasingly takes over women's traditional functions, and women in particular become more dependent on its favors. Thus women would increasingly perceive politics as relevant to their lives; the definition of the political simply expands to include women's traditional concerns.[13]

A "floor effect" might also account for the cross-national variations in rates of change. That is, sex differences may diminish more slowly in countries where the differences are initially smaller, namely, the United States and Canada. A later section examines the floor effect more thoroughly.

Variations by Type of Political Participation   Sex differences have narrowed most strongly for political discussion and for party and campaign work. The diminution is weakest, on the average, for three of the four measures of psychological involvement, namely, partisanship, election concern, and interest in the campaign. More is said on this later.

Variations Within Nations by Type of Political Participation   Those types of activities conducted within political organizations, such as campaign work and party membership, tend to change in unique ways compared to the indicators of psychological involvement and activities undertaken alone or in an informal group. There are two different patterns. In Canada and the United States, the diminution has been greatest for party membership and campaign work. However, for Germany and Sweden the diminution has been weakest for party membership. How the political system accelerates or depresses change in these types of activity will now be considered.

PARTY MEMBERSHIP

The British trends presented in Table 2 strikingly illustrate how changes in methods of recruiting party members affect the sex differences. Sex differences in party membership diminished primarily because of the Labour party's lessening recruitment of men through union subscriptions—from roughly 7 to 9 percent in the 1960s to 3.5 percent in 1974 and then 1 percent in 1983. The proportion of women recruited through unions remained constant at around 0.1 to 0.3 percent. Also remaining constant—at .14 (gamma)—were sex differences in party membership when union-affiliated Labour members are removed from the party member category.

The British results document how sex differences can diminish because of changes in the *interaction* of gender roles with political organizations rather than changes in gender roles per se. The influx of women into the work force and into unions did not translate into increased Labour party membership. Rather, men's advantage due to their preponderance in unions simply shrank with the fall-off in recruitment through unions.

Sweden and Germany illustrate the opposite effect—how factors associated with party organizations can inhibit the reduction in sex differences in party membership. In both countries, the reduction is .002 (gamma) a year, relatively weak in comparison both to other types of participation in these countries and to party membership in other countries. In Sweden, three-quarters of all party members are Social Democrats,[14] and over time this party had been enlarging its collectively affiliated labor unions[15] and losing members in its Women's Federation.[16] Thus the recruitment channels became increasingly more favorable to men. Also probably due to strengthened union recruitment, new members of the German Social Democrat party were increasingly male from the 1950s to the 1960s (when the data end).[17] Official party membership data show the sex differences to have increased in Germany until the early 1970s.[18]

For these European mass-membership parties, with well-developed party institutions and recruitment processes, organizational changes can strongly affect women's representation. In the United States, however, where parties are weakly organized and membership is poorly defined, certain political issues may particularly mobilize women into parties and campaigns. The elections of 1972 and 1980 saw women especially more active than men in campaigns, perhaps because the candidates took distinctive stands on women's economic, political, and reproductive rights. Indeed, the increased salience of these issues in other nations as well may have activated women; in the four countries where data are available, sex differences in party and campaign work diminished quite rapidly in comparison to

Table 2 TRENDS IN PARTY MEMBERSHIP AND UNION MEMBERSHIP

	1964		1970		1974		1983	
	Male	Female	Male	Female	Male	Female	Male	Female
Party member (%)	18.8	9.6	16.2	7.4/6.0	11.6	6.2	8.7	6.3
Labour party member (%)	9.5	1.8	9.9	1.2/1.0	5.0	1.2	2.6	1.4
Local party subscription (%)	3.0	1.5	1.4	1.0/1.0	1.5	1.1	1.6	1.1
Union party subscription (%)	6.5	0.3	8.5	0.2/0.0	3.5	0.1	1.0	0.3
Union member (%)	42.7	7.1	39.9	9.9/10.4	41.4	13.6	36.9	17.6
N of cases	813	970	282	517/308	1107	1124	1727	1945

other kinds of activity. Again, this explanation demonstrates how sex differences are affected by changes in the political system—specifically, in the types of political issues considered important. Significantly, the feminist political movement, by broadening the definition of the political to include many women's concerns, altered the system and women's representation in it.

THE FLOOR EFFECT

The floor effect holds that the larger the initial sex differences, the more rapid the diminution in these differences. As will now be demonstrated, some types of data better support this hypothesis than others.

First, over time, it is not clear that the pace of change slows as sex differences diminish. As mentioned earlier, Sweden and West Germany do show such a curvilinear pattern for some types of participation and involvement. However, many other trends are clearly not curvilinear. In fact, these trend data reveal a serious weakness in the explanatory capacity of the floor effect—its failure to specify the circumstances in which the floor is reached. Does change end when equality in participation is reached? Then why the anomalies for voter turnout in Sweden and partisanship in the United States? In both countries women became increasingly more active than men *after* equality was reached. Another anomaly involves the Swedish and West German trends identified as curvilinear, for there change leveled off before equality was reached.

As for variations within nations by type of political activity, the floor effect expects that change is slowest for those types of participation with the smallest initial sex differences. Thus, sex differences may have diminished more slowly for the three attitudes of psychological involvement because they were relatively small to begin with. However, this hypothesis holds true in some countries but not others. The correlation (Pearson's r) between the initial size of the sex differences and the rate of change is positive (.74) and significant at the .05 level for Norway. The correlation is positive but not significant for West Germany (.61), Britain (.60), Canada (.52) and, weaker still, Sweden (.22). However, the relationship is −.03 in the United States. Particularly anomalous in the United States is the strong diminution for partisanship, where sex differences were initially small, and the lack of change for intellectual efficacy, where sex differences were initially large.

The floor effect best explains the cross-national variations. Sex differences diminished least strongly in the United States and Canada, the two countries averaging the smallest initial sex differences (measured by gamma), .17 and .20, respectively. They diminished most strongly in those countries averaging the largest initial sex differences—West Germany (.56), Norway (.35), and Sweden (.34). The British case is most anomalous, with moderate initial sex differences (.28) but the most rapid rate of diminution.

These examples indicate the necessity of ascertaining the processes involved in the floor effect. Does resistance to change increase as equality is approached, how, and among whom? Does change end when sex differences in political participation disappear? These and other questions require systematic study and testing.[19] Whatever the findings, this analysis demonstrates that the floor effect *alone* cannot explain the variations in rates of change.

IMPLICATIONS FOR THE FUTURE

Table 3 estimates when sex differences would disappear if the past trends are projected into the future. This estimation assumes that the trends are indeed linear and that the floor effect is weak or absent—quite tenuous assumptions. These projections indicate that in half the cases, sex differences will disappear in a gen-

Table 3   ESTIMATED NUMBER OF YEARS AFTER 1990 BEFORE SEX DIFFERENCES DISAPPEAR, BY COUNTRY

Country	Sweden	Norway	West Germany	Great Britain	Canada	USA
Political interest	31	79	46	12	∞	
Campaign interest					∞	84
Election concern				2		64
Partisanship	24	∞	42	=	44	=
Political efficacy			19		∞	34
Intellectual efficacy					24	∞
Follow politics		30				274
Newspaper attention	31	31	50	139		184
Television/ radio attention	30	10	68	3		∞
Political discussion	1	2	43	3		
Political discussion (other)	10		26			
Vote solicitation		13			20	61
Meeting attendance			63	9	8	∞
Campaign work				=	=	30
Party activism	12					
Party membership	189	31	284	21		=
Voter turnout	=	14	17	=	24	19

Notes: The numbers represent the estimated sex differences in 1964 (intercept of the regression equation) divided by the estimated yearly reduction in sex differences (slope of the regression equation), minus 26. An equal sign denotes that sex differences are estimated to have disappeared by 1990. An infinity sign indicates that sex differences are not diminishing.

eration. In fact, the sexes are already equal in 12 percent of these cases.[20] Moreover, in only 20 percent of the cases are sex differences predicted to remain longer than a century.

However, as this study discussed, some processes are at work which do not produce linear trends. For example, the projections predict that sex differences in party membership in Sweden and West Germany will not diminish for several centuries. Yet the party leadership, through deliberate efforts, could increase their recruitment of women. Already, rising proportions of women are being chosen for party offices and party lists of candidates, demonstrating that, if desired, political institutions can accelerate change.

CONCLUSIONS

Although sex differences in political participation have generally decreased, there are considerable variations in the rates of change by nation and by type of participation. The data are too limited and imperfect to allow for precise explanations of these variations. However, they do indicate that factors affecting the rates of change are multiple and complex. This study documented how factors associated with political systems affect the rate of change. Particularly relevant are changes in the institutions that channel individuals into parties and campaign work. Several plausible explanations were offered for the differences in the rates of change between Sweden and Germany, on the one hand, and Great Britain and the United States, on the other.

This study also examined the evidence for a floor effect, where the rate of diminution slows as the sex differences diminish. The evidence was mixed, more valid across nations than within nations and over time. Better understanding of the underlying processes is necessary.

These results have important implications for future trends. First, although sex differences in political participation are diminishing, the pace of change at times can be quite slow. Thus, sex differences in some types of participation are likely to remain significantly large for at least several generations. Second, the pace of future change will not be regular, particularly for those types of participation affected by changes in political institutions and processes. Indeed, in certain cases institutional factors can either prevent or accelerate change. In the final analysis, however, more thorough studies of these trends are required before reliable predictions can be offered.

Notes

1. For discussion of these various types of factors, see Vicki Randall, *Women and Politics: An International Perspective*, 2d ed. (Chicago: University of Chicago Press, 1987), pp. 83–94; and Joni Lovenduski, *Women and European Politics: Contemporary Feminism and Public Policy* (Amherst, MA: University of Massachusetts Press, 1986), pp. 127–135.
2. For an examination of the impact of electoral systems, see Karen Beckwith, "Sneaking Women into Office: Alternative Access to Parliament in France and Italy," *Women and Politics* 9 (3), 1989: 1–15.
3. Carol A. Christy, "American and German Trends in Sex Differences in Political Participation," *Comparative Political Studies* 18 (April 1985): 81–103.
4. Herbert Tingsten, *Political Behavior: Studies in Election Statistics* (London: King & Son, 1937); Maurice Duverger, *The Political Role of Women* (Paris: UNESCO, 1955).
5. Early studies include Marjorie Lansing, "Sex Differences in Political Participation," (unpublished Ph.D. dissertation, University of Michigan, 1970); Kristi Andersen, "Working Women and Political Participation, 1952–1972," *American Journal of Political Science* 19 (August 1975): 439–453; Susan Welch, "Women as Political Animals? A Test of Some Explanations for Male-Female Political Participation Differences," *American Journal of Political Science* 21 (November 1977): 711–730; Susan Welch and Philip Secret, "Sex, Race and Political Participation," *Western Political Quarterly* 34 (March 1980): 5–16; Eileen L. McDonagh, "To Work or Not To Work: The Differential Impact

of Achieved and Derived Status upon the Political Participation of Women, 1956–1976," *American Journal of Political Science* 26 (May 1982): 280–297; Pinky S. Wassenberg, Kay G. Wolsborn, Paul R. Hagner, and John C. Pierce, "Gender Differences in Political Conceptualization, 1956–1980," *American Politics Quarterly* 11 (April 1983): 181–203; and Sandra Baxter and Marjorie Lansing, *Women and Politics: The Visible Majority,* rev. ed. (Ann Arbor: University of Michigan Press, 1983).

6. For Canada, see Jerome H. Black and Nancy E. McGlen, "Male-Female Political Involvement in Differentials in Canada, 1965–1974," *Canadian Journal of Political Science* 12 (September 1979): 471–497; and Barry J. Kay, Ronald D. Lambert, Steven D. Brown, and James E. Curtis, "Feminist Consciousness and the Canadian Electorate: A Review of National Election Studies 1965–1984," *Women and Politics* 8(2), 1988: 1–21.

   For France, see Sylvia B. Bashevkin, "Changing Patterns in Politicization and Partisanship Among Women in France," *British Journal of Political Science* 15(1), 1984: 75–96.

   For Germany, see Christy, cited in note 3.

   For Great Britain, see Pippa Norris, "Gender Differences in Political Participation in Britain: Traditional, Radical and Revisionist Models," *Government and Opposition* 26 (Winter 1991): 56–74.

   For the Netherlands, see Peter Castenmiller and Paul Dekker, "Politieke participatie van vrouwen en mannen in Nederland 1973–1986," *Acta Politica* 22(4), 1987: 409–447, and Monique Leijnaar, *De Geschade Heerlijkheid: Politiek Gedrag van Vrouwen en Mannen in Nederland, 1918–1988* ('s-Gravenhaage, Netherlands: SDU uitgeverij, 1989), chap. 3.

7. These types of participation are examined in Sidney Verba, Norman H. Nie, and Jae-on Kim, *Political Participation and Political Equality: A Seven-Nation Comparison* (Cambridge, England: Cambridge University Press, 1978), and Samuel H. Barnes, Max Kaase, et al., *Political Action: Mass Participation in Five Western Democracies* (Beverly Hills: Sage, 1979).

8. Gamma is the best measure of inequality because, unlike other measures of association, it remains large when activists are few but disproportionately male. Note, however, that sex differences measured by gamma tend to be larger than for other measures of association and that gamma is more vulnerable to sampling error when the marginals are highly skewed.

9. There are some obvious problems associated with this choice of measure, such as the small number of cases and the possibility of curvilinear patterns of change. Interpretation of the results should be consistent with the original trend data.

10. The Allensbach data show the diminution to be linear, not curvilinear. There are several plausible explanations for the discrepancy between the two types of data. The 1953 election study had relatively large deviations in the wording of the measures of partisanship, political efficacy, and, to some extent, attention to politics via the radio. Also, there are relatively few sampling points in the 1950s and 1960s for both types of surveys, and the discrepancies could simply be sampling error. Finally, the discrepancies could be real and could indicate, for example, that certain election campaigns focused on issues that particularly involved one sex.

11. Carol A. Christy, *Sex Differences in Political Participation: Processes of Change in Fourteen Nations* (New York: Praeger, 1987), pp. 97–98.

12. Carol A. Christy, "Gender, Employment, and Political Participation in Eleven Nations," paper presented at the Annual Meeting of the American Political Science Association, Washington, D.C., September 1983.

13. These factors are discussed in Helga Maria Hernes, "Women and the Welfare State: The Transition from Private to Public Dependence," in Harriet Holter (ed.), *Patriarch in a Welfare Society* (0510: Universitetsforlaget, 1984), pp. 26–45; Abby Peterson, "The Gender–Sex Dimension in Swedish Politics," *Acta Sociologica* 27(1), 1984: 3–17; and Randall, chap. 4, cited in note 1.

14. Elina Haavio-Mannila et al., *Unfinished Democracy: Women in Nordic Politics* (Oxford: Pergamon Press, 1985), p. 45.

15. Sten Berglund and Pertti Pesonen, with Gylfi P. Gislason, "Political Party Systems," in Erik Allardt et al. (eds.), *Nordic Democracy* (Copenhagen: Danske Selskab, 1981), pp. 80–125.

16. Hilda Scott, *Sweden's "Right to Be Human,"* (Armonk, NY: Sharp, 1982), p. 51.

17. Mechtild Fulles, *Frauen in Partei und Parlament* (Cologne: Verlag Wissenschaft und Politik, 1969) p. 38.

18. Jane Hall, "West Germany," in Joni Lovenduski and Jill Hills (eds.), *The Politics of the Second Electorate: Women and Public Participation* (London: Routledge & Kegan Paul, 1981), pp.

153–181; Fulles, cited in note 17; and Christy, cited in note 3.

19. Diffusion theory has a well-developed literature on change. See, for example, Lawrence A. Brown, *Diffusion Processes and Location: A Conceptual Framework and Bibliography* (Philadelphia: Regional Science Research Institute, 1968); Everett Rogers, *Diffusion of Innovation,* 3d ed. (New York: Free Press, 1983); and Vijay Mahajan and Robert A. Peterson, "Models for Innovation Diffusion," *Sage University Paper Series on Quantitative Applications in the Social Sciences* (Beverly Hills: Sage, 1985). The floor effect could be explained as the end of the classic S-shaped diffusion curve. However, in the United States, Norway, Sweden, and Canada (Gallup data), I did not find change consistently occurring first among younger, better-educated, and urban residents, as predicted by diffusion theory (Carol A. Christy, "Trends in Sex Differences in Political Participation: Results from the Norwegian and Swedish Election Studies," paper presented at the Annual Meeting of the Southern Political Science Association, 1986, and Carol A. Christy, "Canadian Trends in Sex Differences in Political Participation: 1945–1984," paper presented at the Annual Meeting of the American Political Science Association, 1986).

20. Data from the U.S. Census Bureau (*Current Population Reports,* Population Series P-20, no. 435, February 1989) show sex differences in turnout to have completely disappeared, with women voting more than men since 1980. However, in the survey data presented here, with the exception of 1984, more men than women reported having voted. Men tend to overreport having voted. The more recent presidential election studies have validated the reports of voting, but in order to be consistent over time, the trends presented here are based solely on the invalidated data.

In Quest of African American Political Woman

JEWEL L. PRESTAGE

The complete history of African American women's participation in American politics must recognize not only their involvement in traditional political acts such as registering, voting, and holding office but also those nontraditional activities in which they engaged long before gaining the ballot. Because African American women are simultaneously members of the two groups that have suffered the nation's most blatant exclusion from the normal channels of access to civic life, African Americans and women, their political behavior has been largely overlooked by political scientists, who have tended to focus primarily on those actions that conform to the more restrictive definitions of politics.[1] Because African American women have only recently been granted access to the political arena as voters and officeholders in significant numbers, there is a paucity of information about them in these roles and even less about their nontraditional actions that predated these roles.[2]

The purpose of this article is to begin a full exploration of the types and extent of political participation and behavior in which African American women have engaged. Utilizing extant social science literature and recent survey research findings by political science scholars, this quest for African American political woman will encompass a historical overview in which traditional and nontraditional political actions will be examined. Three basic contentions will permeate and guide the discussion.

The first contention is that throughout their existence on the American continent, African American women have been engaged in political activity, the nature of which has been determined by the legal and cultural circumstances they faced at the time. The second is that African American women's political activities have been directed toward altering their disadvantaged status both as African Americans and as women. Third is the observation that, historically, African American women have escalated their political activity progressively, moving from a predominance of nontraditional activity to a predominance of traditional activity, and have emerged as prime users of these traditional avenues in contemporary American politics.

. . .

THE SECOND RECONSTRUCTION (1944–PRESENT)

One of the mainstays of white political control in the South, the white primary election, was declared unconstitutional in 1944, creating a more positive environment for African Americans to realize their goal of becoming practitioners of traditional politics. Through individual and group initiatives, African Americans mounted an uphill battle against those legal and cultural norms that had militated against their aspirations in previous eras. African American women were made acutely aware of the irrelevance of the Nineteenth Amendment to their enfranchisement desires and earnestly joined in these race-based strategies.

Nontraditional activities were still necessary in the post–World War II broadside against racial discrimination at the polls. In litigation challenging state laws requiring segregation and discrimination in a variety of areas, including voter registration, and in lobbying for legislative remedies at the national level, African American women played prominent roles. Constance Baker Motley, legal counsel for the NAACP, and Thomasina Norford, lobbyist for the American Council on Human Rights in Washington, D.C., are examples. When the "outside of the courtroom" dimension of the movement emerged in the late 1950s and early 1960s, women again played significant roles in grass-roots organizations in local communities, in national coordination structures, and in confrontations with hostile police officers and anti-integration groups and individuals. Studies of demonstrations by African American college students show that 48 percent of those personally involved in sit-ins and freedom rides were female.[3] A study of participation in protests and more traditional antidiscrimination activity by New Orleans African American adults indicated only minimal overall differences between men and women.[4] Among those persons who achieved high visibility as pioneers in integrating previously segregated higher educational settings were African American women like Autherine Lucy, Ada Sipuel, Edith Jones, Vivian Malone, and Charlene Hunter. Other major activists in the civil rights movement were Rosa Parks, Daisy Bates, Fannie Lou Hamer, and Victoria DeLee. In the NAACP leadership ranks were Margaret Bush Wilson, Althea Simmons, and Jean Fairfax.

Writing about the civil rights movement, Professor William Chafe notes the pivotal, initiating role of African American women in defining issues of sex and race liberation for white women.[5] Within the context of the civil rights movement, African American women experienced and chose to consciously confront the issue of sexism. Through church organizations, women's clubs, sororities, and educational organizations, they provided monetary and moral support for civil rights workers, ranging from those registering voters to those engaged in more revolutionary politics.

Voting

With the passage of the 1965 Voting Rights Act, African American women received their first real opportunity to participate in traditional politics, since both the Fifteenth Amendment, which enfranchised men, and the Nineteenth, which benefited women, had in effect excluded them. Underscoring this is a 1966 publication declaring that African American women were, at the time, "frozen out" of the Southern political scene.[6] Clayton, in 1964, found that only a score or so of these women had achieved "success" in politics and that the "less than a dozen" in political offices across the nation had gained them through political parties.[7]

The 1965 Voting Rights Act was significant empowering legislation for African American women. It produced a remarkable escalation in the levels of African American voter registration and voting, especially in Southern states. For example, in Mississippi registration increased from about 8.0 percent to 62.0 percent between 1964 and 1968. In 1964 in Louisiana only 31.7 percent of the African American voting-age population was registered, but by 1970 over 55.0 percent was and by 1975 the figure had reached almost 67.0 percent.[8] These figures represent total registration of African Americans and comparable figures are not available along gender lines. Later voter-registration projections and voter-participation figures that are available along gender lines, however, lend some credibility to a projection that women were significantly represented among these new voters.

Studies of overall African American voter turnout show that it trailed white turnout from 1960 to 1980 and then surpassed it between 1980 and 1984. The total gain in turnout was 5.3 percent.[9] In fact, reported African American voting in 1984 was 5 percentage points higher than reported white voting when state-level political and contextual variables and demographic characteristics are held constant.[10] Clearly there has been a striking increase in overall African American voter turnout.

When the focus is narrowed to recent voting patterns of African American women, studies show that young African American women voted at a higher rate than did young African American men and that the gap in voting between African American men and women overall was less than the gap for whites. African American women from white-collar and manual occupations had slightly higher turnout rates than did their male counterparts until 1976, when parity emerged. While professional women voted at higher rates than did African American men of similar status, rates for the men in farm occupations were higher than for African American farm women. Regarded as undergirding this pattern of male-female voting differences were egalitarian sex-role orientations and assertive behavior of African American women at both the low and high ends of the economic scale. Feminist orientations were also associated with higher voter turnout. No single explanation was offered for the unusual pattern, however.[11] African American women who expressed the highest levels of political cynicism and the lowest levels of political efficacy increased their voting strength at greater levels than did any of the other race-sex groups.

As of 1988, African American women were reported to be 4 percentage points more likely to cast ballots than were African American men of comparable socioeconomic status. Especially remarkable, in historical context, is the finding that African American women who were heads of their households were 11 percent more likely to exercise the franchise than were white males, after controlling for demographic factors.[12]

Current available information would seem to suggest that African American women, the last group to acquire the ballot, have emerged as its prime users.

Holding Office

The holding of political office by African American women is a rather recent experience. The first African American woman elected to a state legislature took office in 1938, the first to ascend to the bench did so in 1939, the first to become a member of the federal bench was appointed in 1966, and the first elected to Congress was elected in 1968. The first roster of African American women officeholders widely available was prepared by the Joint Center for Political Studies in 1973 and contained 337 names. Table 1 reveals the progressive increase in the number of women on the rosters published annually. As of 1989, some 1814 of the 7226 African American elected officials on the roster, or roughly one-fourth, were women.

Probings of the characteristics of African American women officeholders have yielded both selected group profiles and a general profile. African American women state legislators serving in the mid-1970s were found to have mostly Southern origins, to be better educated than their parents and most Americans, to have been elected to office after age 40, to have experienced marriage, and to have children mostly over the age of 18. Most of them had no relative who had held political office. Most had exhibited pre-adult interest in politics, had occupations outside the home, and had little prior political experience and yet felt they took office with special advantage in some policy areas. Overall, women's liberation was not opposed, but it was not given high priority. Support of husbands, children, and other family members was considered important and was reportedly given to them to a great degree. All were Democrats representing urban areas.[13]

African American women judges display many of the same traits as do the legislators. Nearly half were born in the South and identified their background as working-class. Almost all reported affiliation with an organized religious denomination. Most were without a lawyer role model in their families, as only one fe-

Table 1   BLACK WOMEN AS A PERCENTAGE OF BLACK ELECTED OFFICIALS (BEOs)

Year	BEOs (total)	Female BEOs	Female BEOs as a percentage of total	Increase in number of female BEOs as a percentage of total
1969	N.A.	131	N.A.	N.A.
1970	1469	N.A.	N.A.	N.A.
1971	1860	N.A.	N.A.	N.A.
1972	2264	N.A.	N.A.	N.A.
1973	2621	337	12.8	N.A.
1974	2991	N.A.	N.A.	N.A.
1975	3503	530	15.1	N.A.
1976	3979	684	17.2	2.0
1977	4311	782	18.1	1.0
1978	4503	843	18.7	0.6
1979	4607	882	19.1	0.4
1980	4912	976	19.9	0.7
1981	5038	1021	20.3	0.4
1982	5160	1081	20.9	0.7
1983	5606	1223	21.8	0.9
1984	5654	1259	22.3	0.4
1985	6056	1359	22.4	0.2
1986	6424	1469	22.9	0.5
1987	6681	1564	23.4	1.0
1988	6829	1625	23.8	0.4
1989	7226	1814	25.1	1.3

Source: Roster of Black Elected Officials (Washington, DC: Joint Center for Political Studies, published annually).

Note: N.A. = not available.

male lawyer was reported among family members. About half were products of historically black colleges and universities, and a quarter of them received legal training at one of the five law schools at these institutions. The vast majority had experienced marriage and a smaller majority were mothers. Husbands were mostly labeled "overwhelmingly supportive," but for nearly half of the women, self-motivation was the source of inspiration for running for office. With reference to age, the majority were in their thirties and forties. Only one of the jurists gained initial office as a result of election. Appointment was the principal facilitator for access.[14]

When a 1983 study compared African American and white women elected officials with each other and with men, it was found that African American women, as a group, were "highly qualified, politically experienced and self-confident, outdoing women officeholders overall, who are themselves outdoing men."[15] They were also more likely than males and than women overall to have attended college, and they were more likely than men to have come from professional, technical, and managerial/administrative positions. While they were less likely than women overall to have political experience, they were more likely to have had staff experience and campaign experience.

Some race-specific differences in the experiences of African American and white women en route to office emerged. One was that groups and organizations were more important in gaining political access for African American women. Another was that, more than white women, the African Americans cited representation of minorities or civil rights issues and the ability to combat discrimination as the main reasons why they ran for office.

In terms of family characteristics, African American women were less likely to be married, less likely to evaluate spousal support as important in decisions to seek office, more likely to be college professors or lawyers, and less likely to have children, but more likely to have children under the age of 12. African American women overall were more likely than white women to be Democrats.

Like African American officeholders generally and women officeholders overall, African American women are concentrated most heavily in local positions. In fact, of the 1814 currently serving, 501 serve on local school boards, and 651 are members of municipal governing bodies, while 1 serves in the United States Congress, and 99 serve in state legislatures. Among the jurists, only 1 serves on a state court of last resort, 88 are on other courts, and 22 are magistrates or justices of the peace.

African American women officeholders seem to have found their major successes in the same electoral settings in which their male counterparts have achieved.

Even after obtaining access to traditional political channels, African American women continue to be involved in a variety of nontraditional activities. For example, they hold leadership positions in civil rights organizations and in interest groups with special relevance for African Americans.

The 1980s brought into being several organizations to accommodate and promote political activity among African Americans in which women have been quite active. Other organizations have been created exclusively for African American women. In the former category are the Congressional Black Caucus and the National Black Caucus of Local Elected Officials. The organizations especially for women include the National Association of Black Women Legislators and the National Political Congress of Black Women. The National Political Congress of Black Women held its first national assembly in 1985, with Shirley Chisholm, the nation's first black congresswoman, at the helm.

Women's Liberation

African American women's relationship to the contemporary women's liberation movement has been a mixed bag. A few African American women have been in the leadership cadre in the major organization, the National Organization for Women, but for most, the women's movement has not been accorded high priority. As early as 1973, the National Black Feminist Organization was formed as an option for African Americans to address feminist issues not dealt with to their satisfaction within the National Organization for Women. Over the last two decades, white women and African American women have worked together when their interests coincided, but, as Deckard points out, "friction does arise."[16] Despite the friction, African American women legislators, as well as African American male lawmakers, have been mostly supportive of women's issues. Curiously, the lack of high-priority status for the women's liberation movement among African American female officeholders has not translated into a lack of membership in women's liberation organizations. Nearly two-thirds of women state legislators who are African American belong to the Women's Political Caucus, compared to one-third of all women legislators. NOW membership is held by one-third of African American women, compared to only one-fifth of all women.[17]

Political Parties

African American women's political-party membership and work have increased progressively. While no complete authoritative record is available, the high visibility of Democratic women like Patricia Roberts Harris, Yvonne Burke Braithwaite, C. Dolores Tucker, Barbara Jordan, Cardiss Collins, and Maxine Waters as well as Republicans Jewel LaFontant, Gloria Toote, and LeGree Daniels indicates a change in the role of African American women in the major parties. Shirley Chisholm was the first to seriously contest for presidential nomination, but Charlotta Bass had been the vice presidential candidate on the Progressive Party ticket in 1952.

Political Socialization

Some interesting findings have emerged from studies of the political socialization of African American women, especially of those who hold political office. For example, the basic assumption undergirding ambition theory is that wanting political office is a prerequisite for winning office.[18] Studies show no significant difference in the political ambition of African American male and female officeholders, in spite of the overall lower social status, educational level, and occupational status of women.[19] Also, among African American women state legislators in the mid-1970s, only one stated unequivocally that she would not seek reelection or aspire to a higher office.[20] Comparisons of political ambition between African American women and white women indicate parity in ambition, but white women's ambition is more closely linked to nontraditional sex-role beliefs acquired early while African American women's ambition is associated more with their current activities.[21] This would seem to lessen the possible impact on African American women of the suppressive legal prescriptions and community practices that prevailed in the period before passage and implementation of the 1965 Voting Rights Act.

Do African American women possess coping skills that separate them from other women officeholders? Work by several scholars indicates that this is true for African American women professionals[22] and for political activists.[23] One scholar even contends that it was the independence of direction and action exhibited by African American women domestic workers that raised the consciousness of their white middle-class employers.[24]

Some African American women scholars have recently addressed the question of African American women's liberation as an issue separate from that of women's liberation, on one hand, and from African American liberation, on the other. Largely because this kind of perspective has been divisive in both the African Americans' and the women's struggles, African American women have generally opted to pursue a two-pronged struggle without taking a radical or self-interested posture in either of the existing movements. Political scientist Shelby Lewis has advised that African American women must construct and implement an independent liberation strategy, as no help can be expected from either of the three other race-sex groups—not even the admission that African American women are oppressed.[25] For either group to do so would acknowledge their culpability in that oppression. Lewis instructs that independence in thought is a prerequisite for independence in action. Given this line of argument, the extent to which there is an African American gender gap equivalent to that reported among white adults takes on special relevance. Research findings to date reveal no comparable division of African American political attitudes along gender lines, however.[26]

SUMMARY AND CONCLUSION

Historical precedence, as examined in this article, suggests that as long as both race and gender remain critical factors in determining life chances, quality of life, and access to what are considered the preferred values in American society, African American women will continue to respond both as African Americans and as women. The nature of that response will involve creative, innovative structures and strategies if the traditional ones are not available or prove to be ineffective. When and where the traditional channels have opened up, African American women have made optimum use of them. One critical issue that must be subjected to continuing and agonizing reappraisal by these women, however, is the efficacy of the traditional political machinery, to which they have only recently gained access, in the achievement of contemporary social and economic goals. In short, have African American women gained access only to find that access has lost its utility for delivering the resources sought? Are there lessons to be learned from the desertion of the ballot box by white males? Does the existence of powerful single-issue groups signal a fundamental change in American politics to which African American women must adapt?

In the search for indications of African American women's political behavior in the future, it would seem that the contingency orientation that has dominated their political behavior historically, the absence of a gender gap among African American adults, and the finding that race issues rather than gender issues are their priorities provide the best clues.

Notes

1. In Barbara J. Nelson, *American Women and Politics: A Selected Bibliography and Resource Guide* (New York: Garland, 1984).
2. John J. Stucker, "Women as Voters: Their Maturation as Political Persons in American Society," in *Women in the Professions*, ed. Laurily Keir Epstein (Lexington, MA: D. C. Keath, 1975), pp. 97–121.
3. Donald A. Matthews and James W. Prothro, *Negroes and the New Southern Politics* (New York: Harcourt, Brace & Jovanovich, 1966), pp. 416–19.
4. John Pierce, William Avery, and Addison Carey, Jr., "Sex Differences in Black Political Beliefs and Behaviors," *American Journal of Political Science*, May 1973, 422–30.
5. *Women and Equality* (New York: Oxford University Press, 1977), pp. 108–10.
6. Mathews and Prothro, *Negroes and the New Southern Politics*, p. 68.
7. Edward T. Clayton, *The Negro Politician* (Chicago: Johnson, 1964), pp. 122–48.
8. See the discussion in Jewel L. Prestage, "Black Politics and the Kerner Report: Concerns and Directions," *Social Science Quarterly*, 49:453–64 (Dec. 1968).
9. Patricia Gurin, Shirley Hatchett, and James S. Jackson, *Hope and Independence: Blacks' Response to Electoral and Party Politics* (New York: Russell Sage, 1989), p. 53.
10. Gerald Davis Jaynes and Robin M. Williams, Jr., eds., *A Common Destiny: Blacks and American Society* (Washington, DC: National Academy Press, 1989), pp. 234–35.
11. See Majorie Lansing, "The Voting Patterns of American Black Women," in *A Portrait of Marginality: The Political Behavior of the American Woman*, ed. Jewel L. Prestage and Marianne Githens (New York: David McKay, 1977), pp. 379–94; Sandra Baxter and Majorie Lansing, *Women and Politics: The Visible Majority* (Ann Arbor: University of Michigan Press, 1983), pp. 73–112.
12. *Common Destiny*, pp. 234–35.
13. Jewel L. Prestage, "Black Women State Legislators: A Profile," in *Portrait of Marginality*, ed. Prestage and Githens, pp. 401–18.
14. Jewel L. Prestage, "Black Women Judges: An Examination of Their Socio-Economic, Educational and Political Backgrounds, and Judicial Placement," in *Readings in American Political Issues*, ed. Franklin D. Jones and Michael O. Adams (Dubuque, IA: Kendall-Hunt, 1987), pp. 324–44.
15. Susan J. Carroll and Wendy S. Strimling, *Women's Routes to Elective Office: A Comparison with Men's* (New Brunswick, NJ: Rutgers University, Center for the American Woman and Politics, 1983), pt. 1, pp. 141–209.
16. Deckard, *Woman's Movement*, p. 346.
17. Carroll and Strimling, *Women's Routes*, pp. 141–209. See also Susan E. Marshall, "Equity Issues and Black-White Differences in Women's ERA Support," *Social Science Quarterly*, 71:299–314 (June 1990).
18. Joseph A. Schlesinger, *Ambition and Politics: Political Careers in the United States* (Chicago: Rand McNally, 1966), p. 1.
19. Pauline T. Stone, "Ambition Theory and the Black Politician," *Western Political Quarterly*, 33:94–107 (Mar. 1980).
20. Prestage, "Black Women State Legislators."
21. Jerry Perkins, "Political Ambition among United States Black and White Women: An Intergenerational Test of the Socialization Model," *Women and Politics*, 6:27–40 (1986).
22. Cynthia Fuchs Epstein, "Positive Effects of the Multiple Negative: Explaining the Success of Black Professional Women," *American Journal of Sociology*, Jan. 1973, pp. 913–35.
23. Chafe, *Women and Equality*, p. 109.
24. Charles V. Willie, "Marginality and Social Change," *Society*, 12:12 (July-Aug. 1975).
25. Shelby Lewis, "A Liberation Ideology. The Intersection of Race, Sex and Class," in *Women Rights, Feminism and Politics in the United States*, ed. Mary L. Shanley (Washington, DC: American Political Science Association, 1982) pp. 38–42.
26. Susan Welch and Lee Sigelman, "A Black Gender Gap?" *Social Science Quarterly*, 70:120–23 (Mar. 1989).

FURTHER READING FOR CHAPTER 2

Anderson, K. 1975. "Working Women and Political Participation, 1952–1972." *American Journal of Political Science* 19 (August).

Bean, C. 1991. "Gender and Political Participation in Australia." *Australian Journal of Social Issues* 26(4), November.

Christy, C. 1987. *Sex Differences in Political Participation: Processes of Change in Fourteen Nations.* New York: Praeger.

Dalton, R. 1988. *Citizen Politics in Western Democracies.* New Jersey: Chatham.

Darcy, R., S. Welch, and J. Clark. 1987. *Women, Elections and Representation.* New York: Longman.

Duverger, M. 1955. *The Political Role of Women.* Paris: UNESCO.

Githens, M., and J. Prestage. 1977. *A Portrait of Marginality.* New York: Longman.

Haavio-Mannila, E., et al. 1983. *Unfinished Democracy: Women in Nordic Politics.* New York: Pergamon Press.

Hartmann, S. 1989. *From Margin to Mainstream: American Women and Politics Since 1960.* New York: Knopf.

Lovenduski, J. 1986. *Women and European Politics.* Hempstead: Harvester Wheatsheaf.

Norris, P. 1991. "Gender Differences in Political Participation in Britain: Traditional, Radical and Revisionist Models." *Government and Opposition* 26 (Winter): 56–74.

Randall, V. 1987. *Women and Politics.* 2nd ed. Chicago: University of Chicago Press.

Sawer, M., and M. Simms. 1984. *A Woman's Place: Women in Australian Politics.* Sydney: Allen and Unwin.

Sapiro, V. 1983. *The Political Integration of Women: Roles, Socialization and Politics.* Urbana: University of Illinois Press.

Tilly, L., and P. Gurin (eds.). 1990. *Women, Politics and Change.* New York: Russell Sage.

Verba, M., N.Y. Nie, and J. Kim. 1978. *Participation and Political Equality: A Seven-Nation Comparison.* Cambridge: Cambridge University Press.

Welch, S. 1977. "Women as Political Animals? A Test of Some Explanations for Male-Female Political Participation Differences." *American Journal of Political Science* 21: 711–730.

CHAPTER
3

Elections and Political Attitudes

The key question for this chapter is whether gender is a fundamental social cleavage that influences our political attitudes, social values, electoral behavior, and partisan loyalties at mass and elite level. Are women different from men as voters and as politicians?

In the classic theory of Lipset and Rokkan,[1] social class and religion were regarded as the most important political cleavages throughout Europe because they reflect broadly based and long-standing social and economic divisions within society. Contemporary party systems result from complex historical processes, notably the national and industrial revolutions experienced by societies from the seventeenth century onward. In Europe, the division between church and state produced religious support for Christian Democrat parties; the division between landowners and industrialists helped create agrarian parties; and the division between employers and workers generated Social Democrat, Socialist, and Communist parties. In the United States, group support for the Democrats and Republicans is rooted in long-standing and complex historical realignments that were based on successive waves of external and internal immigration, regional divisions over the Civil War and civil rights, the urban-rural split, and the unionized worker–employer cleavage.

In different countries, groups based on social class, religion, language, ethnicity, and region became the primary building blocks for the political system. In contrast, gender was usually regarded as secondary, since women's interests were divided by cross-cutting cleavages such as class and generation. For Lipset and Rokkan the varying pattern of social cleavages across Europe in the nineteenth and early twentieth centuries established the essential framework for contemporary party systems. Lipset and Rokkan suggest that after the systems were established, they "froze" as parties strengthened links with their supporters and absorbed new social cleavages. In many countries women got the right to vote after the modern party system was established, and they were drawn into the existing framework. In recent years theorists like Inglehart[2] have questioned the stability of party systems, suggesting that a new cleavage in society, produced by the "postmaterial" revolution, may generate new parties. But the basic theory—that deep-rooted social cleavages are the foundation of party systems—remains the established theoretical paradigm for understanding electoral behavior. So, is gender a fundamental political cleavage? There are three viewpoints about trends over time.

DIVERGENCE

In the divergence view, gender may be seen as a basic and pervasive political division. During the nineteenth century in the United States and Europe, gender defined legal citizenship, the franchise, and property rights. During the twentieth century, women have become equal citizens but continue to be markedly underrepresented in political elites worldwide (see Chapter 7).

This view suggests that because of the early process of socialization, combined with adult experiences, our social background is intimately related to our social values. Women's life-styles, based on their roles within the family, the labor market, the welfare state, and the community, may be expected to lead to different patterns of political participation, partisan loyalties, and political priorities on a wide range of issues: child care, family support, public transport, the environment, technology, reproductive rights, welfare, education, and defense. Writers such as Carol Gilligan suggest that women have a distinctive set of values, which if articulated will transform traditional morality.[3] Gilligan stresses that this woman's perspective emphasizes personal relationships, "caring" responsibility to others, "nurturing" social compassion, pacifism, and concern about the environment. In contrast, men tend to be more concerned with rights and rules, with justice and fairness.

CONVERGENCE

The convergence model suggests that gender has relatively little impact on political attitudes today. It can be argued that in recent decades, after gaining equal citizenship rights, men and women are now subject to similar political influences through the mass media, the political parties, and the basic constitutional framework. Despite the growth of nontraditional families, many individuals remain within the household unit, sharing common economic and social interests. Furthermore, because of wider educational opportunities, increased participation in the paid work force, smaller families, the expansion of the welfare state, and the secular decline in churchgoing, women's life-styles are increasingly coming to resemble men's. Hence, we might expect gradual political convergence in electoral turnout; in partisan affiliations; in membership in secondary political groups such as unions and civic associations; and, eventually, in participation in local, state, and national elected office. This can be seen as part of a broader pattern of social dealignment—a loosening of the ties between social groups and parties—as policy issues, leadership personalities, and government performance become more important determinants of electoral behavior.[4]

MINIMAL THRESHOLD

The minimal threshold argument suggests that the relevance of gender differences in politics depends upon the broader institutional context. This view holds that when women are in a substantial minority within a legislature, they have to conform to the dominant procedures, practices, and norms of the institution. Hence, women who succeed in the current U.S. House of Representatives, the British House of Commons, or the French Assembly are more likely to resemble men in legislatures than women as a whole. But this may change once women achieve significant numbers within the legislature, as in the Scandinavian countries—once they pass the minimum threshold and are able to find their own voice.

THE GENDER GAP IN VOTING

We need to reexamine which of these alternative perspectives seems to give the most accurate account of American and European politics. The available evidence indicates that during the 1950s, women voters in most countries were consistently more conservative than men by a small margin.[5] In the classic work *The Political Role of Women,* published in 1955, Maurice Duverger found women voters were slightly more right-wing than men in Norway, France, and Germany. In the United States, the Gallup poll registered stronger female support for the Republican presidential candidate in every election from 1952 to 1968. Women's conservatism was commonly explained in terms of their greater longevity and religiosity and their lower trade union membership.[6]

Yet over the years the pattern has become more complex: by the 1980s gender differences in voting had converged in countries like Germany, Italy, and France while the gender gap converged and then reversed direction in the United States, Sweden, and Denmark.[7] Since 1980 American election surveys have repeatedly found women to be more liberal in four dimensions: party identification, presidential evaluations, and presidential and congressional elections.[8] During the 1980s women tended to favor the Democrats while men leaned toward the Republicans. According to exit polls, in 1988 women split their vote evenly between Bush and Dukakis while men gave Bush the winning edge. The difference between the male and female vote is not great—in the region of 4 to 10 percentage points—but it is politically important because it affects millions of votes. The gender difference poses problems for each party. The power of the ballot box was demonstrated in 1992 when the Democrats courted the "women's vote," emphasising a pro-choice, pro-parental leave platform and fielding record numbers of women candidates.

How do we explain the liberal gender gap in the United States? Despite considerable research, the reasons have not been clearly established, and there is much room for debate. In a controversial article, Pamela Conover found that American women as a whole do not seem to differ from men in their political values on issues such as egalitarianism, individualism, and liberal self-identification. Nevertheless, a feminist identity is significantly related to a range of domestic and foreign policy preferences and political values. Conover concluded that becoming a feminist may act as a catalyst, helping women recognize their underlying "female" values.

Nancy Walker compares women voters in Britain, France, and West Germany. She finds that the pattern of party support is mixed, but in general women are no longer more conservative than men, due to changes in age and family structure, work expectations, a decline in church attendance, and new issues in election campaigns. Yet Walker concludes that women in these countries have not become more left-wing, as in the United States. Convergence rather than divergence seems the more appropriate model.

Jo Freeman looks at the impact of the gender gap on American political parties, examining the role of women and the debate about feminism and family values at the Democratic and Republican national conventions in 1992. She argues that in recent decades the parties have become strongly polarized. Issues once seen as peripheral—such as gender roles, sexual behavior, reproduction, the care of children, and the intersection of work and family—have become central to the policy debate.

PIPPA NORRIS

Notes

1. S. Lipset and S. Rokkan, *Party Systems and Voter Alignments* (New York: Free Press, 1967), pp. 1–64.
2. Ronald Inglehart, *The Silent Revolution: Changing Values and Political Styles Among Western Publics* (Princeton, NJ: Princeton University Press, 1977); *Culture Shift in Advanced Industrial Societies* (Princeton, NJ: Princeton University Press, 1990).
3. Carol Gilligan, *In a Different Voice: Psychological Theories and Women's Development* (Cambridge, MA: Harvard University Press, 1982).
4. See Mark Franklin, Tom Mackie, Henry Valen, et al., *Electoral Change: Responses to Evolving Social and Attitudinal Structures in Western Countries* (Cambridge: Cambridge University Press, 1992).
5. For a review see Vicky Randall, *Women and Politics,* 2d ed. (London: Macmillan, 1987), pp. 68–78.
6. S. Lipset, *Political Man* (Garden City, NJ: Doubleday, 1960).
7. See Franklin et al., cited in note 4.
8. See Carol Mueller, *The Politics of the Gender Gap* (Newbury Park, CA: Sage, 1985).

Feminists and the Gender Gap

PAMELA JOHNSTON CONOVER

THE NATURE OF THE GENDER GAP

The term "gender gap" is a catch-all phrase referring to a variety of phenomena (Wirls, 1986). First, there may be gender gaps in levels of *mass participation;* however, recently these gaps have narrowed if not disappeared and consequently currently attract little attention (see Poole and Ziegler, 1985). More interesting are the *electoral* and *partisan* gender gaps. The electoral gap refers to the differing vote choices of men and women. In recent years, women have been more likely than men to support Democratic candidates (see Klein, 1985; Wirls, 1986). Closely related to the electoral gap is the partisan gap which refers to the differences between men and women in their party identifications. During the eighties, women have increasingly given their allegiance to the Democratic party so that currently they comprise a majority of Democratic identifiers (see Frankovic, 1982).

Both the electoral and partisan gaps have been the subjects of considerable research (see for example, Baxter and Lansing, 1983; Burris, 1984; Frankovic, 1982; Gilens, 1988; Klein, 1985; Mansbridge, 1985; Poole and Ziegler, 1985; Smeal, 1984; Wirls, 1986). Yet, although this research has clarified the extent of a gender gap in electoral results and partisan distributions, it has faltered in explaining *why* such gender gaps exist. Most studies point to the changing behavior of women (e.g., Abzug and Keller, 1984; Klein, 1985; Smeal, 1984) though some argue that the changing behavior of men has produced the gaps (e.g., Wirls, 1986). And most accounts hint that underlying these electoral and partisan gender gaps are sex differences in policy preferences and ideology (see Gilens, 1988).

That brings us to the fourth, and perhaps the most critical, variant of the gender gap: the growing disparity in the political attitudes of men and women. This gender gap in public opinion is important for several reasons (Shapiro and Mahajan, 1986). For one thing, to the extent that they are issue-based, the full explanation of the electoral and partisanship gaps becomes dependent upon understanding the gender gap in political preferences. More generally, the gender gap in public opinion may alter the salience of various political issues thus prompting changes in the political agenda. And, as the gender gap widens on particular issues there may be aggregate shifts in the public's preferences which in turn create pressure to change the direction of public policy (Page and Shapiro, 1983). As Robert Shapiro and Harpreet Mahajan (1986) point out, women are such a large group that even the emergence of small sex differences in issue preferences can have substantial consequences on public policy.

Yet, despite the potential importance of the gender gap in public opinion, it has attracted less attention than the other three. Moreover, the research that has been done has concentrated on documenting the existence of this gap rather than on explaining it (e.g., Erskine, 1971; Schneider, 1984; Smith, 1984; an exception to this is Gilens, 1988). In this vein, Shapiro and Mahajan's (1986) study is perhaps the most exhaustive. Their examination of public opinion data collected over the last twenty years reveals sizable and persistent gender differences in attitudes toward issues involving the use of force, and smaller, but growing sex differences toward other policies concerning regulation and public protection, social welfare, and traditional values (Shapiro and Mahajan, 1986). Shapiro and Mahajan (1986, p. 42) go on to conclude that "the salience of issues has increased greatly for women, and as a result differences in preferences have increased in ways consistent with the interests of women and the intentions of the women's movement."

But what accounts for such changes? In addressing this question, two distinct bodies of literature will be brought together: feminist political theory and empirical research on the gender gap. Specifically, insights gleaned from feminist theorists advocating a "woman-centered perspective" will be integrated with empirical evidence on gender differences to produce a fuller interpretation of the origins of the gender gap in public opinion.

"A WOMAN'S PERSPECTIVE"

Most explanations of the gender gap in public opinion are based on the notion that men and women have different political values and priorities which stem from fundamental value differences (see for example, Friedan and Dector, 1982; Shapiro and Mahajan, 1986; Tolleson Rinehart, 1985; and for a related argument, Carroll, 1985). Such an explanation triggers three questions. First, how and why do women's values differ from those of men? Second, how do such value differences manifest themselves in political preferences? And finally, what is the empirical evidence pertaining to a gender gap in political values? Let us address each of these in turn.

The Nature and Origins of "A Woman's Perspective"

The question of whether men and women differ in their fundamental values has concerned feminist theorists for some time. Nineteenth century American feminists often entertained the idea that, compared to men, women naturally embrace morally superior values (Stoper and Johnson, 1977). Writing in the late 1960s and early 1970s, contemporary feminist theorists described basic differences between the sexes as social constructions emanating from the different roles that men and women play in a patriarchal society (see Jaggar, 1983; Firestone, 1970; Millett, 1970). More recently, in analyzing such male-female differences as a source of oppression, feminists began to return to the themes of the nineteenth century and to perceive women's differences from men not as a "form of inadequacy or as a source of inferiority," but instead as a matter of pride, confidence, hope, and superiority (Eisenstein, 1983, p. 46). And so there emerged in the mid-1970s a "woman-centered perspective" focusing on the female experience as an unique source of values for society (see Eisenstein, 1983; Massey, 1985).

Advocates of this woman-centered perspective stress the distinctive aspects of women's lives, the values fostered by such life experiences, and the positive contributions to society that such values can make (see Chodorow, 1978; Dinnerstein, 1977; Rich, 1976; Ruddick, 1980, 1984). Moreover, in the course of these analyses some theorists have shifted away from a view of gender differences as socially constructed toward a perspective which stresses intrinsic, biological differences underlying femaleness and maleness (Eisenstein, 1983). As Marilyn Chapin Massey (1985, p. 7) explains, these radical feminists (e.g., Daly, 1984; Irigary, 1981; Kristeva, 1981) claim that "women speak a new truth arising from their unique physical experience. . .(a truth that) does not complement Western male moral discourse, but instead aims to subvert it."

What is this "new truth" that women speak? In "Maternal Thinking," Sara Ruddick (1980) suggests that women's interests in the preservation, growth, and acceptability of their children shape the way they look at the world. Some also argue that women approach ethical problems differently from men. Perhaps the most influential statement of this kind is Carol Gilligan's (1982): she posits that women are more oriented toward interpersonal relationships, and that this results in a conception of morality that stresses caring and responsibility toward others. In contrast, men are more concerned with rights and rules, and thus they emphasize justice and fairness in their moral decisions (for an examination of Gilligan's argument and more generally the "ethic of caring" see Tronto, 1987; Noddings, 1984).

It is argued, then, that a "woman's perspective" is responsive to growth and accepting of change, embodies compassion and caring for others, and manifests humility in its sensitivity to the realities of the environment (Grimshaw, 1986, p. 241).[1] It is also a perspective with uncertain origins: it might be fostered by different social roles or it might be an intrinsic manifestation of the innate differences between men and women. But, regardless of its origins, the question must be asked: how does a woman's perspective come to influence politics?

Politics and "A Woman's Perspective"

Proponents of a woman-centered analysis argue that an infusion of women's values into the political arena will transform society in a positive fashion (see for example, Daly, 1984; Massey, 1985; Ruddick, 1980). But, as critics have pointed out, it is not altogether clear precisely how this injection of values and subsequent cultural transformation are to take place (see Grimshaw, 1986; Dietz, 1985; Eisenstein, 1983). If it is to be argued that a "woman's" values have the potential to transform politics, some mechanism of transformation must be identified.

From the perspective of some feminists, the most obvious mechanism to fill such a role is a *feminist identity and consciousness*. Specifically, it is argued that in the absence of a feminist identity a woman's values usually lie dormant beneath the male-oriented values of the dominant culture. But, in the process of becoming a feminist, women develop a sense of consciousness that enables them to discover their true values which may then serve as a basis for their politics (see Ruddick, 1980; Rich, 1976). Thus, becoming a feminist helps women "recover" their basic values which, in turn, shape their sense of political consciousness, and ultimately their preferences on political issues.

Some would object, however, that a feminist *political* consciousness rooted solely in a woman's values is not enough to ensure either the infusion of those values into politics or the subsequent adoption of distinctive issue preferences. Instead, they argue that if the public world is to be transformed a woman's values must be coupled with, if not subordinated to, democratic political values (see Grimshaw, 1986; Dietz, 1985, 1987; Eisenstein, 1983). As Mary Dietz (1985, p. 32) asserts ". . . the only consciousness that can serve as a basis for this transformation . . . is a distinctly political consciousness steeped in a commitment to democratic values, participatory citizenship, and egalitarianism."[2] In essence, such theorists posit that if women are going to alter the political agenda, a particular set of political values may be more crucial than a "woman's" values.

These theoretical arguments have several implications that are potentially testable. First, at the aggregate level, they suggest that the widening of the gender gap in the late 1970s may be linked to the growing strength of the women's movement. And indeed, this is an argument that a number of scholars have made though not empirically tested (see for example, Friedan and Dector, 1982; Shapiro and Mahajan, 1986; Tolleson Rinehart, 1985). Second, these theoretical arguments imply that a woman's values should be more readily expressed by feminists and more obviously reflected in their politics. Third, and finally, the injection of a woman's values into politics may be related to a commitment to democratic values.

· · ·

The Gender Gap and a Feminist Identity

Women differ in their political values depending on the degree to which they identify as feminists. Is it mainly feminists, then, whose views explain the gender gap in issue preferences? As a first step toward answering this question, table 1 presents the mean position on the value scales for men, and for feminist and nonfeminist women as defined earlier.

As illustrated in table 1, nonfeminists, like women in general, do not differ from men in political values. The feminists, however, do differ from men significantly on three of the four political value orientations: egalitarianism, symbolic racism, and ideology. Specifically, feminists are more committed than men to the value of equality; they evidence less symbolic racism than men; and they are considerably more liberal than men.

Table 1 VALUE DIFFERENCES BETWEEN MALES AND NONFEMINIST WOMEN
AND BETWEEN MALES AND FEMINIST WOMEN

| Orientations | Males | Mean | | Significance of t-test | |
		Non-feminists	Feminists	Males-non-feminists	Males-feminists
Political value					
Egalitarianism	.54	.34	.62	.69	.00*
Individualism	.54	.58	.55	.08	.65
Symbolic racism	.64	.64	.58	.94	.02*
Liberal-conservative identification	.63	.66	.54	.31	.02*
Basic value					
Moral traditionalism	.49	.54	.48	.01*	.62
Religious fundamentalism	.27	.41	.42	.00*	.00*
Sex roles	.69	.65	.77	.15	.01*
Sympathy for the disadvantaged	.67	.68	.74	.31	.00*

* = $p \le .05$.

With respect to the more basic value orientations, . . . earlier analysis uncovered sex differences in religious fundamentalism and sympathy for the disadvantaged. When men are compared separately to feminist and nonfeminist women, the sex difference in religious fundamentalism persists in both cases. Feminists and nonfeminists alike tend to be more religious than men. For the remaining values, however, the pattern of sex differences changes when women are divided into feminist and nonfeminist groups. Specifically, nonfeminist women compared to men have a stronger sense of moral traditionalism; in contrast, feminists resemble men in their level of moral traditionalism.

But, most important are the findings with regard to sympathy for the disadvantaged. Nonfeminist women are similar to men in their degree of caring for the disadvantaged; the mean value for nonfeminist women is .68 on the disadvantaged scale as compared to .67 for men. By contrast, feminists differ greatly from men in the stronger sense of caring that they display; they average .74 on the sympathy scale. Thus, the gender gap in sympathy for the disadvantaged is due entirely to the more caring posture adopted by feminist women. This finding may be interpreted in several ways. On the one hand, it may indicate that a feminist identity is, indeed, necessary to express in politics a woman's natural tendency toward caring. Alternatively, the high degree of sympathy that feminist women display may be an outgrowth of their other political values (e.g., egalitarianism) and not their femaleness per se. Or, some combination of these two explanations may be at work.

One way of testing these alternative explanations is to compare feminist women to feminist men. If the differences in sympathy persist between these two groups, it would tend to support the argument that women are naturally more sympathetic and caring than men. On the other hand, if the sex differences in sympathy disappear when feminist women are compared to feminist men, it would suggest that the political values associated with feminism help to account for the greater sympathy of feminist women. Unfortunately, the 1985 NES Pilot Study does not include a comparable measure of feminist identity for men. Thus, at this time it is impossible to determine if feminist women are more sympathetic to the disadvantaged than men because of their femaleness or because of their political ideology.

Finally, we can turn to the question of the gender gap in issue preferences. Earlier it was discovered that a feminist identity is associated with a distinctive pattern of issue preferences. This raises the possibility that the gender gap in issue preferences may be mainly due to the liberal policy positions of feminist women. This hypothesis is tested in table 2 where the policy preferences of men are compared to those of nonfeminist and feminist women.

Previous research has demonstrated that consistently the largest gender gap is on foreign policy issues (Shapiro and Mahajan, 1986). With respect to such is-

Table 3.2　DIFFERENCES IN ISSUE PREFERENCES BETWEEN MALES AND NONFEMINIST WOMEN AND BETWEEN MALES AND FEMINIST WOMEN

Issues	Males	Mean		Significance of t-test	
		Non-feminists	Feminists	Males-non-feminists	Males-feminists
Foreign policy					
Conventional war	3.5	3.6	3.0	.60	.01*
Nuclear war	3.5	3.4	3.0	.41	.00*
Central America	2.9	2.4	1.9	.00*	.00*
Defense spending	4.1	4.0	3.7	.42	.00*
Domestic					
Spending On:					
Older people	1.5	1.3	1.3	.00*	.00*
Social security	1.6	1.5	1.5	.07	.01*
Medicare	1.7	1.5	1.5	.02*	.01*
Food stamps	2.2	2.3	2.0	.89	.01*
Unemployed	1.9	1.7	1.5	.00*	.00*
Big cities	2.0	2.0	1.7	.36	.00*
Women	1.9	1.8	1.7	.47	.02*
Child care	1.8	1.7	1.6	.09	.01*
Affirmative action					
for women	2.0	2.0	1.9	.99	.09
Equal opportunity					
for blacks	2.8	2.6	2.3	.08	.00*
Guaranteed jobs	4.5	4.4	3.6	.80	.00*
Abortion	1.1	1.2	1.1	.31	.56
School prayer	2.0	2.6	2.2	.01*	.38

* = $p \le .05$.

sues, nonfeminist women do not differ significantly from men with the exception of the issue of Central America. In contrast again, feminists differ significantly from men on every foreign policy issue. Thus, in most cases, the sizable gender gap on foreign policy issues appears to be due to the antiwar, anti-involvement positions adopted by feminists.

In the domestic policy realm, nonfeminist women differ significantly from men on issues affecting the old (e.g. medicare and spending on older people) as well as spending on unemployment. Beyond that, however, the nonfeminist women resemble men in their spending preferences. In contrast, on virtually every domestic policy issue feminists differ significantly from men, adopting on average more liberal positions than those of both men and nonfeminist women. Only on social policies such as abortion and school prayer do feminists resemble men in their issue preferences. Thus, both nonfeminist and feminist women contribute to the gender gap on domestic issues, but the contribution of the feminist women is by far the greater of the two. Taken together, these findings on domestic and foreign policy issues suggest that the gender gap in policy preferences is only rarely due to widespread differences between men and women as a whole. Instead, on most issues the gender gap in public opinion is a function of the liberal positions that a subset of women—feminists—consistently adopt.

CONCLUSIONS

In recent years, a great deal of attention has been focused on the gender gap in electoral behavior. The appearance of this gap has both intrigued and puzzled analysts. In seeking to explain it, researchers stumbled upon an even more interesting gender gap, a gap between men and women in policy preferences. Various explanations for the gap in policy preferences have been offered: men and women are socialized differently, or, feminist consciousness has altered opinions. Most such explanations share an underlying theme: the idea that, for whatever reason, women have different values and priorities than men. In effect, it is argued that there is a distinctive woman's perspective that shapes how women view politics.

Our findings suggest that, in fact, men and women do not generally differ in their political values. As a group, women are no more or no less egalitarian, individualistic, racist, or liberal than men. Gender differences do exist, however, in more basic value orientations. Thus, women are more committed to fundamentalism than are men; and they have more positive feelings than men do toward the disadvantaged in society. This finding is important because it provides preliminary evidence in support of the argument that there is a distinctive woman's perspective characterized by an ethic of caring.

Yet, the lack of more pervasive value differences between men and women is puzzling and makes the growing gender gap in policy preferences difficult to explain. Feminist theorists provide a key to solving this empirical puzzle by positing that becoming a feminist may be a catalyst that helps women recognize their underlying "female" values.[3] This argument suggests that it is essential to look at differences among women if we are to understand the origins of the gender gap.

Accordingly, I investigated the manner in which a feminist identity influences women's values and policy preferences. This identity proves to be strongly related to political values, to basic value orientations and ultimately to issue preferences. These findings have implications for both our understanding of the gender gap and for feminist theory. With respect to the gender gap, they suggest the possibility that there is not so much a gap between men and women as there is a gap between men and feminist women. When men are compared to feminist women there is a significant gender gap on every type of issue; however, on most foreign policy issues (where the gender gap is largest) and many domestic issues, this gap evaporates when men are compared to nonfeminist women. In effect, a substantial part of the gender gap can be attributed to the liberal issue positions adopted by feminist women. Moreover, while it is not very surprising to find that feminist women are more liberal than men in general, it is startling to discover that there are enough feminists who are liberal enough to create almost on their own the appearance of a widespread gender gap.

With regard to feminist theory, the distinctiveness of feminists' values suggests several things. First, it lends support to the argument that a feminist identity fosters the expression of a woman's perspective. In particular, our analysis reveals a gender gap in sympathy for the disadvantaged that is due almost entirely to feminist women. Thus, *if* there is an underlying woman's perspective that encompasses an ethic of caring, its expression is facilitated by a feminist identity. Second, it is important to recognize that the distinctive policy preferences of feminists do not stem solely from a woman's value perspective; instead, their issue positions are also shaped by a commitment to democratic political values as well as by a strong identification with the Democratic Party. This finding provides empirical support for the theoretical contention of Dietz (1985) and others (e.g., Grimshaw, 1986; Eisenstein, 1983): namely, that to be politically effective a feminist consciousness must embrace not only a woman's values but perhaps more importantly, democratic political values. Only when the two are combined do you arrive at a distinctive set of policy preferences which if pursued would substantially alter the political agenda.

Notes

1. A more specific variant of the "woman's perspective" argument is the "maternalist" argument advanced by such theorists as Ruddick (1980, 1984), Hartsock (1985), and Elshtain (1981).
2. Dietz (1987) goes a step further and argues that there are real dangers inherent in arguing that women are morally superior to men. Among the most serious of these dangers is that such a perspective fosters a vision of politics and citizenship that, in the end, is unlikely to produce the transformation of the political world that feminists desire.
3. It is of course possible that what feminist theorists have called a *woman's* perspective is, in fact, simply a *feminist* perspective. This would provide an alternative explanation of why feminists express the woman's perspective while nonfeminist women do not. Unfortunately, testing the feminists' assertion that a woman's perspective lies dormant in all women until "uncovered" in the process of becoming a feminist would be very difficult outside of an experimental setting. On the other hand, the fact that nonfeminist women also differ from men in some values, issue preferences, and moral orientations (see Gilligan, 1982) suggests both that the expression of a woman's perspective may not be solely dependent on the catalyst of a feminist identity, and that a woman's values are not simply a misnamed version of feminists' values.

References

Abzug, Bella, and M. Kelber. 1984. *Gender Gap*. Boston: Houghton Mifflin Co.

Baxter, Sandra, and Marjorie Lansing. 1983. *Women and Politics: The Visible Majority*. 2d ed. Ann Arbor: University of Michigan Press.

Berman, Marshall. 1983. Feminism, Community, Freedom. *Dissent*, 30:247–55.

Burris, Val. 1984. The Meaning of the Gender Gap: A Comment on Goertzel. *Journal of Politics and Military Sociology*, 12:335–43.

Carroll, Susan. 1985. Gender Schema and Mass Politics. A paper presented at the annual meeting of the Midwest Political Science Association, Chicago, April 1985.

Chodorow, Nancy. 1978. *The Reproduction of Mothering: Psychoanalysis and the Sociology of Gender*. Berkeley: University of California Press.

Conover, Pamela Johnston, Stanley Feldman. 1986. Religion, Morality and Politics: Moral Traditionalism in the 1980s. A paper presented at the annual meeting of the American Political Science Association, Washington DC, September 1986.

Conover, Pamela Johnston, and Virginia Gray. 1983. *Feminism and the New Right: Conflict Over the American Family*. New York: Praeger.

Christenson, James A., and Riley E. Dunlap. 1984. Freedom and Equality in American Political Ideology: Race and Gender Differences. *Social Science Quarterly*, 65:861–67.

Crosby, Faye J. 1982. *Relative Deprivation and Working Women*. New York: Oxford University Press.

Daly, Mary. 1984. *Pure Lust: Elemental Feminist Philosophy*. Boston: Beacon Press.

Dietz, Mary G. 1985. Citizenship with a Feminist Face: The Problem with Maternal Thinking. *Political Theory*, 13:19–38.

———. 1987. Context is All: Feminism and Theories of Citizenship. *Daedalus*, 116:1–24.

Dinnerstein, Dorothy. 1977. *The Mermaid and the Minotaur: Sexual Arrangements and Human Malaise*. New York: Harper and Row.

Ehrenreich, Barbara. 1983. On Feminism, Family and Community. *Dissent*, 30:103–9.

Eisenberg, Nancy, and Roger Lennon. 1983. Sex Differences in Empathy and Related Capacities. *Psychological Bulletin*, 94:100–31.

Eisenstein, Hester. 1983. *Contemporary Feminist Thought*. Boston: G. K. Hall & Co.

Elshtain, Jean. 1981. *Public Man, Private Woman: Women in Social and Political Thought*. Oxford: Princeton University Press.

———. 1982. Feminism, Family and Community. *Dissent*, 29:442–49.

Erskine, Hazel. 1971. The Polls: Women's Role. *Public Opinion Quarterly*, 35:275–90.

Fiorina, Morris P. 1981. *Retrospective Voting in American National Elections*. New Haven: Yale University Press.

Firestone, Shulamith. 1970. *The Dialectic of Sex: The Case for Feminist Revolution*. New York: Bantam Books.

Frankovic, Kathleen. 1982. Sex and Politics—New Alignments, Old Issues. *PS*, 15:439–48.

Friedan, Betty, and Midge Dector. 1982. Are Women Different Today? *Public Opinion*, (5)20, 41.

Gilens, Martin. 1988. Gender and Support for Reagan: A Comprehensive Model of Presidential Approval. *American Journal of Political Science*, 32:19–49.

Gilligan, Carol. 1982. *In a Different Voice: Psychological Theories and Women's Development*. Cambridge, MA: Harvard University Press.

Greeno, Catherine G., and Eleanor Maccoby. 1986. How Different is the "Different Voice"? *Signs*, 11:310–16.

Grimshaw, Jean. 1986. *Philosophy and Feminist Thinking*. Minneapolis, MN: University of Minnesota Press.

Gurin, Patricia. 1985. Women's Gender Consciousness. *Public Opinion Quarterly*, 49:143–63.

Hartsock, Nancy C. 1985. *Money, Sex and Power*. Boston: Northeastern University Press.

Irigaray, Luce. 1981. This Sex Which is Not One. In Elaine Marks and Isabelle de Courtivson, eds., Claudia Reedev, trans., *New French Feminisms: An Anthology*. New York: Schocken.

Jaggar, Alison. 1983. *Feminist Politics and Human Nature*. Totawa NJ: Rowman and Allanheld.

Klein, Ethel. 1984. *Gender Politics*. Cambridge, MA: Harvard University Press.

———. 1985. The Gender Gap: Different Issues, Different Answers. *The Brookings Review*, 3:33–37.

Kristeva, Julia. 1981. Woman Can Never Be Defined. Translated by Marilyn August. In Elaine Marks and Isabelle de Courtivson, eds., *New French Feminisms: An Anthology.* New York: Schocken.

Luria, Zella. 1986. A Methodological Critique. *Signs,* 11:317–25.

Maccoby, Eleanor. 1985. Social Groupings in Childhood: Their Relationship to Prosocial and Antisocial Behavior in Boys and Girls. In Dan Olwens, Jack Block, and Marian Radke-Yarrow, eds., *Development of Antisocial and Prosocial Behavior: Theories, Research and Issues.* San Diego: Academic Press.

Mansbridge, Jane J. 1985. Myth and Reality: The ERA and the Gender Gap in the 1980 Elections. *Public Opinion Quarterly,* 49:164–78.

Massey, Marilyn Chapin. 1985. *The Feminine Soul: The Fate of an Ideal.* Boston: Beacon Press.

Millett, Kate. 1970. *Sexual Politics.* Reprint. New York: Avon Books.

Noddings, Nel. 1984. *Caring: A Feminine Approach to Ethics and Moral Education.* Berkeley: University of California Press.

Page, Benjamin I., and Robert Y. Shapiro. 1983. Effects of Public Opinion on Policy. *American Political Science Review,* 77:175–90.

Poole, Keith T., and L. Harmon Zeigler. 1985. *Women, Public Opinion, and Politics.* New York: Longman.

Rich, Adrienne. 1976. *Of Woman Born: Motherhood as Experience and Institution.* New York: W. W. Norton.

Rokeach, Milton. 1973. *The Nature of Human Values.* New York: Free Press.

Ruddick, Sara. 1980. Maternal Thinking. *Feminist Studies,* 6:342–67.

———. 1984. Preservative Love and Military Destruction: Some Reflections on Mothering and Peace. In Joyce Trebilcot, ed., *Mothering: Essays in Feminist Theory.* Totowa, NJ: Rowman and Allanheld.

Schneider, William. 1984. Opinion Outlook: The Democrats are Counting on the Gender Gap, But it May Not be Much Help. *National Journal,* June 23:1242–43.

Sears, David O., and Leonie Huddy. 1987. Women as a Political Interest Group in the Mass Public. In P. Gurin and L. Tilly, eds., *Women in Twentieth Century American Politics.* New York: Russell Sage Foundation.

Shapiro, Robert Y., and Harpreet Mahajan. 1986. Gender Differences in Policy Preferences: A Summary of Trends from the 1960s to the 1980s. *Public Opinion Quarterly,* 50:42–61.

Smeal, Eleanor. 1984. *Why and How Women Will Elect the Next President.* New York: Harper and Row.

Smith, Tom W. 1984. The Polls: Gender and Attitudes toward Violence. *Public Opinion Quarterly,* 48:384–96.

Stoper, Emily, and Roberta Ann Johnson. 1977. The Weaker Sex and the Better Half: The Idea of Women's Moral Superiority in the American Feminist Movement. *Polity,* 10:192–217.

Tajfel, Henri. 1981. *Human Groups and Social Categories.* Cambridge: Cambridge University Press.

Tolleson Rinehart, Sue. 1985. Political Cognition and Political Style: Differences in Male and Female Orientations to Politics. A paper presented at the annual meeting of the American Political Science Association, New Orleans, September 1985.

Tronto, Joan. 1987. Beyond Gender Difference to a Theory of Care. *Signs,* 12:644–63.

Vaux, Alan. 1985. Variations in Social Support Associated with Gender, Ethnicity and Age. *Journal of Social Issues,* 41:89–110.

Wassenberg, Pinky S., Kay G. Wolsborn, Paul R. Hagner, and John C. Pierce. 1983. Gender Differences in Political Conceptualization, 1956–1980. *American Politics Quarterly,* 11:181–204.

Wirls, Donald. 1986. Reinterpreting the Gender Gap. *Public Opinion Quarterly,* 50:316–30.

What We Know About Women Voters in Britain, France, and West Germany

NANCY J. WALKER

Whenever the consequences of women's suffrage have been studied, it would appear that women differ from men in their political behavior only in being somewhat more frequently apathetic, parochial, conservative, and sensitive to the personality, emotional, and aesthetic aspects of political life in electoral campaigns.

Civic Culture, Almond and Verba, 1963

When *Civic Culture* was written, voting patterns and political attitudes showed women in Europe to be the more conservative—and more Conservative—of the two sexes. According to one popular saying of the time, if women had not been granted suffrage, the Labour party would have held office in Great Britain since the end of World War II.[1] Further, in the early sixties "everyone" knew that women formed the base of support for the Christian parties on the continent. Two and a half decades later, we're about due for a new set of conclusions about gender and politics.

GREAT EXPECTATIONS

German women fought for and won the right to vote in 1919. Propertied British women could go to the polls in 1920, but it was only in 1928 that universal suffrage was put on the books. And the nineteenth amendment to the American Constitution was signed into law in 1920. French women lagged behind their European and North American sisters, waiting until 1944 for the right to cast a

British data are taken from the British Election Studies, which started in the early sixties and are based on national samples of eligible voters. The British Election Studies asked respondents if they had voted, and while the resulting turnout rates are higher than the actual rate, we have no reason to believe that either men or women are more likely to exaggerate. German data, on the other hand, are actual representative election statistics. In some 200 representative constituencies, voters put their ballot papers into boxes according to age and gender, unthinkable concept in the United States or Great Britain, but one that allows for highly accurate electoral analysis based on age and gender.

61

ballot, partly because of strong opposition in the Senate. One anti-suffrage French senator quoted ancient authors to justify his position: "The woman of the Latin race does not think, does not feel, does not develop like the woman of Anglo-Saxon or Germanic races."

Women's entrance into the formal political sphere raised great hopes. They were expected to bring morality into politics and change the conduct of public life by waging battles against corruption, alcoholism, and even war.

Despite raised expectations, turnout among women was initially below that of men in all countries. It increased slowly but steadily with each election. After World War II the turnout gap was still evident, particularly in France, but it continued to narrow. Table 1 shows the percentage of men and women who've gone to the polls since the founding of the Federal Republic of Germany in 1949 and indicates the percentage of British men and women claiming to have voted, from 1964 to 1987. In both cases the gender difference decreased over time, becoming extremely small or disappearing by the mid-sixties. When controlled for age, the gender difference is much smaller among the young and over time has closed among the older age groups, as the older cohort has moved out of the electorate.

The Euro-barometre poll suggests that turnout among French women is not quite as high as among British and German women, possibly because suffrage was

Table 1

TURNOUT BY GENDER
WEST GERMANY, 1953–1987

	1953	1957	1961	1965	1969	1972	1976	1980	1983	1987
Men	88%	90%	89%	88%	88%	91%	91%	88%	89%	84%
Women	85	86	860	85	85	90	90	87	88	82
Difference	3	4	3	3	3	1	1	1	1	2

TURNOUT BY GENDER
GREAT BRITAIN, 1964–1987

	1964	1966	1970	1974	1974	1979	1983	1987
Men	91%	85%	81%	89%	85%	85%	83%	
Women	87	83	82	87	85	86	84	
Difference	4	2	−1	2	0	−1	−1	0

Source: For Germany, Joachim Hofmann-Goettig (1953–1983), Representative Wahlstatistik (1987); For Great Britain, British Election Studies.

granted in France so recently. As in Great Britain and Germany, younger French women are as likely to vote as younger men are.

Voting is only one measure of political participation, and by other gauges women in these three countries still lag behind the men, although the gaps are narrowing. Women are less likely than men to be members of a political party, less likely to give money to a party or candidate, and less likely to work for a political campaign. Among certain social groups, however—the upper and upper-middle classes in Britain, for example—women form the core of Conservative party workers. The Tory party could never manage to complete its mailings and canvassing without the aid of its loyal ladies.

Table 2 INTEREST IN POLITICS BY GENDER IN GREAT BRITAIN, WEST GERMANY, FRANCE

	Great Britain			
	1959	1964	1974	1979
Not interested				
Men	31%	24%	28%	32%
Women	48	35	41	46

	West Germany			
	1952	1959	1965	1980
Men	18%	20%	6%	5%
Women	50	45	28	14

	France		
	1953	1969	1978
Men	28%	34%	13%
Women	60	47	20

Source: For Great Britain, 1959: *Civic Culture* response was "Pay no attention to elections or politics"; 1964: British Election Survey, "Not much"; 1974 October: British Election Study, "Not much" plus "None at all"; 1979 British Election Study, same as 1974. *For West Germany,* 1952, 1965, and 1980: Allensbach Institute; for 1959: *Civic Culture. For France,* 1953, 1969, and 1978: Mossuz-Lavau/Sineau.

POLITICAL AND COMMUNITY PARTICIPATION BY GENDER IN GREAT BRITAIN, WEST GERMANY, FRANCE (RATIO: WOMEN TO MEN)

	Talk Politics		Belong to Group	
	1959	1983	1959	1983
Great Britain	.82	.95	.45	.78
West Germany	.60	.90	.36	.75
France		.98		.74

Source: For 1959, *Civic Culture;* for 1983, Euro-barometre, Men and Women of Europe.

Gender differences also persist in expressions of interest in politics and campaigns. In the early 1950s in Germany and France, women were two and a half times more likely than men to express *no* interest in politics—a majority of women in both countries. The gender difference was not quite so large in Great Britain. By the mid- to late sixties, about a third of all women—but only a fifth of the men—were uninterested in politics. The British gender gap narrowed in the late seventies, when both men and women plummeted into apathy, but even then women were more apathetic than men. This gender difference was always smaller among the younger and college-educated men and women in all three countries, but it persists today.

Talking about politics used to be a male prerogative, but this too has changed with the times. A 1959 question from *Civic Culture* and one from the Euro-barometre (1983) shows that the ratio of women to men who discuss politics has increased in both Great Britain and West Germany. In 1959 sixty German women for every one hundred German men discussed politics, but in 1983 it became ninety to one hundred. The number in Great Britain started out higher, with eighty-two women for one hundred men engaging in political conversations, and ninety-five British women for every one hundred men by 1983. Educated, working, younger women talk politics as often as men do in all three countries (see table 2).

IF POLITICAL, THEN CONSERVATIVE?

Women were long thought to be apolitical, but if they were political then they were supposed to be conservative. Women's greater church attendance was one influence that led in this direction. But women's conservative inclinations seem to be changing.

In Great Britain the Conservative party's lead among women voters had disappeared in 1983, as shown in table 3. The Conservative lead declined during the late 1970s even among older voters (over sixty-five), virtually disappearing in the last two British elections. Younger voters, known to some as "Thatcher's children," display greater gender differences in voting, but in no persistent direction (see table 4). In some elections since 1964, the under twenty-five-year-old women were more likely than the youthful menfolk to support the Conservatives, in others they were more likely to throw their support to Labour. Since the Liberal/Social Democratic Alliance was formed in 1981, it seems that young women are slightly more inclined than young men to take the middle road, as both 1983 and 1987 election results suggest. In 1987 the MORI poll shows a huge lead for the Conservatives among Thatcher's boys, but a lead for Labour among Thatcher's girls. It's too early for definitive statements, though.

In the Federal Republic of Germany the right-of-center Christian Democratic party (CDU) used to boast a significantly higher percentage of women's votes than men's, but since the mid-1970s this lead has dwindled (see table 5). The left-of-center Social Democratic party (SPD) used to assume that more men than

Table 3 PARTY VOTE BY GENDER IN GREAT BRITAIN, 1964–1987

	1964	1966	1970	1974	1974	1979	1983	1987
Conservative								
Men	40%	36%	43%	37%	35%	45%	46%	43%
Women	43	40	48	39	37	49	45	43
Labour								
Men	47	54	48	42	45	38	30	32
Women	47	51	41	40	40	38	28	32
Liberal/SDP								
Men	12	9	7	17	16	15	23	23
Women	10	8	8	21	20	13	26	23

Note: Two elections were held in 1974.

Source: British Election Studies (1964–1983); Market & Opinion Research International (1987).

Table 4 PARTY VOTE BY GENDER AND AGE IN GREAT BRITAIN, 1964–1987

	1964	1966	1970	1974	1974	1979	1983	1987
65 years and over								
Conservative								
Men	48%	40%	45%	47%	46%	52%	50%	47%
Women	46	46	61	51	46	57	51	46
Labour								
Men	46	49	44	38	38	37	32	30
Women	44	50	30	34	37	32	26	33
Liberal/SDP								
Men	7	11	5	13	12	9	17	22
Women	9	4	8	14	16	10	21	20
Under 25 years								
Conservative								
Men	47	43	35	20	17	44	46	42
Women	33	33	40	30	32	36	40	31
Labour								
Men	45	50	51	39	53	38	33	37
Women	56	63	51	44	51	47	29	42
Liberal/SDP								
Men		7	12	28	23	23	19	19
Women		3	6	25	16	15	28	24

Source: See Table 2.

Table 5 PARTY VOTE BY GENDER IN WEST GERMANY, 1953–1987

	1953	1957	1961	1965	1969	1972	1976	1980	1983	1987
SPD										
Men	33%	36%	40%	44%	46%	47%	44%	43%	38%	39%
Women	28	29	33	36	40	46	43	44	39	38
CDU/CSU										
Men	39	45	40	42	41	43	47	44	48	43
Women	47	54	50	52	51	46	49	44	49	45
FDP										
Men	11	9	14	10	6	9	8	11	7	9
Women	10	7	12	9	5	8	8	11	6	8
Greens										
Men								2	6	8
Women								1	5	8

Note: Other parties not shown.

Source: Joachim Hofmann-Goettig (1953–1983); Representative Wahlstatistik (1987).

women voted for it, but since 1972 this is no longer the case, and the SPD is look-ing to younger women to provide its margin of victory in future elections. Men have always been slightly more likely to vote for the liberal-leaning Free Democ-rats (FDP), but the gender difference was never vast. The coming of the left-wing Greens into the Bundestag in 1983 certainly shook up German politics, but de-spite their excellent record on sexual equality, the Greens attract slightly fewer women than men.

The German gender difference in voting patterns is still somewhat evident to-day. Women over sixty did support the CDU in 1987 with much more fervor—and ballots—than older men did. But demographics may explain this as much as anything—there are many, many more women than men over sixty. The youthful vote in Germany started to diverge from the general pattern in 1972, with young women no more likely than young men to vote CDU, unlike the older genera-tions. From 1972 until today, younger women cast more SPD ballots than young men. This margin shrank somewhat in 1987, to the dismay of the Social Democ-rats. The Greens drew their support heavily from the votes of "Kohl's children," with boys and girls in equal proportions (see table 6).

French trends were similar to those in Britain and Germany, with women forming the solid base of support for the Christian right and providing substan-tially fewer ballots than men to the French Communists. A decline in church at-tendance, coupled with an increase in college-educated and working women, helped diminish the gender differences on the right. Since Mitterrand came to power in 1981, the parties of the right no longer have a lead among women voters and are unlikely to regain it . . .

Trends in the three countries suggest that the stereotype of the conservative and Christian woman voter no longer holds. Changes in age and family structure and work expectations, decline in church attendance, and new issues in the politi-

Table 6 PARTY VOTE BY GENDER AND AGE WEST GERMANY, 1953–1987

	1953	1957	1961	1965	1969	1972	1976	1980	1983	1987
60 years and over										
SPD										
Men	30%	32%	36%	41%	42%	43%	42%	41%	40%	38%
Women	25	26	30	33	37	42	42	43	40	37
CDU/CSU										
Men	42	47	43	44	45	50	51	51	51	50
Women	51	57	54	56	56	52	53	49	54	54
FDP										
Men	11	8	13	10	6	7	6	7	7	8
Women	10	7	11	9	4	6	5	8	5	7
Greens										
Men									2	2
Women									1	2
Under 25 years*										
SPD										
Men	34	38	41	43	48	54	49	48	38	38
Women	29	31	35	37	45	55	50	50	41	39
CDU/CSU										
Men	41	46	43	46	40	35	40	36	42	37
Women	48	53	50	53	47	36	40	33	40	35
FDP										
Men	12	8	12	8	7	10	9	11	5	9
Women	10	7	12	8	6	9	9	12	5	8
Greens										
Men								5	14	15
Women								4	14	17

Note: * = under age 30 (1953–1969), Other parties not shown.

Source: See Table 4.

cal marketplace have all contributed to the voting shift in the last twenty to thirty years. There is no reason to assume it will stop here in the late 1980s.

WOOING WOMEN VOTERS

Once the political parties in Britain, France, and Germany realized that women voters were no longer more conservative than men voters, they changed their approach to capture the "women's vote." But the election of June 1987 in Britain and January 1987 in Germany saw the parties of the left making the same mistakes in interpreting these movements that the Democrats in the United States did in 1984. Attempts to woo women voters in France have evolved differently.

Under the conservative government of Valery Giscard d'Estaing, the French established a State Secretariat for the Concerns of Women as early as 1974, which was elevated to ministry status in 1978. The justification was that in post-1968 France, women were starting to become more active politically, making demands about equal rights, divorce, pro-choice legislation, and job opportunities.

At the time, analysts decided that women were going to make their voting decisions on women's issues and that the parties should respond in order to reap the benefits of women's votes. It is probably true that some women decided to support the Socialists in the 1970s and 1980s because of the party's more liberal position on divorce, abortion, and equal opportunity. But the left never persuaded some of the older and more conservative women (or men) to cross party lines because of these positions. The Socialists made appeals to young working women in 1981, a more receptive audience. There is some evidence that turnout among this group increased, to the benefit of the Socialists. This is the correct strategy—appeal to a group of women (or men) who have reasons, usually economic, to cast their ballots for one party or another.

During the most recent British election the Labour party promised to establish a Ministry for Women should they be elected to power. The theory behind the decision, in addition to the belief that a women's ministry should exist, was that it would bring in women's votes. The logic is dubious. The women (and men) who would support the idea of a Ministry for Women are likely Labour supporters anyway. The number of women who might switch from the Alliance to Labour because of this particular campaign promise was small at best (the number of men switching even smaller). In addition, the Labour party did not consider that the promise might lose votes for them among the older (and more socially traditional) Labour supporters who might have felt that this contributed to the image of Labour as a party of special-interest groups.

The Labour party in Britain has a chance to pick up more votes among women, particularly white-collar workers and those in the helping professions. These women have been drawn to the more moderate but less traditional Alliance during the last two elections. Labour, in trying to modernize its image, could target these low-paid women by making the argument that the Labour party is best suited to serve their economic needs. The Labour party failed to make a pitch to older voters, mainly women, who are dependent on the welfare state for their livelihood. . . .

The German Social Democrats did not promise to elevate the women's section of the Ministry for Health, Family, Youth, and Women to a separate ministry. But in a postelection internal memo analyzing the 1987 campaign, they suggested that women's votes could provide the future margin of victory, noting that turnout among younger women had been particularly low in the contest. They discussed a need to promote women's issues as one key to the "women's vote." This might be somewhat successful for the women under thirty-five but would probably not be a big vote winner. The SPD realizes the stark generational difference in voting in the Federal Republic, but they don't go beyond that to note which issues are likely to matter to younger working women or older women who are dependent on social security.

ISSUE DIFFERENCES

The expectation that women—as a bloc vote—would provide the margin of victory for the left is misguided. Women are no more a bloc vote than men are.

Men and women do tend to differ on some issues, even when age, religion, education, and labor force participation are factored out. Women on both sides of the Atlantic are in general less inclined to support government policies that involve the use of force, for example. They are more peace-minded than men on siting cruise missiles in Germany, stationing troops in Northern Ireland, and increasing the defense budget. National interest sometimes overtakes their objections, though: French men and women of the left and right are rather in favor of an independent *French* nuclear deterrent; British women are more inclined than British men to think *American* nuclear missiles are a threat to peace, but a majority of these same women join their compatriots in believing that *British* nuclear weapons increase their overall security.

In Britain during the last two elections, men and women alike saw unemployment as the most important problem facing the country. But women were less likely than men to identify national defense or international relations as the next most important issue. Rather, slightly more women felt that education and the National Health Service should be given greater government attention.

On women's issues such as abortion and equal rights, women as a whole are no more liberal than men. Older women are sometimes more conservative on these issues than are older men. Younger women are sometimes—but not often—more liberal than their contemporaries among men, as younger men today also support liberal abortion legislation and equal rights. The intensity of feeling about women's issues is higher among women, whether in strong support or strong opposition. With the abortion issue, for example, any gain a party makes in picking up a woman voter because of a liberal position on women's issues would probably be negated by comparable losses.

In addition to gender differences of opinion, the persistence of the "Don't Know Woman" is a curious phenomenon. On questions of economics, defense, international relations, and to some extent civil rights, women in these three countries are much more likely than men to answer "Don't Know" or "No Opinion." True in all three countries, the tendency is found in the United States as well. This gender difference is smaller for highly educated women but does not go away entirely. On education, health policy, and local issues, the "Don't Know Woman" is less in evidence. And interestingly, on women's issues, particularly abortion questions, men give more frequent "Don't Knows" than women. Differing "Don't Knows" should provide additional clues to the political parties in attracting women and groups of men as voters.

The biggest change in the women's vote since *Civic Culture* was written a quarter century ago is that women now vote at a rate roughly comparable to the rate for men. They have made a more subtle shift away from predictable conservatism and toward a collection of issue concerns that is not substantially different from men's. This makes the political parties' task more difficult than if women voted as a bloc. For the parties to succeed, they're going to have to woo and win the women just as they do the men.

Feminism vs. Family Values

Women at the 1992 Democratic and Republican Conventions

JO FREEMAN

The 1992 Conventions of the Democratic and Republican Parties saw the culmination of trends which have been developing for twenty years. The two major political parties have now polarized around feminism and the reaction to it. On these issues the parties are not following the traditional pattern of presenting different versions of the same thing, or following each other's lead into new territory.[1]

Although the party platforms and the speeches at the conventions devoted many words to many issues, each party's vision can be summed up in a slogan. The Republicans articulated theirs clearly in the phrase "family values." While their platform does not define this slogan, both the document and the speeches indicate that it stands for programs and policies which strengthen the traditional two-parent, patriarchal family in which the husband is the breadwinner, the wife is the caretaker, and children are completely subject to parental authority. The Democrats attempted their usual strategy of pre-emption and co-optation by borrowing the Republican's phrase to use in a different context, but their very use of it belied its content. In reality the Democrats have incorporated the feminist demand that "the personal is political" and have put on the public agenda issues which were once deemed to be purely personal. The most controversial of these is abortion; the most recent is sexual harassment. In between are a plethora of concerns ranging from wife abuse and incest, to ending discrimination against gays, lesbians and others living nontraditional lifestyles, to proposals to reduce the conflict between work and family obligations.

HISTORY

When the feminist movement emerged in the mid-sixties, the major parties did not view women, let alone feminists, as worthy of notice. Support for the Equal Rights Amendment had been removed from the Democratic Party's Platform in 1960 and the Republican Party's in 1964. By 1968 the sole reference in the Republican Platform was "concern for the unique problems of citizens long disadvantaged in our total society by race, color, national origin, creed or sex." The Democratic Platform did not go that far. The words "women" or "sex" did not appear anyplace.[2]

This changed in 1972. In 1970 the feminist movement became publicly known. In 1971 the National Women's Political Caucus was founded specifically to bring more women into mainstream politics, including the major political parties. At the 1972 national nominating conventions its Democratic and Republican Task Forces organized feminists to put their issues back into the Platforms and to increase the number of women delegates. Although feminist activities at the Democratic Convention were by far the more public and the more publicized of the two, the Task Forces were about equally successful in achieving their goals. The ERA was put back into both parties' platforms; proposed planks on abortion were left out.[3] Women's percent of delegates increased from 13 to 40 percent in the Democratic Convention, and from 17 to 30 percent at the Republicans'. The greater increase at the former was because Democratic women were riding a reform movement within the party to make it more accessible. While this movement to write national rules which would curb the power of the local machines was stimulated more by the Civil Rights and Antiwar Movements than by incipient feminism, it created an opportunity which the NWPC used to women's advantage.[4]

By 1976 feminists were strong enough within both parties to engage in major battles, but they were very different battles. The fight within the Democratic Party was over the "50-50" rule to require that from 1980 on all delegations would have to be half women. This change was proposed because there had been a sharp falloff of women delegates from 40 to 34 percent at the 1976 Convention. It lost in the Rules Committee, but with enough support for a minority report, and thus a potential floor fight. The Carter campaign controlled a majority of the votes and did not support the 50-50 rule. However, neither did it want a bloody floor fight in a year in which the Democrats sensed victory. After several days of negotiations Carter compromised by agreeing to *promote* equal division in future conventions and a floor fight was avoided. In December of 1979 the Democratic National Committee voted to require that all future delegations be half women.

At the 1976 Republican Convention, the fight was over keeping the ERA in the Republican Party platform. Although ostensibly between Phyllis Schlafley's STOP ERA and Republican feminists affiliated with the NWPC, this fight was a surrogate for the struggle between the Reagan and Ford factions of the party, and it was ultimately these two campaigns which decided what would be in the Platform. The Republican Party's Platform Committee meets the week before its national convention, unlike the Democrats who draft their platform in the Spring. In

1976, STOP ERA was gaining momentum in state battles; it mobilized Reagan delegates to remove the ERA clause from the Platform. Defeated in the subcommittee and barely reinstated by 51 to 47 in the full Platform Committee, the ERA was ripe for a major floor fight. However, Reagan only wanted a floor debate on two issues and this wasn't one of them. Thanks to candidates Ford and Reagan, the ERA stayed in the Republican Platform until 1980.

In 1980 neither convention saw much fighting. Yet it was clear from reading the platforms that the polarization over feminist issues that had emerged in 1976 was escalating. Both feminists and anti-feminists had established their hegemony over their respective parties' positions by 1980 and were consolidating their power. The few remaining feminists in the Republican Party had no ties to the victorious Reagan campaign and the ERA was removed from the Platform by a full Committee vote of 90 to 9. Abortion actually received more support than the ERA. A motion for neutral recognition of the right to differ on the issue only lost by 75 to 18. For the Democratic convention minority planks had been filed and floor fights scheduled on both the ERA and abortion, but the issue was not support, but how much support. Feminists wanted "the Democratic Party [to] offer no financial support . . . to candidates who do not support the ERA" and to go on record in favor of government funding of abortions for poor women. Though the Carter campaign supported neither of these, both were passed by the Convention itself without much debate—the former by acclamation and the latter by a two to one margin.

By 1984, both feminists and anti-feminists had so thoroughly permeated the two national parties that they could truly be called insiders in the dominant Presidential campaigns. NOW's Action Vice President was put on the Democratic Platform Committee by Mondale's campaign with "sign off" authority on all planks of interest to feminists. Phyllis Schlafly sat on the national defense subcommittee of the Republican Platform Committee but gave directions on the language she wanted in other subcommittees through Eagle Forum supporters. Nothing on women was put in the platform without her agreement. Feminists focused their energies on persuading Mondale to run with a woman; once they succeeded, they celebrated at the convention. Republican feminists boycotted their convention as futile; the few who tried to testify on the ERA at the platform hearings were questioned about Geraldine Ferraro's family finances. Outside the convention, NOW did not even march in protest as it had in 1976 and 1980. 1,700 people came to Schlafly's fundraiser, where prominent feminists were parodied.

Conflict re-emerged in the 1988 conventions, but it was subtle, muted by the desires of feminists in both parties to win the Presidency and to be on good terms with the winners. The Democrats wrote a feminist platform in consultation with representatives of several national organizations, but only after initial drafts that left out mention of the ERA and abortion. NOW moved from being a powerful insider in 1984 to commenting from the fringes that women were still being neglected; other women's organizations told the press that women were now such insiders that they didn't have to be catered to as in the past. At the Republican Convention, abortion, which had been shunned by GOP feminists in the 1970s, became *the* issue. However, most of the earlier Republican feminists were no longer involved with the Party, or were part of the Bush team and more interested in avoiding divisiveness than making policy. Thus it was mostly a new group of women, and men, who opposed support for the human life amendment in the Republican platform and tried to remove language which declared that "the unborn child has a fundamental right to life which cannot be infringed." They lost by 55 to 32. Instead of taking the issue to the convention floor, several had a press conference in which they lauded the "progressive platform" and declared their support for George Bush.

The ease with which feminists and anti-feminists could have their respective positions adopted by the two major parties was facilitated by major transformations occurring within each party. The reform movement within the Democratic Party changed it from a coalition of state parties and local machines into one of national constituencies. Organized labor retained its traditional clout, but over time it was joined by organized minority groups, women, gays and lesbians and others who won acceptance within the party by their ability to elect delegates, raise money and conduct quadrennial struggles over platform planks and rules changes.

The Republican Party saw the emergence of a powerful interest group, the New Christian Right, despite a political culture that was traditionally hostile to organized interest groups within it. In the 1970s several well known ministers were recruited by hard right Republicans looking for troops. They in turn persuaded their deeply religious followers to overcome their repugnance of party politics as well as their traditional Democratic voting habits. Politicized by the legalization of abortion, evangelical Christians began to move into the Republican Party in 1980 to support Ronald Reagan. Pat Robertson's 1988 Presidential campaign organized them to become delegates to that convention. Not warmly received by more traditional Republicans who found them rather déclassé, their persistence, organization and numbers compelled their reluctant acceptance. The following year Robertson organized his campaign supporters into the Christian Coalition. Aided by a $64,000 grant in October 1990 from the National Republican Senatorial Committee, by 1992 the CC claimed 550 chapters in 50 states with thirteen million dollars in donations from 250,000 members. Using what executive director Ralph Reed Jr. described as "stealth" tactics to avoid the stigma attached to religious activism, it claims to have taken over the state Republican Party in at least a dozen states and to have elected dozens of its candidates in state and local races.[5] Although the Christian Coalition only claimed 300 delegates at the 1992 convention, including 20 members on the Platform Committee, the Christian right had the same hegemony over social issues within the Republican Party that the liberal constituency groups did in the Democratic Party. They not only wrote the Platform, but the party line.

THE 1992 CONVENTIONS

Despite running rapidly in the opposite directions, the Democratic and Republican Parties had several themes in common at the 1992 Conventions. Foremost was harmony on the inside.[6] Most of the protests, and there were more than usual this year, were on the outside by groups for whom the conventions were primarily a press availability, not a chance to educate delegates from all over the country. Abortion was the reigning issue; no longer seen as just a "women's issue," or even a debatable one, it has become a deep moral conflict on which elections can be won and lost and on which deviance from each party's official line is tantamount to treason. To the women in the parties, however, electing more of their own took up more time than talking about the right to choose. Showcasing candidates and raising money to elect more women were emphasized far more than in any previous convention.

Harmony There was very little fighting in part because each convention's most contentious delegates (except Jerry Brown's) either felt their concerns were adequately met by the winning candidates, or there were not enough of them to mount an effective protest. The newest claimant in the Democratic Party coalition, the Lesbian and Gay Caucus, with 104 "out" delegates most of whom weren't pledged to Clinton, felt it had "tremendous access."[7] Feminists had no complaint. They liked the platform. They liked the speeches. Unlike Dukakis in 1988, Clinton honored the party's women by making his only off-the-floor speech at their Tuesday morning gathering. NOW, which usually provided at least a voice of disagreement, stayed outside. The only dissident voice was Jerry Brown's, who was largely ignored.

At the Republican Convention, there was a lot of press play over abortion, but it was mostly smoke; the few pro-choice delegates did not come organized or even inclined to oppose their President on this issue. "Embarrassing" the President through public dissent is not considered proper behavior for Republicans; it often results in ostracism. The Right kept quiet because even before the convention began it had been given the platform, several prime time spots on the program, frequent invitations to the Presidential box, and Vice President Dan Quayle as the featured speaker at a God and Country revival hosted by Rev. Pat Robertson. The most lively moments at the GOP convention were the several occasions when ACT-UP activists, disguised as press or Republicans, disrupted a speech or other event. They were quickly dragged out.

Abortion Internal harmony did not prevent abortion, pro- or con-, from being a dominant motif, but only at the Republican Convention was there even token dissent from established orthodoxy; Massachusetts Governor William Weld was allowed to leave a pro-choice line in his convention speech, though he was booed for his boldness. As in the past, the Democrats permitted a quiet floor demonstration with "Pro Choice, Pro Clinton" signs passed to the delegates on the floor. This one was held while six pro-choice Republican women endorsed Clinton from the podium. Their presence emphasized the fact that the Democrats no longer see the issue as a matter of principle or even as deference to one of its constituency groups. Democrats are now convinced that it's the way to win elections. Convention chair Ann Richards denied Pennsylvania Governor Robert P. Casey's request to speak against what he claimed was the Platform's support of "abortion on demand."[8] She herself set the tone when she began her own opening remarks Monday night by declaring "I'm Pro-Choice and I vote." Virtually every speaker in the four day marathon pledged fealty to choice and received thunderous applause. Just in case the Democrats lost, the National Abortion Rights Action League (NARAL) and Planned Parenthood lobbied for the Freedom of Choice Act, by which Congress would limit the state's ability to impose restrictions on abortion.

The full Platform deliberations of both parties each saw a futile motion by one delegate to remove all language on abortion. The speeches that followed could hardly be called debate; they were overwhelmingly in favor of keeping the issue in both platforms, largely expressed in emotional and personal terms. Of course the opinions were for the opposite positions, as was the vote in each Platform Committee. However, the Republicans' refusal to remove their pro-life language got more press because they voted in Houston the week before their convention, in full view of hungry reporters, while Operation Rescue was blocking clinics around the city. The Democratic Platform Committee voted in Washington a month before the New York convention when no one was paying much attention. Thus, dissent was less disruptive for the Democrats.

Protests As usual, people came from all over the country to march in the streets or stand outside the convention hall holding signs. And as has been true since the bloody conflicts with police at the 1968 Democratic convention in Chicago, the protests were tightly controlled. Both NOW and NARAL used the Republican protest site for major rallies, the former two days before the convention began, and the latter while President Bush was being renominated inside. Neither organized marches at the Democratic convention, though a committee of New York City NOW did. According to Jill Ackerman, members of NOW-NYC's Women's Anti-Violence Committee were frustrated at their inability to get an anti-violence plank into the Democratic Party platform, or to even present testimony on it at the Platform Committee's May hearing. Therefore they invited New York City's many feminist groups to weekly meetings to plan a march around this theme, and its numerous feminist luminaries to address the crowd. Over 6,000 marched a mile on July 13, during the first convention session, to hear a very long list of speakers give personal and political testimony late into the night.

Candidates The importance of running for office and winning was the one issue on which Republicans and Democrats could agree, and the one issue which divided feminists in the Democratic Party from pro-choice Republicans. The big events at both conventions were receptions and press conferences to introduce women candidates and parties to raise money for them. The NWPC held a "Salute to Women of Color" for select Democratic candidates, funded with $5,000 from Avon and AT&T, attended by hundreds, and a press conference for Republican women attended by dozens. It wasn't alone. DNC Vice Chair Lynn Cutler's office put out a three page Calendar of Women's Events with 13 events for candidates, some to raise money, some to introduce candidates, and some to toast fundraisers. The 128,000 member National Federation of Republican Women, which was founded in 1938 and has focused on electing Republicans, not women, printed its own three pages with eight candidate events, *not* including the NWPC's or those of pro-choice Republicans.

By 1992 there were eleven national political action committees (PACs), which gave money predominantly to women candidates or functioned with a predominantly female donor base. The oldest is the bipartisan Women's Campaign Fund (WCF), which started in 1974. The best known is Emily's List (Early Money Is Like Yeast). Founded only in 1985 to support Democratic women candidates for federal or statewide offices, it was a chief beneficiary of women's anger at the 1991 Hill/Thomas hearings making it one of the most powerful political organizations in Washington.[9] Several had convention events. Emily's List said it raised $750,000 at its convention reception. Its Republican counterpart, WISH (Women in Senate and House), which was only formed in 1992, said it raised $200,000 for pro-choice Republican women.[10] According to the NWPC, 29 of the 57 Republican women running for Congress were pro-choice. Emily's List and WISH supported women who ran against each other. In addition several organizations have PACS and even the Parties are getting in on the act. The Democratic Senatorial Campaign Committee has established a Women's Council and the Republicans have the Women's Leadership Network and the Women's House Republican Victory Committee.[11]

Reflecting the interest in raising money for women candidates rather than raising feminist consciousness or even training women in political skills is the fact that Emily's List boasted 15,000 "members," who paid $100 just to receive a newsletter and recommendations on which women should receive donations to their campaigns. The NWPC, a bipartisan membership organization committed to train women to run for office, only had 10,000 "governing members," many of whom resent the national body's pre-emption of candidate endorsements and lack of membership services. Both Emily's List and the WCF made the Federal Election Commission's "top-50" PAC list in 1992. Neither NOW nor the NWPC did.

Delegates In the past, the convention press offices issued news releases with statistics describing the delegates, usually written to emphasize the diversity of the Democrats and hide the homogeneity of the Republicans. Not in 1992. However the DNC delegate tracker did provide a printout of delegates (but not alternates) on request. Although Party rules mandate that half of all state delegations be women, the large number of Superdelegates, who are public or party officials, creates some discrepancies. Of the 4319 delegates to the Democratic Convention, 2146 were female and 2173 were male. Only those elected at the District level were truly 50-50; the Superdelegates were 70% male and the at-large delegates were 70% female. Racial breakdowns showed that the 70% who were white and the 2.4% who were Asian/Pacific were more likely to be male; the 7.6% Hispanics, 1.2% Native American and 18% African Americans were more likely to be female. Surveys by news organizations indicate, as has been true for many decades, that Democratic delegates, even Superdelegates, are more liberal than Democratic voters on both economic and social issues. Unfortunately, the surveys did not provide delegate responses by sex. The 50-50 requirement came at the time that women became a significant majority of Democratic voters. Among those who identified themselves as Democrats in 1992, there are 30% more women than men.

The Republican convention press office would not even admit there was a delegate tracker, let alone provide statistics in 1992. However, the Associated

Press contacted 2206 of the 2210 known delegates, and some other news organizations did sample surveys. AP's figures show that 41% of the GOP delegates were women; CBS estimated 43%. Males predominated in all racial groups, 83% of whom were white (CBS says 86%). Mirroring the Democrats, the surveys showed that delegates were much more conservative than Republican voters. CBS said they were "possibly the most conservative since CBS began polling delegates on this question in 1976." A cursory review of answers to the CBS poll questions indicates that the Platform Committee members were *much* more conservative than the Republican delegates, especially on abortion.

Speakers Since the conventions are media events, the parties use their speakers to create an image, as well as to reward important people and acknowledge key players. It is sometimes difficult to know which role is being played by whom. The Democratic Party emphasized its pro-choice position by bringing Republican women on to the podium and by showcasing a large number of women candidates Tuesday night. The press dubbed this Women's Night, joking that the Democrats were featuring women when men would be watching the All-Star baseball game. More notable was the prominence of women on Monday night when Ann Richards, Barbara Jordan and Barbara Mikulski all spoke and the women Senate candidates were introduced. No one said this was showcasing women; it was simply another Democratic show. The Republicans also had a few key women speakers, but even those that were pro-choice (e.g., Secretary of Labor Lynn Martin) carefully avoided any reference to anything that might be identified as feminist. Instead the Republicans staged a "family values" night, whose message was conveyed through addresses by the first and second ladies on the importance of electing their husbands. The Republicans used a nontraditional mode (speeches by wives) to impress on viewers their concern with traditional values.

The Platform The Democratic Party's Platform writing process is less public than that of the Republicans. The Platform Committee finishes its work the month before the convention, while the Republicans have continued the tradition of deliberating on a draft the week before. In 1992 the Democrats began later than usual, holding the first and only hearing in Cleveland, Ohio on May 18. There was no open mike. Organizational representatives and individuals who received permission to speak included Bella Abzug, NARAL, NWPC, BPW and the YWCA. In past years these organizations and others have joined together to negotiate specific language with the platform committee or the campaign; occasionally individuals representing feminist organizations have been appointed to the Platform Committee. Neither happened in 1992. Instead most members of the Platform Committee were sufficiently conscious of feminist issues to put them in automatically. Half of the 15 person drafting committee was appointed by the Clinton campaign, and half by DNC Chairman Ron Brown. The campaign had an especially close working relationship with NARAL, and was particularly concerned with health issues. Consequently, the women on the committee, such as San Francisco Supervisor Roberta Achtenberg, made a special effort to put in planks on women's health issues, such as breast cancer, while more traditional feminist issues, such as the ERA and pay equity, barely got an honorable mention.

This time there was no separate section on women, though there were on "choice" and on "strengthening families." Feminist concerns were blended into these paragraphs and those on worker's rights, civil rights, health care, crime and community.

Like the Democrats, the Republican Party has required that members to the Platform Committee be half female since 1944. But unlike the Democrats, they must also be delegates, and there can be no more than two members per state.[12] Also like the Democrats, the GOP holds regional hearings in the Spring. In 1992 there were four; the one in Salt Lake City on May 26 allocated twenty minutes to abortion. Mary Dent Crisp of the National Republican Coalition for Choice and Ann Stone of Republicans for Choice gave the pro-choice position; Phyllis Schlafly and Beverley LaHaye of Concerned Women for America spoke for pro-life. Despite an effort to minimize attention to the issue, the presence of demonstrations meant it was the only one which made the headlines.[13] Everyone thought the confrontation in Salt Lake foreordained Houston. Stone announced to the press that she would have enough support for a floor fight and sent out direct mail letters soliciting contributions to change the party platform. In late July she sent a "pro-choice caravan" from Washington to Houston intending to rally the faithful along the way. It was a flop. The media and abortion opponents outnumbered supporters. Stone explained the low turnout by disclaiming "Republicans don't do rallies; that's not our thing."[14]

The Platform Committee, largely chosen after the hearings were over, was so packed with pro-lifers that there was never any possibility that 27 members would sign a minority plank. Nor was there any great effort to plan a Platform strategy. According to Eleanor S. Nussley, an outspoken pro-choice Platform Committee-woman from New Jersey, none of the pro-choice groups contacted her before coming to Houston. "I wrote Ann Stone, but she didn't reply," she said. "We (the pro-choicers) found each other after we got here. . . . The others didn't hear from anyone either." John Carroll of Vermont had been asked to "carry the ball" by Planned Parenthood, but he was on the wrong subcommittee and out of town making a speech. While the pro-choice Platform Committee members did meet with Stone and Crisp during the week, a minority report was never a possibility and its discussion only a tease.

The GOP dispensed with the usual first day of hearings and went right to sub-committee deliberation in hopes of wrapping up the platform early. Abortion was in the Subcommittee on Family Values, Education and Health Care, as was most of the press, but there were no surprises. The 1988 language was adopted by 17 to 3 after minimal discussion. The following day the full committee voted 84 to 16 against removing the same language, followed by voice votes on other changes in the wording, such as one exempting victims of rape or incest.

Throughout the week a certain amount of drama was maintained by both sides, who brought their supporters to hand out stickers. Spokeswomen regularly retreated to the hallways to hold mini press conferences claiming that "pro-choice delegates are being intimidated" (Stone) or "being a turncoat is a loser" (Schlafly). Stone regularly told the press how close she was to getting a commitment from six state delegations for a minority plank, the other means of generating a floor fight, but this was also not realistic. Bush operatives quickly dampened any sign of rebellion and fed the few pro-choicers a tidbit from Barbara Bush that abortion was "a personal decision" that should be omitted from the platform. Everyone assumed the President was trying to have it both ways—give the Right the Platform and the pro-choicers a pat on the head.[15] This did not smooth any feathers. After the Platform was finalized on Thursday, August 13, New York pro-choice delegate Tanya Melich, who has been to every GOP convention since 1952, turned in her credentials and went home.

Some of the most interesting debate was in other subcommittees on such subjects as AIDS, health and education. Outside the glare of public scrutiny, many delegates were trying to think out what their values meant when applied to concrete situations. Others appeared to be operating from a script, sticking in such pat phrases as "Judeo-Christian heritage" every place it could fit. The result was lauded by Pat Robertson as "the most conservative platform ever." The final version, elegantly printed with illustrations and photographs in striking contrast to the Democrats' mimeo version, inverted the usual Republican priorities. The section on "Uniting Our Family" came before national defense.

Platforms are read by few voters; they generally act more as a window through which to view factional fights and a means to assess their relative strength. If this holds true in 1992, the influence of the Christian Right is larger than its acknowledged delegate strength would suggest. Fear of homosexuality, which was not even mentioned in the 1988 platform, is pervasive. Concern with maintaining parental authority over children is prominent. "[E]fforts of the Democratic Party to redefine the traditional American family," or "to include sexual preference as a protected minority receiving preferential status" are denounced. Even traditional Republican issues such as taxes, government and bureaucracy, and newer ones such as tort reform, are discussed in terms of their impact on the family. The Party which traditionally favored limited government urged "State legislatures to explore ways to promote marital stability."

ASSESSMENT

Symbolically and substantively the parties sent clear messages that they represent distinct approaches to American politics. Long gone is the day when they chased each other to occupy the middle road, becoming variations on the same theme. The Democrats were heralded for nominating a team of two Southern white males with strong ties to the moderate Democratic Leadership Council. Yet in the platform and their speeches, this same team articulated values and policy positions that only twenty years ago were viewed as radical (abortion) or even unthinkable (gay rights), and did so as though they really believed them.[16] The Republican slate combined a product of their old politics with a creature of their new. Yet even their Eastern Establishment has learned to speak with a Christian Right accent, however artificial it sounds, and many of the contenders for the 1996 nomination will be native speakers.

Although the Republicans are running one, maybe two, election cycles behind the Democrats, they too are being thoroughly transformed by the entry of new players with their own agenda. But it was done by a somewhat different process reflecting the different structures and the different cultures of the parties.[17] The Democratic Party is pluralistic, with multiple power centers which compete for membership support in order to make demands on, as well as determine, the leaders. When challenged by the social movements of the sixties, it followed its usual strategy of co-opting them into the Democratic coalition—changing the nature of the coalition in the process. These groups in turn were sufficiently well organized and committed to claim hegemony over those issues that were their primary concern. Feminists in particular, though not in isolation, put the "personal" on the political agenda and convinced the Democrats that government had a responsibility for righting the wrongs of private life and balancing the burdens of an inequitable social structure.

The Republican Party is a hollow shell. Run by an economic and social élite which uses money, professional expertise and institutional position to elect its candidates and determine policy, its state organizations are very weak, as reflected in their inability to control state legislatures even while regularly electing a Republican President. In the late 70s and early 80s Christian Right leaders were courted by the national Party, not to curb challenges as the Democrats did, but to gain new workers and voters sufficient to enable the Republican Party to challenge Democratic dominance in Southern states. In exchange, Party leaders and the Reagan and Bush administrations ceded authority over anything touching on issues of family and sexuality, a policy arena unimportant to Party operatives but central to evangelical religious doctrines. Initially tutored in political strategy by more experienced hard Right leaders, Christian Right leaders eventually became sufficiently sophisticated to demand that their issues be placed at the top of the party's agenda; "family values" became the major theme.[18]

During the last twenty years an élite realignment has taken place within and between the major parties. New players were brought into the national party coalitions, for different reasons and at different times, with opposing agendas. Each succeeded in capturing control of those policy arenas which were most important to it. Consequently the parties have polarized around issues—gender roles, sexual behavior, reproduction, care of children, family structure, intersection of work and family obligations, military service—which twenty years ago were either not considered proper political issues, or were not partisan ones. Other issues which already were on the public agenda—race, welfare, education—have been transformed by the new ones. As a result, Presidential candidates in both parties have changed their views to become politically correct. Among ordinary party workers, dissidents from the dominant themes have dropped out or been drummed out. And voters are beginning to switch: feminists vote for Democrats and evangelicals vote for Republicans.

During the next twenty years, or less, these changes will work their way down through the party and political structure, eventually realigning the electorate. Feminists have a head start. Although not as well organized on the local and state as on the national level, they nonetheless have a lot of influence. A lot of women have been trained in political skills; a lot of money has been raised to elect them; a lot of men run on feminist issues—or at least don't oppose them—in order to win elections. As was clear from the 1992 Democratic convention, electing women, preferably feminists, to public office is high on the priority list. When women are elected to state and local offices, some studies show, their issue priorities are different. They are much more concerned with the same cluster of concerns as are the evangelicals.

The Christian Right has also recognized the importance of electing sympathetic public officials on the local level. Much more than feminists, it is seeking to use the existing party structure to attain its policy goals. In 1989 Pat Robertson created the Christian Coalition to obtain "working control" of the Republican Party from the bottom up. Access to Washington only affected national policy; many matters of concern to Christians were decided on the local level. Control of the Republican Party would provide a respectable vehicle through which to "return America" to "her Christian roots."[19] To do this the CC combined a traditional tactic of Democratic insurgents, grass-roots organizing of committed ideologues through the network of evangelical churches, with a Republican one, ties to prominent national figures. Given the lack of participation in most local Republican bodies, and the pre-existing network of evangelical churches, it has not been hard to take them over. The more traditional Republicans who don't like the Christian Right's style and agenda by and large have no troops.

"Family values" did not turn out to be a winning issue in 1992; it was eclipsed by the sorry state of the economy. But for the Christian Right, family values is not merely a slogan with which to win elections; it summarized why they got into partisan politics in the first place. The cluster of issues this slogan represents is fundamental to their religious beliefs. Pat Buchanan, a Catholic who comes from the old hard right, not the new religious right, best articulated their view when he told the Republican delegates "this election is about much more than who gets what. It is about who we are. It is about what we believe, it is about what we stand for as Americans. There is a religious war going on in our country for the soul of America. It is a cultural war, as critical to the kind of nation we will one day be—as was the Cold War itself. . . . [R]adical feminism [is] the agenda Clinton & Clinton would impose on America—abortion on demand, a litmus test for the Supreme Court, homosexual rights, discrimination against religious schools, women in combat. . . . It is not the kind of change we can tolerate in a nation that we still call God's country."

If Buchanan is right, and I think he is, the realignment of the next twenty years will transform the nature of partisan competition from a mere fight for office to a surrogate civil war. Each party, and its candidates, will be the carrier of a conflicting cluster of values. The winner will get to decide the role of government, or each of the many governments in our federal system, in promulgating those values. Culture, not class or economics, will define the great political debates of the twenty-first century.[20]

Notes

1. Party platforms traditionally show a "cyclical movement" in which one party leads on an issue, and the other follows within an election or two. Polsby, Nelson W. and Aaron Wildavsky, *Presidential*

Elections, New York: Scribner's Sons, 6th edition, 1984, pp. 240, 258–9. Pomper, Gerald M., *Elections in America: Control and Influence in Democratic Politics,* New York: Dodd, Mead, 1971, Chapters 7 and 8.

2. Past Party platforms can be found in Donald Bruce Johnson and Kirk H. Porter, *National Party Platforms,* Urbana: U. Ill. Press, multiple dates. This failure to mention women was not because no one asked. Betty Friedan testified on "A Bill of Rights for Women in 1968" at both parties' platform hearings, and the National Women's Party asked for an ERA endorsement. 3:3 *NWP Bulletin,* Fall 1968, 2–3, and Spring/Summer 1968, 2–3; Reel 158, NWP papers; Party Platforms, 734, 749; minutes of NOW Board meeting, Sept. 14–15, 1968, author's files.

3. At the time of the conventions abortion was still illegal in all but a few states, though reform (not repeal) bills were under consideration in many more. *Roe v. Wade* was not decided until January 23, 1973.

4. Shafer, Barry, *The Quiet Revolution: Party Reform and the Shaping of Post Reform Politics,* New York: Basic Books, 1984, Chapter 17. Jo Freeman, "Whom You Know Versus Whom You Represent: Feminist Influence in the Democratic and Republican Parties" in Mary F. Katzenstein and Carol M. Mueller, eds., *The Women's Movements of the United States and Western Europe,* Philadelphia: Temple U. Press, 1987, pp. 222–5.

5. Frederick Clarkson, "Inside the Covert Coalition", *Church & State,* November 1992, pp. 220–223.

6. *National Journal Convention Daily,* July 14, 1992, p. 31. *New York Times,* July 15, 1992, p. 1:6.

7. *National Journal Convention Daily,* July 14, 1992, pp. 10, 14.

8. *National Journal Convention Daily,* July 15, 1992, p. 22. Casey did testify at the May 18 Democratic Platform Committee hearings in Cleveland, Ohio; *The Boston Globe,* May 19, 1992, p. 8.

9. The other national PACs are: ANA-PAC (American Nurses Association), Hollywood Women's Political Committee, Leader Pac, National Federation of Business and Professional Women's PAC, National Organization for Women PAC, National Women's Political Caucus PAC, WISH List, Women in Psychology for Legislative Action, and the Women's Council for the Democratic Senatorial Campaign Committee. There were also thirty-one state PACs. In 1992 the Center for the American Woman and Politics at the Eagleton Institute asked the 42 women's PACs how much money they had contributed to candidates. Thirty-five reported giving $11,558,712 to women candidates. In 1990, 26 such PACs had given $2,695,354. 9:1 *CAWP News and Notes,* Winter 1993, p. 10–11. These do not include the many PACs who specifically support pro-choice candidates.

10. Emily's List was widely reported as raising and contributing $6.2 million to Democratic women candidates in 1992. *CAWP News and Notes* p. 13 and *CO Weekly Report,* October 17, 1992, pp. 3270. However the final report of the Federal Election Commission for the 1991–92 election cycle showed that *for federal candidates* Emily's List reported receiving $4,139,346 and contributing $365,318 to federal candidates out of total disbursements of $3,389,276. The Women's Campaign Fund raised $1,980,430 and disbursed $1,976,482, of which $512,067 went to federal candidates. WISH List reported receiving $300,345 and disbursing $288,520 of which $67,191 went to federal candidates. *Federal Election Commission* press release of April 29, 1993, and inquiry of the FEC Press Office on August 23, 1993. Campaign money was also raised by state affiliates of national organizations, none of which are included in these figures.

11. *National Journal Convention Daily,* August, 19, 1992, p. 23. *CAWP News and Notes* p. 18 reports that the Women's Council "distributed $1.5 million to 10 Democratic, pro-choice women candidates in the general election." It didn't say whether these were federal, state or local candidates, but the Women's Council is not on the FEC's top 50 PAC list for any category.

12. Rule 17, *The Rules of the Republican Party,* 1992. "State" includes the District of Columbia and Puerto Rico. In addition Guam, American Samoa and the Virgin Islands can send one delegate for a total of 107 members.

13. *The New York Times,* May 27, 1992, p. 1:5. Kate Michaelman of NARAL was not allowed to testify at the GOP hearing.

14. *The New York Times,* August 2, 1992, p. 24.

15. "Beyond Bush's Mixed Abortion Signals," *The New York Times,* August 15, 1992, p. 1:3. "Anti-Abortion With an Asterisk," *National Journal Convention Daily,* August 20, 1991, p. 6.

16. Many in the Party's left wing expressed satisfaction with Clinton's agenda. Frank Watkins of the National Rainbow Coalition claimed his domestic program was taken from the NRC platform;

Salim Muwakkil, "Keeping Clinton's Feet to the Fire," *In These Times,* Nov. 30–Dec. 13, 1992, p. 20.

17. See my "Political Culture of the Democratic and Republicans Parties," *Political Science Quarterly,* Vol. 101, No. 3, Fall 1986, pp. 327–356.

18. Duane Oldfield, *The Right and the Righteous,* Ph.D. dissertation, University of California, Berkeley, 1990.

19. Quoted in *The Washington Post,* Sept. 10, 1992, p. 1:3.

20. Byron Shafer came to a similar conclusion after observing the 1984 conventions. "The New Cultural Politics," *PS,* Spring 1985, pp. 221–231.

References

The Boston Globe. 19 May 1992.

Clarkson, Frederick. 1992. "Inside the Covert Coalition." *Church & State.* November.

Freeman, Jo. 1986. "Political Culture of the Democratic and Republican Parties." *Political Science Quarterly* 101(3) (Fall): 327–56.

The Legal Times. 16 March 1992.

National Journal Convention Daily. 14 July 1992, 15 July 1992.

National NOW Times. August 1992.

The New York Times. 27 May 1992, 15 July 1992, 2 August 1992.

Oldfield, Duane. 1990. "The Right and the Righteous." Ph.D. diss., University of California, Berkeley.

Polsby, Nelson W., and Aaron Wildavsky. 1984. *Presidential Elections,* 6th ed. New York: Scribner's Sons.

Pomper, Gerald M. 1971. *Elections in America: Control and Influence in Democratic Politics.* New York: Dodd, Mead.

Shafer, Byron. 1985. "The New *Cultural* Politics," *PS* Spring 18(2): 221–31.

The Wall Street Journal. 5 November 1991.

The Washington Post. 1992. "The GOP's Abortion-Rights Upstart," 4 April.

The Washington Post. 10 September 1992.

FURTHER READING FOR CHAPTER 3

Carnaghan, E., and D. Bahry. 1990. "Political Attitudes and the Gender Gap in the USSR." *Comparative Politics* 22(4), July:379–400.

Kelly, R. M. 1991. "Female Public Officials: A Different Voice?" *Annals of the American Academy of Political and Social Science* 515 (May):77–87.

Mueller, C. 1985. (Ed.). *The Politics of the Gender Gap.* Newbury Park, CA: Sage.

———. 1991. "The Gender Gap and Women's Political Influence." *Annals of the American Academy of Political Science* 515 (May):23–37.

Norris, P. 1993. "The Return of the British Gender Gap." In D. Denver et al. (ed.), *British Parties and Elections Yearbook, 1993.* Hempstead: Harvester Wheatsheaf.

Randall, V. 1987. *Women and Politics: An International Perspective,* 2d ed. London: Macmillan.

Renzetti, C. M. 1987. "New Wave or Second Stage? Attitudes of College Women Towards Feminism." *Sex Roles* 16 (5/6):265–277.

Simon, R., and J. Landis. 1989. "Women's and Men's Attitudes About Woman's Place and Role." *Public Opinion Quarterly* 53:265–276.

Shapiro, R. Y., and H. Mahajan. 1986. "Gender Differences in Policy Preferences: A Summary of Trends from the 1960s to the 1980s." *Public Opinion Quarterly* 50:42–61.

Skard, T., and E. Haavio-Mannila. 1985. Women in Parliament. In Haavio-Mannila, et al. (eds). *Unfinished Democracy: Women in Nordic Politics*. New York: Pergamon Press.

Thomas, S., and S. Welch. 1991. "The Impact of Gender on Activities and Priorities of State Legislators." *Western Political Quarterly* 44(2), June:445–456.

Welch, S. 1985. "Are Women More Liberal than Men in the U.S. Congress." *Legislative Quarterly* Vol. x, 1, pp. 125–134.

CHAPTER
4

Political Recruitment

From the time women gained equal citizenship rights until the 1960s, in most western democracies there have been few women in political elites—legislative, judicial, and executive. This phenomenon was so universal some thought it an iron law, one of the few in political science. Since the 1960s there is evidence of progress. The number of women in elected national office has grown significantly in many countries. Nevertheless, this generalization requires three important qualifications.

First, in all countries, even Scandinavian societies with the most rapid change, women continue to be underrepresented in proportion to their size in the electorate. In 1991 women made up 38.5 percent of the Finnish Eduskurta, the highest proportion in any single legislative chamber worldwide, yet women were 52 percent of the population. In a worldwide survey that compared 150 countries in 1991, women were only one in ten members of legislatures (11 percent of the lower house and 9 percent of the upper chamber).[1]

Second, progress over time is not linear. In countries such as Japan, the marked absence of women in national elected office has remained largely unchanged over forty or fifty years. In others, such as France, the number of women has increased in some elections only to fall again later, after changes in the electoral system.[2] In countries like Poland and Hungary, the process of democratization in the transition from communist rule has, ironically, led to a sharp decline in the number of women in parliament. The use of gender quotas, associated with the ancien régime, was abandoned at the very moment these parliaments assumed real power. The evidence indicates there are no grounds to assume that change will be automatic, uninterrupted, or steady, let alone fast.

It tends to be true as a broad generalization that the higher the level of politics, the fewer the women. Women are usually better represented in local or state government than in national legislatures, in government cabinets, and as heads of state. There have been some notable exceptions to this pattern; women have been national leaders as head of government or state in Norway (Gro Brundtland),

Israel (Golda Meir), Ireland (Mary Robinson), India (Indira Gandhi), France (Edith Cresson), the United Kingdom (Margaret Thatcher), the Philippines (Corazón Aquino), Bolivia (Lidia Geiler), Pakistan (Benazir Bhutto), Nicaragua (Violeta Chamorro), Portugal (Maria de Lourdes Pintasiglo), Argentina (Isabela Peron), Iceland (Vigdís Finnbogadottir), and Sri Lanka (Siramavo Bandaranaike). But these are the exception, not the rule; in 1991, 13 out of 150 countries had a woman as head of state or government.[3]

In the United States change has been most significant at the local level. From 1975 to 1988, the number of women in county offices quadrupled, from about 451 to 1600.[4] The number of women city mayors increased at a comparable rate during these years to just under 10 percent of the total, with women elected in such major cities as San Francisco, Houston, Chicago, San Jose, San Antonio, San Diego, and Dallas.

There are slightly fewer women at the state level. In 1991 women were governors in Kansas (Joan Finney), Arizona (Rose Mofford), Texas (Ann Richards), and Oregon (Barbara Roberts); six women were lieutenant governors; and four were attorneys general. Between 1975 and 1989 the number of women in state legislatures doubled, from 604 to 1260 (going from 8 to 17 percent). Female representation varies significantly from state to state; it is strongest (about one-third) in Arizona, Maine, Colorado, Wyoming, New Hampshire, Vermont, and Washington, while it is weakest in Louisiana (2%), Kentucky (5%), Alabama (6%), Arkansas (7%), and Mississippi (7%).

Change in American politics has been slowest at the top. The proportion of women elected to Congress has gradually improved, but the absolute numbers remain remarkably low compared with most western democracies. The proportion of women in the United States House of Representatives rose from 12 women (2.8%) in 1971 to 29 (6.7%) in 1990. Following the November 1992 elections the House contained 48 women (11%) representing 27 states, while there were 6 women in the U.S. Senate.

EXPLANATIONS FOR FEMALE UNDERREPRESENTATION

What are the major barriers to female representation? This puzzle is deepened since we have already seen that in the electorate, gender differences in political participation are small and have been diminishing over time. Explanations are controversial. One way to understand the pattern of recruitment is to see it as a three-stage process.

In the first step on the election ladder, people have to be willing and able to enter the pool of eligibles. Eligibility is determined by socialization (political attitudes such as ambition and confidence) and structural constraints (such as occupational patterns, financial resources, and educational qualifications). In the second step, people have to get support from gatekeepers to office: party members and leaders; interest groups and community associations; financial backers; media commentators, journalists, and editors; campaign volunteers and professionals; and grass roots supporters who contribute toward an effective election. The recruitment process, and hence the key gatekeepers, vary in different political systems. In most European countries formal party organizations control the recruitment process, but in the United States the growth of primaries has led to more open, "candidate-centered" campaigning. And in the third step, nominees need to obtain the support of voters.

The recruitment process operates inside a wider political system that contains three institutional factors which stand out as critical. First, the electoral system is important. First-past-the-post plurality systems with single-member districts, used in the United States, Canada, and the United Kingdom, seem to disadvantage women. Women tend to do better under party list systems of proportional representation. Second, party and legislative competition, including patterns of incumbency and turnover, may be significant. In multiparty systems with high turnover there are more points of access to public office. And third, the political culture of a country, whether egalitarian or traditional, may play a role. The interaction of these factors helps to explain the considerable cross-national variation in women's representation.

The key questions are therefore: Are women reluctant to run? Are women less successful in getting campaign support from political elites? Are women less popular with the electorate? And, are institutional barriers critical?

Robert Darcy, Susan Welch, and Janet Clark analyze the barriers to women running for the U.S. Congress, including the barriers to women winning and the barriers to women running. The authors conclude that if more women ran, more would be elected.

Eliza Carney focuses on the role of women's fund-raising groups in providing the essential "seed corn" for successful races.

Janet Clark focuses on changes over time in women's representation in local and state government in the United States. She compares theories that explain the underrepresentation of women on the basis of political culture, sex role socialization, explicit party discrimination, voter discrimination, and institutional constraints. Recent trends, she concludes, give grounds for optimism that women will have an increased role in American public office in future, even though the past record is not encouraging.

Marjorie Randon Hershey considers whether 1992 represented the "year of the woman." She explains the expansion in opportunities for women in terms of anti-incumbent sentiment, redistricting, renewed abortion-rights activism, the Clarence Thomas–Anita Hill hearings, and the expanded pool of women candidates.

The importance of the electoral system is confirmed by the last reading in this chapter. Pippa Norris compared electoral systems and found that party lists tend to be best for women. She argues, however, that electoral reform should not be seen as a mechanical panacea; in countries such as Israel, Belgium, and Portugal, few women are elected despite the use of party lists. Accordingly, what matters is the electoral system combined with the party selection system.

PIPPA NORRIS

Notes

1. "Distribution of Seats Between Men and Women in National Parliaments: Statistical Data from 1945 to 30 June 1991," Inter-Parliamentary Union, Series *Rapports et Documents* no. 18, Geneva, 1991.
2. See Karen Beckwith, "Sneaking Women into Office: Alternative Access to Parliament," *Women and Politics* 9(3), 1989:1–15.
3. "Women and Political Power: Survey Carried Out Among the 150 National Parliaments Existing as of 31 October 1991," Inter-Parliamentary Union, Series *Reports and Documents* no. 19, Geneva, 1992, p. 157.
4. Figures are supplied by the Center for the American Woman in Politics, Rutgers University, New Brunswick, New Jersey.

Women, Elections, and Representation

R. DARCY, SUSAN WELCH, AND JANET CLARK

OPENING UP POLITICAL LIFE TO WOMEN

By noting that "where power is, women are not," Elizabeth Vallance has aptly summed up the traditional fate of women in American politics.[1] Yet . . . the role of women in American politics is changing; as barriers drop, women are running for office in record numbers. Some of them are winning, assuming a prominent role in the political life of their city, state, and nation.

But progress has been slow. The increase of women has not been constant at all levels; at the national level it has been minute. The increase in the number of winning women candidates has not really kept pace with the increased number of candidates. . . .

In seeking to explain why there are so few women in politics, analysts have turned to two kinds of explanations. One is that women cannot win when they run; the other is that not enough women run. Let us examine each of these two reasons in turn.

Can Women Win When They Run?

Voters There is a popular belief that women are discriminated against by many voters, that a woman candidate automatically loses a lot of votes merely because of her sex. In fact, public opinion polls indicate that less than 20 percent of the public says they will not vote for a woman for president; this is a substantial number, but fewer than admitted they would not vote for a Catholic in 1960. The proportion agreeing they would not vote for a woman for lesser office, including the House of Representatives, is much lower: only around 10 to 11 percent.

Despite this admission of prejudice, . . . it is difficult to detect any penalty levied against women candidates. Once party and incumbency are taken into account, women candidates do as well as men in both primary and general elections. Whereas in the 1950s and 1960s women were discriminated against at the polls, at least in some places, this has become largely a historical, rather than a contemporary, problem.

Of course, some voters vote against women because of prejudice against them. Older, conservative voters who hold traditional religious beliefs are somewhat more likely to be against women taking a role in politics. Given the overall success of women who run, it appears that these antiwomen voters are equaled by those who go out of their way to cast a vote for a woman. It is also likely that some prejudice expressed to a pollster may not be carried out in actual voting when faced with the choice of a woman of one's own party or a man of the opposition party.

Party Leaders   Another popular explanation for the lack of women's success is that party leaders discriminate against them. Traditionally, party leaders who had some influence on party slating could deny women a place on the slate. In situations where party leaders did not have this power (as where party nominations were decided by primaries), party leaders could have refused to encourage women candidates to run or actively discouraged them. There is no question that there were such actions in the past. There is little question that there will be such actions in the future as well. But our systematic evidence from before the 1970s is scanty, and there are many stories of party leaders working against the aspirations of male candidates as well. Our more recent systematic evidence does not find that party leaders discriminate against women candidates. Women do not appear to be running disproportionately for unwinnable seats. And women are just as likely as men, and in some cases more likely, to say that party leaders encouraged their candidacy.[2]

Incumbency   A major reason for the slow entrance of women into political office, particularly at the national level, is the power of incumbency. . . . Incumbents have a tremendous advantage in House elections. About 90 percent of all House members who run are reelected, and almost the same is true in state legislatures. This advantage, combined with the fact that only a small minority of members voluntarily give up their seats in any one election, means that newcomers in legislative bodies are rare. This is particularly true for the House of Representatives, where the number of open seats for any election is only about 10 percent of the total.

The power of incumbency and turnover is an excellent explanation for two puzzling phenomena. First, it helps explain why women are entering state legislatures faster than the House of Representatives. While both bodies have extremely high rates of incumbency election success, in the state legislatures voluntary turnover is much higher. State legislators are much more likely than members of the House to decide to return to private business or run for higher office. Thus women can run for more open state legislative seats and win a fair share of them. The power of incumbency also explains why, at the national level, so many fewer women are winning elections than are running. Most women candidates for the House of Representatives (like most nonincumbent male candidates) are running against incumbents, not for open seats. Thus their chances of electoral victory are very low.

Overall, then, it appears that while voter discrimination now plays at best a small part in keeping women out of office, the impact of incumbency and low turnover for many offices is a major explanation. This incumbency factor is in turn a consequence of changes in the structure of American politics begun early in this century.[3] As more women run, more will benefit from incumbency. Women incumbents have just about the same advantage as male incumbents.

Why Don't More Women Run?

If every woman who ran won, we would still not have proportional representation for women. Women still represent only a small proportion of the new political candidates. Thus we must turn to a consideration of why more women do not run for office.

Trying to figure out who constitutes a pool of potential candidates and then learning the members' reasons for running or not are nearly impossible tasks. So our conclusions about why women do not run must be based more on inference and less on direct evidence than our conclusions about what happens to women when they do run.

Fear of Losing   One explanation for the small number of women candidates is that women who are potential candidates believe that voters and party elites will not support them because they are women. This fear may have had some basis as recently as 20 years ago, but it is certainly no longer the case. Nonetheless, if it is believed, some women candidates will be discouraged.

Women candidates may also believe that should they become candidates, they will encounter opposition from party leaders, political activists, and fund-raisers simply because they are women. Again, this fear may be rooted in historical fact. As we have indicated, it has not been too many years since party leaders were quite blatant about admitting that they did not want a woman on their tickets. Further, many women candidates, even now, report difficulty with fund-raising.

Yet again, these beliefs have been disproved in systematic investigations of recent campaigns. As we have shown at both the congressional and state legislative levels, women candidates do just as well as men candidates in raising funds. Investigations of patterns of candidacies for men and women have illustrated that women are not more likely to be found running for hopeless seats. These findings indicate a relative equity between male and female candidates. Our research shows that women candidates will not have to carry an extra burden because they are women. We hope these findings will make it easier for more women to decide to become political candidates.

Patterns of Women's Socialization   Some people have suggested that rather than blaming the voters or party leaders for the reluctance of women to become political candidates, it is the victims themselves who are to blame. This very global explanation has at least three components. One is that women were socialized to believe that politics is a man's game and hence to stay away from it. In recent U.S. history, this explanation falls short. Women have participated at the grass-roots level as much as men, have been the backbone of many political campaigns, and have taken part in all sorts of political activities at the same rates as men.

However, women, as well as men, have only recently come to believe that women can and should play a leadership role in political life. In some surveys, for example, the proportion of people saying that men are better suited for politics than women fell from 47 percent to 36 percent between 1974 and 1983.

Occupational Segregation   Women have traditionally been directed into only limited occupational channels. . . . The very occupations that lead to politics—law and business—are the ones that traditionally contained few women. The absence of women from these stepping-stones to political office does explain a good portion of women's underrepresentation in public office.

Very much related to this is that women in our society are traditionally given primary child-care responsibility. The impact of that role on political office-holding is probably great, and we have a good deal of indirect evidence for that. We know that women are much more likely to be elected to local offices, where time away from home is more limited than at the state and national levels. We know that women tend to defer political careers until children are in school. We know that the distance from the statehouse is related to the proportion of women elected as state representatives. But what we do not know is how many women have completely dropped aspirations for a political career in favor of a homemaker role.

However, we must not assume that the stepping-stones into politics are set in concrete, as it were. There is no necessity that the stepping-stones used by men must also be used by women. Research is beginning to show that women who are elected to state legislatures and to the House of Representatives, for example, do have somewhat different backgrounds from those of their male colleagues. Though many women in these bodies are lawyers and business executives, many others come to the legislature from more traditional women's roles, including homemaking. More research is needed on how women can enter political life using their existing backgrounds and experiences.

Impact of the Electoral System on Women

The electoral system is a factor related to both the absence of women running for office and their electoral fate when they do run. . . . Women are more likely to be elected in multimember districts than in single-member systems. The difference is fairly great when one compares nations with multimember proportional election systems with nations such as the United States with a predominantly single-member district system. Even in the United States, however, where multimember plurality systems are used, women do somewhat better than in the single-member plurality systems. Though the strength of the relationship varies, this pattern obtains at both the state and local levels. It appears that our system of single-member districts leads to a focus on finding the "best man for the job" rather than forcing us to seek ways to represent community diversity.

This pattern is particularly interesting and somewhat disturbing because it is counter to the pattern for geographically segregated racial and ethnic minorities.

In areas where they form a significant minority, minority males benefit from single-member districts, especially at the local level. Finding an electoral system that is politically acceptable while being fair both to women generally and to minority men may prove to be a challenge, but it is a challenge our political system will have to meet.

. . .

Notes

1. Elizabeth Vallance, "Where the Power Is, Women Are Not," *Parliamentary Affairs* 35 (Spring 1982): 218–219.
2. Sophonisba P. Breckenridge cites examples of both party support for women candidates and party opposition to women candidates from the early 1920s in *Women in the Twentieth Century* (New York: McGraw-Hill, 1933), 327–332.
3. See David R. Mayhew, *Congress: The Electoral Connection* (New Haven, Conn.: Yale University Press, 1974); Morris P. Fiorina, *Congress: The Keystone of the Washington Establishment* (New Haven, Conn.: Yale University Press, 1977).

Weighing In

ELIZA NEWLIN CARNEY

Dozens of women-run groups have thrown their . . . full weight behind female candidates this year. From the National Organization for Women (NOW) to the National Association of Female Executives, groups of all stripes have virtually dropped everything to push for an electoral breakthrough.

"If we are ever going to make a change on any of our issues—reproductive freedom, health, violence, workplace reform—we've got to change the faces," said NOW president Patricia Ireland. "If there was any object lesson out of [the] Clarence Thomas–Anita Hill [hearings], it was that we cannot rely on anybody else to represent us. We have to be there to represent ourselves. And it's got to be now."

Professional groups that were once largely apolitical have launched campaign training sessions, volunteer drives and election fund-raisers. Feminist groups that long squabbled over legislative priorities have found a rallying point in an effort to elect more women. Republican women, long overshadowed by Democrat-dominated groups, have started a raft of new organizations. And women-run political action committees (PACs) have cashed in on a wave of enthusiasm for female candidates.

Several factors appear to make 1992 potentially a banner year for women, including redistricting, retirements, anti-incumbent sentiment, renewed abortion-rights activism, a widely held perception of women as "outsiders" and an impressive pool of female contenders. . . . The emerging influence of women's groups, however, goes beyond this year's special circumstances. Once bogged down with fund-raising and image problems, women's groups have widened their appeal, dramatically increased their financial reserves and adopted a tougher, more professional approach.

"If you are a woman and you want to run for national office, i.e., the Congress or the U.S. Senate, going to Washington and seeing the women's groups is basically a mandatory stop," said Gerald J. Austin, a senior partner with the Democratic media consulting firm of Austin Sheinkopf. . . . "Getting their 'Good Housekeeping' seal of approval is very important back in your home state and [in] opening doors in Washington."

But for all the euphoria among feminist leaders, not everybody is celebrating. As women's groups come into their own politically, they are attracting a lot more scrutiny—and in some cases a lot more criticism. Increasingly sought after and fought over, women's PACs face painful choices about which candidates to support, and their decisions are not always popular. As women's groups gain clout, some candidates complain that they are becoming as elitist and exclusive as the male-dominated parties they claimed were locking women out.

More generally, many "bipartisan" groups remain vulnerable to the charge that they are mostly interested in electing Democrats. Emerging Republican groups, too, are taking some heat as they walk the line between supporting female newcomers and defending GOP incumbents. Republican pro-abortion-rights groups are on a collision course with party leaders as they prepare for a showdown at the Republican National Convention in Houston. And as women's leaders from both parties gain notoriety, they face a chorus of questions about whom they endorse, what they stand for and where the money is going.

"I think their focus is really too narrow," said Donna Peterson, a Texas Republican who is challenging Democratic Rep. Charles Wilson and who has been shunned by women's groups of both parties because she opposes abortion. "If you are really attempting to promote women, then promote women. Those organizations, to an outsider, almost look as if they're really promoting abortion and not promoting women."

MONEY'S SURGING

Historically, women's groups have done quite a bit more than raise money for political candidates. The Fund for the Feminist Majority, headed by former NOW president Eleanor Smeal, has no PAC but vigorously recruits and endorses candidates. The bipartisan National Women's Political Caucus hosts hundreds of political training sessions for women each year.

In fact, many leaders of women's organizations say the past grooming of women for local school boards, boards of supervisors and other stepping-stone political positions is paying tremendous dividends in this year's campaign season.

"You are seeing the benefit of women having held lower-level office, either in county supervisor, assembly or senate roles in their states, and they are now running for federal office," said Margery Tabankin, executive director of the Culver City (Calif.)–based Hollywood Women's Political Committee.

Increasingly, groups such as Tabankin's are finding a niche in raising impressive sums for federal candidates. The Hollywood Women's Political Committee, formed six years ago to back "progressive" causes, has come to specialize in mega-fund-raisers that bring in as much as $1.5 million in a single night. Since its 1984 launch, the group's PAC has donated $4 million to liberal-leaning candidates, with the priority on women.

Seven of the major women's PACs more than doubled their contributions to female candidates from 1988–90, according to a recent survey by the Center for the American Woman and Politics at Rutgers University.

And many PACs expect to double their money again this year. Women's groups say they were inundated with contributions after Supreme Court Justice Clarence Thomas's stormy confirmation hearings last fall, and the money surge hasn't stopped.

EMILY's List, for example, a Democratic PAC for women who are pro-abortion-rights, raised $1.5 million for federal candidates in 1989–90 and expects to increase that to $3 million in this cycle. Membership has jumped from 3,000 last year to 12,000, boosted in part by a glowing *60 Minutes* report. The National Women's Political Caucus gave $96,000 to female federal candidates in 1989–90 and expects to give $250,000 this time. The Women's Campaign Fund, launched in 1974 and the oldest bipartisan PAC for women, predicts its state and local contributions will hit $1 million this year.

"Women have become accustomed to the idea that they should give political money," said Celia Morris, author of *Storming the Statehouse: Running for Governor With Ann Richards and Dianne Feinstein* (Macmillan Publishing Co., 1992). "[Women] don't have the tradition of political giving—they have given to charities, they have given to cultural things. But all of that is changing now."

Driving that change is support from women who might otherwise reject the "feminist" label but who are happy to give money to a woman who's running for office. Some women's leaders, aware that an untapped pool of women responded to the Thomas hearings, have moved quickly to fill the gap. Among other projects, the National Women's Political Caucus is working with St. Louis–based McDonnell Douglas Corp. on a series of political seminars for corporate women.

"Because of what we learned from that outburst, we recognized that it was a lesson for us as well as for the Senate," said caucus president Harriett Woods, a Democrat who is former lieutenant governor of Missouri and ran twice unsuccessfully for the Senate. "There are a lot of women we haven't reached, who are mainstream women, who now understand they have to get women into office."

EMILY's List—the acronym stands for Early Money Is Like Yeast—is also credited with helping to alter the political landscape for women. By "bundling" checks written by members directly for candidates, the List gets beyond the $5,000 federal contribution limits and can infuse big money into women's races.

"What EMILY's List has done is lift the ceiling of what was possible. It has proved dramatically that we are way beyond the bake sale now," said Ann F. Lewis, a Boston-based political consultant and former political director of the Democratic National Committee.

OVERLY SELECTIVE HELP?

But some political analysts say that EMILY's List is too exclusive, endorsing only candidates who fit a narrow profile and belong to its "insider" political network. The PAC's stamp of approval goes only to Democratic women who support abortion rights and back the Equal Rights Amendment. A prevalent complaint is that EMILY's List and other women-run election groups function essentially as arms of the Democratic Party. Some critics wonder where the women's groups were when six high-profile Republican women ran for the Senate last time around—and all but the sole incumbent (Nancy Landon Kassebaum of Kansas) lost. Some of the Republican women won backing from women's PACs, but many ran into problems.

Female PAC leaders insist that they work hard to recruit Republican candidates, and note that there are considerably fewer GOP women in the field. Others point to abortion rights—a litmus test for virtually all the major women-run PACs—as a sticking point for Republican women.

A look at the PAC dollars, however, reveals that Democrats are cleaning up. NOW gave $141,320 directly to federal candidates in the last election, 87 per cent of it to Democrats, according to FEC reports. The Hollywood Women's Political Committee gave $106,000 to Democrats; Republicans got zero. For her part, EMILY's List president Ellen R. Malcolm is unapologetic about the PAC's decision to support only Democrats.

"It was very clear to us that politics at its base is partisan," Malcolm said. "And we believe that women and families are much better off when Democrats control the Congress."

But Republican women are starting to get the message. The WISH List, run by former *Michigan Woman* editor Glenda Greenwald, has already raised more than $180,000 for Republican candidates since its launching in January. Modeled after EMILY's List, the WISH List also requires that candidates support abortion rights and has virtually the same rules.

Other up-and-coming Republican organizations are the National Republican Coalition for Choice, headed by former Republican National Committee co-chair Mary Dent Crisp, and Republicans for Choice, headed by Republican direct-mail fund raiser Ann Stone. Both groups were formed in the wake of the Supreme Court's 1989 *Webster v. Reproductive Health Services* ruling, which allowed states more leeway in restricting abortions. And both are engaged in a well-financed grass-roots advertising and lobbying effort to change the GOP's anti-abortion platform.

"We give a home to pro-choice Republicans who felt they had nowhere to go before," Crisp said of her coalition. "Most Republicans feel more comfortable working within the Republican Party."

Whatever the party, however, many groups struggle with conflicting demands. Some Republican women are angry that Stone's group and the WISH List—unlike the National Republican Coalition for Choice—are unwilling to go after GOP incumbents in primary races. The charge points up a fundamental dilemma for women's groups allied to a single party: Should such PACs support a female primary challenger at the expense of an incumbent who's in the same party?

Often, the answer is no. Of the 30 candidates that EMILY's List has recommended to its members this year, for example, only a handful are running against Democratic incumbents. The rest face Republicans or open seats. Sen. Alan J. Dixon, D-Ill., may have gotten kid-gloves treatment in Illinois, say critics, noting that EMILY's List was hardly "early" in its support of challenger Carol Moseley Braun, who beat Dixon. The PAC gave a last-minute $5,000 to Braun's Senate campaign a week before the March 17 primary.

EMILY's List also ruffled some feathers with its endorsement of Ferraro over New York City Comptroller Elizabeth Holtzman, who is vying with her for the Democratic nomination to challenge D'Amato. Holtzman, a longtime feminist leader (and a former House Member who narrowly lost to D'Amato in the 1980 Senate campaign), charged that EMILY's List was "playing politics instead of playing its conscience," noting that Ferraro's polling and consulting staff had ties to EMILY's List.

Malcolm said that the List picked Ferraro only after a costly, exhaustive review, and chose to rally behind one of the women lest both of them lose. Interestingly, the Women's Campaign Fund endorsed both Ferraro and Holtzman, while the National Women's Political Caucus took no position.

Malcolm said that the List's success is partly a function of its selectivity.

"I think the bottom line is how many women we can get elected," she said. "We could have recommended twice as many candidates in 1990. I believe that if we had done that, we would have had fewer victories and not more, because all of them would have gotten half as much money."

The WISH List, too, has grappled with conflicting demands. Rep. Robert K. Dornan, R-Calif., a staunch abortion opponent, cornered Republican women Members at the WISH List's Washington launch in March to complain that WISH backed his primary opponent, California Superior Court Judge Judith Ryan. As it turned out, Wish hadn't endorsed Ryan.

Greenwald said the point was moot anyway, because WISH was formed too late to get involved in this year's primaries. But the group quickly made it clear that it won't challenge GOP incumbents. That left Ryan in a stew.

"I was disappointed . . . that they took the response that they did," said Ryan, an abortion-rights advocate who said she was pressured by California GOP leaders to back out of the race (and who lost in the June 2 party primary). Ryan, interviewed before the primary, added that Republican women Members, who were all for women candidates at NOW's April abortion-rights rally, "are not standing up for the things they espouse."

DEFINED BY ONE ISSUE

A more common complaint is that the new GOP women's groups, not unlike Democrat-run PACs, tend to define themselves in terms of abortion. Enter the Women's Leadership Network, a new Republican group for women not tied to the debate about abortion.

"Most of us are sick to death of women's groups addressing so-called women's issues. We care about the environment, foreign policy, energy, economics, health care, budget policy as much as any other group," said Deborah L. Steelman, a Washington lawyer and former campaign adviser to President Bush, who's a Network officer.

The group hasn't raised a fortune through its Leader PAC since its launch in mid-March. But the network does boast a powerhouse membership roster that includes Mimi Weyforth Dawson, former deputy Transportation Secretary in the Reagan Administration and coalitions director of the Bush-Quayle reelection campaign, and Washington lawyer Mary Jacob (Honey) Skinner (who's married to White House chief of staff Samuel K. Skinner). Not to mention honorary co-chairwoman Marilyn Quayle.

"We really thought we had an opportunity to greatly increase the number of women in the Senate last time, and we thought we were fairly successful in raising money in that effort," said network president Judy A. Black, a former Reagan adviser who's now vice president of the International Council of Shopping Centers. "But they didn't win. And I think that's when a lot of us realized that we needed something that was ongoing and concentrated on a variety of different areas."

Some analysts predict that the Women's Leadership Network will have trouble raising money without a single, driving issue—like abortion—to rally the troops. But female activists of all stripes agree that the diversity among women's groups is a strong point. While some groups recruit the candidates, others provide the training, pressure the parties or raise the money.

For all the disagreement over the role women's groups should play, the controversy underscores the fact they are being taken seriously. And for female candidates who fit the profile, women's groups can hold the one card that matters—the difference between winning and losing. Both Sen. Barbara A. Mikulski, D-Md., and Gov. Ann W. Richards, D-Texas, credit EMILY's List with putting their campaigns over the top.

To Geraldine Ferraro, . . . groups like the American Nurses Association, the Women's Campaign Fund and EMILY's List are critical allies. "They are important for the money, they are important for the message that they send," she said. "Especially in this atmosphere, when women are being looked at as the candidates that can make a difference."

Getting There:
Women in Political Office

JANET CLARK

In the seventy years since the ratification of the Nineteenth Amendment, which gave women the right to participate fully in the American political system, few women have actually held elective office. While women have gradually increased their participation in terms of voting and other forms of activism, they still remain woefully underrepresented in all levels of government. A key question concerns the importance of having women hold public office in a democracy. What difference does it make that women, who comprise half of the American population, constitute less than 20 percent of all political officeholders? What benefits can be derived for women and for the political system itself by placing more women in public office?

THEORIES OF REPRESENTATION

In terms of maximizing legitimacy, there are benefits in having the personnel in governmental bodies resemble the general population in regard to key characteristics such as sex and race. Theories of descriptive representation argue that the exclusion of any group from positions of power may distort policy decisions and political outcomes.[1] Representative government is justified on the assumption that the representative body is a microcosm of the entire population and can be readily substituted for a democratic convocation of the whole people. The presumption is that an officeholder represents constituents whose social characteristics he or she shares. The leader, hence, empathizes with that constituency and identifies its interests with his or her own. Legitimacy is enhanced because members of the group feel represented just because one of their own holds office.

Pitkin points out that descriptive representation does not form a complete theory of democracy. There are two issues in using this method of defining representation.[2] The first concerns the question of which social characteristics are politically relevant and deserving of representation. Second, there is the problem that members of relevant groups may not entirely share substantive opinions, and the political leader representing the group may not vote as the majority of its members would on specific policies.

In terms of the first consideration, political scientists long believed that women did not hold attitudes and opinions that were significantly different from those of men; hence they were not a politically relevant group. It was thought that they tended to vote for the same candidates for many of the same reasons as men did. The development of the women's movement in the 1960s has altered this assumption. Sapiro argues that women do form a distinct political group that has a distinct position and shared set of problems, although they may not be fully conscious of their difference from men nor disagree with men on policy issues.[3] The relatively large difference that emerged in presidential voting between men and women during the Reagan administration suggests that women may be developing a consciousness of their shared position and problems.[4] Differences in the political attitudes between women and men have appeared in such areas as social compassion, protection of the environment, and basic economic issues; they joined the differences regarding public morality and the use of violence in domestic and international relations, which had long separated men and women.[5]

In terms of the second consideration, female officials do appear to be committed to supporting women's issues. Their presence in office provides not only descriptive but also instrumental representation. Studies of women candidates and officeholders show that substantial proportions of both are committed to the goals of the women's movement and feel that they are more sensitive to the needs of women than are their male counterparts.[6] Women in state legislatures are more likely than men legislators to give top priority to bills focusing on women.[7]

Another normative issue regarding the number of women in political office involves the impact of participation upon women themselves. Classical democratic theory assumes that citizen participation in all aspects of public affairs is essential to the full development of individual capacities.[8] Further, the paucity of women in public office indicates that the system is being deprived of the contribution of more than half of its citizens.[9] Finally, in practical terms, the paucity of women begets future underrepresentation. Women in office provide two types of stimulants for women's candidacies. First, their presence in government serves as role models to other women. Many women officeholders indicate that their interest in holding office came from seeing other women in office. More directly, they also received their first practical political experience in working for women in office.[10] When there are few women in public office, there are few role models and few opportunities for political experience for future women.

HISTORICAL UNDERREPRESENTATION OF WOMEN

Historically, only minuscule numbers of women have been elected to public office. The struggle for women's suffrage and political efforts to change public policy to promote greater social and economic equity for women did not result in widespread efforts by women to take public office. Rather, few suffragists sought public office in 1920. They clearly saw the vote as a vehicle for lobbying male representatives or as a means of bypassing elected officials through use of the initiative and referendum.[11] As a result, women have been underrepresented at all levels of American government.

Women's representation in state legislatures grew slowly but not necessarily steadily in the years between 1920 and 1970. The gradual progress in numbers achieved in the decade of the 1920s halted during the depression in the 1930s.

The number of women's candidacies increased again during World War II and continued to grow through the 1950s. Another decline in the actual numbers of women legislators occurred in the 1960s, however, so that women made up less than 4 percent of state legislators by 1970.[12]

The pattern of slow and fluctuating progress made by women in achieving seats in state legislatures was followed in other political offices as well. Few women have ever served in the U.S. Senate. The first, Rebecca Latimer of Georgia, was appointed to fill the vacancy caused by the death of the incumbent in 1922. To date, a total of 16 women have served in the Senate. Women's representation in the House of Representatives preceded the passage of the Nineteenth Amendment when Montana elected Jeannette Rankin in 1916. Since then, 120 women have been U.S. representatives. Twelve women have served as governors of their states. The first was Nellie Ross of Wyoming, who was elected in 1924 to replace her deceased husband. Ella Grasso of Connecticut, who served from 1975 to 1980, was the first woman of eight to be elected governor of a state in her own right. The first woman lieutenant governor was Consuelo Bailey of Vermont, who was elected in 1954. Twenty-three women have served in this post.[13] Women have also held a variety of other statewide elected positions.

Finally, women have gradually increased their representation in county and municipal government. Bertha Landes of Seattle was the first woman to be elected mayor of a major city, in 1926. Chicago is the largest U.S. city to have had a woman mayor, Jane Byrne, who served from 1979 to 1983.[14] It is at the local level of government where women have perceived advantages in terms of their interests and the convenience of serving near home. Consequently, it is among the myriad local governments where they have occasionally achieved a majority of the legislative seats.[15] Yet, on the average, women still constitute less than 20 percent of the local government officials. In recent years, more women have been running for and holding office, but equity is still a long way off.

THE CONTEMPORARY PICTURE

Since the early 1970s, women have gradually increased their representation on local governing councils and in state legislatures and executive branches. In 1990, women attained their greatest representation in Congress. Table 1 summarizes the recent steady growth of women's representation at all three levels of government. The data suggest two things. First, the women's movement has been accompanied by greater political involvement by women. Mueller argues that it has increased the legitimacy of women's political ambition.[16] Second, there is a tendency for women to achieve greater representation in the lower-level offices. Women's representation in Congress lags far behind the progress in state legislatures and local bodies. Two women are currently in the Senate: Nancy Kassebaum of Kansas and Barbara Mikulski of Maryland. There are 29 women in the House, the highest number ever. Since 1969, the proportion of women in state legislatures has more than quadrupled. The number of women on county and municipal boards has tripled since 1975.

Table 1   PERCENTAGE OF AMERICAN ELECTIVE OFFICES HELD BY WOMEN

Level of office	1975	1977	1979	1981	1983	1985	1987	1989	1991
U.S. Congress	4	4	3	4	4	5	5	5	6
Statewide elective offices[a]	10	8	11	11	13	14	15	14	18
State legislatures	8	9	10	12	13	15	16	17	18
County governing boards	3	4	5	6	8	8[b]	9	9[c]	9[c]
Mayors and municipal or township governing boards	4	8	10	10	N.A.	14	N.A.	N.A.	N.A

Source: Center for the American Woman and Politics, National Information Bank on Women in Public Office, Eagleton Institute of Politics, Rutgers University, 1991.

a Includes only popularly elected officials to the executive branch.

b 1984.

c 1988.

The American national government has only two elected members of the executive branch.* No woman has ever served as president of the United States or as vice president. The three most recent presidents have become sensitive to the demands of the women's movement for greater representation and have appointed more women to their cabinets and to other high administrative positions than had previous administrations. To date, six presidents have appointed women to their cabinets. Nine women have held actual cabinet posts, constituting 2.0 percent of the cabinet members since 1789.[17] Women received 13.5 percent of President Carter's appointments to full-time positions requiring the confirmation of the Senate. They received 9.0 percent of President Reagan's appointments.[18] By October 1989, President Bush had appointed them to 9.6 percent of such positions.[19]

While these figures demonstrate overall progress in women's representation in America, they mask great variations between the fifty states. Some states have excelled in granting office to women while others have rarely elected women to high office. New York has had the most women elected to Congress, a total of 15, while 10 states have never sent a woman to Congress: Alaska, Delaware, Iowa, Mississippi, New Hampshire, North Dakota, Vermont, Virginia, Wisconsin, and Wyoming.[20] New Hampshire has generally led in the proportion of women in its state legislature. Louisiana has the smallest.[21] Again New Hampshire has the largest percentage of women on its county boards, and Mississippi has the lowest. The District of Columbia, Hawaii, and Michigan lead with the highest proportion of women in municipal office.[22] Table 2 shows the public offices currently held by women in each of the states. On average, women have gained the highest levels of representation in the New England and western states and their lowest in south-

Editor's Note: This pattern has changed under the Clinton administration. Five of the nineteen members of his cabinet are women: Hazel R. O'Leary, Donna Shalaha, Janet Reno, Carol Browner, and Madeline Albright.

Table 2   WOMEN HOLDING PUBLIC OFFICES IN THE AMERICAN STATES, 1990

State	Congress House (N)	Senate (N)	State Executive (N)	State Legislature[a] (percentage)	County Board[c] (percentage)	Mayor and Board[b] (percentage)
Alabama	0	0	1	5.7	2.0	11.0
Alaska	0	0	0	20.0	25.0	23.1
Arizona	0	0	2	30.0	14.6	17.6
Arkansas	0	0	2	7.4	9.3	11.9
California	3	0	2	15.8	19.2	17.8
Colorado	1	0	3	29.0	9.4	16.5
Connecticut	3	0	2	21.9	d	18.7
Delaware	0	0	1	16.1	10.5	17.5
District of Columbia[e]	1	—	—	—	—	50.0
Florida	1	0	1	16.3	14.3	13.3
Georgia	0	0	0	10.2	4.3	7.8
Hawaii	1	0	0	23.7	24.2	30.0
Idaho	0	0	1	24.6	10.6	13.2
Illinois	1	0	1	18.6	10.0	N.A.
Indiana	1	0	2	14.0	3.5	N.A.
Iowa	0	0	3	16.7	9.7	12.9
Kansas	1	1	2	25.5	7.7	11.9
Kentucky	0	0	0	5.8	3.0	N.A.
Louisiana	0	0	1	2.1	4.9	11.7
Maine	1	0	0	31.2	6.3	10.4
Maryland	3	1	0	22.9	17.8	15.2
Massachusetts	0	0	0	17.0	9.3	11.3
Michigan	1	0	1	14.9	17.3	27.5
Minnesota	0	0	2	18.4	8.4	12.8
Mississippi	0	0	0	5.8	2.0	10.5
Missouri	1	0	1	14.7	4.7	N.A.
Montana	0	0	2	18.0	10.0	14.4
Nebraska	0	0	2	20.4	6.6	7.6
Nevada	1	0	3	22.2	17.0	16.1
New Hampshire	0	0	0	32.1	26.7	10.7
New Jersey	1	0	0	10.8	11.3	13.2
New Mexico	0	0	1	13.4	15.7	16.3
New York	3	0	0	10.9	12.3	14.4
North Carolina	0	0	0	14.1	9.1	12.2
North Dakota	0	0	2	15.1	5.0	8.5
Ohio	2	0	1	12.9	9.5	16.5
Oklahoma	0	0	2	8.7	2.2	10.2
Oregon	0	0	3	20.0	17.2	22.2
Pennsylvania	0	0	2	6.7	16.4	N.A.
Rhode Island	0	0	1	15.3	d	12.8
South Carolina	1	0	1	8.8	11.7	12.2
South Dakota	0	0	2	19.1	5.3	8.9
Tennessee	1	0	0	9.9	6.8	7.1
Texas	0	0	2	10.5	2.9	12.8
Utah	0	0	0	11.5	2.3	11.5

Vermont	0	0	0	33.3	d	6.3
Virginia	0	0	1	10.7	9.8	13.3
Washington	1	0	1	29.3	11.3	19.3
West Virginia	0	0	0	19.4	6.5	13.6
Wisconsin	0	0	1	25.8	12.7	N.A.
Wyoming	0	0	2	23.4	7.3	17.8

Source: Center for the American Woman and Politics, National Information Bank on Women in Public Office, Eagleton Institute of Politics, Rutgers University, 1990.

[a]1989.
[b]1988.
[c]1984.
[d]No counties in Connecticut, Rhode Island, or Vermont.
[e]The District of Columbia has only a nonvoting member of the House of Representatives and a mayor and city council.

ern and border states. Maryland is an interesting exception. Although a border state, it has the largest delegation of women in Congress and ranks thirteenth among the states in terms of women state legislators, fifth in terms of women on county governing boards, and fourteenth in terms of women mayors and city council members.

Yet, despite the growing representation of women in American government, the United States lags behind other societies in terms of the numbers of women in national legislatures. Table 3 shows that the percentage of women in Congress is about half their average representation in national bodies. Women's representation in the formerly socialist regimes exceeded 20 percent. It was close to 30 percent in the Scandinavian countries. Only the countries of the Far East and Middle East had lower proportions of women in their national assemblies. Nevertheless, women in all types of society are greatly underrepresented in public office.

THEORIES EXPLAINING WOMEN'S LOW REPRESENTATION

Several broad theories have been developed to account for the fact that women have not achieved proportional representation in the United States in the seventy years since the passage of the suffrage amendment. The wide variation between the fifty states in terms of the numbers of women elected to office provides the foundation for theories based on differing political cultures and environments. Using Elazar's classification of the states into three cultural types—moralistic, individualistic, and traditionalistic[23]—researchers have found that women's representation is higher in moralistic states, where political participation is encouraged, while it is lower in individualistic state cultures, where competition for office is great, and lowest in traditionalistic cultures, which emphasize continuity of elite control.[24] Other research has found that women's representation has been related to party dominance. Women have fared better in Republican as opposed to Democratic states.[25] Apparently, the control of the Democratic Party by eastern and southern European ethnics and blue-collar unions in many states led to lim-

Table 3   PERCENTAGE OF WOMEN IN NATIONAL LEGISLATURES, 1984

World	10
USSR and Eastern Europe	22
Developing socialist states[a]	22
Western Europe	13
United States	5
Other developed countries[b]	7
Developing Latin America	8
Developing South Asia	5
Developing Africa	5
Developing Far East	3
Developing Middle East	2

Source: Adapted from Ruth Sivard, *Women: A World Survey* (Washington, DC: World Priorities, 1985), pp. 35–37. © 1985 World Priorities.
[a]China, Cuba, North Korea, Mongolia, Vietnam.
[b]Australia, Canada, Israel, Japan, New Zealand.

ited roles for women.[26] Recent findings, however, indicate that these relationships are no longer valid. Although women are still poorly represented in the South, where traditionalistic political culture predominantly exists and where the Democratic Party still controls local and state politics, in the other regions of the country, individualistic culture and dominance by the Democratic Party no longer impede the election of women to public office.[27]

A second set of theories stresses sex-role socialization as the cause of women's low representation in public office. According to these theories, women and men are taught to accept different kinds of roles in life. Women are trained to be passive and home oriented. Men are taught to be independent, assertive, and achievement oriented. Consequently, politics and public life in general are seen as a man's world while the home is the woman's domain. As a result of this type of sex-role socialization, which begins in childhood and continues and is reinforced in adult life, women who challenge their designated role and actively seek public office will suffer psychological pain because they can no longer identify with nonpolitical women and are not accepted by their male colleagues.[28] Consequently, only a few women, those who have experienced "counter socialization," will seek public office.[29]

Another perspective on role conflicts focuses simply upon the extent to which women's family responsibilities limit their political participation. Women devote themselves to their homes and families; therefore, they do not have the time or energy for active participation in politics. Their situation as homemakers prevents their taking on the rigor of public office. A study of elected officials found that support from spouse and family was one of the three most important factors in the decision to seek public office. Married women were more likely than married men to place spousal and family support as of uppermost importance.[30] Furthermore, political aspiration and the ambition to hold public office still seem to be more constrained among women than men. Studies of the politically active women who make up the party elites in America have shown that they are less likely than the male leaders to desire elected office. The differences in the level of political ambition have been declining in recent years, however.[31]

Research has shown two of the ways in which some women in public office have avoided role conflicts between being homemakers and politicians. Jeane Kirkpatrick found that women in American state legislatures delayed the start of their careers until their children were in school.[32] Thus, on the average, women legislators were older than their male counterparts. A study by Carol Nechemias indicates that women's ability to hold office may depend on convenience. For example, the women in her study of 16 American state legislatures were more likely than the men to come from districts that were closer to the state capital.[33]

Another way that sex-role socialization is hypothesized to limit women's political participation is structural. By concentrating on homemaking to the exclusion of other occupations and roles, women are not found in the professions from which politicians inordinately are chosen—the law and other broker-type businesses. Therefore, they do not achieve the higher socioeconomic status that forms the "eligibility pool" for elective office.[34] Susan Welch investigated the limitations asserted by career on women's representation in American state legislatures. The findings were mixed. Although there were far fewer women than men in the key professions that provide the career backgrounds for legislators, their levels in these eligibility pools were greater than predicted by their numbers in office.[35] Furthermore, the road to public office for women seems to diverge from that for men. Women may be able to compensate for their lower socioeconomic status by working harder in voluntary groups and political parties to prove their competence.[36]

Socialization barriers, however, are coming under increasing challenge from the women's movement and from women's increasing assumption of professional jobs. For example, a recent poll showed that while only a third of American women considered themselves feminists, 62 percent believed that feminists had helped women and over 80 percent believed that the women's movement had helped women become more independent and improve their lives.[37] These attitudes certainly indicate support from a large majority of women in the United States for challenging traditional role stereotypes and socialization patterns.

A third explanation attributes the low representation of women in public office to explicit discrimination against them. This so-called male-conspiracy theory is derived from feminist ideology. Women do not achieve equality with men because men discriminate against them. Party and interest group leaders are men, and they prevent women from achieving equality. Feminists who adopt a Marxist perspective see private property and male ownership of the means of production as the cause of women's inequality. Radical feminists believe that the subjugation of women is the most basic form of discrimination. Men dominate women because they enjoy the power it gives them.[38]

Evidence of discrimination against women by political elites has not been conclusive. Lamson, Mandel, and the Tolchins have all suggested that American women candidates face this obstacle in running for office.[39] Yet, others have not concurred. Studies of party leaders in various states and of national and state legislative races have shown that a candidate's gender has not been a significant factor in raising and spending campaign funds, and there is little evidence that party elites have been withholding campaign funds from women candidates in recent races.[40] Apparently, discrimination by party gatekeepers has been receding in recent years as the increased legitimacy of women politicians make overt discrimination potentially costly.

Voter discrimination is another factor seen as limiting the access of women to public office; here, voters may perceive women as less qualified than men to hold public office. But voter discrimination against female candidates seems to be on the decline. While there is evidence of past voter discrimination in the United States, this problem seems to have largely vanished. At least according to public opinion polls, the general populace's acceptance of and support for women's officeholding has grown considerably since the late 1960s.[41] More important, the difference in voter support for male and female candidates in actual elections has declined to an insignificant level since the mid-1970s. Once the candidates' party and incumbency status are controlled, voters are now as likely to vote for women as for men in both local and national elections.[42]

Institutional constraints have also been adduced as a barrier to the election of women. One obvious constraint is implicit in the previous findings that women candidates do as well as their male competitors once incumbency is controlled. Political incumbents have a tremendous electoral advantage in running for most offices because of the political resources that officeholders control, their sheer advantage in name recognition, and the fact that previous victories demonstrate an ability to appeal to the voters. To the extent that incumbents enjoy a considerable advantage in elections, women are certainly disadvantaged. Since women are much less likely than men to be incumbents, who are known to and respected by constituents, it will take decades for them to achieve equality in office in most nations if the normal advantages of incumbency continue to operate.[43] The news about the effects of incumbency is not entirely negative, however, because once women do succeed in winning election in a district, state, or nation, their example evidently makes it easier for other women to win elections later.[44]

The nature of electoral systems themselves may be limiting the election of women to public office; the evidence is that women clearly do better in some types of elections than others. For instance, Wilma Rule found that the proportion of women elected to the lower house of the national legislature in 23 industrial democracies at the beginning of the 1980s was much higher in districts with multiple seats, proportional representation, and a party list of candidates than in single-seat, winner-take-all systems.[45] Darcy et al. have found that women candidates do better in larger, multiseat districts in U.S. state and local elections.[46]

Several reasons have been advanced for women's advantage in multi-seat districts. First, parties may be more willing to place women on the ballot when there are more seats available. They can reward both active men and active women in these districts.[47] Second, voters may be more willing to elect women when they have several votes and can also vote for men. Finally, in campaigns in multi-seat districts, candidates focus on their own accomplishments rather than attacking opponents', and more women may be willing to run for election in such an environment.[48]

Finally, the power and prestige of the political office also seem to be factors in determining the level of representation of women. That is, the more desirable the office and/or the greater the competition for the office, the less likely that women will be well represented. In legislatures that are large relative to the population represented, women have more seats. Also the degree of the professionalism of the legislature determines the relative representation of women. In legislatures where the members sit full-time, receive a relatively large salary, and hold greater prestige, there will be fewer women.[49] The hypothesis that the level of competitiveness and prestige of the legislative body affects the number of women in office seems to be confirmed by the fact that there are more women in local and state offices than in national offices. Also, even at the same level of government, women have been more likely to be elected in places where the office is considered less desirable.[50]

IMPLICATIONS FOR THE FUTURE

Although the record of the United States in getting women into public office has not been outstanding, current trends are encouraging. Since 1975, increasing numbers of women have entered government office at all levels in each successive election. Many factors are operating simultaneously to maintain the slow but steady rise in women's representation. First, the society that created domestic sex roles for women has irreversibly changed. The family is no longer a haven for women who can depend on their husbands for support. The continuous rise in the divorce rate, the reduction in the birthrate, and economic realities have all contributed to a changing life-style for women. Most adult women are an integral part of the labor force. Most have experienced job discrimination, and many live in relative poverty. These women have developed a feminist consciousness and support the issues of the women's movement. They recognize the need to elect and will vote for public officials who recognize and empathize with the problems of women.[51] The education levels of women have increased, and more are entering the professions from which public officials are drawn, so the number of women in the eligible pool is growing. The ambition of women active in political parties is increasing. Younger women are more willing to consider running for public office than they were in the past. As an example of their greater political competitiveness, women ran for governor in eight states in 1990: Alaska, California, Kansas, Nebraska, Oregon, Pennsylvania, Texas, and Wyoming.[52] As a result, while the number of women governors in office remained the same, the number of women who had ever been governor increased by more than 33 percent in just one year. Finally, there is a greater number of women in public office now who will enjoy the advantages of incumbency in running in future elections. These women serve as role models and provide political experience for other women who may seek office in the future.

Notes

1. Hanna Fenichel Pitkin, *The Concept of Representation* (Berkeley: University of California Press, 1967), chap. 4.
2. Ibid., pp. 86–91.
3. Virginia Sapiro, "Research Frontier Essay: When Are Interests Interesting? The Problem of Political Representation of Women," *American Political Science Review,* 75:703–4 (Sept. 1981).
4. "The Gender Gap in Presidential Voting: 1980–88" (Report, Center for the American Woman and Politics, National Information Bank on Women in Public Office, Eagleton Institute of Politics, Rutgers University, 1989).
5. "The Gender Gap" (Report, Center for the American Woman and Politics, 1987).
6. Susan J. Carroll, *Women as Candidates in American Politics* (Bloomington: Indiana University Press, 1987), p. 321.
7. Susan J. Carroll and Ella Taylor, "Gender Differences in Policy Priorities," *CAWP News & Notes,* 7:3–4 (Winter 1989).
8. Peter Bachrach, *The Theory of Democratic Elitism: A Critique* (Boston: Little, Brown, 1967), p. 3.
9. Susan J. Carroll, "Woman Candidates and Support for Feminist Concerns: The Closet Feminist Syndrome," *Western Political Quarterly,* 37:307 (June 1984).
10. "Bringing More Women into Public Office" (Report, Center for the American Woman and Politics, 1984).
11. Robert Darcy, Susan Welch, and Janet Clark, *Women, Elections and Representation* (New York: Longman, 1987), p. 11.
12. Martin Gruberg, "From Nowhere to Where? Women in State and Local Politics," *Social Science Journal,* 21:6 (Jan. 1984).
13. "Statewide Elective Executive Women 1990" (Report, Center for the American Woman and Politics, 1990).
14. "Women in Municipal Office 1990" (Report, Center for the American Woman and Politics, 1990).
15. Darcy, Welch, and Clark, *Women, Elections and Representation,* p. 29.
16. Carol M. Mueller, "Feminism and the New Women in Public Office," *Women & Politics,* 2:9 (Fall 1982).
17. "Women Appointed to Presidential Cabinets 1989" (Report, Center for the American Woman and Politics, 1989).
18. Susan J. Carroll, "New Strategies to Bring More Women into Office: Organized Efforts to Increase the Number of Women Appointed to Recent Presidential Administrations in the United States" (Paper delivered at the "Vater Staat Und Seine Frauen" Conference in Berlin, West Germany, 1988).
19. *Facts on File: World News Digest,* 49:783 (Oct. 1989).
20. "Women in the U.S. Congress 1990" (Report, Center for the American Woman and Politics, 1990).
21. "Women in State Legislatures 1990" (Report, Center for the American Woman and Politics, 1990).
22. "Women in Municipal Office 1990."
23. Daniel J. Elazar, *American Federalism: A View from the States* (New York: Thomas Y. Crowell, 1966), pp. 86–94.
24. Darcy, Welch, and Clark, *Women, Elections and Representation,* pp. 13–14.
25. Ibid., pp. 21–22.
26. Ibid., p. 50.
27. Wilma Rule, "Why More Women Are State Legislators: A Research Note," *Western Political Quarterly,* 43:443 (June 1990).
28. Robert D. Hess and Judith V. Torney, *The Development of Political Attitudes in Children* (Chicago: Aldine, 1967), chap. 8; Virginia Sapiro, *The Political Integration of Women: Roles, Socialization, and Politics* (Urbana: University of Illinois Press, 1983); Marianne Githens and Jewel L. Prestage, eds., *A Portrait of Marginality: The Political Behaviour of the American Woman* (New York: David McKay, 1977), chap. 1.
29. Diane L. Fowlkes, "Ambitious Political Woman: Counter Socialization and Political Party Context," *Women & Politics,* 4:7–10 (Winter 1984).

30. Susan J. Carroll, "The Personal Is Political: The Intersection of Private Lives and Public Roles among Women and Men in Elective and Appointive Office," *Women & Politics,* 9:57 (Summer 1989).

31. Janet Clark, Charles D. Hadley, and R. Darcy, "Political Ambition among Men and Women State Party Leaders: Testing the Countersocialization Perspective," *American Politics Quarterly,* 17:196 (Apr. 1989).

32. Jeane J. Kirkpatrick, *Political Woman* (New York: Basic Books, 1974), p. 38.

33. Carol Nechemias, "Changes in the Election of Women to U.S. State Legislative Seats," *Legislative Studies Quarterly,* 12:125–42 (Feb. 1987).

34. Kristi Andersen, "Working Women and Political Participation, 1952–1972," *American Journal of Political Science,* 19:439–53 (Aug. 1975).

35. Susan Welch, "Recruitment of Women to Office: A Discriminant Analysis," *Western Political Quarterly,* 31:372–80 (Sept. 1978).

36. Harold D. Clarke and Allan Kornberg, "Moving up the Political Escalator: Women Party Officials in the United States and Canada," *Journal of Politics,* 41:454 (May 1979).

37. Claudi Wallis, "Onward Women," *Time,* 4 Dec. 1989, pp. 80–89.

38. Barbara S. Deckard, *The Women's Movement: Political, Socioeconomic, and Psychological Issues,* 3d ed. (New York: Harper & Row, 1983), chap. 14.

39. Peggy Lamson, *Few Are Chosen: American Women in Political Life Today* (Boston: Houghton Mifflin, 1968); Ruth B. Mandel, *In the Running: The New Woman Candidate* (New Haven, CT: Ticknor & Fields, 1981); Susan Tolchin and Martin Tolchin, *Clout: Woman-power and Politics* (New York: Capricorn, 1976).

40. Robert Darcy, Margaret Brewer, and Judy Clay, "Women in the Oklahoma Political System: State Legislative Elections," *Social Science Journal,* 21:67–78 (Jan. 1984); Barbara Burrell, "Women's and Men's Campaigns for the U.S. House of Representatives, 1972–1982: A Finance Gap?" *American Politics Quarterly,* 13:251–72 (July 1985).

41. Susan Welch and Lee Sigelman, "Changes in Public Attitudes toward Women in Politics," *Social Science Quarterly,* 63:312–22 (June 1982).

42. Susan Welch et al., "The Effect of Candidate Gender on Electoral Outcomes in State Legislative Races: A Research Note," *Western Political Quarterly,* 38:464–75 (Sept. 1985).

43. Kristi Andersen and Stuart Thorson, "Some Structural Barriers to the Election of Women to Congress: A Simulation," *Western Political Quarterly,* 37:143–56 (Mar. 1984).

44. Susan A. McManus, "A City's First Female Officeholder: 'Coattails' for Future Female Officeholders," *Western Political Quarterly,* 34:88–99 (Mar. 1981).

45. Wilma Rule, "Electoral Systems, Contextual Factors, and Women's Opportunity for Election to Parliament in Twenty-Three Democracies," *Western Political Quarterly,* 40:477–98 (Sept. 1987).

46. Darcy, Welch, and Clark, *Women, Elections and Representation,* chap. 6.

47. Carroll, *Women as Candidates,* p. 41.

48. R. Darcy, Susan Welch, and Janet Clark, "Women Candidates in Single- and Multi-Member Districts," *Social Science Quarterly,* 66:951 (Dec. 1985).

49. Irene Diamond, *Sex Roles in the State House* (New Haven, CT: Yale University Press, 1977), chaps. 1–3.

50. Richard L. Engstrom, M. D. McDonald, and Bih-Er Chou, "The Election of Women to Central City Councils in the U.S." (Paper delivered at the Seventh Annual Meeting of the International Society of Political Psychology, Toronto, 1984).

51. Ethel Klein, *Gender Politics* (Cambridge, MA: Harvard University Press, 1984), pp. 1–8.

52. "1990 Women Candidates" (Center for the American Woman and Politics, 1990).

The Year of the Woman?

MARJORIE RANDON HERSHEY

Conventional wisdom suggests that there are so few women in Congress because incumbents, the great majority of whom are male, have so many advantages in winning reelection, not merely because voters discriminate against women candidates.[1] Redistricting and retirements in 1992 opened up unprecedented avenues into Congress for the growing number of women public officials at the state and local levels. Even the prevalence of gender stereotyping seemed to benefit women campaigners in 1992; given the high levels of public frustration with Congress, the stereotyping of women as more moral and less tainted by "politics as usual" put women, the ultimate congressional outsiders, in just the position that most male candidates were working to attain.

In addition to the opportunity, events of 1992 provided the motive for some women to run. The confirmation hearings on the nomination of Clarence Thomas, widely broadcast on radio and television, were a defining moment for many politically involved women. Some were propelled into candidacy by the sight of an all-male Senate Judiciary Committee grilling Professor Anita Hill on her charges of sexual harassment against Thomas. One was Lynn Yeakel, head of a fund-raising organization for women's issues. Yeakel's decision to run against Senator Arlen Specter (R-Pa.) was prompted by her disgust at the way in which Specter led the Judiciary Committee's charge against Hill. Another was Carol Moseley Braun, a Cook County, Illinois, official who astonished the political professionals by winning the Democratic Senate nomination from incumbent Senator Alan J. Dixon.

As the primary season advanced, the number of women running for Congress increased. At the end of May there were 150 women candidates for the House—the largest number in history, by a considerable margin—106 of whom won their party's nomination in the primaries. A record eleven women won nomination to the Senate. Most were Democrats: seventy in the House races and all but one in the Senate. These candidates were greatly helped by the contributions of other women, which expanded substantially in 1992.[2]

But the two faces of incumbency were a potential hazard for these new women candidates. Although many women benefited from their image as outsiders, untainted by the scandals and the gridlock that dominate current perceptions of Congress, their outsider status could also, in the hands of a skilled opponent, be portrayed as a lack of experience and aggressiveness in bringing home benefits to the district. As Ellen Goodman wrote: "Gradually and predictably, The Year of the Woman became the year of individual women, each on her own turf, with her own strengths and weaknesses."[3]

In the end, the "year of the woman" turned out to be the year of *some* women. Four new Democratic women won Senate seats: Boxer and former San

Francisco Mayor Dianne Feinstein in California, State Senator Patty Murray in Washington, and Braun in Illinois, the first black woman ever to serve in the Senate. They joined incumbents Barbara Mikulski (D-Md.), who won reelection easily, and Nancy Landon Kassebaum (R-Kan.) to push the number of women in the Senate to six—enough to convince the Senate to construct the first women members' restroom just off the Senate floor.

Lynn Yeakel, however, lost her initial lead during the summer and was unable to regain it during the fall, partly because of Specter's effective emphasis on his record of constituent service. One reporter wrote: "He struts his incumbency like a bodybuilder displaying his biceps . . . and [he has] a way of squeezing blood out of the federal turnip that impresses even Democrats."[4] In addition to Yeakel, six other women Senate candidates lost their races.

The number of women voting members in the House jumped from twenty-eight in the 102nd Congress to forty-seven in the 103rd.[5] Other minorities greatly expanded their representation as well. The new House included a record number of African Americans (thirty-eight) and Hispanics (seventeen), many of whom ran in new districts drawn especially to help elect more minority representatives. Five southern states—Alabama, Florida, North and South Carolina, and Virginia—elected black House members for the first time since Reconstruction.

But the gains, particularly for women, must be kept in perspective. In order for women to hold about the same percentage of congressional seats as their proportion of the population as a whole, voters would have needed to elect 194 new women House members, not 19; and 49 new senators, not 4 (see table 1). Analysts may dispute whether parity in numbers between women and men in Congress is a worthwhile goal; but the striking *lack* of parity certainly suggests that women remain seriously disadvantaged in the effort to win House and Senate seats, to a much greater extent than do blacks and Hispanics.

And the gap will close only slowly, if at all; a Voting Rights Act intended to benefit geographically concentrated minorities cannot be used to increase women's representation. Being a woman candidate clearly did not result in the free ride to victory that a trend-happy press had trumpeted. Mary Rose Oakar and two other female incumbents, Joan Kelly Horn (D-Mo.) and Liz Patterson (D-S.C.), were defeated for reelection (as was Beverly Byron, D-Md., in the primary) along with fifty-five of the seventy-nine nonincumbent women who ran in House races. Only two of the women House newcomers defeated male incumbents; all the other winners had contested open seats. Similarly, only two of the four new women senators had run against incumbents, one of whom had been appointed to the Senate only two years before; the others won open seats. All the other women Senate candidates who ran against incumbents lost. Many women candidates, in short, owed their seats to the great wave of incumbent retirements and primary defeats in 1992—an occurrence unlikely to recur with any regularity.

The new congressional women were not a group of political neophytes. A full three-quarters of those elected to the House had previously served in elective office. So had an even higher proportion of the new black and Hispanic House members; the least politically experienced group, in fact, was the new white male representatives. In the Senate, all four of the newly elected women members had

Table 1   REPRESENTATION OF WOMEN, BLACKS, AND HISPANICS IN CONGRESS, 1973–93

	WOMEN		BLACKS		HISPANICS	
	%	N	%	N	%	N
1973						
% of population	51.3		11.1		4.6	
% of House membership	3.7	16[b]	3.4	15	1.1	5
% of Senate membership	0.0	0	1.0	1	1.0	1
Representation ratio [a]		.06		.27		.24
1983						
% of population	51.4		11.7		6.4	
% of House membership	5.1	22[c]	4.8	21	2.3	10
% of Senate membership	2.0	2	0.0	0	0.0	0
Representation ratio		.09		.33		.30
1993						
% of population	51.3		12.1		9.0	
% of House membership	10.8	47	8.7	38	3.9	17
% of Senate membership	6.0	6	1.0	1	0.0	0
Representation ratio		.19		.60		.35

Sources: U.S. Bureau of the Census, *Congressional Quarterly Weekly Report.*

[a] The ratio of the percentage of women (or blacks or Hispanics) in Congress (including both House and Senate) to the percentage of that group in the general population.
[b] Includes two women members elected in special elections.
[c] Includes one woman member elected in a special election.

previous experience in elective office, compared with five of the seven newly elected men. Political experience, it would seem, is even more central to the success of minority challengers than it is for white male challengers.

Will these demographic changes make any difference in congressional action? Some policy impact is likely: For example, every one of the newly elected women supports abortion rights. There may be some impact on the congressional agenda as well. A survey of half of all state legislators in 1991 found that "even when men and women shared the same party and ideology, women were much more likely to expend their energies on health care, children's and family questions and women's rights issues."[6] The survey also found that women public officials tended to bring government business out from behind closed doors and to involve private citizens in governmental processes, more than their male counterparts did. To the extent that women's life experiences differ from men's, the eyes through which Congress sees the nation could indeed have a different focus.

Notes

1. R. Darcy, Susan Welch, and Janet Clark, *Women, Elections, and Representation* (New York: Longman, 1987).
2. Beth Donovan, "Women's Campaigns Fueled Mostly by Women's Checks," *Congressional Quarterly Weekly Report,* 17 October 1992, 3269–73.
3. "A Mood of Political Activism May Reveal Itself this Election," *Herald-Times* (Bloomington, Ind.), 9 October 1992, A8.
4. Dale Russakoff, "Arlen Specter on the Case," *Washington Post National Weekly Edition,* 14–20 September 1992, 9.
5. Eleanor Holmes Norton, the nonvoting delegate from Washington, D.C., is the forty-eighth.
6. R. W. Apple, Jr., "Steady Local Gains by Women Fuel More Runs for High Office," *New York Times,* 24 May 1992, sec. 4, p. 5.

The Impact of the Electoral System on Election of Women to National Legislatures

PIPPA NORRIS

More and more women have been elected to national office in some countries while progress in others seems slow or nonexistent (see Table 1). Why is this? Many blame party members. Others blame voters. Some believe that women do not come forward as candidates. This article argues that two interacting institutional factors are critical for women's access to elected office:

- The electoral system
- The party selection system

THE ELECTORAL SYSTEM

Electoral systems vary substantially in different countries, but the main alternatives are simple plurality or first past the post (FPTP), alternative vote (AV), single transferable vote (STV), additional member system (AMS), and party list systems.

Simple Plurality: First Past the Post

The FPTP system is currently used in the United States and countries of the "old commonwealth," including the United States, Britain, New Zealand, and Canada. The system uses single-member constituencies, in which the candidate with a simple plurality of votes (more than any other) is elected. Voters cannot prioritize their choice but must cast a simple ballot with a single preference for one candidate (X).

Alternative Vote

The AV system is used in elections to the Australian House of Representatives. Australia is divided into single-member constituencies. Instead of a simple X, voters number their preferences among candidates (1, 2, 3 . . .). To win, candidates need an absolute majority of votes. Where no candidate gets over 50 percent after first preferences are counted, then the candidate at the bottom of the pile is eliminated and those votes are redistributed among the other candidates according to second preferences. The process continues until an absolute majority is secured.

Single Transferable Vote

The STV system is currently used in Ireland and Malta and in elections to the Australian Senate. Ireland is divided into multimember constituencies, each with about four or five members of parliament (MPs). Parties put forward as many candidates as they think can win in each constituency. Voters number their preferences among candidates (1, 2, 3, . . .). The total number of votes are counted, and this total is divided by the number of seats in the constituency to produce a quota. To be elected, candidates must reach the minimum quota. If no candidates reach the quota when the first preferences are counted, then the person with the least votes is eliminated and those votes are redistributed according to second preferences. This process continues until all seats are filled.

Party List Systems

Electoral systems based on party lists are widespread throughout Europe. These lists may be open, as in Norway, Finland, the Netherlands, and Italy, in which case voters can express preferences for particular candidates within the list. Or they may be closed, as in Israel, Portugal, Spain, and Germany, in which case voters can select only the party, and the ranking of candidates is determined by the

Table 1   WOMEN IN ELECTED OFFICE IN DEVELOPED DEMOCRACIES, 1991

Country	Percentage of women	Year	System
	Proportional party lists		
Finland	38	1991	Regional list
Sweden	38	1988	Regional list
Norway	36	1989	Regional list
Denmark	33	1990	Regional list
Iceland	24	1991	Regional list
Austria	22	1990	Regional list
Netherlands	21	1989	National list
Germany	20	1990	AMS
Switzerland	16	1991	Regional list
Spain	15	1989	Regional list
Luxembourg	13	1989	Regional list
Italy	13	1987	Regional list
Israel	7	1990	National list
Portugal	8	1987	Regional list
Belgium	8	1987	Regional list
Greece	5	1990	Regional list
	Plurality systems		
New Zealand	16	1990	FPTP
Canada	13	1988	FPTP
United States	6	1990	FPTP
UK	6	1987	FPTP
	Majority systems		
Australia	7	1990	AV
France	6	1988	Second Ballot
	Semiproportional systems		
Ireland	8	1989	STV
Malta	3	1987	STV
Japan	2	1990	SNTV

Note: AMS, alternative member system; AV, alternative vote; FPTP, first-past-the-post system; STNV, single nontransferable vote; STV, single transferable vote.

Source: Distribution of Seats between Men and Women in National Assemblies, June 1991 (Interparliamentary Union, Geneva, 1987).

political party. The rank order on the party list determines which candidates are elected—for example, the top 10 to 15 names. Party lists may also be national, as in Israel, where the country is one constituency divided into 120 seats. Or party lists may be regional, as in Belgium, where seven regions are subdivided into 2 to 34 seats each. Votes are allocated to seats on the basis of the minimum quota, which can be calculated in a number of ways. In the simplest form (the Hare quota), the total number of valid votes is divided by the total number of seats to be allocated.

Additional Member System

The AMS combines characteristics of the single-member and party list systems. This system is used in Germany, where electors have two votes. Half the Bundestag is elected in single-member constituencies based on simple plurality voting. The remaining members are elected from regional party lists. Parties that receive less than a specified minimum threshold of votes (5%) are not entitled to any seats. The total number of seats a party receives in Germany is based on the Niemeyer method, which ensures that seats are proportional to votes. For example, a small party that received 10 percent of the vote but did not win any single-member seats outright is topped up through its party list to receive 10 percent of all the seats in the Bundestag.

THE IMPACT OF ELECTORAL SYSTEMS ON WOMEN

What difference does these systems make for women? Comparative studies suggest that three factors in electoral systems affect women's representation, in the following order of priority:

- Ballot structure (whether party list or single-candidate)
- District magnitude (the number of seats per district)
- Degree of proportionality (the allocation of votes to seats)

All other things being equal, women tend to do best under multimember constituencies with a high number of seats per district. It follows that national party list systems tend to be the most favorable for women. The STV system falls somewhere in the middle, depending upon the number of representatives per district. In contrast, FPTP and AV systems are least favorable to the representation of women. What evidence is there for this?

Evidence from Countries That Use Different Electoral Systems

Australia uses the alternative majoritarian vote in single-member electoral divisions for the House of Representatives and uses multimember state-level districts with proportional quotas for the Senate. In the 1990 general election, women MPs made up 7 percent of the House but one-quarter of the Senate. Similar contrasts can be drawn in Japan, which uses the single nontransferable vote (SNTV) system for the house of representatives (Shugi-In) and the district party list system for the upper house of councilors (Sangi-In). In the 1989 general election, women were far less successful in the house of representatives (2%) than in the upper house (13%). The classic case used to confirm this argument is Germany, where in federal elections half the seats in the Bundestag are allocated by majoritarian single-member districts and the rest by proportional land (regional) party lists. In 1990 women represented 20 percent of the Bundestag. Some 80 percent of these women entered the Bundestag through the land list route. Clearly, then, in simultaneous elections in the same country, women do far better under party list systems.

Evidence from Countries That Changed Their Electoral Systems

The classic case in this instance is France: between 1945 and 1956, and again in 1986, for the National Assembly the French used proportional representation with Département party lists without preference voting. Although it was proportional, the system used in France in 1986 employed few seats per Département; hence, it resulted in a relatively high number of seats per district. In contrast, in the national elections from 1958 to 1981 and again in 1988, the system was changed so that candidates were elected by a single-member first-ballot majority system, with a second runoff plurality ballot. As a result, with the exceptions of elections in 1981 and 1988 more women were elected each term to the National Assembly by proportional representation than to any assembly using the majoritarian system.

Evidence from Cross-national Comparisons

We can compare the representation of women in the lower house in a range of 25 developed democracies, classifying electoral systems into four categories: proportional party list and semiproportional, majority, and plurality systems.

The results in Table 1 confirm that in 1991 there were few women in Parliament under FPTP plurality systems, particularly in Britain and the United States, although the situation was better in Canada and New Zealand. In contrast, female representation is strongest in countries using party lists with a high level of proportionality. The contrast is stark: women make up 38 percent of MPs in Finland and Sweden, compared with only 6 percent in Britain.

WHY WOULD PARTY LIST SYSTEMS BENEFIT WOMEN?

Party list systems increase gender representation for three main reasons: use of balanced tickets, affirmative action programs, and legislative turnover.

Balanced Ticket

In single-member constituencies, local parties pick one standard-bearer. When selection committees consider women an electoral risk, they may hesitate to choose women candidates. There is a different "logic of choice" under proportional systems, where voters are presented with a list of candidates for each party. Here parties have a rational incentive to present a balanced ticket. It is unlikely that any votes will be lost by the presence of women candidates on the list. And their absence may cause offense by advertising party prejudice, thereby narrowing the party's appeal.

Affirmative Action

The affirmative action argument holds that if parties want to help women candidates, selection quotas, positive training mechanisms, or financial assistance are easiest to implement where there are national or regional lists of candidates.

Legislative Turnover and Party Competition

Greater proportionality increases the number of seats that change hands and fosters party competition. This improves access for any group currently underrepresented in government, including women.

PARTY REFORMS

Therefore the adoption of multimember constituencies would probably increase the number of women officeholders in simple plurality systems. Nevertheless, electoral reform should not be treated as a mechanical panacea that will automatically bring women into politics. There are no "quick fixes." In some countries, such as Israel, Belgium, and Portugal, few women are elected despite the use of party lists, because of the candidate selection process within parties. Therefore what matters is reform of the electoral system and the party selection system. So, what practical steps can parties take? In simple plurality systems where selection takes place at the local level, parties can consider a number of reforms:

- *Candidate training*. Parties can produce training packages to develop candidates' techniques in public speaking, presentational skills, and personal confidence.
- *Selection interviews*. In the selection process, parties can use a variety of techniques to evaluate applicants—for example, supplementing formal interviews with small group discussions among applicants, role-playing exercises, and written forms of evaluation.
- *Equal opportunity*. Parties can introduce equal opportunity training for selectors, standardize the application process, and bring gender monitoring into each level of the process.
- *Active recruitment*. Parties can do more to encourage potential applicants rather than assuming that women will be self-starters. Parties can make more information available and give advice about how to run for office, making the rules formal and explicit.
- *Civic education*. Parties can increase their educational function in the broadest sense, encouraging supporters to participate in all aspects of democratic life.

- *Positive action.* Parties can consider using affirmative action or positive discrimination.
- *Financial assistance.* Parties can provide financial assistance to cover candidates' personal expenses associated with running for office.

CONCLUSIONS

The number of women elected under simple plurality systems shows evidence of slow improvement. Under the present system, parties have been gradually changing their selection procedures to facilitate the entry of women. More women have been coming forward as applicants, and eventually as candidates. But progress toward gender equality in these systems has often lagged behind gains in other democracies. The essential problem with single-member districts is that no matter how much parties say they want to change, no matter how loudly party members and voters say they would like to have more women in office, the mechanisms are difficult to reform so long as the final decision rests in the hands of separate constituencies.

FURTHER READING FOR CHAPTER 4

Beckwith, K. 1989. "Sneaking Women into Office: Alternative Access to Parliament in France and Italy." *Women and Politics* 9(3): 1–15.

Carroll, S. 1985. *Women as Candidates in American Politics.* Bloomington: Indiana University Press.

Costantini, E. 1990. "Political Women and Political Ambition: Closing the Gender Gap." *American Journal of Political Science,* 34 (3), August: 741–770.

Cranford, John R. 1992. "The New Class: More Diverse, Less Lawerly, Younger." *Congressional Quarterly* November 7, pp. 7–9.

Flammang, J. (Ed.) 1984. *Political Women.* Newbury Park, CA: Sage.

Geddes, A., Lovenduski, J., Norris, P. 1991. "Candidate Selection: Reform in Britain." *Contemporary Record* April, pp. 19–22.

Haavio-Mannila, E., et al. (ed.) 1985. *Unfinished Democracy.* New York: Pergamon Press.

Lovenduski, J., and Norris, P. 1989. "Selecting Women Candidates: Obstacles to the Feminisation of the House of Commons." *European Journal of Political Research* 17: 533–562.

Lovenduski, J., and Norris, P. (eds.). 1993. *Gender and Party Politics.* London: Sage.

Lovenduski, J., and Norris, P. 1991. "Party Rules and Women's Representation: Reforming the British Labour Party." In I. Crewe, P. Norris, D. Denver, and D. Broughton (eds.), *British Elections and Parties Yearbook 1991.* Hempstead: Harvester Wheatsheaf.

Norris, P. 1985. "Women's Legislative Participation in Western Europe." *West European Politics,* 8(4): 90–101.

Rule, W. 1990. "Why More Women Are State Legislators." *Western Political Quarterly* 43 (2), June: 436–448.

Rule, W. 1987. "Electoral Systems, Contextual Factors and Women's Opportunity for Election to Parliament in Twenty-three Democracies." *Western Political Quarterly* 40: 477–486.

Rule, W. 1981. "Why Women Don't Run: The Critical Contextual Factors in Women's Legislative Recruitment." *Western Political Quarterly* 34 (March): 60–77.

Rule, W., and Zimmerman, J. (eds.). 1992. *The United States Electoral Systems: Their Impact on Women and Minorities*. New York: Greenwood Press.

CHAPTER
5

Political Issues

Although sweeping generalizations about the conditions and experiences of all women imply the possibility of genuine comparison, a closer examination of women in particular societies indicates considerable difference and variation in their situations. This is especially true in the area of public policy, where the national setting establishes the tone of the policy debate and defines available options. Bearing this caveat in mind, it is still possible to identify some *leitmotivs* in the policy concerns articulated by European and American women. These shared concerns stem largely from some similarities in societal changes which have taken place in Europe and America over the past two centuries.

In the preindustrial societies of Europe and the United States, there were distinctive roles based on gender, but there was no gender differentiation in the location of work. Men and women lived and worked in the same place. Men usually performed the physically demanding tasks of farming while women were primarily responsible for the children and the household.[1] This pattern was profoundly altered by the advent of the industrial revolution, which radically changed both the source of wealth and the nature of the workplace. Work and home became separated, with men working outside the home. The changes were more complicated for women. Work outside the home was simply added to home and family obligations. Many women discovered that they now had two jobs: one in the labor market outside the home and the other in the home, caring for family and children. The burdens imposed on women by industrialization were made still worse by the disintegration of the agrarian, extended family system. Women could no longer count on others to share the burden of caring for the home and family.

The repercussions of these changes on the lives of women were recorded in the journals, diaries, and papers of the period. American women affiliated with the Settlement House Movement, like Florence Kelly and Alice Hamilton, wrote detailed accounts of the plight of the women factory workers, many of whom were compelled to bring their infants and toddlers with them to the poorly lit, ill-ventilated, and unheated buildings. There these women worked, often for fourteen or sixteen hours a day, afterward returning home to do household chores. European women recounted similar experiences.

Industrialization redefined a wide variety of behavioral norms, including those governing gender roles. Assumptions surfaced, positing the existence of specific gender spheres that reflected the bifurcation of work and home. The male world of economic activity was outside the home, and the realm of women was the world of the home and family. The woman at home, with her husband leaving each day to go out to work, was posited as the ideal. Both social custom and public policy reinforced this image. Better-paying jobs were reserved for men, and women's role in the labor market was depicted as trivial and marginal.

For a variety of reasons, not least of which was economic necessity, some women continued to participate in the labor force. However, the woman at home was the ideal held up for all to emulate, and it was the fundamental assumption on which public policy was based in both Europe and the United States. For example, in the garment industry in America, the common practice was for women to do piecework at home. Although there was clearly an economic basis for this practice, it also supported gender stereotypes. The at-home mother status masked the exploitative employment of women and reinforced the prevailing norms for appropriate gender roles. To be sure, when there were shortages in the work force during World Wars I and II, these norms were overlooked; women were quickly absorbed into the job market. As soon as the men returned to civilian life and the labor shortage abated, however, the women were pressured to return home. Thus, the ideal of the woman in the home persisted and was used as an excuse for giving to women the lower-paying, lower-status positions carrying few benefits.

Changes in the last decades of this century have also transformed women's lives. At the beginning of the century, about 25 percent of the women in the United States worked, and they were likely to be young and unmarried. The present profile of the working woman is in sharp contrast: 56 percent of all American women are now in the labor market, and they are likely to be married, widowed, separated, or divorced and to have children.[2] Not only are more women working, but they are also likely to be working the equivalent of full time. The total number of full-time hours women work (41.3) is only slightly less than that of men (45.1). Similar changes have occurred in Europe. Within the past twenty years, large numbers of European women have also entered the labor market. Except in Great Britain, where the percentage is slightly lower, more than 40 percent of all European women now work outside the home. Like their American counterparts, European working women are more likely now than was the case at the beginning of the century to be married, separated, divorced, or widowed; to have children; and to seek continuous employment.

The influx of women into the work force has challenged the validity of the notion that men must go out to work and women must stay at home. The idea that women's place is in the home no longer jibes with reality; women are now an ongoing part of the labor force, not merely casual, marginal workers temporarily seeking employment. There is a widespread consensus among women that public policies predicated on the notion of the at-home wife need to be replaced. Feminists have targeted prejudice against women in the areas of pay, promotions, and benefits and gender-biased job classifications. Similarly, advocates want policies assuring women opportunities in the workplace and establishing an environment supportive to them, especially policies barring sex discrimination and sexual harassment in the workplace.

Discrimination against women in the workplace and the issue of sexual harassment are not the only policy concerns of women. Another obstacle to women's work is that women are still assigned the primary responsibility for the care of children and family; this imposes extraordinary pressures on working women. The support systems that women workers require—such as effective maternity leave policies, flexible work schedules, and child care, as well as leave policies acknowledging the role of women in caring for aged parents—are either nonexistent or inadequate. Although there is considerable variation from one country to another, with the United States lagging far behind Europe, the needs of women workers have not been fully met anywhere. Consequently, new policies reflecting the dual role of women have been the focus of campaigns in both Europe and America.

The problems confronting working women who are also responsible for caring for a family have been compounded by recent transformations in family structure. A sharp increase in the number of marriages ending in divorce and the growth in the number of single-headed households conflict with public policies based on the assumption that each household contains an intact nuclear family and an at-home mother. With the number of women as sole breadwinners growing, the consequences of poorly paying jobs for women cannot be overstated. In the United States, the impoverished are most likely to be women and children, with the most rapidly expanding poverty group being children in single-parent households. Over one-third of all female-headed households in America fall below the poverty line, and this proportion increases to 47.8 percent for female-headed households with children under age 18.[3] Obviously, poorly paid employment for working mothers has negative effects on the succeeding generation. We need to change present inequities that contribute to low pay for working women and policies that define unemployment and retraining in terms of male workers' needs.

Issues involving safety and violence against women have also gained attention. As long as women remain particularly susceptible to violence and abuse, they are in jeopardy. There have been some successes, as well as failures, in confronting existing norms that ignore, accept, and justify violence against women. In the United States, for example, there have been some changes in the legal treatment of rape prosecutions and sentencing. However, violence against women continues. Both in America and in Europe, campaigns against domestic violence attempt to force government authorities to deal with it as a serious crime. Although there are considerable differences between European and American feminists on the issue of pornography, the linkage between defining women as sex objects and the perpetuation of women's inferior status has been widely acknowledged.

Finally, women's attention has focused on their role in reproduction. The issue of abortion has played a prominent role in both European and American politics. In countries such as the United States, Germany, and Ireland, the question of abortion continues to be hotly debated, whereas in Britain and France the issue is largely resolved. Policies regarding the use of fetal tissue and in vitro fertilization, however, are of increasing concern in both Europe and the United States.

The selections contained in this chapter focus on these policy concerns. The first set of readings examines the problems resulting from the failure of existing public policy to accurately reflect the changes in nature of the contemporary family. Although national settings affect the language and context of the policy debates and make comparisons difficult, common assumptions define women in terms of the traditional family and assume that women are available for child care and domestic responsibilities. Women's role as principal breadwinners has been ignored or minimized. These outdated views continue to be the basis for much of the social welfare policy in Europe and America. As a consequence, women face the feminization of poverty, inadequate provision for the care of children and the elderly, the persistence of sex discrimination in employment, and sexual harassment in the workplace. Diane Sainsbury's article on welfare policies in Sweden, Britain, and the United States, and Gertrude Schaffner Goldberg and Eleanor Kremen's article "The Feminization of Poverty: Not Only in America" examine the implications of European and American social welfare policies based on notions of the traditional family.

Embedded in women's struggle to achieve equality is the issue of their reproductive freedom, particularly their right to obtain an abortion. The women's movement, along with feminists scholars such as Petchesky and Eisenstein, has claimed that the very foundation of patriarchy is the definition of woman as mother. To what extent has the issue of abortion been resolved in Europe and the United States? Joni Lovenduski and Joyce Outshoorn provide an overview of the abortion debate in Europe, while Dorothy McBride Stetson looks at abortion policy in Russia, the United States, and France.

As women become more visible in the marketplace, the issue of their safety assumes a high priority. Efforts have been made both to reform legal procedures for the prosecution of rape and to protect women from domestic violence through the funding of shelters for battered women. How successful have these attempts been? In "Unfinished Business in Rape Law Reform," Carole Goldberg-Ambrose contends that despite legal reforms, old attitudes about gender, sexuality, and coercion continue to play a role in the disposition of rape cases. Similarly, Amy Elman and Maud Eduards report that prevalent attitudes about the seriousness of domestic violence have a considerable bearing on efforts to assist battered women in Sweden.

MARIANNE GITHENS

Notes

1. In the United States, these distinctions in gender role were not observed among slaves. On many plantations, women slaves were expected to do the same kind of heavy work as the men, and although the slave codes prescribed a reduced work load for pregnant slaves, this rule was often ignored and virtually impossible to enforce.
2. Cynthia Taeuber (ed.), *Statistical Handbook on Women in America* (Phoenix: Oryx, 1991).
3. Taeuber, pp. 195; 210.

Gender and Comparative Analysis: Welfare States, State Theories, and Social Policies

DIANE SAINSBURY

SOCIAL POLICY
AND THE INFLUENCE OF FAMILIAL IDEOLOGY

Feminist theory has underlined the crucial role of ideological constructs in shaping women's lives, and this emphasis has informed feminist accounts of the welfare state. More specifically, feminist analysis has stressed the influence of familial ideology in structuring social policies and reproducing the division of labour between the sexes. Two separate but interlocking dimensions of familial ideology can be identified: the breadwinner ideology and what might be called the caring ideology. The breadwinner ideology underlines the norm that the man is responsible for earning a living and providing for the family. The caring ideology stresses the woman's inherent domesticity and her duties in nurturing and caring for members of the family in the form of unpaid labour in exchange for the support of her husband.

One problematical feature of feminist thinking about the welfare state is that not much attention has been paid to diversity among welfare states and social policies. This tendency has also been strengthened by a major current in feminist theory which views the state as an epiphenomenon of patriarchy, thus ruling out significant variations between specific states and the possibility of variations that might be beneficial to women. Furthermore, the specific contexts of theorizing and policy studies have overwhelmingly been the Anglo-Saxon countries. An inherent danger of such a concentration is that the experiences of these countries will be taken as representative of universal phenomena—and to some degree this has happened. It is thus imperative to extend the horizon of feminist theory and comparisons, and feminists have begun to consider the implications of different state formations for women and to draw on the experiences of a variety of countries (Sasoon 1987, Hernes 1987, Ruggie 1984). However, since so few rigorous empirical comparisons have been made, a basic problem is that we really do not know what the differences and similarities are between various welfare states with respect to gender, and this ignorance tends to reinforce a generic approach based on theorizing that is grounded in the experiences of individual countries.

An essential question must be addressed: Are the central ingredients of feminist theorizing on the welfare state possibly variations? For example, how prevalent and how important is or was the breadwinner ideology in shaping legislation? In seeking to answer this question, I want to explore its importance in four welfare states: the United States, the United Kingdom, the Netherlands, and Sweden. The choice of these countries is based on a desire to include welfare states that differ in important ways (Sainsbury, 1991). Although it would be exaggerated to view this choice as entailing a "most different" design, it does contrast with several existing comparative studies that have adopted or reflect a "most similar" design—that is, they included similar countries such as the Anglo-Saxon countries or the Scandinavian countries. The comparison takes the early 1980s as a baseline for comparing the four countries and for comparing developments until 1990.

Even the most cursory of comparisons across nations and over time reveals substantial variations. In 1980 the influence of the breadwinner ideology was strongest in the Netherlands and least in Sweden, with the UK and the United States occupying the middle ground. During the decade, however, Dutch legislation was extensively revised so as to eliminate (at least officially) most of the worst elements of discrimination against married women.

The Netherlands

The influence of the male breadwinner ideology has been most clearly evidenced in major social insurance schemes—rather ironically, especially in those schemes that are national in character rather than the employee insurance schemes, with the exception of the compulsory health insurance (Ziekenfondswet, ZFW). The most blatant discrimination against married women was found in general disablement benefits (Algemene Arbeidsongeschiktsheidswet, AAW), the basic old-age pension (Algemene Ouderdomswet, AOW), and extended unemployment insurance benefits (Wet Werkloosheidsvoorziening, WWV). Married women originally had no individual entitlement to benefits under these programs. Equal benefits for women and men were written into the legislation and came into effect with respect to general disability insurance in 1980, the basic old-age pension in 1985, and unemployment benefits in 1987. Despite this legislation, little change has occurred in the proportion of women receiving disability benefits (Emanuel et al., 1984: 424; *Statistisch zakboek,* 1988: 355). In contrast to this harsh treatment of married women, the compulsory health insurance automatically covered family members *without an income* with no additional contributions required until recently (Roebroek & Berben, 1987:689).

The influence of the breadwinner ideology can be detected in the construction of benefits—both social assistance (Algemene Bijstandswet, ABW), including unemployment assistance benefits (Rijksgroepsregeling voor Werkloze Werknemers, RWW), and several social insurance benefits. Social assistance benefits are calculated according to personal circumstances—which more exactly refers to maintenance or family responsibilities. As distinct from Britain, the construction of benefits has been based on support of the family as the norm rather than centered on the individual with supplements for dependents, and assistance providing a social minimum has been linked to the minimum wage. Accordingly, the social minimum in the 1980s was roughly equivalent to the net minimum wage for couples and 90 percent for single-parent families, with lower rates for single persons and for young adults living at home. The benefits of several social insurance schemes are also linked to the minimum wage and have a similar construction.

The concentration on the family as the recipient unit of social benefits seems to have resulted in the lack of a family policy, apart from an elaborate system of child allowances differentiated according to the number and age of the children. The norm of the male family provider also shaped child or family allowances, which, unlike in Britain and Sweden, are in the form of social insurance transfers and not a noncontributory benefit. Family allowances are paid to the insured person, who is often the head of the household—that is, generally the father. This arrangement originally excluded unmarried mothers, who were not entitled to the allowance until 1950 (Roebroek & Berben, 1987: 690–94).[1]

In fact, one is struck by the lack of benefits attached to motherhood in the Netherlands. Although sickness insurance (Ziektewet, ZW) provides generous maternity pay (100% of one's pay up to a ceiling for 16 weeks since 1990), women do not have a statutory right to maternity leave beyond this, and there are no maternity grants or other benefits for nonworking mothers. Day care facilities are also a sorry story. Nursery schools are available for children from the age of 3, but a European Community (EC) questionnaire on availability of day care for children under 3 in the early 1980s revealed that the Netherlands had the fewest places of all the EC countries (EC, 1983: 125).

At first glance, tax reforms of the 1980s seem to indicate a reduction of the importance of the traditional male family provider as an ideal in structuring taxes. Prior to 1984, tax relief for married people was enormously skewed in favour of married men, who had a standard deduction of 12,716 guilders compared to 2529 guilders for married women; single persons had an exemption of 7381 guilders (or 9921 guilders if they were 35 years or older). The Dual Wage Earners Act of 1984 introduced a measure of individualization in that everyone received the same basic personal allowance of 7168 guilders (SCP, 1985: 54–55; OECD, 1984: 173–174). However, the act left intact a generous spouse deduction for nonworking married women (7168 guilders). Furthermore, although the husband loses this deduction if his wife works, a working wife can transfer any unused portion of her tax allowance to her husband. Also, it does seem that there is a two-earner-family penalty. Because of a supplement for one-person households, two single earners would have higher reductions than a married couple. An interesting feature of the reform is special tax relief for single parents. They receive a reduction of 5735 guilders for support of a child and an additional reduction of 4333 guilders if they work outside the home (OECD 1986: 185, 189).

The United Kingdom
The breadwinner ideology was an integral part of Beveridge's thinking (cf. Lewis, 1983: 33, 44–46, 67, 90–92), and it left an indelible mark on the national insurance

scheme in several ways. First, until 1978 the married women's option excluded women from certain benefits and enhanced their dependency on their husbands. More specifically, married women could opt out of paying full contributions and instead rely upon their husbands' contributions, and in the process they forfeited their claim to benefits in their own right. Because of the unified approach inherent in the national insurance scheme, the married women's option worked to excluded women from *all* social insurance benefits. Its utilization resulted in not only the loss of an individual pension but also other benefits, such as the sickness benefit, the injury benefit, the invalidity (disability) benefit, and the unemployment benefit. The option was widely used, and in the early 1970s three-fourths of married women had opted out of the national insurance scheme. The Social Security Pensions Act of 1978 eliminated the married woman's option, except for those women already utilizing it. However, this exemption means that the effects of the option will linger into the next century (Land, 1985: 56–57). For example, in 1982 an estimated 45 percent of married women continued to use it (MacLennan and Weitzel, 1984: 206).

Second, the breadwinner ideology also affected the rates of benefits under the national insurance scheme for married women who chose to pay full contributions until 1978 (Groves, 1983). Three rates of benefit existed, and married women were entitled to the highest rate only if they were main breadwinners; otherwise they received the middle rate despite paying full contributions. Third, in the case of married couples, only men could apply for supplementary benefit (public assistance) until November 1983. For the most part, these regulations imposed penalties upon wives working outside the home. On the other hand, a fourth feature of the national insurance scheme—adult dependent allowances—act as incentives for women to stay in the home and thus tend to reinforce the traditional division of labour in the family.

And fifth, social legislation has reinforced the notion of the wife's duty to provide care and service in the home without remuneration. Until 1986 married women were ineligible to receive the invalid care allowance, which had been introduced to compensate people for having to give up employment to care for the infirmed. The housewives' noncontributory invalidity pension (abolished in 1984) also imposed more rigorous qualifying conditions than the regular noncontributory pension. Besides being incapable of work, housewives also had to be unable to perform normal household duties.

The norm of the traditional family with the husband as the financial head of the household and keeper of his wife's income also pervaded tax legislation. Until 1990/91 joint taxation of spouses tended to be the rule. In this instance, a couple in 1985 was entitled to substantial marital status tax relief—a basic allowance of £2205 and a married man's allowance of £1250. This tax relief was largely unaffected by the wife's employment, and the working wife received a tax allowance which was equivalent to the basic allowance: £2205. Furthermore, a couple could *jointly* choose individual taxation of the wife's earnings, but the husband was taxed on the remainder of the joint income, *including any unearned income of the wife* (OECD 1986:239, 242). The main disadvantage of opting for separate taxation was a reduction in tax relief due to the loss of the married man's allowance.

The recent tax reform marked the introduction of "independent" taxation of spouses but also the celebration of marriage. All earners are entitled to the same basic allowance, but the married man's allowance was transformed into the married couple's allowance, giving preferential treatment to couples who are married compared to those who are living together. Furthermore, the allowance goes automatically to the husband, although he may transfer it to his wife. Thus the married man usually receives greater tax relief than his working wife, reaffirming the notion of the male as primary provider.

The United States

The two areas of U.S. legislation most strongly influenced by the breadwinner ideology are social security and taxation. In the Old-Age, Survivors and Disability Insurance (OASDI) program—the pillar of social security legislation—the most striking evidence of the breadwinner ideology is the spouse benefit. Working married women have not been penalized as their British counterparts were prior to the Social Security Pension Act of 1975. As early as 1950 many provisions that treated working women differently from men were removed (Aaron, 1986: 31). Currently, working wives upon retirement can choose between a spouse benefit equalling 50 percent of their husbands' benefits or a benefit based on their own earnings—but not both, that is, the spouse benefit plus a benefit based on their own earnings. However, married women have dual entitlement if their social security benefits based on their own earnings are less than their spouse benefit, and they receive a secondary benefit that makes up the difference.

Controversy over the spouse benefit concerns two issues: dissimilar treatment of women as housewives and as workers—and women's dependency on their husbands. First, the spouse benefit often works to the advantage of the traditional family with a single (male) breadwinner and to the disadvantage of the two-earner family (cf. Bergmann, 1986: 223).

In many cases when these two types of families have roughly the same earnings, the family with the single breadwinner will receive a larger pension. The one-earner family wins additionally because the spouse benefit is a noncontributory benefit. In other words, the traditional family enjoys a larger pension and pays lower social security taxes.

Secondly, women's dependency is reflected in a welfare provision based on claims via their husbands. The magnitude of the dependency is evidenced in the proportion of women whose claims are solely or partially via their husbands; in 1980, 43 percent of women receiving social security benefits made their claims solely as wives or widows while another 15 percent who had dual entitlement made their claims partially on the basis of their husbands' earnings (SSB, February 1985: 28). In other words, nearly 60 percent of women's claims to social security benefits reflected dependency on their husbands as breadwinners.

A similar pattern of favouring the traditional family, particularly to the disadvantage of working wives and single parents, shows up in income taxation in three ways. First, although married couples can choose between individual and joint taxation, the system actually encourages joint taxation of spouses. Joint returns generally receive preferential tax rates, and deductions are less beneficial to two-earner families compared to families with a sole provider and or single individuals. For example, in 1991 the deduction in the case of joint taxation was $5700 irrespective of one or two earners. However, in a two-earner family, each spouse was entitled to a deduction of $2850, whereas a single person's deduction was $3400. Second, the sole-earner family gets the same reduction in taxes as the two-earner family, which virtually amounts to deduction for a dependent spouse. Third, single-parent families do not enjoy the same deduction as a sole provider with a spouse. The single parent receives the same deduction as a single individual (OECD, 1986: 244–5, 1989:239–243). These three features of the tax system have been aptly described as (1) the two-earner marriage penalty, (2) the housewife bonus, and (3) the single-parent penalty (cf. Bergmann, 1986: 218–220). As we have seen, both the Dutch and the British tax systems are starting to recognize the financial plight of single parents and provide special tax relief for them, but this is not the case in the United States.

Finally, the United States is renowned for its lack of a family policy. As distinct from the other three countries, no system of family allowances exists, although there are tax deductions for children. Nor is there any provision of statutory maternity benefits at the national level, which has resulted in fragmented coverage through disability insurance provided either by a few states or by employers. In the early 1980s fewer than 40 percent of employed women received paid disability leave of six weeks or more after they gave birth (Gelb and Palley, 1987: 172). Apart from tax relief in connection with maintenance of children and for day care, the sole semblance of a program related to family policy is Aid to Families with Dependent Children (AFDC), with means-tested benefits targeted to the guardians of needy children.

Sweden

Evidence of the breadwinner ideology has been much less prominent in Swedish social legislation compared to the other countries. It has surfaced primarily in the forms of wife's supplements in unemployment insurance and widow's benefits in the public pension schemes. Instead, in contrast to the other three countries, and perhaps uniquely, married women were incorporated in major social insurance schemes with individual entitlement to benefits, although not necessarily equal benefits.[2] In Sweden's first national old-age insurance, adopted in 1913, all women irrespective of marital status were included as paying members of the scheme. The importance of this arrangement in the long term was to establish the principle of individual entitlement to a pension regardless of sex, marital status, or labour market status. When compulsory sickness insurance was introduced in 1955, coverage was not restricted to employees and the self-employed, as in the Netherlands and Britain. In addition, spouses at home (originally housewives but subsequently also husbands) and single parents at home with children under 16 years old were entitled to minimum cash benefits. In other words, all women were incorporated in the compulsory insurance system, and they were included as beneficiaries in their own right—and not as the raison d'être of benefit supplements for men as in Britain. Furthermore, under the same program, maternity benefits were not limited to working women but included a fairly generous flat-rate grant to all mothers. These measures can be interpreted as a modest recognition that work in the home qualified for entitlement to social benefits.

In the area of taxation of earnings, individualization has become the guiding principle. In 1970 joint taxation of spouses' earnings was abolished. Even earlier, however, the idea of tax deductions for dependents had been eroded. Already in 1946, in connection with the introduction of universal family allowances for each child, major tax exemptions for children were abolished. In the 1980s the tax system offered quite modest allowances. If both parents worked, the one with lowest income could receive a tax reduction of 2000 Swedish krona (SEK). Single parents received a tax reduction of 1800 SEK. Also, a spouse allowance amounting to 1800 SEK existed in cases where the spouse had no taxable income, i.e., earnings above 6000 SEK.

The size of the spouse deduction is paltry compared to those in the other countries, and it can scarcely be regarded as a monetary incentive or penalty. To get an idea of its modest nature, we can compare standard tax relief for married couples as a percentage of the average earnings of a production worker. In 1985 the Swedish spouse allowance amounted to 1.8 percent; for the United States the "housewife bonus" was 11 percent and standard deductions for married couples totalled 28 percent; for the UK the marital allowance was 15 percent and the total standard tax relief for a married couple was 40 percent; and in the Netherlands the sole-earners supplement equalled nearly 20 percent and total deduction was slightly under 40 percent of the average earnings of a production worker (calculated from OECD, 1986).

CONCLUSION

In conclusion, looking at the influence of the breadwinner ideology, we find significant diversity. In recent years, programs have been modified to eliminate the most pronounced inequities. Nonetheless, the strength of the breadwinner ideology varies across the four countries, and four fairly distinct patterns emerge. An interesting issue is the extent to which legislation reflecting the male breadwinner ideology has reinforced the traditional division of labour in the family, with the husband as provider and the wife as homemaker.

In the Netherlands, married women, because they lacked breadwinner status, were excluded from the right to general disability benefits, an individual pension, and extended unemployment benefits. Furthermore, working wives received only a minimal tax allowance, and in 1982 they were excluded from minimum wage legislation if they did not have breadwinner status. Overall, legislation seems to reveal a pattern of penalties combined with no rewards for married women entering the labour market, encouraging either no participation or marginal participation. In view of this legislation it is hardly surprising to find that the Netherlands has one of the lowest rates of female employment among the advanced industrial countries. In the early 1980s women's labour market participation rate was just under 40 percent in the Netherlands, compared to around 60 percent in the UK and the United States and slightly over 75 percent in Sweden. Dutch women also had the highest rate of part-time employment of the four countries (Side by Side, 1985: 12).

Married women in the labour market in Britain were not entirely stripped of their rights to a pension and other benefits as in Holland, but they were clearly denied equal rights. Furthermore, the married women's option insidiously encouraged wives to renounce their rights. Given the fact that the choice was really no rights and half obligations (i.e., contributions) versus only half rights and full obligations, it is hardly surprising that so many married women settled for the option.

Despite the removal of the married women's option and major improvements in establishing formal equal status of the sexes to entitlement, the breadwinner ideology persists, primarily in four ways. First, as documented, the married women's option tenaciously lived on through exemptions in the 1980s. Second—ironically, because of the ideal of uniform benefits provided by a single national insurance program—a system evolved that included spouse allowances covering more contingencies than in the other countries. Furthermore, the construction of the allowance in relative terms (but not absolute terms) has been fairly generous. The allowance provides 60 percent of the benefit of a man or single woman. Third, married women without sufficient contributions toward the basic pension can rely on their husbands' contributions. Fourth, the male breadwinner ideology assumes a main breadwinner who has full-time employment, and many income maintenance programs are designed to provide benefits primarily for full-time employees. The programs of the UK seem most zealous in incorporating this assumption.

In the United States the breadwinner ideology is manifested in rewarding the wife who stays at home. The spouse benefit in absolute terms is quite generous, and the survivor's benefit is even more generous, totalling 100 percent of the husband's benefit. Over half of all women's claims to social security benefits are either wholly or partially in the form of dependents' benefits. The tax system also provides a housewife bonus, although not as generous as in Britain and the Netherlands.

However, perhaps the most distinctive aspect of the U.S. case is that the spirit of the breadwinner ideology, combined with the ideal of social protection, pervades and has given rise to an entire social assistance program for dependents (mothers and children). Simultaneously with the incorporation of dependents' benefits into the pension system in the late 1930s, Aid to Dependent Children (now AFDC) was established. Universalist policies are almost entirely lacking in the United States, and a two-tier system of welfare provision has developed. In one of the tiers, entitlement is based on labour market status along with contributions, benefits are earnings-related, and claims for benefits are heavily dependent upon men's earnings. In the other tier, need determines entitlement and beneficiaries are overwhelmingly women (Sainsbury, 1993).

In Sweden the influence of the breadwinner ideology has been comparatively weaker in the area of income maintenance programs, and the height of its influence appears to have been in the 1940s. A determining factor militating against this influence has been one of the unique features of the Swedish welfare state—its universalist aspects. Entitlement is a right of citizenship, and the system relies on communitarian funding rather than individual contributions. First, providing a basic individual pension for married women made a spouse allowance superfluous. Second, family policy has been primarily child-oriented, with the child allowance (*barnbidrag*) as one of its chief instruments. It is perhaps revealing that the allowance was named "child allowance" and not "family allowance" as in the UK. Again, and importantly, the principles of universalism shaped the construction of the child allowance. As distinct from the Netherlands and the UK, as well as most other countries, the allowance from its inception in 1948 covered *all* children. Especially when first introduced, the child allowance had a major impact on family income and tended to counteract discussion of a family wage. Its introduction also eroded the principle of tax exemptions for dependents, which was not the case in Britain. Third, universalism in the form of social citizenship as the basis of entitlement also left its stamp on the compulsory sickness insurance scheme by incorporating all women—both the economically active and housewives. Interestingly, in justifying the repeal of the wife supplement attached to unemployment allowances, policy makers held up sickness insurance as a model.

In summary, we can say that the impact of the breadwinner ideology on social legislation often perpetuates women's dependency on their husbands inasmuch as their claim to social benefits is via their husbands. The resulting patterns include incentives for women staying at home and penalties for married women entering the labour market, and this does seem related to the extent of women's economic activities. In any event, in the Netherlands, where penalties were very harsh, women's labour participation rate is very low. Conversely, in Sweden, women have entered the labour market in huge numbers since the late 1960s. Thus, the pattern of incentives and penalties in social legislation constitutes a threshold to women's entry into the labour market, and when labour market status is the basis of entitlement to social benefits, the familial ideology also operates in a more indirect manner to limit women's access to social benefits. Finally, the norms of the traditional division of labour between the sexes, embedded in familial ideology, may also affect roles in the family, and in this way they influence women's claims to social benefits. In attempting to combine tasks in the home with outside work, women often take part-time employment. When social legislation excludes part-time workers or includes earnings requirements and substantial work tests, these women workers are ineligible for benefits.

Notes

1. The insurance principle has led to overlapping entitlement as women have entered the work force; that is, both parents are insured and in theory can claim two allowances for the same child. Dual claims are regulated by the care principle: the parent caring for the child (or if there is disagreement in joint households, the woman is awarded entitlement) (SZW, 1990: chap. 3: 4.7).

2. A wife's supplement to the unemployment benefit was introduced in 1941. A means-tested supplement had initially been proposed, but it was modified and accepted as a wife's supplement (Heclo 1974: 129). The supplement was abolished in 1964, on the grounds that this would harmonize social benefits and that the principle of income replacement ought to prevail, as it did in the case of

sickness benefits (SOU, 1963: 40). Moreover, as distinct from the British dependents' benefit, the Swedish wife's supplement prior to its abolishment constituted a mere 10 percent of the benefit. The national pension reform of 1946 and the general supplementary pension (ATP) reform of 1959 included widow's pensions, which are now in the process of being phased out. As distinct from the national or basic pension, the supplementary pension required a woman to be married in order to be eligible for the widow's pension. The abolishment of the widow's pension largely deviates from the policy pursued in other countries, namely, equalization by introducing widower's pensions.

References

Aaron, Benjamin. 1986. 'Fifty Years of Labor Law and Social Security: Main Developments and Prospects in the United States' in *Fifty Years of Labour Law and Social Security*. Deventer: Kluwer.

Bergmann, Barbara. 1986. *The Economic Emergence of Women*. New York: Basic Books.

Berkowitz, Monroe, et al. 1976. *Public Policy toward Disability*. New York: Praeger Publishers.

Dahlerup, Drude. 1986. 'Confusing Concepts–Confusing Reality: A Theoretical Discussion of the Patriarchal State', in Anne Sassoon (ed.), *Women and the State*. London: Hutchinson.

EC. 1984. Report on Social Developments Year 1983. Brussels: European Communities.

Emanuel, Han, et al. 'Disability Policy in the Netherlands', in Robert H. Haveman, et al. (eds.); *Public Policy toward Disabled Workers*. Ithaca: Cornell University Press.

Gelb, Joyce and Palley, Marian. 1987. *Women and Public Policies*. Princeton: Princeton University Press.

Groves, Dulcie. 1983. 'Members and Survivors: Women and Retirement-Pensions Legislation' in Jane Lewis (ed.).

Heclo, Hugh. 1974. *Modern Social Politics in Britain and Sweden*. New Haven: Yale University Press.

Hernes, Helga. 1984. 'Women and the Welfare State: The Transition from Private to Public Dependence', in Harriet Holter (ed.), *Patriarchy in a Welfare Society*. Oslo: Universitetsforlaget.

Land, Hilary. 1985. 'Who Still Cares for the Family? Recent Developments in Income Maintenance', in Clare Ungerson (ed.), *Women and Social Policy*. London: Macmillan.

Lewis, Jane (ed.). 1983. *Women's Welfare, Women's Rights*. London: Croom Helm.

MacLennan, Emma and Weitzel, Renate. 1984. 'Labour Market Policy in Four Countries: Are Women Adequately Represented?', in Gunther Schmid and Renate Weitzel (eds.), *Sex Discrimination and Equal Opportunity*. Aldershot: Gower.

OECD. 1992. *The Tax/Benefit Position of Production Workers 1988–1991*. Paris: OECD.

OECD. 1989. *The Tax/Benefit Position of Production Workers 1985–1988*. Paris: OECD.

OECD. 1986. *The Tax/Benefit Position of Production Workers 1981–1985*. Paris: OECD.

OECD. 1984. *The Tax/Benefit Position of Production Workers 1979–1983*. Paris: OECD.

Roebroek, Joop and Berben, Theo. 1987. 'Netherlands', in Peter Flora (ed.), *Growth to Limits*, Vol. 4. Berlin: Walter de Gruyter.

Ruggie, Mary. 1984. *The State and Working Women*. Princeton: Princeton University Press.

Sainsbury, Diane. 1993. 'Dual Welfare and Sex Segregation of Access to Social Benefits', *Journal of Social Policy* 22, 69–98.

Sainsbury, Diane. 1991. 'Analyzing Welfare State Variations', *Scandinavian Political Studies* 14, 1–30.

Sassoon, Anne. 1986. (ed.), *Women and the State*. London: Hutchinson.

SCP. 1985. *Women on the Move*. Rijswijk: Planning and Cultural Office.

Side by Side. A Report on Equality between Women and Men in Sweden 1985. Stockholm: Ministry of Labour.

SOU 1963:40. *Arbetslöshetsförsäkringen*. Betänkande avgivet av 1960 års arbetslöshetsförsäkringsutredning. Stockholm: Idun.

Statistisch zakboek. 1988. Voorburg: Central Bureau of Statistics.

SSB. *Social Security Bulletin*. Various years.

SZW. 1990. *Social Security in the Netherlands*. The Hague: Ministerie van Sociale Zaken en Werkgelegenheid.

The Feminization of Poverty: Not Only in America

GERTRUDE SCHAFFNER GOLDBERG
AND ELEANOR KREMEN

UNDER WHAT CONDITIONS
DOES THE FEMINIZATION OF POVERTY OCCUR?

The feminization of poverty occurs wherever there are insufficient efforts to reduce poverty either through labor market or social welfare policies and where single motherhood is sufficiently widespread. Both these conditions have been met in the United States. The rate of single motherhood has risen to nearly one-fifth of all families with children, and women are assured neither a fair market wage nor a decent social wage. In fact, nearly half of single-mother families are poor, and they comprise three-fifths of all poor families, more than meeting our definition of the feminization of poverty.

In the United States it has long been assumed that there is a direct link between poverty and family composition or single motherhood. However, Sweden has gone far toward breaking this link—a notable achievement. Single motherhood is about as prevalent in Sweden as it is in the United States. By using a combination of labor market and social policies, developed and pursued for at least four decades, Sweden has achieved a relatively low rate of poverty for single-parent families. In the only study for which there are standardized figures on poverty, American single parents were shown to be nearly six times as likely to be poor as their Swedish counterparts (Smeeding, Torrey, and Rein, 1988, p. 113). Nonetheless the Swedish poverty rate of 7.5 percent, twice the overall rate for families with children, does not indicate the absence of poverty for single-parent families.

Japan is the other country in the sample where the feminization of poverty is not in evidence. Japan presents a very different picture from Sweden, however, in that women are extremely disadvantaged in the labor market. Their labor force participation rates are relatively low and their employment careers interrupted not only for motherhood but often a second time for elder care. In a system that rewards seniority, women are at a severe disadvantage. They are rarely hired by the large firms that provide such enviable wages, fringe benefits, and job security. The wage gap between Japanese women and men is even wider than it is in North America. In order to offset these disadvantages in the labor market, the state would need to provide a very generous system of income transfers. At present Japan has a very minimal social assistance program, and its other benefits—such as health insurance and means-tested family allowances—do not lift the single mother out of poverty.

What prevents the feminization of poverty in Japan is a very low rate of single motherhood—about one-fourth the rate found in Sweden and the United States. It appears that the economic prospects of Japanese women are so bleak that relatively few of them can risk the economic independence that divorce entails. Those few women who do support themselves in Japan are probably at greater risk of poverty than in any of the other countries studied. While single motherhood does not appear to be on the increase at this time, social and economic policies in Japan are ill-prepared to cope with increases in the rate of divorce and separation that characteristically occur in most industrialized societies. It should be noted that the U.S. rate of single motherhood in 1960 was not much greater than that of Japan in the 1980s. Between 1960 and 1987, however, the U.S. rate almost tripled.

While the feminization of poverty may be a distant prospect in Japan, it is a distinct possibility in Canada. Single motherhood is still not as prevalent there as it is in the United States and Sweden, but it is 13 percent and growing. Single-mother families already comprise over 40 percent of all poor families in Canada. If divorce rates continue to rise, so, we believe, will the feminization of poverty. Canadian women have relatively high rates of unemployment, a wage gap about equal to that of American women, and little progress has been made in overcoming occupational segregation. Canada however differs from its North American neighbor in having a wider range of social welfare programs, although these benefits are not sufficient to offset the disadvantages of a single wage and a woman's wage. Canada now appears to be moving toward more restrictive social policies that could result in even less protection against the economic liabilities of single motherhood.

It has been more difficult to state with confidence whether France, Poland, and the Soviet Union are experiencing a trend toward the feminization of poverty. In all three countries there is an absence of national data on family poverty. What we do know about the combination of market and social welfare income in France leads us to be guardedly optimistic about the prevention of poverty there. Compared to Canada, Japan, and the United States, France is clearly the more generous welfare state. The range of benefits for families is comparable to Sweden, although the adequacy of these benefits is lower. Available studies suggest that the antipoverty impact of French social programs is considerable. In any case, single parenthood, though it has increased measurably in France since the 1960s, is still relatively low. Even with increasing rates of single parenthood, it is less likely that feminization of poverty will occur in France than in Japan or Canada. One area of concern, however, is persistently high unemployment rates for French women. Since French social policy assumes that single mothers earn part of their income through employment, the high unemployment rate poses a threat to the adequacy of their income.

. . .

Women's Policy and the Single-Mother Family

The findings of our crossnational study suggest some measures to reduce the poverty and inequality that single-mother families experience. Our first inclination would be to adopt a labor market approach that would enable the female breadwinner to support herself and her family. However, we cannot avoid the recognition that the single breadwinner, even if male, is a vanishing breed. We must continue to seek parity for women in the labor market through enlarging opportunities for them to enter higher paying jobs, eliminating discriminatory practices, stimulating employment through macroeconomic interventions, and assuring more equitable pay through minimum wage and comparable worth policies. In Sweden where most of these labor market policies have had a fair trial, social welfare benefits, including public assistance, must be used extensively to forestall poverty for single-parent families.[1] One important conclusion that we draw is that it is necessary to pursue a combination of work and social welfare policies to prevent the poverty of women. We want to distinguish our proposal from current welfare reform in the United States, which restricts the right to relief for mothers with young children and forces them into a labor market with limited jobs and low wages. Although we favor expansion of social welfare benefits and a minimum standard beneath which no person should fall, we believe that every effort should be made to remove inevitably stigmatized and usually inadequate social assistance from the repertoire of social welfare policy.

Social welfare benefits need not be directed solely to the single-parent family. . . . It is useful to think of four levels of provisions, only one of which is specifically for the single-parent family. These are:

1. subsidies or benefits to help all citizens pay for the costs of basic goods and services such as housing or health care;
2. benefits that protect against threats to income security arising from unemployment or underemployment;
3. benefits that reduce the costs of parenthood such as family allowances and paid parental leave; and
4. benefits specifically geared to single parenthood such as government-assured child support, special income maintenance measures, and priorities for services.

There are severe deficiencies in the adequacy and scope of U.S. social welfare programs at all four levels of provision. The absence of national health insurance, the failure to treat housing as an entitlement, restricted coverage and low replacement of earnings in unemployment insurance, and the lack of paid maternity leaves and family allowances create hardships for single-parent families. One U.S. program, the Earned Income Tax Credit (EITC), attempts to compensate both for low wages and the costs of parenthood through a tax reduction or rebate. Although benefits are low and do not reflect the number of children in a family, Congress is considering measures that would both raise benefits for all recipients and provide higher credits for families with two and three or more children. With modifications, the EITC could be a substantial aid to all employed parents, including single mothers. An advantage would be the use of the relatively neutral tax system to determine income eligibility.

Although programs that aid all individuals and families reduce the economic deprivation of single-mother families, the experience of other countries suggests that programs targeted specifically to single parents are also necessary. Government-assured child support, a program adopted by both advanced welfare states in this study, France and Sweden, provides a minimum child support payment in advance of collecting the support from the noncustodial parent. One inference drawn from the Swedish experience is that the father's contribution, even when it is obtained, is often not sufficient to provide minimally adequate child support and must be subsidized by the state.

In view of the increased incidence of single parenthood, the consequent risks to the welfare of children and the need to resort to the use of public or social assistance for single parent families, it seems prudent to reconsider the proposal for fatherless child insurance made years ago by Alvin Schorr (1966). His proposal would extend social insurance to children who are "socially orphaned"—fatherless as a result of divorce, separation, or nonmarriage of parents.

In the United States the approach to the poverty of single mothers has tended to focus on demographic factors and on the attempt to restrict the growth of single parenthood. We recognize that rising rates of single parenthood occur in nearly all industrialized societies and that efforts to combat this complex phenomenon, short of restoring women's total economic dependence on men, are likely to be futile. There is, however, a form of single parenthood that is itself born of poverty, the result of limited employment opportunities and low earnings of both women and men. Such economic deprivation strains marriages or prevents them from forming in the first place. The prevention of this form of single parenthood is within the legitimate purview of social policy.

. . .

POLITICAL RESOURCES FOR PREVENTING THE FEMINIZATION OF POVERTY

Our ultimate objective is the adoption of policies that would reduce the feminization of poverty in the United States. We therefore conclude with a discussion of the political resources that could contribute to the requisite policy changes.

The labor market, equalization, and social welfare policies that appear to prevent and reduce the feminization of poverty in other countries will not be easy to achieve. In the United States, as elsewhere, long-term trends in the labor market are creating more contingent work, less steady and secure employment, and fewer jobs with full fringe benefits for women (for most men as well). Affirmative action and antidiscrimination policies have lost the support of the federal government, and some recent Supreme Court decisions have reversed earlier rulings that furthered desegregation, both gender and racial. Pay equity strategies have had some success at the state level among public and unionized employees, although the lower courts have tended to regard comparable worth settlements as counter to free market principles. Minimum wage policies benefit the lowest paid workers and have been used to reduce the wage gap in other countries. Yet, during the 1980s, the federal government did not increase the statutory minimum wage for nine years.

Crossnational comparison, however, indicates that it is in social welfare policies that the United States is particularly deficient. Unfortunately, antipathy to the welfare state runs deep, expressing the value American society still places on individualism and economic self-reliance. Fueling and reflecting these attitudes are journalistic misrepresentations and distortions of welfare programs and their recipients. Inadequate, inequitable, and punitive, American welfare programs are unlikely to inspire support, even among prospective beneficiaries. Further, the United States still lacks programs for people of working age that could aid and draw the allegiance of the nonpoor—programs such as paid maternity leave, children's allowances, and national health insurance.

There is another reason why women of various social classes may be wary of the welfare state. It has been argued that the English poor law and its successors—particularly the very reluctant American welfare state—have been geared to "regulating the lives of women," with the state's role being primarily one of social control rather than social provision (Abramovitz, 1988; Ursel, 1986). Yet, it is possible to envision a more benign, dependable, and less controlling welfare state. Reflecting their more positive experience, Scandinavian women regard government benefits as creating an "alliance" between women and the state, a relationship that offers them more choice and more freedom than the traditional patriarchal family (Siim, 1988; Hernes, 1987).

Despite the overwhelmingly negative perception of welfare in the United States, there is historical evidence of an attempt by women to expand the welfare state. In the 1960s, poor women, with allies in civil rights, religious, labor, academic, and antipoverty organizations, mobilized to defend and redefine their rights as recipients of public assistance. Through vigorous protest and demonstration strategies, they pressed local authorities to reduce restrictive requirements and to expand benefits. Ultimately the proponents of welfare rights, many of them black as well as poor, lobbied for a guaranteed national income (West, 1981; Piven and Cloward, 1977; Steiner, 1971). Although a few welfare rights groups continue to function, the welfare rights movement lasted less than a decade. In the 1980s, when the federal government was conducting a virtual "war on welfare," recipients, lacking some of their former resources and allies, were in no position to mount an effective resistance.

The second wave of the movement for women's equality that began in the 1960s has accomplished significant changes in public policy, fostered political participation of women, and deepened women's understanding of their role in society. However, the American women's movement, in contrast to its Canadian counterpart, has, on the whole, distanced itself from the struggle to defend and expand the welfare state. This may be related to the fact that American feminism, though it has tried to unite women on the basis of common gender oppression, has not yet been able to transcend the divisions of class and race (Degler, 1980).[2] Yet, it is apparent from our crossnational study that women, particularly those who support themselves, need the welfare state both to escape poverty and to achieve greater equality. Even in Sweden, with its full employment and solidarity wage policies, one-third of single-parent families would be poor without government transfers (Smeeding, Torrey, and Rein, 1988, p. 113).

Since the 1960s increasing numbers of American women of all strata have faced the risk of single parenthood, which, in turn, has exposed them to the full force of their inequities in the labor market. Although social insurance has taken firm, it belated, root on American soil, growing incrementally and adding risk upon risk, it has not addressed the new economic vicissitudes that confront women. Widespread recognition of their common economic vulnerability and of the consequent need for a decent social as well as economic wage could be the basis for a new mobilization of American women. Perhaps the organization of women on the basis of the risk of single parenthood that so many will face at some time during their adult lives could contribute to such a mobilization.

To change the position of the federal government in the United States, particularly one that has become more adversary than advocate of disadvantaged constituencies, women would need to mobilize themselves and join with potential allies who are already advocating for workplace, labor market, social welfare, and equalization policies. There is no dearth of such allies, but there are obstacles to coalescing with each of them. Although inequities overlap, there is potential for conflict of interest among those who press for the reduction of gender, class, or racial inequities.

However weakened and unresponsive, even resistant, to the needs of women in the past, organized labor is a potential ally of women in the workplace. There is indeed evidence of successful drives by labor to organize women workers and of union support for issues such as pay equity. A number of trade unions, in fact, are represented on the board of the National Committee on Pay Equity. An increasing number of women in trade unions, moreover, can be a force for exerting pressure from within. In addition to the labor movement itself, there are independent organizations of and for working women such as Wider Opportunities for Women and 9 to 5: National Organization of Working Women (Gelb, 1990, p. 281). These organizations can be allies in supporting a broad range of labor market and equalization policies.

Although we favor expansion and improvement of the welfare state, the task in the 1980s was largely to prevent its dismantling, particularly to save programs that reach the very poor. A diverse group of human needs advocates has struggled to preserve the social safety net and to build some foundation for future expansion. These organizations include the Children's Defense Fund, the Center on Budget and Policy Priorities, the Coalition on Human Needs, the National Association of Social Workers, and other lobbies, task forces, or coalitions concerned with such critical problems as hunger and homelessness. As women recognize the extent to which their interests are linked to government programs or the welfare state, these human needs advocates will be their potential allies.

Another potential ally for women is the civil rights movement whose gains have certainly benefited women as well as people of color. Sometimes forced to compete for scarce resources, these two constituencies have had an uneasy relationship. Some political leaders are achieving moderate success in creating coalitions that encompass civil rights and women's organizations.[3] Separate organizations may well permit women of color to define and give voice to their "double disadvantage."

A potential and largely untapped ally is the elderly, predominantly women, who may have organized effectively to protect and expand social security. Many older women have direct experience with labor market inequities and social welfare inadequacies. A recent study by the Older Women's League (OWL) found that despite the mass entry of women into the labor market, many younger women may be not better protected by social security than their mothers (Loeb, 1990). This warning by an organization of older women identifies a welfare-state issue that could be pursued by both younger and older women. To an even greater degree than younger women, the elderly face the risk of being single. A movement based on this common risk could unite and mobilize women of all ages.

Obviously the electoral process is a means to advancing economic justice for women. Nowhere are women fully integrated into the central decision-making apparatus of their governments so that labor market, social welfare policies, and certainly major economic and strategic decisions are made without them. In the United States, the underrepresentation of women in the national legislature is especially egregious, although there has been more progress at the state and local levels of government. One of the organizations that seeks to achieve an equal voice and role for women in government is the National Women's Political Caucus whose stated purpose is to oppose "racism, sexism, institutional violence, and poverty through the election and appointment of women to public office" (Mueller, 1990, p. 97, citing Feit, 1979).[4] Voter registration drives geared to extending the franchise to poor people, including the many women who are public welfare clients, are an attempt to change the composition of the American electorate and to elect government officials who are more responsive to the needs of disadvantaged groups (Piven and Cloward, 1988).

The unexpected and profound political and economic changes that have reduced the tensions between the United States and the Soviet Union offer an opportunity to utilize some of the vast resources formerly appropriated for armaments to address the enormous social deficits that have developed. As we write, a "peace dividend" network comprised of a very wide range of interest groups is forming. Whether women disadvantaged by social class, race, or family composition do collect a much-deserved peace dividend depends in large measure upon the extent to which women recognize both the economic and social risks they face and take action to achieve a just economic and social wage, in their own right.

Notes

1. About 40 percent of single-mother families in Sweden received social assistance in 1985, and the average length of time during which they received this help was four and a half months (Nordic Council of Ministers, 1988, p. 97).
2. Referring to the "first wave" of American feminism, historian William L. O'Neill writes that organized women "shared the dominant values of their class and failed to see that, unlike bourgeois men, they stood to benefit directly from the welfare state" (1971, p. 166).
3. Jesse Jackson, former presidential candidate, formed the Rainbow Coalition during his election campaign, an attempt to include all economically depressed groups across racial and ethnic lines. He has also been a speaker at rallies for abortion rights.

4. Former Representative Bella Abzug, one of the founders of the National Women's Political Caucus (NWPC), was not interested in "getting just any woman elected." The main goal, she felt, should be "to build a political movement of women for social change that would simultaneously help elect more women, minorities, and other underrepresented groups and build an electoral bloc strong enough to influence male politicians to support our programs" (1984, p. 21). In this regard she claims to have differed from Betty Friedan, another founder of NWPC and author of *The Feminine Mystique*, who was primarily interested in electing women to political office "with fairly minimal guidelines" (1984, p. 21).

References

Abramovitz, M. (1988). *Regulating the Lives of Women: Social Welfare Policy from Colonial Times to the Present.* Boston: South End Press.

Abzug, B., with M. Kelber (1984). *Gender Gap: Bella Abzug's Guide to Political Power for American Women.* Boston: Houghton Mifflin.

Degler, C. N. (1980). *At Odds: Women and the Family in America from the Revolution to the Present.* New York: Oxford University Press.

Feit, R. F. (1979). "Organizing for political power: The National Women's Political Caucus." In B. Cummings and V. Schuck, eds. *Women Organizing.* Metuchen, NJ: Scarecrow Press.

Gelb, J. (1990). "Social movement 'success': A comparative analysis of feminism in the United States and the United Kingdom." In M. F. Katzenstein and C. M. Mueller, eds. *The Women's Movements of the United States and Western Europe.* Philadelphia: Temple University Press.

Hernes, H. (1987). *Welfare State and Woman Power.* Oslo: Norwegian University Press.

Lewis, D. K. (1983). "A response to inequality: Black women, racism, and sexism." In E. Abel and E. K. Abel, eds. *The Signs Reader: Women, Gender, and Scholarship.* Chicago: University of Chicago Press.

Loeb, L. (1990). *Heading for Hardship: Retirement Income for American Women in the Next Century.* Washington, DC: Older Women's League.

Milwaukee County Welfare Rights Organization (1972). *Welfare Mothers Speak Out: We Ain't Gonna Shuffle Anymore.* New York: W. W. Norton & Company, Inc.

Mueller, C. M. (1990). "Collective consciousness, identity transformation, and the rise of women in public office in the United States." In M. F. Katzenstein and C. M. Mueller, eds. *The Women's Movements of the United States and Western Europe.* Philadelphia: Temple University Press.

Nordic Council of Ministers (1988). *Kvinnor och Man i Norden: Fakta om Jamstalldheten 1988 (Women and Men in the Nordic Countries: Facts on Equal Opportunities 1988).* Copenhagen: Nordic Council of Ministers.

O'Neill, W. L. (1971). *Everyone Was Brave: A History of Feminism in America.* New York: Quadrangle/The New York Times Book Co.

Organisation for Economic Co-operation and Development (OECD). (September 1988). *Employment Outlook.* Paris: OECD.

Piven, F. F., and R. A. Cloward (1977). *Poor People's Movements: Why They Succeed, How They Fail.* New York: Pantheon Books.

———— (1988). "New prospects for voter registration reform." *Social Policy* 18 (3): 2–15.

Protzman, F. (November 20, 1989). "The Germanys as an economic giant." *New York Times,* pp. 1, 14.

Schorr, A. L. (1966). *Poor Kids.* New York: Basic Books, Inc.

Scott, H. (1984). *Working Your Way to the Bottom: The Feminization of Poverty.* London: Pandora Press.

Sidel, R. (1986). *Women and Children Last. The Plight of Poor Women in Affluent America.* New York: Viking.

Sieber, S. D. (1974). "Toward a theory of role accumulation." *American Sociological Review* 39 (August): 567–578.

Siim, B. (September 1988). *Reproductive Politics, Gender Politics, and the Political Mobilization of Women.* Paper presented at the Conference on Public Policies and Gender Policies, Social Science Research Council and Wagner Institute, City University of New York.

Smeeding, T., B. B. Torrey, and M. Rein (1988). "Patterns of income and poverty: The economic status of children and the elderly in eight countries." In J. L. Palmer, T. Smeeding, and B. B. Torrey, eds. *The Vulnerable.* Washington, DC: The Urban Institute Press.

Sorrentino, C. (1990). "The changing family in international perspective." *Monthly Labor Review* 103 (3): 41–58.

Steiner, G. Y. (1971). *The State of Welfare.* Washington, DC: The Brookings Institution.

Sundström, M. (August/September 1989). *Part-time Work: Trends and Equality Effects in Sweden and EEC.* Paper presented at the 9th World Congress of the International Economics Association, Athens.

UNICEF (United Nations Children's Fund) (1989). *The State of the World's Children.* New York: Oxford University Press.

Ursel, J. (1986). "The state and the maintenance of patriarchy. A case study of family, labour, and welfare legislation in Canada." In B. Russell and J. Dickinson, eds. *Family, Economy, and State: The Social Reproductive Process under Capitalism.* New York: St. Martin's Press.

West, G. (1981). *The National Welfare Rights Movement: The Social Protest of Poor Women.* New York: Praeger.

Wilson, W. J. (1987). *The Truly Disadvantaged: The Inner City, the Underclass, and Public Policy.* Chicago: University of Chicago Press.

World Bank (1988). *World Development Report 1988.* New York: Oxford University Press.

The New Politics of Abortion

JONI LOVENDUSKI AND JOYCE OUTSHOORN

Most Western democracies liberalized their abortion politics during the 1960s and 1970s. The process involved and the political circumstances in which new policies emerged were often very similar, although the content of the new laws varied considerably. In general the political systems did not welcome the abortion issue. Those which were organized around socio-economic cleavages were ill suited to cope with abortion politics. Neither did those countries whose major institutions expressed cultural cleavages fare well.

From the mid-1960s onwards liberal, medical, social welfare and feminist pressures impacted upon religious, natalist and traditionalist concerns to produce abortion law reform movements prepared to use a range of strategies in order to achieve their objectives. These movements began from different starting points. In Europe and in the United States restrictive laws had been passed during the nineteenth or the early twentieth centuries. Some of these laws had been moderated by the mid-1950s. In Scandinavia, for example, a limited availability of abortion was acceptable to popular feelings as a result of a long process of legitimation. There, further reform met with relatively little resistance. Elsewhere attempts to liberalize abortion laws generated widespread public debates and complex political conflicts, as in Great Britain, the Netherlands, France, Italy, and the USA. In Ireland the issue led to a constitutional amendment prohibiting abortion law reform. In Belgium the political system avoided action, neither altering existing statutes nor enacting new laws on the issue.

In West European politics abortion is unusual in that it cuts across the dominant socio-economic or Left–Right dimension of party politics. Parties in such systems rarely developed a specific stance on abortion before it arose as a political issue. Discomfited, they find the abortion issue difficult to link to their main corpus of doctrine. Confessional parties too have their problems with the matter. Doctrinal indicators notwithstanding, political expediency has led religious parties to the prioritization of economic matters. The constraints of coalition building, as well as purely electoral considerations, dispose them to downplay their stands on abortion. Only when religious parties are essential to the formation of government are they in a position to follow their doctrinal inclinations on abortion policy.

The cross-cutting nature of the abortion controversy may have consequences not only for the way in which the issue is perceived but also for the political system itself. In multi-party systems conflict over abortion policy has led to additional conflicts in coalition formation. This has been the case in Belgium, the Netherlands, Italy and Norway. In general, politicians have been reluctant to press the issue. The exceptions are the leaders of both the major Irish confessional parties (who compete for Catholic support) and the leaders of the small parties of the European religious right.

Three major strategies have characterized political responses: abstinence, postponement, and de-politicization. Abstinence occurs where governments, parties and leaders refrain from taking a stand. Postponement is less straightforward. Ostensibly simply a delaying tactic, it may also result from a perception that reform groups will be unable to sustain mobilization. De-politicization may take a number of forms. Most commonly, abortion is redefined as a technical issue enabling politicians to pass responsibility to experts. Few governments have been able to sustain strategies of abstinence or postponement for long. De-politicization offers greater flexibility but depends both on the complicity of the designated experts and on the government's capacity to maintain its definition of the issue. However, as medical practitioners and courts have indicated their preference for clear guidelines from the state, de-politicization strategies have become less feasible.

But the major challenge has been over the way in which the issue is defined. The criminalization of abortion during the nineteenth century had made it a penal matter. Church interest added a moral dimension. In some countries it became a medical matter and in most it developed into a polarized political and philosophical issue, a matter of competing notions of rights. More than many other issues, abortion has been subject to continuous redefinition.

Redefinition first occurred in the early 1960s when both medical practitioners and liberal reformers sought a restricted legalization in many countries. At this stage it was considered that demand for the termination of pregnancies would be limited to a few special cases. Essentially, leave was sought to perform abortions in the event of particular pathologies: psychiatric, medical and, more rarely, social indicators were to be used. The aim here was to prevent 'deserving cases' from having to seek backstreet abortions. It was widely agreed that this was best achieved by providing legal, medical terminations. These arguments were accepted and reform was achieved early in Scandinavia, Great Britain and some US states.

The first reforms left the matter very much in the hands of the experts, a pattern which prevailed until feminism re-emerged as a political force in the late 1960s and 1970s. Precipitating incidents such as the Bobigny trial in France, the White amendment in Britain and Dolle Mina demonstrations in the Netherlands focused feminist attention on the issue. The result was in many cases, a further redefinition. The right of women to decide whether to have an abortion became an issue. Seen from such a perspective abortion restrictions were instruments of social control and experts were the agents of that control. It was redefinition of this kind which finally undermined government de-politicization strategies.

Meanwhile, those who opposed the extension of abortion rights stressed what they regarded as the moral dimensions of the issue, eventually redefining abortion in terms of the rights of the unborn. In this they have had considerable support from the churches, particularly the Roman Catholic church. Church activity was most apparent where the religious dimension was organized into politics. In such cases a traditional social institution came to be opposed by a social movement espousing modern values.

The redefinitions of the issue offered by both the women's movement and the groups opposing legalization had the effect of making abortion a matter on which the public felt competent to judge. This widened discussion, considerably enlarging both the scope and terrain of conflict. Once this point was arrived at, mass mobilization became possible. A whole range of groups became active on the issue and many new groups emerged. In several countries (the Netherlands, Italy, Norway) social movement organizations prevailed, while in Britain and to a lesser extent West Germany, traditional interest group politics predominated.

In all countries except Sweden debate over abortion policy was virulent, divisive and protracted. As the dispute gained momentum governments were forced to deal with it. But in most cases when the matter came before the legislature a 'free vote' was allowed, even where, as in France and West Germany, the legislation was government-sponsored. Only in the Netherlands and Norway were parliamentarians expected to toe a liberalizing party line and there only because of special circumstances. In the United States, Congress was not involved in the resolution of the issue which was decided in the courts. A national referendum forced the issue on the Italian Chamber of Deputies, while in Britain and Belgium private members' bills brought the matter before the legislature.

Religious variables had a considerable effect upon the mode of resolution. In predominantly Roman Catholic countries the issue was resolved, if at all, in a formal and legalistic manner with practice often bearing little resemblance to statute. In Protestant countries more of a coincidence between law and policy could be observed.

In all of the countries considered in this volume the effects of abortion legislation have in many respects been marginal. The most important variable in the availability of abortion to a particular population of women is not the law, but the independent existence of a network of good medical facilities organized either by the state or the private sector. Sweden and the United States supply a useful contrast on this point. Both countries have liberal policies. In Sweden the scrupulous provision of adequate facilities makes access to abortion a reality for women. In the United States, on the other hand, access to abortion is often severely restricted. There free access to abortion is merely an abstract principle for many women. Such examples show that implementation is as important an issue as legalization. In many countries abortion policy is of the 'posturing' variety, often subject to the vagaries of the political climate.

The various pressures which surround abortion policy are ongoing ones and in none of the countries discussed below may the issue be said to be resolved. Groups on both sides remain vigilant and developments in medical technology may lead yet again to redefinition. And redefinition, as we have seen, has been the main strategy for placing abortion on the political agenda. Its capacity for being redefined may therefore be sufficient to ensure that the abortion issue continues to challenge established political arrangements.

Abortion Rights in Russia, the United States, and France

DOROTHY MCBRIDE STETSON

The purpose of this paper is to compare the process of reproductive rights in Russia, the United States, and France by pointing out similarities and differences in three aspects of abortion policy: (1) the circumstances of legalization; (2) the official definition of abortion laws in relation to women's rights; and (3) the participation of women's rights advocates in the debate over abortion policy. Then, the conclusion will compare the reproductive rights of women.[*]

---

[*]This brief comparison requires the use of generalizations to characterize aspects of abortion politics. Readers are urged to consult works in the bibliography to learn more about details and nuances of reproductive issues in each country.

CIRCUMSTANCES OF LEGALIZATION

In legalizing abortion, policymakers in all countries responded to a common problem: the failure of criminalized abortion laws to work. The Soviet government had prohibited abortions in 1936, except for a few restrictive medical conditions. In 1955, the Presidium of the Supreme Soviet repealed the 1936 law, stating simply that the rise in illegal abortions was so great that it endangered women's health and fertility. The U.S. laws prohibiting abortions except to protect the life or health of the mother dated back to the nineteenth century. In 1973, when the Supreme Court declared these laws unconstitutional in *Roe v. Wade,* participants in the policy debate agreed that the old laws were inadequate, although the parties disagreed on their vision for a new law. In France, legislators had greatly hoped that strict enforcement of criminal abortion laws of 1920 and 1923 would reverse the decline in the birth rate. By 1975, when the National Assembly legalized abortion in the first 10 weeks of pregnancy, even the pronatalists recognized the inability of the courts to enforce the laws and their ineffectiveness in increasing the birth rate.

Feminists and physicians were active in the debates preceding legalization in both France and the United States. Second-wave feminist movements considered a woman's right to make choices about pregnancy and childbirth as fundamental to both liberation and equality. In France, especially, feminists seemed to be effective in changing the terms of the public debate about the issue (Jenson, 1987). At the same time, French medical groups gained doctors the right to refuse to perform abortions on moral grounds. The medical profession also took a prominent role in the U.S. debates. However, the American Medical Association sought only to expand the list of medical conditions to include rape, incest, and fetal deformity. U.S. feminists successfully countered that conditional laws would not satisfy women's needs for abortion.

Although there were no women's advocacy organizations in Soviet Russia when abortion was legalized, the Soviet Medical Encyclopedia ("Abort," 1956) reports that women initially proposed legalization after World War II. Despite the closed nature of Soviet decision making in the 1950s, policymakers were aware of women's interest in the issue. The medical profession was probably the most influential group, however, in gaining the repeal of the 1936 laws. They had long debated the issue, voicing their concern about the health consequences of illegal abortions.

OFFICIAL DEFINITIONS OF ABORTION

Since legalization, policymakers in France, Russia, and the United States have defined abortion as a woman's right, at least in part. They vary in their commitment to this right and in the priority they give it with respect to other motives for legal abortion. Russian lawmakers initially paid attention to the importance of abortion to women's lives by including the following statement in the 1955 law: "In order to give women the opportunity to decide for themselves the question of mother-hood. . . " (translated in Savage, 1988: p. 1053, n. 135). But authorities were more concerned, then and now, with the importance of abortion to women's roles as mothers. The state's major objective is to discourage abortions through programs of maternal-infant protection. Officially, public health bureaucrats recognize that prevention of abortion will require adequate contraceptive services, but they have not succeeded in convincing top policymakers of the need to provide adequate information and services on effective contraceptive techniques.

In the United States, the Supreme Court is the institution that has articulated the basic legal framework for abortion law; its opinions set forth detailed reasoning underlying the official definitions of the issue. On the basis of these opinions, the U.S. authorities initially recognized the rights of women to make decisions about abortions, but as only one of several interests that must be balanced. In *Roe v. Wade,* women's choice was placed in a zone of privacy that included physicians; in fact, abortion was defined primarily as a medical matter and physicians' rights had priority. Since the *Roe* case, however, the Court has retreated from the medical definition of abortion; justices have refused to require public health programs to pay for most abortions. In the 1992 decision in *Planned Parenthood v. Casey,* abortion was presented as first and foremost a woman's right; doctors were not even mentioned. Still, physicians and hospitals can refuse to perform abortions, and local and regional jurisdictions may act to impede ready access to abortion by placing administrative hurdles, such as 24-hour waiting periods, in the path of women seeking services.

The French cabinet presented the abortion reform bill in France in the 1970s and, in the parliamentary debate, affirmed that abortion was essential to woman's rights. The law states that a woman who is in "distress" from pregnancy is permitted to obtain an abortion, and it is the woman, not the doctor, who determines whether such distress exists. Doctors, on the other hand, were given the right to refuse to perform abortions if the procedure went against their moral beliefs. Since 1979, when the parliament reaffirmed legal abortion, the government has acted to help women exercise their rights to abortion. The Ministry of Woman's Rights, a new cabinet-level agency established by Socialist President François Mitterrand in 1981, persuaded the government to reimburse women for abortion services under the national health insurance scheme. The ministry also worked to increase the number of hospitals that would perform abortions. In 1990, the Minister of Health ordered that the abortion pill RU-486, which provides an alternative to surgical abortion and is banned in the United States, be made available because it "belonged" to the women of France (Beaulieu, 1990).

Initially, policymakers in all three countries recognized the importance of abortion to the status and rights of women. However, as abortion policy has evolved, the place of those rights in the overall definition of the issue and the government's commitment to achieving it have varied. French leaders have done the most to further the effective use of legalized abortion for women as part of an overall policy of reproductive rights. The Russian and American governments tend to leave women to fend for themselves in finding and using abortion services.

PARTICIPATION OF WOMEN
IN ABORTION POLICY DEBATES

Women's rights advocates have taken a major place in the debate on abortion policy in France and the United States. They have not been active in Russia. Most of
the Russian debates over abortion take place in the medical and public health
journals. There, physicians have often recognized the importance of the effect of
unwanted pregnancies on women's educational, work, and family lives. After
1985, official and unofficial women's organizations formed and entered the public
policy process; they did not, however, bring up abortion or reproductive rights issues. Despite the continued lack of contraceptive services, deteriorating health
conditions, and painful surgical procedures, on the few occasions when women
write about abortion, they are likely to emphasize the dangers of abortion to fertility rather than criticize the public health system for failing to provide contracep-
tives and improved procedures. Women's most effective means of influencing
abortion policy debates in Russia remains their continuing demand for the procedure regardless of the pronatalist preferences of elites, the indifference of the
economic planners, or the self-interest of gynecologists.

In both France and the United States, where the right to abortion on demand
was a major demand of the second-wave feminist movements, women's rights advocates have been major participants in abortion policy debates. In France, feminists were united on the issue and acted effectively in the early 1970s to bring
abortion to public attention and to point out the ineffectiveness and injustice of
the criminal law (Stetson, 1987). Later, feminists of the Socialist Party in power at
the Ministry of Woman's Rights (1981–1986) encouraged mass action through
street demonstration to break a deadlock within the government over reimburse-
ment of abortion services. Abortion was one of few issues that brought together
the diverse "tendencies" of the women's rights movement in France. Since the
early 1980s, politicians have occasionally tested public opinion for the salience of
an anti-abortion stand among voters but have found few electoral benefits. Current abortion policy and practice is congruent with the contemporary political culture. Without a major challenge to their rights, advocates for French women's
rights have moved to other issues.

In the early days of the U.S. women's liberation movement, the demand for
abortion was articulated as the right to control one's body. By challenging the
medical definitions of abortion, these feminists were successful in changing the
terms of debate: instead of asking whether to expand the list of medical conditions
to include fetal deformity, incest, and rape, they asked whether a woman had a
right to terminate an unwanted pregnancy for whatever reason she chose.

U.S. feminist leaders, confronted with a strong anti–abortion rights campaign,
may look to France with some envy. Since the 1970s, American anti–abortion
rights groups have succeeded in winning support from one of the two major political parties and have installed sympathetic policymakers in the national administrations of Presidents Ronald Reagan and George Bush. So far the pro-choice organizations have prevented the rollback of legal abortion. But under the pressure
of a fractious debate between pro– and anti–abortion rights groups, the govern-

ment has retreated far from providing resources to help women gain access to abortion services.

CONCLUSION

Russian women confront no legal impediments to obtaining abortions. But the cost of these services may be high, due to the monopoly of the centralized public health bureaucracy over the procedure and the indifference of political elites to the health concerns of women. Doctors, as employees of this centralized bureaucracy, cannot technically deny a woman an abortion, but they are fully empowered to talk her out of it or to perform one without anesthesia. With privatization, doctors may organize clinics to perform safer and less painful "mini-abortions" and may charge rates above what many women can afford. Further, women in Russia have few family planning alternatives to abortion.

U.S. women may, depending on the state they are in, face administrative hurdles, but legally, these may not be an "undue burden" on their access to abortion services. Still, they may find it difficult to locate a doctor who will perform the procedure. The government offers almost no assistance to women to pay for abortions and authorizes doctors and hospitals to refuse requests for other than a limited set of medical conditions. The U.S. obstetrics and gynecological profession considers abortions to be a rather shady aspect of their work. Abortions are rarely performed in hospitals and are usually assigned to private abortion clinics, mostly in urban areas. The result is a severe shortage of services available for women who seek to exercise their right to choose to terminate their pregnancies.

French women, too, face some legal hurdles in seeking abortion services. They must receive counseling and satisfy a waiting period. Access to RU-486 is closely monitored by the government. However, the government has acted to empower women to secure safe abortion, expand services, and, at the same time, to secure contraceptive techniques to avoid unwanted pregnancies.

Once abortion is formally legalized, what aspects of the policy process are associated with reproductive rights? The foundation of abortion policy is the relationship between the official definition of the issue, the level of government activism, and the attention of women's rights activists. In this brief comparative study three different patterns are represented:

1. The Russian pattern finds the government defining legalized abortion as necessary primarily to prevent the bad effects of widespread illegal abortion. Only secondarily does the government recognize the importance of women's choice. Central government authorities show little interest in the abortion issue and give the public health bureaucracy and doctors employed by it full control over provision of services; there is little attention to the broad range of family planning services and contraception. Voices of women's rights activists are not present in the public debate on abortion. The effect of the Russian pattern is that abortion services are available to women, but there is little effective reproductive choice.

2. The U.S. pattern finds the government defining legal abortion as a woman's right, using the concept of right to mean privacy from government interference. There is a low level of government activism to help women obtain abortion services. Some parts of the public administration system have responded to the strong anti–abortion rights groups to limit assistance. Women's rights activists are central in the abortion debate, but they must concentrate on fending off efforts to criminalize abortion once again. The U.S. pattern means that women's reproductive rights depend on their own educational, social, and financial resources and on the willingness of physicians to provide services to them.

3. The abortion policy in France combines the official definition of abortion as an important right of women with government action to expand services for both abortion and contraception. The abortion debate has receded from public attention, and feminists, who were at one time major participants on behalf of legalization and public assistance, have been able to move to other issues. The French pattern is most successful in securing reproductive rights for women, exercised with government advocacy and regulation.

References

"Abort." 1956. *I bol'shaya meditsinskaya entsiklopediia* (Great medical encyclopedia), vol. 1, col. 22–47.

Beaulieu, Etienne Emile, with Mort Rosenblum. 1990. *The "Abortion Pill."* New York: Simon & Schuster.

Ershova, E. N., and Novikova, E. E. 1988. *SSSR-SShA: Zhenschina i obshchestvo; Opyt sravnitel'novo analiza* (USSR-USA: Woman and society; A comparative analysis). Moscow: Profizdat.

Imber, Jonathan B. 1990. "Abortion Policy and Medical Practice." *Society* 27 (July-August): 27–34.

Jenson, Jane. 1987. "Changing Discourse, Changing Agendas: Political Rights and Reproductive Policies in France." In Mary F. Katzenstein and Carol M. Mueller, *The Women's Movements of the United States and Western Europe*, pp. 64–88. Philadelphia: Temple University Press.

Ladrière, Paul (ed.). 1982. "La libéralisation de l'avortement." *Revue Française de Sociologie* 23(3):351–548.

Lovenduski, Joni, and Joyce Outshoorn (eds.). 1986. *The New Politics of Abortion.* London: Sage.

Luker, Kristin. 1984. *Abortion and the Politics of Motherhood.* Berkeley: University of California Press.

Mouvement français pour le planning familial. 1982. *D'une revolte a une lutte; 25 ans d'histoire du planning familiale.* Paris: Editions Tierce.

Planned Parenthood of Southeastern Pennsylvania v. Casey. 1992. 91–744.

Roe v. Wade. 410 U.S. 113, 1973.

Sachev, Paul (ed.). 1988. *International Handbook on Abortion.* New York: Greenwood.

Savage, Mark. 1988. "The Law of Abortion in the Union of Soviet Socialist Republics and the People's Republic of China: Women's Rights in Two Socialist Countries." *Stanford Law Review* 40 (April): 1027–1065.

Stetson, Dorothy McBride. 1987. *Women's Rights in France.* Westport, CT: Greenwood Press.

United Nations. 1992. "Abortion Policies: A Global Review." *Population Newsletter* 53 (June): 1–8.

Unfinished Business in Rape Law Reform

CAROLE GOLDBERG-AMBROSE

Substantial and widespread changes in federal and state rape laws, designed to advance the concerns of feminists and law enforcement interests, have gone into effect over the past 15 years. Some researchers who have tried to assess the effects of these reforms believe the changes have thwarted feminist goals; others have found little impact on case processing or victims' experiences; still others have pronounced the reform efforts a success. There are many obstacles to measuring and achieving rape reform, the most notable being the need to eliminate juror misconceptions about rape and its victims. Contemporary research and law reform should focus on the trial process, especially on how rules of evidence and methods of constructing a rape case relate to social perceptions about gender, coercion, and sexuality.

As their interests converged in the mid-1970s, feminists and law-and-order forces secured passage of countless state and federal laws broadening the definition of rape and altering the procedures followed in rape trials (for surveys of these laws, see Berger, Searles, & Neuman, 1988; Galvin, 1986; Searles & Berger, 1987). Accompanying these changes was a vast body of feminist literature criticizing traditional rape law for fostering inappropriate conceptions of women and men, for denying legal protection to female victims who failed to adhere to conventional standards of propriety, for disregarding women's experience of sexual violation, and for inflicting emotional distress on rape victims who report and prosecute rape charges (Berger, 1977; Brownmiller, 1975; Clark & Lewis, 1977). Although they sometimes disagreed about the mechanisms at work, these feminist authors all viewed traditional rape law as contributing significantly to a system of male dominance.

. . .

RESEARCH FINDINGS ON RAPE LAW REFORM

Interestingly, the judgments of those researchers prepared to render a verdict run the full gamut. At one extreme are some feminists, such as Bumiller (1987), who view the law as having produced changes, but for the worse. According to Bumiller, these laws (particularly those redefining the crime) did not go far enough in making women's experience of sexual violation the touchstone for rape; consequently, they have delegitimized women's experience, and provided legitimacy for males' claims to sexual access and overall dominance.

Closer to the center of the spectrum are writers who doubt whether the law has had any impact at all, either on attitudes, street crime, or the operation of the criminal justice system. Some of these authors question whether the laws have been implemented as legislators intended them to be. For them, the lack of impact can be chalked up to the lack of real reform outside the law books. Like Adler (1987), who studied English rape trials, they may focus on restrictive judicial interpretations of laws designed to broaden the definition of the crime or to restrict introduction of evidence concerning the victim's sexual history. Studies from Canada, Australia, and the United States have depicted how subjective interpretations of events by a mostly male judiciary override concern with the victim's treatment (Horney & Spohn, 1991; LaFree, 1989; Osborne, 1985; Soshnick, 1987; Tempkin, 1987). Other authors emphasize police and prosecutorial unwillingness to pursue complaints that are clearly within the scope of the law. Chappell (1984), for example, found that one major prosecutor's office did not change its conservative case-filing practices following rape law reform, and Loh's (1980) study of Washington State confirmed those data and also found a slight *decrease* in prison sentences during the period studied.

In five of the six jurisdictions studied by Horney and Spohn (1991) (Chicago, Houston, Washington, DC, Philadelphia, and Atlanta), rape reform did not produce an increase in victim reports and did not affect case processing. In the sixth city (Detroit), reform had only limited effects, and rates of conviction and incarceration remained unchanged. The authors' interviews with criminal justice personnel suggested to them that the explanation for inertia lay in the laws' failure to address broad realms of prosecutorial and judicial discretion. For example, they discovered that the elimination of corroboration and resistance requirements had had little effect on the likelihood of prosecution and conviction, and they hypothesized that the reason for this lack of change was the failure of prosecutors to invoke their discretion to file charges where corroboration or resistance were absent, or to ask for jury instructions explaining the lack of need for corroboration or evidence of resistance.

Another group skeptical about the legal impact of rape reform doubts whether the laws attempted as much as people thought. They express concern that the reform laws became so diluted in going through the legislative process— because of ideological differences between feminists and their law enforcement coalition partners—that the legal changes never truly represented major feminist reform (e.g., Berger et al., 1988). Such a position necessarily assumes that there is widespread agreement among feminists about whether particular rape law reforms advance feminist goals. However, the debates among feminists about whether to abandon the term "rape" in favor of "sexual assault" call that assumption into question.

In contrast with observers who doubt the ambitiousness of law reform are those who contend that reform made little difference because reform-oriented changes had been occurring through court decisions long before formal reform was instituted by statute. For example, judges and lawyers from six states surveyed by Horney and Spohn (1991) could recall few, if any, cases before the advent of rape shield reforms in which attorneys sought to harass victims by introducing evidence of their sexual history. They also claimed that pre-reform case rulings had accomplished much of what rape shield laws and laws eliminating corroboration and resistance requirements were designed to do.

From still another angle, Estrich (1987) discounts the impact of rape law reform because she believes that even the most aggressive state law reform efforts were clumsy or misguided; but if the laws (particularly those defining the crime) had been better formulated, the goals of rape law reform might have been achieved. Her position seems to be that laws defining rape will produce change only if they are drafted to provide a clear and correct symbolic message to those charged with interpreting them.

At the positive end of the spectrum, a number of writers seem more sanguine about realizing the promise of rape reform law. In an exhaustive review of court decisions implementing "rape shield" laws (ones that prohibit the use in trials of certain evidence of the victim's sexual history), Galvin (1986) concluded that the laws and the judges have functioned well in excluding impermissible evidence, even if the laws themselves were not always well drafted. Galvin, it should be noted, believes sexual history *should* be admissible when its admission does not depend on some invidious inference of "unchaste character" (1986, p. 809). Hence, she is less likely than some other commentators to be offended by many court decisions admitting such evidence.

Other researchers have found improvements in arrest, clearing, prosecution, or conviction rates, in the sentences meted out to convicted rapists, or in the experiences of rape victims at trial. For example, in her study of prosecutorial decisions in one Michigan county over a three-year period following the enactment of reform legislation, Caringella-MacDonald (1985) found an increase in the percentage of cases accepted for prosecution (from 10% in 1973 Detroit to 46% in 1975–1977 Kalamazoo). At the same time, the loss of these accepted cases through findings of nonguilt, dismissals, and nolles (refusals to prosecute further) decreased from 45% in 1973 Detroit to approximately 20% in both Detroit and Kalamazoo after passage of rape reform. The conviction rate for authorized cases rose from 55% in 1973 Detroit to 70–73% in 1975–1979 Detroit. Marsh, Geist, and Caplan's (1982) comprehensive study of the impact of Michigan's reform effort indicated that reporting rates had not been affected (they were increasing, but not because of the legal change), arrest rates had increased, both absolutely and relative to other serious crimes, and conviction rates had risen considerably. According to the overwhelming majority of criminal justice personnel, the rape reform law, particularly the rape shield provision, had also made the victim's experience with the criminal justice system less traumatic. Horney and Spohn's (1991) data on Detroit contradicted the findings of Marsh, Geist, and Caplan for Michigan as a whole, but they substituted some positive findings of their own: Reform produced increases in victim reporting rates, indictment rates, and the length of sentences for convicted rapists (an average increase of about 63 months).

One study conducted in California (reported in Marsh et al., 1982, p. 38) found convictions on rape charges had increased in a statistically significant way after California's rape shield law was adopted and the cautionary instruction was eliminated. (The cautionary instruction was a traditional warning that judges gave to jurors, before the jury deliberations, about the vulnerability of rape prosecutions to false accusations by the complaining witness.) Another California study, by Polk (1985), found a modest increase in the percentage of arrests for rape that resulted in the filing of a felony complaint, and hence an increase in the percentage of rape felony convictions per arrest. Polk's most dramatic finding was the increase over time in the probability that a rape offender would be sentenced to a state institution (from 58% in 1975 to 81% in 1982). The significance of these data is tempered, however, by the fact that California created a new sentencing system during the 1970s that resulted in increases in time served for *all* serious felons. Like the researchers who studied Michigan, Loh (1980) found a substantial increase in the number of rape complaints presented to prosecutors for charging following Washington State's rape law form. His findings of no increase in the percentage of cases charged as rape and a slight decrease in prison sentences counter the Michigan and California results, however.

Although aggregate American statistics cannot measure the effect of changes in individual state laws, they do offer some indication that the rate of reporting rape has increased since rape reform legislation was passed. Between 1970 and 1980, reports of rape doubled, from 18.7 to 36.4 per 100,000 population (Bourque, 1989, p. 11). Yet between 1972 and 1980, the National Crime Survey showed a drop in the incidence of rape per 100,000 population over age 11, from 77 to 40 for completed rapes, and from 238 to 120 for attempted rapes (Bourque, 1989, pp. 22–25). These data suggest an increase in the rate of reporting rape, which could possibly be attributable to legal changes designed to ameliorate the experience of the rape victim. National statistics also showed an 18% increase in the number of rape reports cleared by arrest between 1976 and 1980 (Bourque, 1989, pp. 34–35).

Elsewhere in the world, research in New South Wales (Temkin, 1987) found a sizable increase in police acceptance of rape complaints following rape law reform, a stable conviction rate, a marked rise in custodial sentences, and a sharp decline in the number of court cases in which sexual history evidence was admitted. An English study (Lloyd & Walmsley, 1989) supported Polk's findings in California with data showing that, for all convicted rapists between 1973 and 1985, there were significant increases in the likelihood and length of incarceration, even controlling for changes in the characteristics of offenders and the circumstances of crimes.

• • •

FOCUSING ON THE TRIAL PROCESS: CHALLENGES AND NEW DIRECTIONS FOR RESEARCH

Because of lessening confidence in the value of substantive changes in the definition of rape, the rape law reform movement seems to be turning its attention to events at trial, and how rules of evidence and methods of constructing a rape case relate to social perceptions about gender, coercion, and sexuality. That change of focus to the trial process suggests the need for much more research about how the race of the victim bears on jurors' perceptions. Data from the *Uniform Crime Re-*

ports and National Crime Surveys, supported by some but not all community studies, show that Black women have a disproportionately higher risk of being raped (Bourque, 1989). Research also demonstrates that jurors are less likely to convict for rape when the victim is Black (Field & Bienen, 1980; LaFree, 1989). Yet surprisingly, no research has examined whether legal reforms are equally effective in rape cases with Black and White victims. The absence of attention to this issue contrasts sharply with the intense scrutiny that has been given to the question of whether Black *men* are treated more harshly than White men charged with raping White women (LaFree, 1989). More emphasis on the race of the victim would be consistent with research on the imposition of the death penalty, which has shown that the race of the victim is more important than the race of the perpetrator in predicting sentencing decisions (Kennedy, 1988). History also suggests the importance of focusing on the victim's race. In the pre–Civil War South, for example, rape of a Black woman carried the sentence of a fine or imprisonment at the court's discretion, while the sentence for rape of a White woman was at least two years in prison, and could be death if the defendant was Black (Kennedy, 1988).

Contemporary feminist theorists have stressed the need for attention to the variety of women's experiences, taking account of differences in race, class, and religion. There is good reason for attention to these differences when studying rape law reform. For example, the history of American race relations suggests that rape myths about Black women may be different from the myths about rape generally (Wyatt, [1992]). What implications should that have for the effectiveness of evidence regarding the rape trauma syndrome or rape myth acceptance? Should distinctive testimony be introduced about rape myths concerning Black women? Is more research needed as a basis for such expert testimony?

The goal of rape reform legislation that seems most difficult to achieve is change in knowledge, values, and attitudes about gender and sexuality. Loh (1980), in his study of Washington State's rape law reform, indicated that criminal justice personnel were applying the previous standards to rape cases, regardless of alterations in the law. But changing the perceptions and values of jurors may be most difficult of all; indeed, police and prosecutors often state that they would modify their practices if they perceived a change in jurors' responses at rape trials (Estrich, 1987; Marsh et al., 1982). The evidentiary changes mentioned above may contribute to such a transformation in juror reactions to rape trials, at least if the courts begin to admit expert testimony on rape trauma syndrome and rape myth acceptance.

At the same time, the symbolic or ideological component of rape law reform, be it substantive or evidentiary, may also affect jurors' perceptions and conclusions. Indeed, some notable participants in the rape law reform movement (Bienen, 1983; Chappell, 1984; Nordby, 1980) identify symbolic/educative effects as the most important (and sometimes the *only*) consequences of legal change. Yet little is known about which kinds of legal changes are most effective in inducing attitudinal change. Caringella-MacDonald (1985) suggested that any measure that improves arrest, prosecution, and conviction rates could have a positive effect on attitudes, because attrition in these aspects of rape cases confirms and perpetuates rape myths about false accusations. Yet she also acknowledged that the attitudes she hoped to change were the very source of difficulty in reducing attrition rates. As Field and Bienen (1980) pointed out, "Legislation . . . cannot destroy the social function which the traditional rules [of rape law] performed. As long as large numbers of men and women believe that women are inferior and should be kept in their place through forced submission to sexual acts, the law will reflect that view" (p. 162). Thus, reforms that address the trial process, and hence the attitudes of individual jurors rather than society as a whole, may be more promising as vehicles for achieving feminist goals. Of course, the longer that research waits to assess legal impacts, the more difficult it may become to attribute changes in practice or attitudes to any specific law reforms.

All of these problems and complications suggest the need for careful longitudinal research, comparing complaint and case outcomes, as well as victim experiences and public perceptions of rape, before and after law reform, and using different states to study different types of reform. In fact, given the amount of rape reform legislation that has been enacted, the total amount of before-and-after research is surprisingly limited. Michigan has been the focus of the best and most sustained work (Caringella-MacDonald, 1985; Marsh et al., 1982; Nordby, 1980). Washington State and California have also been studied in this way, as have some foreign countries with British common law traditions, most notably Australia.

However, most research on rape documents a particular condition (be it the victimization rate, the reporting rate, the conviction rate, or the attitudes of jurors or victims) as of a given time, with no attempt to assess change over time generally, let alone to study change as a function of revisions in the law. Sometimes that is not a problem, as when Galvin (1986) studied the practices of state court judges in admitting sexual history evidence. There a safe assumption was that before the law was changed, all such evidence came in at trial, so comparison was possible with just an "after" study. But on other issues, knowing whether the situation has improved would be important. In some instances, commentators may be prepared to say that a given condition is unacceptable even though it constitutes an improvement over the past. But on many topics that judgment would be quite difficult without knowing how much of an improvement occurred and what was required to achieve it. If most of the significant rape law revisions have already been adopted, some of this kind of research may be impossible, for there is no longer a "before" to compare with the "after." However, a number of valuable studies on such topics as victims' experiences and police attitudes toward rape were undertaken in the early years of the rape reform movement. These studies could now be replicated, and comparisons drawn.

With their time-series analyses of six different urban jurisdictions, Horney and Spohn (1991) have made real progress in constructing useful research on rape law reform and suggesting testable hypotheses to explain its general lack of legal impact. Their study fails, however, to examine the full range of rape reforms, particularly those attempting to affect the construction of events at trial.

Ultimately, there are some problems with rape that the legal system cannot hope to fix, at least without compromising bedrock values of fairness to the victim or defendant. For example, to the extent that victims do not report the crime because of concerns with privacy, or to the extent that having to appear at trial under any conditions anguishes victims and deters them from reporting rape, law reform cannot make a difference. Social science research has not yet come up against that brick wall, however. There is still much unfinished business for research in studying problems with rape that the legal system may be able to remedy.

CONCLUSION

Despite the intense effort that has gone into rape law reform, we have insufficient and conflicting information about the difference that these laws make for victims, for the criminal justice system, and for the treatment of women generally. The variety of law reform approaches and goals in different states both complicates the assessment process and offers opportunities for comparative research. Given the key role of juror values and perceptions in determining how rape complaints will be dealt with, future research could profitably focus on the trial process—especially on how widespread perceptions about gender, sexuality, and coercion interact with legal rules regulating the presentation of a rape case. Such a focus will require greater sensitivity to victims' race and class, as well as other factors that may bear on juror perceptions.

References

Adler, Z. (1987). *Rape on trial.* New York: Routledge & Kegan Paul.

Bennett, L., & Feldman, M. (1981). *Reconstructing reality in the courtroom.* New Brunswick, NJ: Rutgers University Press.

Berger, R., Searles, P., & Newman, W. (1988). The dimensions of rape reform legislation. *Law and Society Review, 22,* 329–349.

Berger, V. (1977). Man's trial, woman's tribulation: Rape cases in the courtroom. *Columbia Law Review, 77,* 1–103.

Bienen, L. (1983). Rape reform legislation in the United States: A look at some practice effects. *Victimology: An International Journal, 8,* 139–151.

Borgida, E. (1980). Evidentiary reform of rape laws: A psycholegal approach. In P. Lipsett & B. Sales (Eds.), *New directions in psycholegal research* (pp. 57–75). New York: Van Nostrand Reinhold.

Bourque, L. (1989). *Defining rape.* Durham, NC: Duke University Press.

Brekke, N., & Borgida, E. (1988). Expert psychological testimony in rape trials: A social-cognitive analysis. *Journal of Personality and Social Psychology, 55,* 372–386.

Brownmiller, S. (1975). *Against our will.* New York: Simon & Schuster.

Bumiller, K. (1987). Rape as a legal symbol: An essay on sexual violence. *University of Miami Law Review, 42,* 75–91.

Caringella-MacDonald, S. (1985). Sexual assault prosecution: An examination of model rape legislation in Michigan. In C. Schweber & C. Feinman (Eds.), *Criminal justice politics and women: The aftermath of legally mandated change* (pp. 65–82). New York: Haworth.

Chappell, D. (1984). The impact of rape legislation reform: Some comparative trends. *International Journal of Women's Studies, 7,* 70–80.

Clark, L., & Lewis, D. (1977). *Rape: The price of coercive sexuality.* Toronto: Women's Educational Press.

Estrich, S. (1987). *Real rape.* Cambridge, MA: Harvard University Press.

Field, H., & Bienen, L. (1980). *Jurors and rape.* Lexington, MA: Heath.

Fischer, K. (1989). Defining the boundaries of admissible expert psychological testimony on rape trauma syndrome. *University of Illinois Law Review,* 691–734.

Frazier, P., & Borgida, E. (1988). Juror common understanding and the admissibility of rape trauma syndrome evidence in court. *Law and Human Behavior, 12,* 101–122.

Galvin, H. (1986). Shielding rape victims in the state and federal courts: A proposal for the second decade. *Minnesota Law Review, 70,* 763–916.

Handler, J. (1978). *Social movements and the legal system: A theory of law reform and social change.* New York: Academic Press.

Handler, J. (1986). *The conditions of discretion.* Beverly Hills, CA: Sage.

Holstein, J. A. (1985). Jurors' interpretations and jury decision-making. *Law and Human Behavior, 9,* 83–100.

Horney, J., & Spohn, C. (1991). Rape law reform and instrumental change in six urban jurisdictions. *Law and Society Review, 25,* 117–153.

Kennedy, R. (1988). *McCleskey v. Kemp:* Race, capital punishment, and the Supreme Court. *Harvard Law Review, 101,* 1388–1443.

LaFree, G. (1989). *Rape and criminal justice.* Belmont, CA: Wadsworth.

LaFree, G., Reskin, B., & Visher, C. (1985). Jurors' responses to victims' behavior and legal issues in sexual assault trials. *Social Problems, 32,* 389–407.

Lloyd, C., & Walmsley, R. (1989). *Changes in rape offenses and sentencing.* London, England: Her Majesty's Stationery Office.

Loh, W. (1980). The impact of common law and reform rape statutes on prosecution: An empirical study. *Washington Law Review, 55,* 543–652.

Marsh, J., Geist, A., & Caplan, N. (1982). *Rape and the limits of law reform.* Boston: Auburn House.

Nordby, V. (1980). Reforming the rape laws: The Michigan experience. In J. Scutt (Ed.), *Rape law reform* (pp. 3–34). Canberra: Australian Institute of Criminology.

Osborne, J. (1985). Rape law reform: The new cosmetic for Canadian women. In C. Schweber & C. Feinman (Eds.), *Criminal justice politics and women: The aftermath of legally mandated change.* New York: Haworth.

Polk, K. (1985). Rape reform and criminal justice processing. *Crime and Delinquency, 31,* 191–205.

Rowland, J. (1985). *The ultimate violation.* Garden City, NJ: Doubleday.

Scutt, J. (1980). Evidence and the role of the jury in trials for rape. In J. Scutt (Ed.), *Rape law reform* (pp. 90–114). Canberra: Australian Institute of Criminology.

Searles, P., & Berger, R. (1987). The current status of rape reform legislation: An examination of state statutes. *Women's Rights Law Reporter, 10,* 25–43.

Soshnick, A. (1987). The rape shield paradox: Complainant protection amidst oscillation trends of state judicial interpretation. *Journal of Criminal Law and Criminology, 78,* 644–698.

Temkin, J. (1987). *Rape and the legal process.* London, England: Sweet & Maxwell.

Tetreault, P. A. (1989). Rape myth acceptance: A case for providing educational expert testimony in rape jury trials. *Behavioral Sciences and the Law, 7,* 243–257.

Wyatt (1992). The sociocultural context of African American and White women's rape. *Journal of Social Issues, 48(1),* 173–185.

Zimring, F. (1987). Legal perspectives on family violence. *California Law Review, 75,* 521–539.

Unprotected by the Swedish Welfare State

A Survey of Battered Women and the Assistance They Received

R. AMY ELMAN AND MAUD L. EDUARDS

INTRODUCTION

According to Swedish police statistics for 1989, approximately 39 women are battered daily and one woman is killed every 10 days by a man known to her (Statistics Sweden, 1989). Yet as alarming as these statistics seem, authorities concede that underreporting remains a serious analytic problem; available measurements are still too low. In an attempt to account for under estimation, a report from the Delegation for Equality Research (JämFo) estimated that a woman is battered every 20 minutes by a man with whom she is having (or has had) an intimate relationship (Leander, 1989).

Despite this evidence, it is often assumed that woman battery is neither a serious nor pervasive problem in Sweden. It is, after all, generally believed that equality between women and men has advanced further in Sweden in comparison to most other western industrialized states (Adams & Winston, 1980; Norris, 1987; Ruggie, 1984; Scott, 1982; Sidel, 1986; Verba, 1987). Those who focus on the egalitarian achievements of this welfare state, however, have been reticent to analyze sexual inequality or welfare in terms of violence against women.

While the above figures hint at the prevalence of woman battery, there is a dearth of primary research concerning violence against women in Sweden. This may result from the tendency of Swedes to analyze oppression almost exclusively in terms of class (Eduards, 1986). Until quite recently, woman battery was deemed both academically irrelevant and unworthy of political analysis. To date, for example, only one highly criticized doctoral thesis has been written about the subject (Bergman, 1987)[1] and modern legislative reforms have been adopted only within the last 8 years.

In the past, the Swedish state did not consider beating women a criminal act. It was not until 1864 that men lost the right to batter their wives and woman battery was legislatively recognized as a criminal assault. Yet, while it became possible for the criminal justice system to take action against men who battered women, batterers rarely received sanctions. Recently, the Swedish parliament adopted two legislative reforms in an effort to correct this injustice.

The first reform, adopted in 1982, made woman beating a public offence (SFS 1981: 1313). This made it possible for others, besides the battered woman herself, to take action against the perpetrator. Additionally, police were empowered to take a batterer into custody if they suspected that he would continue to harm the woman. The second reform was adopted in 1988. It provides women with orders of protection (besöksförbud) against their assailants. The orders were adopted for the express purpose of providing women immediate protection from their abusers (SFS 1988: 688).

Until now, researchers (BRÅ, 1989:2; Socialstyrelsen, 1990) have mainly analyzed reforms and services for abused women from the perspective of service providers, often neutralizing the severity of the problem. This approach essentially ignores the victims for whom these services were developed. A recent investigation concerning orders of protection, for example, surveyed prosecutors and some shelter workers to determine if the law providing for orders of protection was being successfully implemented (BRÅ, 1989:2). As battered women were not surveyed, we do not know if women find the necessary procedures complex and alienating or whether the orders truly deterred further assaults. In addition, the Department of Welfare recently completed an investigation of the services provided by the battered women's movement (Socialstyrelsen, 1990). Yet, once again, no attempt was made to survey battered women about the assistance they received at shelters and/or through other channels.

Although we do not deny the intrinsic value of the above mentioned studies, one will never accurately judge the effectiveness of reforms and services the state affords battered women if studies continue to focus only on the service providers. The issue of battery must also be approached from the perspective of those in whose name reforms were adopted and public programs exist. Therefore, we constructed a survey that asked battered women, themselves, about the effectiveness of state intervention and assistance. In addition, we briefly surveyed the staff at shelters who often serve as an intermediary between women and various state authorities. When one examines the services provided by the Swedish authorities from the perspective taken here, one is afforded an opportunity to either maintain or transform traditional characterizations of the Swedish state as both interested and effective in pursuing sexual equality.

· · ·

DISCUSSION

Subjects and Methods

It is, undoubtedly, a difficult task to assess the net balance of formal and informal assistance the state provides to battered women. While most, if not all, previous scholars have focused on the perceptions of service providers and law enforcement personnel, we attempted to transcend this by focusing on what battered women in shelters thought of the various forms of (official) assistance they received. There are two reasons for limiting our sample in this manner. First, shelters provide an accessible survey population of battered women. Women in shelters are safer and calmer than they would otherwise be in hospitals or courts. Second, shelters are formally organized to specifically meet the needs of battered women and often serve as an intermediary between women and the authorities. For this reason, we also surveyed the shelter staff with the hope that they could provide an overview of the obstacles battered women face and what can be done to best meet the needs of these victims.

Background

The brutality and prevalence of woman battering in Sweden casts aspersions on the state's reputation for sexual equality. This could account for the unwillingness of Swedes and their foreign admirers to concede the seriousness and universality of the problem in Sweden. According to one battered woman in this survey, "In the (daily news) papers they write only about foreign men and battering. Swedish men's behavior is apparently taboo."

Focusing on immigrant men's contempt for and violence against women may be merely an attempt to sustain an impressive political reputation that is increasingly challenged by Swedish feminists (Elman, 1990).[2] Of the battered women we surveyed, 79% stated that they were abused by Swedish men. There was, however, a slight overrepresentation of immigrants in our sample as both men and women immigrants separately constitute approximately 12% of the general adult Swedish population. The overrepresentation is probably due to the relatively few social and economic resources immigrants possess. For this reason both immigrant women and Swedish women who are battered by immigrant men may be more likely to rely on the support of shelters for assistance. Yet, even with the presence of immigrants within our sample, our research confirms the experiences of battered women and their advocates who argue that women battery is not a foreign import.

Unlike any other oppressed group, women are harmed most often by those they have been taught to love and trust. Without exception, all 82 of our respondents were beaten by men with whom they were presently or previously having an intimate heterosexual relationship. Nearly all of these respondents shared a residence with their abuser, which facilitated the privacy of the abuse.

Unlike any other form of violence, violence committed against women is typically fused with sexuality (Barry, 1984; MacKinnon, 1987; Millett, 1969). Our finding that 76% of the abusers forced their victims to have sex supports this notion and is consistent with other studies concerning sexual abuse and battery (Dobash & Dobash, 1979; Lundgren, 1989; Watts, 1990).[3]

Given the extreme conditions to which battered women are subjected, there remains the question of why women do not simply leave the men who abuse them. In fact, the only primary research done on woman battery in Sweden focused on this question. The researcher, psychiatrist Bo Bergman, depicted battered women as mentally imbalanced, irrational, and psychiatrically morbid (Bergman, 1987). This woman-blaming research insists that women are masochists who precipitate the abuse men inflict on them. Contrary to this thinking, most of our respondents wanted to leave but cited the fear of worse violence and even murder if they attempted to do this. When one considers that a woman is killed every 10 days in Sweden by a man she knows, this fear is not irrational. Perhaps it would be more reasonable to say that battered women would be "mentally imbalanced" if they did not experience some "morbidity" as a result of the cruelty to which they are subjected. Women fear leaving the men who brutalize them precisely because the abuse is so bad. Moreover, the very threat of violence is effective in the suffocation of women's dissent and assertion of self. These factors, along with the sexual aspect and private context of the abuse, serves to distinguish woman battery from other forms of violence while it concomitantly dissuades state intervention.

Woman Battery and the State

Although the existing legal system could provide battered women relief, laws are meaningless if they are not enforced. One of our respondents explained that "in cases of women battery the ordinary rules are not followed." After she had filed the police report she had to convince both the police and prosecutor that she had really been battered by the man in question. She states "I got the feeling at an early stage that they believed me less than they did him. According to my view of justice, a crime that is reported should be duly investigated. Who would question that my car had actually been stolen?" As the results of our survey further confirmed (see Table 1), authorities entrusted with the public's safety and welfare rarely offered women options that recognized the criminal dimensions of woman battery.

Table 1   SUGGESTIONS WOMEN RECEIVED REGARDING POSSIBLE CRIMINAL SANCTIONS AGAINST THEIR ASSAILANT

Suggestion	Police ($n = 60$)[a]	Prosecutor ($n = 24$)[a]	Social worker ($n = 51$)[a]
Arrest	17% (10)	29% (7)	10% (5)
Police report	12% (7)	8% (2)	0
Protection orders	10% (6)	25% (6)	0

[a]n = number of respondents who were in contact with respective authorities. Note that they may have received more than one piece of advice.

The Police   More women contacted the police for assistance than any other authority. The police are the only public agency easily accessible in times of crisis. Unfortunately, however, women were highly dissatisfied with them (see Table 3). Many respondents told us that the police neglected to provide protection, trivialized their harm, and seldom believed their accounts. For example, when we asked "is there anything else you would like to say," a battered woman states that during an investigation, a police officer inquired "How come an educated and alert woman like you was beaten?" Many women wrote of waiting hours before the police arrived to help. Another respondent writes, "I wish the police would listen more to what women say when they (the women) have come so far to finally report their husbands." In fact, research indicates that when police do listen to battered women it may deter future violence. An American study of arrest policies found that in the cases where police took the time to listen to battered women in front of their assailants, only 9% of the men arrested were violent again (Sherman & Berk, 1984).

Swedish police were, however, not only slow in responding to calls for help and unlikely to offer support, they were often reluctant to proceed with any action that displayed that they consider woman battery a crime. For example, only 17% of police officers suggested arrest when 31% of the women themselves had made the request. Police were more likely to favor extracriminal actions that would not require their attention (compare Tables 1 and 2). This may, in part, result from police identifying with male assailants. According to an American study of police intervention, "police officers are socialized in precisely the same manner as the citizens we are supposed to protect." Moreover, the researcher notes an "extreme paradox of delegating to police officers the role of arbiters" given the machismo of the professional (Bannon, 1975, p. 1).

The Prosecutors   As prosecutors have been the foremost conduits of reforms in Sweden, we were concerned with their response to the needs of battered women. Only prosecutors, for example, are empowered to issue arrests and provide women orders of protection. Yet the proper use of the latest legislative reforms concerning arrest and protection orders are made difficult given that only 33% of the battered women we surveyed ever spoke to a prosecutor.

There are numerous factors that complicate the use of Sweden's order of protection reform. Among these we found a general reluctance of all authorities, including the prosecutor, to suggest they be issued. The reluctance of authorities to

Table 2   THE AUTHORITIES' EXTRA-LEGAL ADVICE

Advice	Police (n = 60)[a]	Prosecutor (n = 24)[a]	Social worker (n = 51)[a]
Leave man	48% (29)	17% (4)	41% (21)
Obtain new residence	22% (13)	8% (2)	53% (27)
Divorce	15% (9)	12% (3)	25% (13)
Medical assistance	12% (7)	12% (3)	8% (4)
Therapy	17% (10)	8% (2)	45% (23)
None	28% (17)	37% (9)	20% (10)

[a]n = number of respondents who were in contact with respective authorities. Note that they may have received more than one piece of advice.

suggest protection orders is exacerbated by the fact that the reform explicitly states that women living with their assailants are unable to receive one.[4] According to this stipulation, only four of the women we surveyed would have been considered eligible for a protection order. That so few of our respondents would have been considered eligible calls into question the assistance battered women derive from a law that was adopted to benefit them. This also explains the frustration of shelter staff, 35% (23/65) of whom stated that one of the obstacles they faced in assisting battered women was their inability to help women receive protection orders. In fact, a government study found that 38% of all those who applied for protection orders were denied them (BRÅ, 1989:2).

It is significant that so few women have contact with those whose job it is to offer them the security an arrest or protection order can provide. Although few battered women may understand their abuse as criminal, public authorities exacerbate this by rarely acknowledging that woman battery is a crime. This is so for both public authorities within the criminal justice system and those outside of it.

The Social Workers   While social workers are not part of the criminal justice system, women frequently request help from them. Of the state authorities in our survey, however, social workers were, unfortunately, the most inclined to take a therapeutic approach and the least willing to acknowledge the criminal dimensions of battery. None of the social workers with whom the women in this survey spoke mentioned that the women should file a police report, let alone apply for an order of protection; furthermore, only 10% suggested arrest as a viable option (see Table 1).

The suggestions that battered women stated that social workers made most often concerned women changing residences (see Table 2). The Social Welfare Department has a policy of giving battered women preference for public housing. This is quite effective considering that the most frequently mentioned request of battered women was a change of residence. Yet, with the exception of being able to provide women with access to a preferred position in the housing queue, social workers appeared ill equipped to meet the other needs of battered women.

Battered women suggested that social workers possessed little knowledge of the obstacles they faced. For example, when asked "what more should have been done to help you?" a woman replied that "everything would have been easier had the social worker not demanded that I return home after 2 months to collect my belongings in my (lover's) presence." The social worker failed to comprehend the

Table 3   THE MEAN RANKING OF THE ASSISTANCE WOMEN RECEIVED[a]

Authority/Service provider	Mean ranking
Police (n = 58)[b]	2.5
Prosecutor (n = 24)[a]	2.3
Social worker (n = 46)[b]	2.7
Shelter staff (n = 69)[b]	4.7

[a]On a scale of 1 to 5, with 1 being poor and 5 being best.

[b]n = number of respondents.

psychological trauma and physical danger in which she placed the woman. Other women simply commented that social workers were uninterested in helping them. One women wrote that the "social welfare office was slow and did not want to help." These examples help to explain the low rankings social workers received from battered women (see Table 3).

Women in the battered women's movement are also consistently skeptical of the support social workers provide. We were recently informed by shelter volunteers in Alingsås that a social worker told a battered woman, "You can't leave your husband after 20 years—what of the children?" In another community a social worker cautioned the woman that it would be best to endure the beatings because housing is difficult to find.

The Shelters   "If it had not been for the women's shelter, I would not have been alive today," was a common sentiment among the women in our survey. In response to the open-ended question, "is there anything else you would like to say," one woman provided the following insight:

> There is chaos in Sweden when it comes to justice. Men who batter may get a few months (in jail). Men who kill a year or so. Men who rape get fines. . . . The women live with the memories all their lives. The only things that exist for us are the shelters . . . if we come that far.

We find it significant that these women gave shelters a higher rating than any other service provider (see Table 3).

The data confirmed what many women's advocates assert: while battered women are often in need of immediate housing and some counseling, there is no substitute for the provision of these services within shelters.[5] Shelters provide a community within which battered women are no longer isolated and feel the need to conceal their abuse. Shelters are also distinguished from traditional social services by their staff. Refuges for battered women are staffed exclusively by women, providing battered women with an even greater sense of self and security. More important, the Swedish shelters are primarily staffed by committed volunteers who have, over the years, developed tremendous expertise in assisting battered women.

Although battered women possessed a most favorable view of the services they received within the shelters, shelter women themselves held a more modest view of their effectiveness. After all, when asked to judge themselves on a scale similar to that by which they were judged, shelter staff held themselves to higher standards; they rated themselves lower than battered women ranked them.[6]

Shelter workers are under considerable strain to provide the assistance that others are poorly equipped to deliver. In working so closely with battered women, shelter staff possess a greater awareness of their limitations and possibilities and are not always able to accomplish all that they desire. For example, one shelter volunteer asserts that the staff is committed to raising the consciousness of authorities and the public at large. She, however, notes that they are "so involved in the work with the women in the shelter that it is difficult to get the time to inform the public about the problem to the extent that we wish to."

According to shelter workers and numerous feminist activists, the greatest obstacle in assisting battered women is public consciousness. They believe this could be overcome if violence against women became a political issue in Sweden. They realize that if the police and other authorities are to respond adequately to battered women, Sweden's political parties must provide leadership. Shelter staff believe that having a commitment to sexual equality necessitates recognizing that woman battery constitutes an obstacle to obtaining it.

CONCLUSION

In the past, discussions regarding male brutality were kept so private that public solutions and state interventions were considered inappropriate. Most Swedes and their foreign onlookers have been more inclined to deny or ignore violence against women than to change it. Yet, as the oppression of women became incorporated into daily public discourse, the state became a site of conflict. Women in Sweden began to assert that, as citizens, they were entitled to protection from the men who terrorized them. And, state authorities increasingly intervened, occasionally even to the benefit of women. Battered women's shelters received public funding, reforms were instituted, and penalties and various other restraints were imposed on men.

Perhaps this was done, in part, to counteract the contradictions that became more apparent as women in Sweden discussed their compromised safety and status within a state that holds out the prospect of sexual equality. To account fully for the determinants of reform is, however, an impossible task. Although reforms may be mere concessions from those who have power (Wilson, 1977) or thinly disguised adjustments necessary for the patriarchal status quo (Dahlerup, 1987), to deny any improvement that reforms may have for women displays a calloused indifference to welcomed relief. And it is this relief that inspires the Swedish battered women's movement to seek redress through public authorities.

Unfortunately, however, while Sweden's Statistics Bureau concedes that violence that takes place within the victim's home is the most serious (1981), our data shows a disappointing responsiveness of the state to the needs of battered women. Although Swedish law no longer regards woman beating as a male prerogative, the criminal justice system has been slow to provide women with protection against it. Even social workers do little to hinder the dangers battered women face.

Sweden enjoys the pretense of providing for the general well-being of its citizens, yet it has shown a limited capacity and determination in mitigating male violence against women. There is both a strong contradiction and an element of hypocrisy in this highly esteemed state. As long as progress in women's conditions is defined exclusively in terms of gainful employment and shared parenthood rather than in terms of sexuality, violence and power, sexual equality will remain illusory for women in Sweden.

Notes

1. On the basis of 22 interviews with battered women in a hospital emergency room, Bergman depicted most of them as mentally imbalanced. For an in-depth critique see Lundgren and Eriksen (1988).
2. For specific details of recent protests see Elman (1990).
3. Researchers found that over half of all battering incidents occur in the bedroom and much of it is precipitated by sexual jealousy (Dobash & Dobash, 1979, pp. 14–21). In interviewing numerous batterers, Eva Lundgren notes that the men explicitly state that they get sexual satisfaction from battering their wives and girlfriends (Lundgren, 1989). Moreover, a British men's crisis center notes that 25% of the batterers that contacted them *admitted* they forced their partners to have sex (Watts, 1990).
4. In the United States a majority of states have laws explicitly permitting eviction of batterers from their own homes. The 1986 Illinois Domestic Violence Law, for example, explicitly states that even when a batterer can claim a legal right to possession of his residence, the court *must* exclude him if the risk of his future abuse interferes with the petitioner's safe and peaceful occupancy ("New Illinois Domestic Violence Law," 1987, p. 7). Although this law and others similar to it have been challenged, they have, without exception, been upheld. A woman's right to the safety of her home outweighs the rights of the man who, in his criminal behavior, denies the woman of her freedom.
5. A British study, for example, found that most battered women prefer staying in a refuge before being immediately rehoused (Binney, Harkell, & Nixon, 1985, p. 172).
6. Battered women ranked shelter workers with a 4.7 and shelter workers gave themselves a 3.7.

References

Adams, Carolyn, & Winston, Kathryn. (1980). *Mothers at work*. New York: Longman.

Bannon, James. (1975). Law enforcement problems with intra-family violence. Paper presented to the American Bar Association Convention, August 12, 1975, Montreal, Canada.

Bard, Morton. (1971). The study and modification of intra-familial violence. In J. L. Singer (Ed.), *The control of aggression and violence: Cognitive and psychological* (pp. 149–168). New York: Academic Press.

Barry, Kathleen. (1984). *Female sexual slavery*. New York: New York University Press.

Bergman, Bo. (1987). *Battered wives: Why are they beaten and why do they stay?* Stockholm: Repro Print AB.

Binney, Val, Harkell, Gina, & Nixon, Judy. (1985). Refuges and housing for battered women. In Jan Pahl (Ed.), *Private violence and public policy: The needs of battered women and the response of public services* (pp. 166–178). London: Routledge & Kegan Paul.

BRÅ, PM (1989:2). Lagen om besöksförbud: En Uppföljning [The order of protection law: A Follow-up Study]. Stockholm: BRA, Rapport.

Dahlerup, Drude. (1987). Confusing concepts—Confusing reality: A theoretical discussion of the patriarchal state. In Anne Showstack Sasson (Ed.), *Women and the state* (pp. 93–127). London: Hutchinson.

Dobash, Rebecca, & Dobash, Russel. (1979). *Violence against wives: A case against patriarchy*. New York: Free Press.

Eduards, Maud. (1986). Kön, stat och jämställdhetspolitik [Sex, state and equality policy]. *Kvinnovetenskaplig Tidskrift*, 3, 4–15.

Elman, R. Amy. (1990, March). Swedish politics. *off our backs*, 4–5.

Leander, Karen. (1989). Misshandlade kvinnors möte med rättsapparaten [Battered women meet the justice system]. *Kvinnomisshandel*. Stockholm: JämFo Rapport nr 14.

Lundgren, Eva, & Eriksen, K. (1988, April). Fördomsfult om kvinnormisshandel [Prejudices about women battering]. *Socialt Arbete*, 18–21.

Lundgren, Eva. (1989). Våldets normaliseringsprocess. Två parter—Två strategier [Normalizing violence: Two parties—Two strategies]. *Kvinnomisshandel*. Stockholm: JämFo Rapport nr 14.

MacKinnon, Catharine. (1987). *Feminism unmodified: Discourses on life and law.* Cambridge, MA: Harvard University Press.

Millett, Kate. (1969). *Sexual politics.* New York: Avon Books.

New Illinois Domestic Violence Law. (1987, January) *The Women's Advocate,* 7.

Norris, Pippa. (1987). *Politics and sexual equality: The comparative position of women in western democracies.* Boulder, CO: Riener.

Öhrman, S. (1990, January 29). 38 procent får inte besöksförbud [38 percent do not get orders of protection]. *Aftonbladet.*

Ruggie, Mary. (1984). *The state & working women: A comparative study of Britain and Sweden.* Princeton, NJ: Princeton University Press.

Scott, Hilda. (1982). *Sweden's "Right to be Human."* New York: Sharpe.

SFS 1981: 1313 Lag om ändring av brottsbalken [Public Prosecution Law].

SFS 1988: 688 Lag om besöksförbud [Order of protection Law].

Sidel, Ruth. (1986). *Women & children last.* New York: Penguin Books.

Sherman, Lawrence, & Berk, Richard. (1984). The specific deterrent effects of arrest for domestic assault. *American Sociological Review, 49,* 261–272.

Socialstyrelsen, et al. (1985). *Misshandel och sexuella övergrepp mot kvinnor och barn* [Battery and sexual abuse against women and children]. Stockholm: Liber Information.

Socialstyrelsen. (1990). Kartläggning av kvinnojourerna och mänsjourerna i Sverige [A survey of women's and men's crisis centers]. Stockholm: Author.

Statistics Sweden. (1981). *Victims of violence and property crimes #24.* Stockholm: SCB.

Statistics Sweden. (1989). *Yearbook of judicial statistics.* Stockholm: SCB.

Verba, Sidney (et al.). (1987). *Elites and the idea of equality: A comparison of Japan, Sweden and the United States.* Cambridge, MA: Harvard University Press.

Watts, J. (1990, February 25). Men say why they batter women. *The Observer.*

Wilson, Elizabeth. (1977). *Women and the welfare state.* London: Tavistock.

FURTHER READING FOR CHAPTER 5

Allen, I. 1988. "Ageing as a feminist issue," *Policy Studies,* Vol. 9, No. 1–2.

Boneparth, E., and E. Stoper. 1988. *Women, Power and Policy.* Riverside, NJ: Pergamon Press.

Diamond, I. 1983. *Families, Politics and Public Policy.* New York: Longman.

Eisenstein, Z. 1981. *The Radical Future of Liberal Feminism.* New York: Longman.

Evans, S., and B. Nelson. 1989. *Wage Justice: Comparable Worth and the Paradox of Technocratic Reform.* Chicago: University of Chicago Press.

Francome, C. 1984. *Abortion Freedom: A Worldwide Movement.* London: Allen and Unwin.

Gelb, J., and M. Palley. 1987. *Women and Public Policies,* rev. ed. Princeton: Princeton University Press.

Gordon, L. (ed.). 1990. *Women, the State and Welfare.* Madison: University of Wisconsin Press.

Hernes, H. 1987. *Welfare State and Women Power: Essays in State Feminism.* Oslo: Norwegian University Press.

Kendrigan, M. 1991. *Gender Differences: Their Impact on Public Policy.* New York: Greenwood Press.

Lovenduski, J., and J. Outshoor (eds.). 1986. *The New Politics of Abortion.* London: Sage.

MacKinnon, C. A. 1979. *Sexual Harassment of Working Women: A Case of Discrimination.* New Haven: Yale University Press.

Meehan, E. 1992. *Citizenship in the European Community.* London: Sage.

Petrie, P. 1991. "School-age child care and equal opportunities," *Women's Studies International Forum*, Vol. 14, No. 6, pp. 527–537.

Schaffner Goldberg, G., and E. Kremen (eds.). 1990. *The Feminization of Poverty: Only in America?* New York: Praeger.

Scott, H. 1984. *Working Your Way to the Bottom: The Feminization of Poverty.* London: Pandora Press.

Sidel, R. 1986. *Women and Children Last: The Plight of Poor Women in Affluent America.* New York: Viking.

Spallone, P., and D. Steinberg. 1987. *Made To Order: The Myth of Reproductive and Genetic Progress.* Oxford: Pergamon Press.

Stetson, D. McBride. 1991. *Women's Rights in the U.S.A.* Pacific Grove, CA: Brooks/Cole.

Wilson, E. 1977. *Women and the Welfare State.* London: Tavistock.

CHAPTER
6

The Women's Movement

In the West, the 1960s was a decade for questioning old values, a decade for proposing alternative views of the world and the way people could lead their lives, a decade during which the voices of many people previously relegated to the margins of society shouted to be heard. As if from nowhere, there emerged a "youth culture" which insisted that young people should play a role in shaping social values. Student movements in both the United States and Europe pressed for institutional change in what they deemed to be constrictive, elitist educational systems. On both sides of the Atlantic, ethnic and racial movements demanded an appreciation and an acceptance of diversity and an expanded role in the political system. In the midst of this vortex the contemporary women's movement surfaced.

This was, of course, not the first time women had participated in a social movement to achieve a change in their status. In the preceding century a women's movement dedicated to obtaining legal and political rights had existed in both Europe and North America. Indeed, by the first decade of this century there was an international organization explicitly devoted to the purpose of advancing the cause of women's suffrage. However, the women's movement of the 1960s differed from its predecessor; its doctrine, its ideology, its linchpin was feminism. Described as second-wave feminism, it sought to raise women's consciousness of the oppressive conditions that governed their lives. Its rallying cry, "The personal is political," urged American and European women to protest against the patriarchal structures of the existing social, economic, and political order.

Although most agreed that the women's movement was the "conscious, collective activities of women fighting for feminist goals," it was easier to define what feminism was against than to achieve consensus about its objectives.[1] From the start, there were significant philosophical and ideological disagreements about the meaning of feminism as well as about appropriate strategies. Within each country there were differences of opinion based on the traditional left-right political continuum. Some segments of the women's movement adopted socialist principles while others endorsed incremental reforms within a capitalist framework. Stressing reforms that promoted equality, liberal feminism was primarily concerned with giving women the opportunity to compete with men on an equal footing. Its proponents pushed for the enactment of laws and policies that would end discrimination in the workplace. Socialist feminism, in contrast, argued that women's oppression was inexorably linked to capitalism and contended that fundamental structural changes should be made in the economy, particularly in those elements that justified the inequitable distribution of wealth and property. Laws banning sex discrimination in the workplace were, according to this view, a band-aid solution at best. Furthermore, this group argued that since liberal feminism was insensitive to the dynamic of class, it could never adequately address the oppression of working-class women. Although accepting some of the same premises as socialist feminism, radical feminism attributed women's oppression to patriarchy and to the male domination it justified.[2] For radical feminists, neither incremental changes in the existing order nor a Marxist transformation of the economy would eradicate the subjugation of women. Patriarchal structures had to be dismantled. To accomplish this, it was necessary to move away from the concept of woman as "other," as deviant, as someone who must be judged against male norms. Unlike liberal feminism and socialist feminism, radical feminism accepted and celebrated women as different.

Given these diverse interpretations, it was no wonder that even within a particular nation, the women's movement often found it difficult to agree on a common agenda or strategy. In addition, the women's movement was influenced by each national culture. Hence, it varied considerably from one country to another in structure, style, and operation. As Gelb put it, "the 'political opportunity structure' or institutions, alignments and ideology of each nation structure the development, goals, and values of feminist activists."[3]

In spite of these variations both within and among the second-wave women's movements, they all challenged the foundations of the existing order. First, the women's movement disputed the distinction between a public and a private sphere and asserted that this division contributed to the second-class status of women. Second, the women's movement called for an end to discrimination in education and employment. It also urged the creation of support systems, such as child care centers, that would enable women to participate in the work force. And third, it questioned the right of one half of the population, men, to control the processes by which social values were determined. In short, despite political and philosophical differences, there was some consensus about the need for change. There were common themes, such as reproduction, employment discrimination, and violence against women, around which all could mobilize. All segments of the various women's movements wanted to eliminate those conditions that perpetuated women's inferior position in the economic, social, and political domains.

Any call for a basic change in power relationships is bound to create hostility and crystalize opposition. The experience of the women's movement proved no exception. Before long, a backlash sought to discredit the women's movement and to depict its adherents in terms of negative social and sexual stereotypes. In the United States, the women's movement came to be portrayed in the media as a bunch of "bra-burning women's libbers," malcontents whose demands threatened the stability not only of the family but of the nation as a whole. Hostile depictions of the members of women's movement surfaced elsewhere. For example, the Greek women's movement was viewed with animosity by the parties of the left, which often accused the women of irrational extremism.[4] Other typical accusations were that women were guilty of extremism, irrationality, and the destruction of prevailing moral and social values.

As might be expected, the consequence of these attacks was that some women disassociated themselves from the women's movement. For example, during the 1970s, American women who feared the negative impact the women's movement might have on their election to public office attempted to distance themselves from it in public.[5] "I'm not a feminist, I'm just pro-people" was a remark women politicians often made.[6] Many ordinary women, too, remained detached and aloof, in some cases actively condemning the women's movement and what it stood for.

In America, second-wave feminism is now close to thirty years old. In Europe it has existed for almost as long. In retrospect, what can be said about the women's movement? Did it have a lasting impact? What were its contributions? Has it empowered women? Has it transformed political dialogue? Does it have a future? Have the problems identified by the movement changed? Have they disappeared? Is the women's movement no longer relevant? Is it, in other words, just a bit of history?

The selections included here attempt to address these questions. The first two articles deal with the extent to which the women's movement has extended the parameters of public dialogue in Europe and the United States. In "The Diffusion of Consciousness in the United States and Western Europe," Ethel Klein examines the relationship of the new roles and experiences of American women with the growth of feminist consciousness, then contrasts this with the development of a feminist consciousness in Europe. She concludes that although there is greater support for feminism and the women's movement in the United States than in Europe, the political party structures in Europe might provide a better opportunity for implementing feminist policies.

In empowering women to structure a new collective identity, and to develop a discussion that underscores gender differences, the women's movement has not stressed the traditional, maternal role as did first-wave feminism. Rather, it has highlighted the concept of women as individual and autonomous. It has facilitated a dialogue in which women may see themselves as independent from the family and men, in control of their reproduction, and able to act against the forces that have marginalized them. In the early days of the women's movement this strategy generated a very negative response. The women's movement, feminism, and feminists were often denounced. To what extent has this separated women and closed off dialogue? In "Women Who Do and Women Who Don't, Join the Women's Movement," Robyn Rowland discusses the characteristics of feminists and antifeminists and the ensuing conflicts. In the author's view, reconciliation is to some extent dependent on the ability of the women's movement to get its message across more clearly.

Many of the old controversies have disappeared or decreased in importance. Many divisions that were clear-cut in the early days are now less obvious. Yet the women's movement needs to adjust its emphasis if it is to speak to the needs and concerns of ethnic and racial minorities. The final two selections in this chapter deal with minority groups, the women's movement, and feminism. The first discusses the Chicana feminist movement in the United States and the "double jeopardy" of being both female and Hispanic. Alma Garcia chronicles the problems Hispanic women have faced in defining an agenda that responds to both their sexual and ethnic oppression, comparing the Hispanic woman's experiences to those of other women of color—Asian Americans and African Americans. Eleonore Kofman and Rosemary Sales address the difficulties immigrant women have experienced in placing their problems on the public agenda in Europe.

MARIANNE GITHENS

Notes

1. Drude Dahlerup, *The New Women's Movement* (London: Sage, 1986), p. 6.
2. Joni Lovenduski, *Women and European Politics: Contemporary Feminism and Public Policy* (Hempstead: Harvester Wheatsheaf, 1986); Jane Jenson, "Struggling for Identity: The Women's Movement and the State in Western Europe," in S. Bashevkin, *Women and Politics in Western Europe* (London: Cass, 1985).
3. Joyce Gelb, "Feminism and Political Action," in R. J. Dalton and M. Kuechler, *Challenging the Political Order New Social and Political Movements in Western Democracies* (New York: Oxford University Press, 1990), p. 137.
4. Eleni Stamiris, "The Women's Movement in Greece," in Ellen Boneparth and Emily Stoper (eds.), *Women, Power and Policy: Toward the Year 2000,* 2d ed. (Elmsford, NY: Pergamon Press, 1988).
5. Susan Carroll, *Women as Candidates in American Politics* (Bloomington: Indiana University Press, 1985).
6. Marianne Githens, "Spectators, Agitators or Lawmakers: Women State Legislators," in M. Githens and J. Prestage, *A Portrait of Marginality* (New York: Longman, 1977).

The Diffusion of Consciousness in the United States and Western Europe

ETHEL KLEIN

DIFFUSION OF FEMINIST CONSCIOUSNESS IN THE UNITED STATES

The tremendous growth in feminist consciousness since the emergence of the women's movement rises out of the educational efforts of the movement itself, as well as out of the continued integration of women into nontraditional lifestyles. Feminist leaders have incorporated discussions of social equality and sex discrimination into a coherent ideology, which identified sex discrimination as women's problem, held the government responsible for ending this unfair treatment, and offered a plan of action to ease women's burdens. By 1980 the majority of men (54 percent) and women (58 percent) came to believe that differences in men and women's experiences were due to the way they were raised rather than to basic physical differences or innate abilities. Women were placing a higher priority on self-fulfillment. Only 48 percent of women in 1985, compared to 64 percent in 1974, regarded being taken care of by a loving husband as more important than making it on one's own. Most women in the late 1980s are working to help support themselves and their families, but the majority (66 percent) see their adult roles in the workplace and would continue to work even if they were financially secure.[1]

Americans have embraced many of the new roles brought about by the changing division of labor. When people think of the ideal ways to combine work, marriage, and children, a marriage where husband and wife share responsibilities is deemed preferable to the traditional division of breadwinner and housewife by the majority of men (50 percent) and women (57 percent) as compared to a scant minority of men (44 percent) and women (46 percent) in 1974. There is a general sense that women have gained more respect through recent efforts to change their status. When the movement first emerged, some men (40 percent) and women (38 percent) already felt that women were more respected in 1970 than a decade earlier. A decade later, 53 percent of men and women thought that women were more respected in 1980 than in 1970. By 1985 this assessment was even stronger, with 60 percent believing that women today are more respected.

People expect this trend toward greater role equality to continue. Most men and women (75 percent) believe that women's roles in the future will be very different from their roles in 1985 with only 10 percent believing that women will revert to more traditional roles. Moreover, most Americans (68 percent) believe that women's roles *should* continue to change, even if the consequences are unpredictable. This is a substantial increase from just five years earlier, when 57 percent favored continued change.

In the course of the last 15 years there has been a greater recognition of sex discrimination. In 1985 the majority of women felt that they did not have an equal chance with men in becoming business executives (57 percent), entering prestige professions (55 percent), or obtaining top jobs in government (57 percent). More women felt that they were excluded from leadership responsibilities in 1985 (46 percent) than in 1970 (31 percent), and the sense that women had less access to skilled jobs grew from 40 percent in 1970 to 51 percent in 1985. Overall, the percentage of women arguing that there are more advantages to being a man than a woman increased from 31 percent in 1974 to 49 percent in 1985.

Changing views on women's roles and opportunities have been accompanied by increased support for political efforts to strengthen women's status in general and the feminist movement specifically. Public support for efforts to advance women's rights increased from 44 percent of men and 40 percent of women in 1970 to most men (69 percent) and women (73 percent) in 1985. People were also considerably more positive toward the efforts of women's organizations than they had been in the past. In 1980 many more people (53 percent) felt that feminist organizations were helpful than had thought so in 1970 (34 percent). Public support for the women's liberation movement increased from 49 percent in 1972 to 60 percent in 1979. In 1985 most men and women (72 percent) strongly agreed that over the past 20 years the women's movement had helped rather than hurt working women, but many (42 percent) also believed that it made little difference in the lives of homemakers. Still, more people thought the movement had helped homemakers (33 percent) rather than hurt them (20 percent).

Trends in attitudes toward appropriate sex roles, perceived discrimination, and support for efforts to further women's rights reveal a tremendous growth and diffusion of feminist support between 1970 and 1985. Efforts toward improving women's status were initially endorsed by women with nontraditional experiences, but support then spread to other segments of the population.

· · ·

Ideas of the feminist movement have long found support among Black women. Contrary to what is often heard in public discussion, Black women have been the most supportive constituency of feminist principles. In 1970, when only 37 percent of white women embraced feminist activism as necessary, 60 percent of Black women favored feminist efforts. This gap had narrowed by 1985, but Black women were still more favorable toward women's rights than white women (78 percent versus 72 percent).

· · ·

Adherence to the ideology of sex equality is not synonymous, however, with a sense of membership in the women's movement or an endorsement of all its policies. Most Black feminists are working outside of mainstream feminist organizations to create space for discussing the problems facing Black women. There are long-standing Black women's clubs, sororities, and organizations—such as the National Council of Negro Women—that were addressing the concerns of Black women prior to the emergence of the feminist movement. As the debate over women's place became more radical, Black women lent their voice by forming the National Black Feminist Organization (1973), the National Alliance of Black Feminists (1976), and the National Association of Black Professional Women (1976). Black feminists also pressed for the establishment of the Mary McLeod Bethune Memorial Museum, the National Archive for Black Women's History, and the National Institute for Women of Color to establish the Black woman's rich history and enlighten discussion of current public policy. At the community level, most Black women address feminist concerns through their local clubs, churches, the YWCA, or neighborhood organizations rather than through newly established feminist groups (Giddings 1984; Hooks 1981).

. . .

By 1980 many more working-class women were supportive of feminist principles. In looking at the roots of sex role differentiation in society, working-class women were almost as likely as middle-class women to attribute the cause to socialization rather than biology (57 percent compared to 59 percent) and to argue that sex discrimination made it more advantageous to be a man than a woman (40 percent compared to 45 percent). These changes in role orientation and recognition of discrimination among working-class women increased support for efforts to strengthen women's role and status from 42 percent in 1970 to 54 percent in 1980 to 63 percent in 1985. Support among middle-class women increased from 57 percent in 1970 to 73 percent in 1980 to 79 percent in 1985.

. . .

FEMINIST CONSCIOUSNESS IN WESTERN EUROPE

If feminism in the United States grew in response to dramatic changes in the sexual division of labor, then one would also expect women's movements to emerge in European countries. In fact, feminist organizations did surface in most Western European democracies during the early 1970s, including France, West Germany, Italy, Holland, and Great Britain. By the end of the 1970s feminist movements had appeared in Greece and Spain as well. All of these movements have raised the issue of role equality and sex discrimination. They have taken a variety of forms and met with different degrees of success (Hills and Lovenduski 1981; Randall 1982).

Feminist concerns have also made it onto the agenda of the European Community as a whole. The Commission of the European Communities has conducted three studies in an attempt to understand the attitudes of men and women toward some of the problems their countries face. In 1983 the commission conducted a study of men and women's attitudes on women's employment situation and their role in society. The findings of this study illustrate the extent of feminist consciousness in Europe and its possible roots and consequences for feminist politics.[2]

Feminism builds on the rejection of the traditional division of labor in favor of more egalitarian roles. Most citizens of the European Community (64 percent) agree that there should be fewer differences between the respective roles of men and women. Yet when it comes to choosing work and family roles, Europeans are less likely than Americans to see an egalitarian marriage as ideal. . . . Members of the European Community divide among three scenarios for job and family roles: one where both partners have absorbing jobs and share equally in household and child care (36 percent); another where the wife works at a less demanding job and thereby takes greater responsibility for the household (30 percent); and the traditional division where the husband works and the wife runs the home (28 percent).

. . .

Approximately one-third of women in the European Community are currently employed, yet two-thirds of women say that—given a choice—they would prefer to be employed. Most women (60 percent) in the labor force say they would continue to work even if they had enough money to live as comfortably as they wished. It is important to note, however, that a significant number of women in Europe work part time (39 percent) and that most of these women (78 percent) prefer to continue with part-time work.

These patterns are similar to those found in the earlier years of the feminist movement in the United States, when support for gender equality was first embraced by younger cohorts and men and women with nontraditional experiences, and later diffused to the more traditional segments of the population. European women—and to a lesser extent, men—no longer see traditional arrangements as viable or even ideal; they welcome women's entry into the workplace but have not, as yet, fully accepted women as equals in the marketplace. In fact, most men (61 percent) and women (59 percent) tend to agree that in a period of high unemployment a man has a greater right to work than a woman. Still, acceptance of work as man's privilege is influenced by a woman's age and education. Young women are much less likely to acknowledge men's prior right to employment than older women (33 percent compared to 73 percent). Similarly, women with high levels of education are less likely to grant men preference than women who are less educated (40 percent compared to 73 percent).

The overall pattern, then, of people's assessments of traditional roles versus gender equality is related to generational differences and exposure to nontraditional experiences. However, European attitudes on gender roles also vary a great deal from country to country. For example, while there is majority agreement that differences between men and women's roles need to be reduced, there is greater support for this proposition among citizens of Greece (75 percent), France (74 percent), and Luxembourg (68 percent) than in the Netherlands (62 percent), United Kingdom (58 percent), or Belgium (55 percent). Egalitarian marriages were much more popular in Greece (51 percent), Denmark (46 percent), and France (40 percent) than in Luxembourg (25 percent), Belgium (31 percent), or Ireland (30 percent).

The multiple causes underlying these national differences need to be explored further in order to understand the constraints and opportunities for feminism in Europe. Part of the explanation is structural, rooted in birthrates, divorce rates, employment patterns, expansion of the industrial and service sector, and degree of urbanization. But this is only a partial explanation, since one finds tremendous support for feminist roles in Greece, a relatively less industrialized country with a higher birthrate and lower female labor force participation than the United Kingdom, where nontraditional roles are not as favored.

In countries such as Greece and Ireland, there is a significant domestic economy in which women produce goods, work in family businesses, and take in boarders. These activities contribute to both the family and the national economy but are not reflected in the rates of labor force participation. It would be important to explore the extent to which domestic production hinders or promotes the growth of feminism. Religion, as a means of tapping the penetration of traditional culture, is often offered as a factor hindering the acceptance of role equality and hence the emergence of feminist movements, yet one finds relatively strong feminist sentiments in such Catholic countries as France and Italy. There are undoubtedly political explanations: legal rights based on the family as opposed to the individual; the passage of social policies such as parenting leaves, family allowances, day care services, and antidiscrimination legislation that preempt political mobilization: or, from a more historical perspective, the political controversy surrounding the enfranchisement of women. These hypotheses raise a broad research agenda aimed at understanding both the general conditions that allow or push for a redefinition of women's roles—which is necessary for the emergence of feminism in any country—and country-specific constitutional and historical arrangements that facilitate or repress movement formation.

In the United States the basic tenets of feminism, belief in gender equality and acknowledgment of sex discrimination, are accepted by both men and women. While there has been little exploration of the significance of this male support, it has provided the American feminist movement with an important constituency (Klein 1984). It is unclear how feminist politics would have evolved in the United States in the face of male opposition to role equality. On the whole, European men and women also tend to agree on reducing role divisions and on images of the ideal marriage, but there are some countries where sex differences emerge. Women are considerably more egalitarian than men in Ireland (59 percent versus 71 percent) and Germany (58 percent versus 68 percent), while men are somewhat more egalitarian in the Netherlands (65 percent versus 59 percent) and the United Kingdom (62 percent versus 54 percent). The implications of these gender differences for the growth of feminism in these countries need to be explored.

The political consequences of the rejection of traditional role prescriptions depend on whether that rejection leads to the reevaluation of social and legal arrangements and a recognition of discrimination. Europeans acknowledge that men are more advantaged than women in the workplace. The majority of men (57 percent) as compared to a minority of women (27 percent) say their sex is an advantage for the work they do; women are more likely to see their sex as a disadvantage (15 percent versus 2 percent). Women argue that sex makes no difference to their work more often than men (53 percent compared to 37 percent). Comparing these responses to people's assessments in 1977 of whether their sex was an advantage to employment reveals a large shift away from a sense that women are economically advantaged by their sex in Ireland (55 percent to 20 percent), Luxembourg (55 percent to 29 percent), Belgium (41 percent to 23 percent), and Germany (37 percent to 14 percent). European men have maintained their sense of advantage, with the exception of Belgium (60 percent to 40 percent) and Ireland (83 percent to 71 percent).

While most people agree that men have a prior right to work and that men are more advantaged in the workplace, there is also a sense that women face discrimination and that this needs to be remedied. Europeans believe that women face discrimination when it comes to the number and range of jobs available to them (51 percent), salary (51 percent), prospects for promotion (51 percent), and, to a lesser extent, job security (42 percent).

Perceptions of discrimination were highest in Germany, Denmark, and France. These were also the countries where women were much more likely to be aware of discrimination than men. In Denmark, women see greater sex discrimination in salary (14 percent difference), job security (11 percent difference), and promotions (17 percent difference). German women are more likely to feel unfair treatment in the number and range of available jobs (13 percent difference), training (23 percent difference), job security (20 percent), and promotion (17 percent): French women are more aware of discrimination in job security (7 percent) and promotions (16 percent).

Having acknowledged discrimination, 65 percent point out that there are laws in their country allowing women to demand equality of treatment at work; however, more than half (58 percent) believe that these antidiscrimination laws are not applied in practice. People who believe in gender equality and show concern over employment discrimination provide a constituency for feminist movements.

Women's movements are popular in some countries and highly unpopular in others. A substantial number of people (18 percent) have no opinion about movements for women's liberation in their country, but on the whole, positive assessments (45 percent) outweigh negative judgments (37 percent) among those aware of feminist activism. More women support the movement than oppose it (47 percent versus 33 percent), while men divide evenly for and against (42 percent versus 43 percent). Feminist movements find their greatest support among women who are 15 to 39 years old or have high levels of education, while resistance is strongest among men with high levels of education.

. . .

Europeans are much more likely to support the aims of women's movements than the movements themselves. . . . Most favor fighting against prejudice

(68 percent), want to obtain true equality between men and women in their work and careers (81 percent), believe political parties should give women the same chances as men to reach positions of power (78 percent), argue for parenting leaves to care for sick children (67 percent), and agree that housewives should be compensated for caring for children (60 percent). Few people, however, favor organizing women into an independent movement aimed at transforming society (21 percent).

The majority of even the oldest and least-educated groups support feminist aims, but there is significantly greater feminist support among the young and better-educated. Sex differences emerge for 15- to 24-year-olds, with women taking a more feminist position than men on equality in politics (10 percent difference) and sharing the care of sick children (10 percent difference). Similarly, there is an average of 8 percent difference in fighting prejudice, equality at work and politics, and sick care among 40- to 54-year-olds. There are no sex differences on these four goals among people with low levels of education, but as education levels increase, women are on average (8 percent) more feminist.

In most of these countries, feminist movements grew out of the protest movements of the late 1960s and have continued to be much more radical and socialist than contemporary American feminism. Thus opinions of movements for women's liberation are more favorable in countries with active socialist movements, such as France, Italy, and Greece, than in those where socialist governments have been turned out of power, such as England and Germany.

All of these countries, however, have class-based parties that inhibit feminist organizing, arguing that feminism is a special interest that undercuts the unity of the working class and undermines the strength of labor parties. Many feminist demands—including abortion, divorce, domestic violence shelters, and rape crisis centers—fall outside the agendas of most labor movements, which traditionally eschew taking stands on social policies. Economic issues are the primary concerns facing most Europeans, particularly in this period of high unemployment and inflation. When asked to rank the importance of sex equality as a political concern, the majority (55 percent) feel it has some importance, 20 percent rank it as very important, and 21 percent see it as having little importance. This is a decline in support since 1975, when 32 percent rated gender equality as a very important issue. This decline is partly in response to the growing fiscal crisis of European states and partly due to the belief that the situation for women has been improving.

Again, the importance attached to the problems of women is a function of age, education, and sex. The problem of women's situation is seen as more important in Greece, Italy, and France than in Denmark, the United Kingdom, or the Netherlands. To what extent are these political differences due to the strength of revived socialist movements as compared to that of long-standing labor parties? Are the differences due in part to social policies that have helped incorporate women into the labor force as part of an emphasis on workplace concerns rather than concern for women's rights?

There has been a greater diffusion of support for feminism, women's movements, and feminist politics in the United States than in Europe. There is, however, a sizable feminist constituency in Europe similar to that found in the United States in the mid-1970s. The rate of increase in feminist consciousness in Europe will depend partly on how fast and in what ways changes in the sexual division of labor force men and women to question traditional arrangements. High unemployment rates are likely to dampen movement toward feminism; increased divorces and female-headed households will accelerate the process.

The politicization of women's consciousness in the United States has been limited by the social diversity of women. The fact that the United States lacks institutions such as strong parties or unions has meant that the women's movement has been unable to aggregate and coordinate activities across its diverse constituency base. This is particularly evident in efforts to organize the women's vote, where there is agreement on the overall policy agenda but serious differences—based on race and class—in the priorities given to these issues. Currently, there is no broad-based organizational vehicle—feminist organization, political party, or labor union—that is capable of organizing this vote to its full potential.

In Europe, the presence of strong socialist parties or labor unions provide potential organizational vehicles for implementing feminist policies. These organizations are often hostile to feminist claims, however, because such claims are seen to challenge the primacy of politics organized around issues of class. In those European countries where feminist movements have successfully organized outside the parties (Italy is a prime example), feminists have been able to exert enough pressure to change the political agenda in part by having their issues co-opted by the parties (Ergas 1982). Ironically, the future of feminist politics in the United States is dependent on the development of strong political organizations that can mobilize its diverse constituency, while in Europe it will require challenging strong institutions because they refuse to acknowledge interests that are not directly linked to traditional class-based issues.

Notes

1. The data discussed in this section are largely from a series of surveys conducted by the Roper organization for the Virginia Slims American Women's Opinion Poll in 1970, 1972, 1974, 1980, and 1985.
2. The analysis presented in this section is based on a study by the Commission of the European Communities entitled *European Women and Men in 1983*. The survey was conducted in ten countries of the European Community (at the request of the Directorate for Information of the Community) as a supplement to the Eurobarometer Survey no. 19, conducted in March–April 1983. The same questionnaire was put to representative samples of the population aged 15 years and over in each country. The total sample size was 9,790, all of whom were personally interviewed. The study was carried out by ten professional research companies, all members of the "European Omnibus Survey."

References

Baxter, Sandra, and Marjorie Lansing. 1983. *Women and Politics: The Visible Majority*. Ann Arbor: University of Michigan Press.

Clymer, Adam. 1983. "If Anything, Gender Gap Is Becoming Even Wider." *New York Times,* 11 December, p. E5.

Ergas, Yasmine. 1982. "1968-1979—Feminism and the Italian Party System: Women's Politics in a Decade of Turmoil." *Comparative Politics* 14 (April):253–80.

Frankovic, Kathleen. 1982. "Sex and Politics—New Alignments, Old Issues." *PS* 15:439–48.

Gelb, Joyce, and Ethel Klein. 1983. *Women's Movements: Organizing for Change in the 1980's.* Washington, D.C.: American Political Science Association.

Giddings, Paula. 1984. *When and Where I Enter: The Impact of Black Women on Race and Sex in America.* New York: Bantam Books.

Gittell, Marilyn, and Nancy Naples, 1982. "Activist Women: Conflicting Ideologies." *Social Policy* 12 (Summer):25–27.

Hills, Jill, and Joni Lovenduski. 1981. *The Politics of the Second Electorate: Women and Public Participation.* London: Routledge & Kegan Paul.

Hooks, Bell. 1981. *Ain't I A Woman: Black Women and Feminism.* Boston: South End Press.

Ketter, Scott, 1985. "Public Opinion in 1984." In Gerald Pomper et al., *The Elections of 1984: Reports and Interpretations.* Chatham, N.J.: Chatham House.

Klein, Ethel. 1984. *Gender Politics.* Cambridge, Mass.: Harvard University Press.

———. 1985. "The Gender Gap: Different Issues, Different Answers." *The Brookings Review* 3 (Winter):33–37.

Miller, Arthur H., and Oksana Malanchuk. 1983. "The Gender Gap in the 1982 Election." Paper presented at the Annual MEH.

Oberschall, Anthony. 1973. *Social Conflict and Social Movements.* Englewood Cliffs, N.J.: Prentice-Hall.

Randall, Vicki. 1982. *Women and Politics.* New York: St. Martin's Press.

Schroedel, Jean Reith. 1985. *Alone in a Crowd: Women in the Trades Tell Their Stories.* Philadelphia: Temple University Press.

Shapiro, Robert Y., and Harpreet Mahajan. 1986. "Trends in Gender Differences in Policy Preferences." *Public Opinion Quarterly* 50 (Spring):42–61.

Smith, Tom W. 1984. "The Polls: Gender and Attitudes Toward Violence." *Public Opinion Quarterly* 48:384–96.

Useem, Michael. 1975. *Protest Movements in America.* Indianapolis: Bobbs-Merrill.

Wertheimer, Barbara. 1977. *We Were There: The Story of Working Women in America.* New York: Pantheon.

Women Who Do and Women Who Don't, Join the Women's Movement: Issues for Conflict and Collaboration

ROBYN ROWLAND

METHODOLOGY

Women Who Do and Women Who Don't, Join the Women's Movement ... explored the experiences and personal statements of pro- and antimovement women, attempting to clarify why some women choose feminism and others reject it. Twenty-four women from five countries (the United States, England, Canada, Australia, and New Zealand) contributed, and their backgrounds varied across race, class, age (17 to 75 years), marital status, sexual preference, and whether they had children or not. Selecting the sample was difficult, but I aimed for as wide a diversity across the above variables as was possible.

RESULTS AND DISCUSSION

The results of the explorations ... are at times startling, not least of all because of the impossibility of drawing a distinct line between feminist and antifeminist women. ...

The antifeminists *do* argue that sex differences are innate and biologically determined, and feminists claim social conditioning as causal. This issue is important because it determines the position taken by both groups concerning the concept of equality. Antifeminists want to be "equal but different" and see feminists as wanting to be the *same* as men, as forefeiting their uniqueness. This leads antifeminists to scorn the use of nonsexist language, and the implementation of similar education for girls and boys. They are ignorant of the arguments with respect to sexist language, and fear a sameness between girls and boys, girls thus losing sight of the values of motherhood and the power within this role as perceived by antifeminists.

Surprisingly, the antifeminists often claim to be the true feminists and to represent stage III of the women's movement. Stage I was emancipation, stage II is liberation (equal pay and opportunities), and stage III is recognition for "uniquely female roles." They express no understanding of oppression and have no sense of being part of the social group "woman," which Juliet Mitchell points out . . . is a prerequisite for feminist consciousness. Antifeminists see their own success in terms of their individual merit, and the assumption is strong that if a woman has "failed" or is unhappy, there is something wrong with her, and not with society.

Feminists reject the idea of "uniquely" sex-typed roles, seeing this as a ploy by which men opt out of child rearing and women are excluded from the work force. They have experienced the oppression of woman as an individual and as group, and have a group consciousness and a belief in cooperative action.

Relationships with men were discussed. Antifeminists argue that feminists hate men and marriage. They invariably describe their husbands as "wonderful" and "loving." They profess to like men, yet see them as untrustworthy, less worthy and moral, "slightly inferior," and as users of women. They express the fear that the removal of the protective role from men would lead to "risks to the group, in particular the female, from the isolated nonresponsible male." Men thus need the moral guidance and control of women and family; otherwise, they are a threat. Any woman, therefore, who threatens this view of woman as moral, would place the power base and therefore antifeminists, at risk. There is a naive division of men into two groups; the married, loving, and controlled husbands; and the un-married, childless, and irresponsible men. Dworkin has suggested that the an-tifeminist woman sees the violence in man and has devised a way of controlling it. She bargains continuously with the male not to use his power over her, and be-lieves "liberalism" leads to greater violence against women "often in the name of humanism and freedom" (Dworkin, 1983b, p. 34). The antifeminist arguments against pornography would be an example of this. In my book, the antifeminists certainly give the impression that "good" husbands are the results of good man-agement and a reflection, therefore, of their own greater worth as women.

For feminists, too, men are a problem. Contrary to the antifeminist belief, most of the feminists expressed a desire to relate to men, but at differing levels, and not at a cost to their selfhood. The experiences of some contributors with in-cest, man's violence during and after war, and the study of rape, illuminate the re-ality of woman as victim of male violence. It is the violence and cruelty of men that feminists loathe. Antifeminists seem either to ignore this, or believe it only exists in the "odd" case. As Scutt points out. . . , "the real problem for the women's liberation movement is that we care about men too much" (p. 220). In fact, if women were strong enough to withdraw support from men, change would be eas-ier to effect.

Men's attitudes to sexuality offended feminists and antifeminists alike. An-tifeminists see feminists as colluding in the sexual revolution; however, most fem-inists see that period as a man's revolution, with massive sexual exploitation of women's bodies. Both Purdue (antifeminist) and Spender (feminist) advocate celibacy as a potential life-style.

Relationships with other women varied among antifeminists. Some state that they find men more interesting, while others had always had close women friends. But "women's libbers" are attacked virulently as a threat to home and family, and to the identity of antifeminists as women and mothers. In comparison, feminists speak of the joy and really fulfilling experience of that first occasion when they "made the simple but momentous discovery that I *liked* women" (Spender, p. 222).

Antifeminists argue that feminists devalue motherhood and family life, forcing women into the work force. It is clear, however, that feminists value the *experience* as opposed to the *institution* of motherhood and that this provides them with a real dilemma: how to recreate family life so that it does fulfill the needs of people for "security, commitment and continuity" (Curthoys, p. 224), without destroying a woman's self-identity in the process.

The complexities of racial and cultural differences also emerged. The racism inherent within the women's movement itself, particularly in Australia, is reason enough for alienating black and migrant women from the movement, as Skyes and Fesl point out. Alternatively, Te Awekotuku placed male oppression of all women as primary, over white woman's collusion in black oppression. A similar issue emerges with respect to class. Feminists are aware of both these realities within the lives of women and the problems they pose for a united women's movement. The issues were not mentioned by antifeminists.

Abortion was obviously the most divisive issue. The orientation of antifeminists to the abortion debate takes the position of the unborn child as preordinate. The feminist debate centers on concern for the woman and her right to decide on abortion. Antifeminists misrepresent the "pro-choice" view of feminists as "pro-abortion." All antifeminists discussed this issue. Landolt points out that it divided the women's movement in Canada, and Purdue comments that "this is the dividing line." Both these antifeminists see women as conned by men on this issue, with Landolt commenting: "I believe that feminists have fallen into a male trap. They are attempting to adapt women to a wombless male society, instead of adapting society to meet the needs of women" (p. 225). Feminist Barbara Ehrenreich has elsewhere described the issue as double-edged, noting that freer abortion may further undercut "male responsibility towards women and children" (1981, p. 99).

CONCLUDING COMMENTS

. . . This brief summary gives an indication of the development of conflict between feminist and antifeminist groups of women. The goals to which members are committed differ both in their ideological base and also in their socioeconomic base, which is important. Feminists, in their challenge of the economic base, make middle-class antifeminists adamant about protecting their position. It is not expressed this way in the antifeminist literature, but the issues of class and race are on the whole ignored, which is a political position in itself.

Concomitant with this is a genuine fear of power loss on the part of antifeminists. If a woman's sense of personal power lies in her role as mother in the family, she needs to defend this base from threat. If she has other sources of power, for example, in her work, her identity is different. Self-esteem, self-identity, a sense of personal control, of being important and needed in her chosen role, are necessary to *all* women and they will defend the perceived source of these feelings. Ehrenreich has commented:

> It is almost as if the economic stresses of the seventies split women into two camps: those who went *out* to fight for some measure of economic security . . . and those who stayed at home to hold on to what they had. (1981, p. 99)

And what feminism offers as a sense of personal power may involve women in upheaval or turmoil before they achieve a sense of relief and power. Antifeminists opt to accommodate to patriarchy, rather than fight it, because they fear the results of the failure of the fight more than they desire the changes that ensue. Dworkin puts the issue of power succinctly when she writes of antifeminists:

> The powerless are not quick to put their faith in the powerless. The powerless need the powerful, especially in sex oppression because it is inescapable, everywhere. . . . Because feminism is a movement for liberation of the powerless by the powerless in a closed system based on their powerlessness, right-wing women judge it a futile movement. Frequently they also judge it a malicious movement in that it jeopardizes the bargains with power that they can make; feminism calls into question for the men confronted by it the *sincerity* of women who conform without political resistance. (her emphasis, 1983, p. 33)

• • •

In terms of reducing ideological conflict, three basic differences are operating. Feminists work to eliminate sexism, while antifeminists reject the theory of male oppression as a feminist paranoia and see no sexism operating. Secondly, feminists stress the social conditioning of the sexes, and reject innate and immutable sex differences, while antifeminists stress the "naturalness" of sex differences based on biological differences. Thirdly, feminists see women as part of a social group sharing the experience of oppression; antifeminists see the individual woman as responsible for her situation and her life. Therefore, any problems experienced by a woman are *her* problems and not representative of a shared powerlessness. These inform the campaigns of the groups and will continue to create conflict while they are firmly held.

• • •

Women's liberation is often deliberately misrepresented. But it could be, too, that the movement has failed to get its message across clearly enough. Dialogue is essential. Antifeminists may work to undermine all the positive changes women have made. But if they continue to support antifeminist men, they may lose more than they bargained for, and find, like Anita Bryant, that they have given men the ammunition they need to fire at *all* women—including homemakers. They may find that: the education they do want for their daughters is no longer available for women, who are "naturally" mothers and need no further education; they are refused jobs because a lower qualified man needs one; or find that their divorced daughter is unable to obtain credit because we have gone back to the good old days when men supported women—except that their daughter's husband turns out *not* to be "decent" and leaves her with three children to support, no money, and no maintenance.

The one continuing link between feminists and antifeminists is the reality of our shared oppression. Hope lies in this reality of common struggle and the possibility that antifeminists may be challenged by their own internal conflicts.

References

Bardwick, J. *In transition.* New York: Holt, Rinehart & Winston, 1979.

Dworkin, A. *Right-wing women: The politics of domesticated females.* London: The Women's Press, 1983. (a)

Dworkin, A. Antifeminism. *Trivia: A Journal of Ideas,* 1983, Spring, 6–35. (b)

Ehrenreich, B. The women's movements: Feminist and antifeminist. *Radical America,* 1981, *15,* 93–101.

Firestone, S. *The dialectic of sex: A case for feminist revolution.* London: Paladin, 1972.

Friedan, B. *The feminine mystique.* U.S.A.: Penguin, 1963.

Gerlach, L., & Hine, V. *People, power, change: Movements of social transformation.* Indianapolis, Ind.: Bobbs-Merrill, 1970.

Heberle, R. *Social movement: An introduction to political sociology.* New York: Appleton-Century-Crofts, 1951.

Mitchell, J. 1984. In Robyn Rowland's *Women who do and women who don't, join the women's movement.* London: Routledge and Kegan Paul.

Rowland, R. Directions in sex role research: Past, present and future. *Australian Psychologist,* 1980, *15,* 419–426.

Rowland, R. An exploratory study of the childfree lifestyle. *Australian and New Zealand Journal of Sociology,* 1982, *18*(1), 17–30.

Rowland, R. (Ed.), *Women who do and women who don't, join the women's movement.* London: Routledge and Kegan Paul, 1984.

Schlafly, P. *The power of the positive woman.* New York: Arlington House Press, 1977.

Scutt, M. 1984. Quoted in ch. 7 in Robyn Rowland's *Women who do and women who don't, join the women's movement.* London: Routledge and Kegan Paul.

Sherif, C. W. *Orientation in social psychology.* New York: Harper & Row, 1976.

Sherif, M. *Group conflict and co-operation: Their social Psychology.* London: Routledge and Kegan Paul, 1966.

Sherif, M., & Sherif, C. *An outline of social psychology.* (Revised ed.) New York: Harper & Row, 1956.

Snyder, D., & Tilly, C. Hardship and collective violence in France, 1830–1950. *American Sociological Review,* 1972, 37, 520–532.

Spender, D. *Women of ideas and what men have done to them.* London: Routledge and Kegan Paul, 1982.

Toch, H. *The social psychology of social movements.* London: Menthuen, 1966.

The Development of Chicana Feminist Discourse, 1970–1980

ALMA M. GARCIA

DEFINING FEMINISM FOR WOMEN OF COLOR

A central question of feminist discourse is the definition of feminism. The lack of consensus reflects different political ideologies and divergent social-class bases. In the United States, Chicana feminists shared the task of defining their ideology and movement with white, Black, and Asian American feminists. Like Black and Asian American feminists, Chicana feminists struggled to gain social equality and end sexist and racist oppression. Like them, Chicana feminists recognized that the nature of social inequality for women of color was multidimensional (Cheng 1984; Chow 1987; Hooks 1981). Like Black and Asian American feminists, Chicana feminists struggled to gain equal status in the male-dominated nationalist movements and also in American society. To them, feminism represented a movement to end sexist oppression within a broader social protest movement. Again, like Black and Asian American feminists, Chicana feminists fought for social equality in the 1970s. They understood that their movement needed to go beyond women's rights and include the men of their group, who also faced racial subordination (Hooks 1981). Chicanas believed that feminism involved more than an analysis of gender because, as women of color, they were affected by both race and class in their everyday lives. Thus, Chicana feminism, as a social movement to improve the position of Chicanas in American society, represented a struggle that was both nationalist and feminist.

Chicana, Black, and Asian American feminists were all confronted with the issue of engaging in a feminist struggle to end sexist oppression within a broader nationalist struggle to end racist oppression. All experienced male domination in their own communities as well as in the larger society. Ngan-Ling Chow (1987) identifies gender stereotypes of Asian American women and the patriarchal family structure as major sources of women's oppression. Cultural, political, and economic constraints have, according to Ngan-Ling Chow (1987), limited the full development of a feminist consciousness and movement among Asian American women. The cross-pressures resulting from the demands of a nationalist and a feminist struggle led some Asian American women to organize feminist organizations that, however, continued to address broader issues affecting the Asian American community.

Black women were also faced with addressing feminist issues within a nationalist movement. According to Dill (1983), Black women played a major historical role in Black resistance movements and, in addition, brought a feminist component to these movements (Davis 1983; Dill 1983). Black women have struggled with Black men in nationalist movements but have also recognized and fought against the sexism in such political movements in the Black community (Hooks 1984). Although they wrote and spoke as Black feminists, they did not organize separately from Black men.

Among the major ideological questions facing all three groups of feminists were the relationship between feminism and the ideology of cultural nationalism or racial pride, feminism and feminist baiting within the larger movements, and the relationship between their feminist movements and the white feminist movement.

CHICANA FEMINISM AND CULTURAL NATIONALISM

. . . Throughout the seventies, Chicana feminists viewed the struggle against sexism within the Chicano movement and the struggle against racism in the larger society as integral parts of Chicana feminism. As Nieto Gomez (1976, p. 10) said:

> Chicana feminism is in various stages of development. However, in general, Chicana feminism is the recognition that women are oppressed as a group and are exploited as part of *la Raza* people. It is a direction to be responsible to identify and act upon the issues and needs of Chicana women. Chicana feminists are involved in understanding the nature of women's oppression.
>
> It is not surprising that more and more Chicanas are forced to go to work in order to supplement the family income. The children are farmed out to a relative to baby-sit with them, and since these women are employed in the lower income jobs, the extra pressure placed on them can become unbearable.

Thus, while the Chicano movement was addressing the issue of racial oppression facing all Chicanos, Chicana feminists argued that it lacked an analysis of sexism. Similarly, Black and Asian American women stressed the interconnectedness of race and gender oppression. Hooks (1984, p. 52) analyzes racism and sexism in terms of their "intersecting, complementary nature." She also emphasizes that one struggle should not take priority over the other. White (1984) criticizes Black men whose nationalism limited discussions of Black women's experiences with sexist oppression. The writings of other Black feminists criticized a Black cultural nationalist ideology that overlooked the consequences of sexist oppression (Beale 1975; Cade 1970; Davis 1971; Joseph and Lewis 1981). Many Asian American women were also critical of the Asian American movement whose focus on racism ignored the impact of sexism on the daily lives of women. The participation of Asian American women in various community struggles increased their encounters with sexism (Chow 1987). As a result, some Asian American women developed a feminist consciousness and organized as women around feminist issues.

CHICANA FEMINISM AND FEMINIST BAITING

. . . Chicana, Black, and Asian American feminists experienced similar cross-pressures of feminist-baiting and lesbian-baiting attacks. As they organized around feminist struggles, these women of color encountered criticism from both male and female cultural nationalists who often viewed feminism as little more than an "anti-male" ideology. Lesbianism was identified as an extreme derivation of feminism. A direct connection was frequently made that viewed feminism and lesbianism as synonymous. Feminists were labeled lesbians, and lesbians as feminists. Attacks against feminists—Chicanas, Blacks, and Asian Americans—derived from the existence of homophobia within each of these communities. As lesbian women of color published their writings, attacks against them increased (Moraga 1983).

• • •

In the 1970s, Chicana feminists reconciled their demands for an end to sexism within the Chicano movement and their rejection of the saliency of gender oppression by separating the two issues. They clearly identified the struggle against sexism in the Chicano movement as a major issue, arguing that sexism prevented their full participation (Fallis 1974; Gomez 1976). They also argued that sexist behavior and ideology on the part of both Chicano males and Anglos represented the key to understanding women's oppression. However, they remained critical of an analysis of women's experiences that focused exclusively on gender oppression.

Chicana feminists adopted an analysis that began with race as a critical variable in interpreting the experiences of Chicano communities in the United States. They expanded this analysis by identifying gender as a variable interconnected with race in analyzing the specific daily life circumstances of Chicanas as women in Chicano communities. Chicana feminists did not view women's struggles as secondary to the nationalist movement but argued instead for an analysis of race and gender as multiple sources of oppression (Cotera 1977). Thus, Chicana feminism went beyond the limits of an exclusively racial theory of oppression that tended to overlook gender and also went beyond the limits of a theory of oppression based exclusively on gender that tended to overlook race.

• • •

Although Chicana feminists continued to be critical of building coalitions with white feminists toward the end of the seventies, they acknowledged the diversity of ideologies within the white feminist movement. Chicana feminists sympathetic to radical socialist feminism because of its anticapitalist framework wrote of working-class oppression that cut across racial and ethnic lines. Their later writings discussed the possibility of joining with white working-class women, but strategies for forming such political coalitions were not made explicit (Cotera 1977; Marquez and Ramirez 1977).

• • •

Chicana feminists continued to stress the importance of developing autonomous feminist organizations that would address the struggles of Chicanas as members of an ethnic minority and as women. Rather than attempt to overcome the obstacles to coalition building between Chicana feminists and white feminists, Chicanas called for autonomous feminist organizations for all women of color (Cotera 1977; Gonzalez 1980; Nieto 1975). Chicana feminists believed that sisterhood was indeed powerful but only to the extent that racial and class differences were understood and, above all, respected. As Nieto (1974, p. 4) concludes:

> The Chicana must demand that dignity and respect within the women's rights movement which allows her to practice feminism within the context of her own culture. . . . Her approaches to feminism must be drawn from her own world.

References

Almaguer, Tomas. 1974. "Historical Notes on Chicano Oppression." *Aztlan* 5:27–56.

Balderama, Sylvia. 1981. "A Comprehensive Bibliography on La Chicana." Unpublished paper, University of California, Berkeley.

Barrera, Mario. 1974. "The Study of Politics and the Chicano." *Aztlan* 5:9–26.

———. 1979. *Race and Class in the Southwest*. Notre Dame, IN: University of Notre Dame Press.

Beale, Frances. 1975. "Slave of a Slave No More: Black Women in Struggle." *Black Scholar* 6:2–10.

Cade, Toni. 1970. *The Black Woman*. New York: Signet.

Candelaria, Cordelia. 1980. "Six Reference Works on Mexican American Women: A Review Essay." *Frontiers* 5:75–80.

Castro, Tony. 1974. *Chicano Power*. New York: Saturday Review Press.

Chapa, Evey. 1973. "Report from the National Women's Political Caucus." *Magazin* 1:37–39.

Chavez, Henri. 1971. "The Chicanas." *Regeneracion* 1:14.

Cheng, Lucie. 1984. "Asian American Women and Feminism." *Sojourner* 10:11–12.

Chow, Esther Ngan-Ling. 1987. "The Development of Feminist Consciousness Among Asian American Women." *Gender & Society* 1:284–99.

Combahee River Collective. 1981. "A Black Feminist Statement." Pp. 210–18 in *This Bridge Called My Back: Writings by Radical Women of Color*, edited by Cherrie Moraga and Gloria Anzaldua. Watertown, MA: Persephone.

Cordova, Teresa et al. 1986. *Chicana Voices: Intersections of Class, Race, and Gender*. Austin, TX: Center for Mexican American Studies.

Cotera, Marta. 1973. "La Mujer Mexicana: Mexicano Feminism." *Magazin* 1:30–32.

———. 1977. *The Chicana Feminist*. Austin, TX: Austin Information Systems Development.

———. 1980. "Feminism: The Chicana and Anglo Versions: An Historical Analysis." Pp. 217–34 in *Twice a Minority: Mexican American Women*, edited by Margarita Melville. St. Louis, MO: C. V. Mosby.

Davis, Angela. 1971. "Reflections on Black Women's Role in the Community of Slaves." *Black Scholar* 3:3–13.

———. 1983. *Women, Race and Class*. New York: Random House.

Del Castillo, Adelaida. 1974. "La Vision Chicana." *La Gente:* 8.

Dill, Bonnie Thornton. 1983. "Race, Class, and Gender: Prospects for an All-Inclusive Sisterhood." *Feminist Studies* 9:131–50.

Dunne, John. 1967. *Delano: The Story of the California Grape Strike*. New York: Strauss.

Fallis, Guadalupe Valdes. 1974. "The Liberated Chicana—A Struggle Against Tradition." *Women: A Journal of Liberation* 3:20.

Flores, Francisca. 1971a. "Conference of Mexican Women: Un Remolino. *Regeneration* 1(1):1–4.

———. 1971b. "El Mundo Femenil Mexicana." *Regeneracion* 1(10):i.

Fong, Katheryn M. 1978. "Feminism Is Fine, But What's It Done for Asian America?" *Bridge* 6:21–22.

Freeman, Jo. 1983. "On the Origins of Social Movements." Pp. 8–30 in *Social Movements of the Sixties and Seventies*, edited by Jo Freeman. New York: Longman.

———. 1984. "The Women's Liberation Movement: Its Origins, Structure, Activities, and Ideas." Pp. 543–56 in *Women: A Feminist Perspective*, edited by Jo Freeman. Palo Alto, CA: Mayfield.

Garcia, Alma M. 1986 "Studying Chicanas: Bringing Women into the Frame of Chicano Studies." Pp. 19–29 in *Chicana Voices: Intersections of Class, Race, and Gender,* edited by Teresa Cordova et al. Austin, TX: Center for Mexican American Studies.

Garcia, F. Chris and Rudolph O. de la Garza. 1977. *The Chicano Political Experience.* North Scituate, MA: Duxbury.

Gomez, Anna Nieto. 1971. "Chicanas Identify." *Hijas de Cuauhtemoc* (April):9.

———. 1973. "La Femenista." *Encuentro Femenil* 1:34–47.

———. 1976. "Sexism in the Movement." *La Gente* 6(4):10.

Gonzalez, Sylvia. 1980. "Toward a Feminist Pedagogy for Chicana Self-Actualization." *Frontiers* 5:48–51.

Hernandez, Carmen. 1971. "Carmen Speaks Out." *Papel Chicano* 1(June 12):8–9.

Hooks, Bell. 1981. *Ain't I a Woman: Black Women and Feminism.* Boston: South End Press.

———. 1984. *Feminist Theory: From Margin to Center.* Boston: South End Press.

Joseph, Gloria and Jill Lewis. 1981. *Common Differences: Conflicts in Black and White Feminist Perspectives.* Garden City, NY: Doubleday.

Kushner, Sam. 1975. *Long Road to Delano.* New York: International.

LaRue, Linda. 1970. "The Black Movement and Women's Liberation." *Black Scholar* 1:36–42.

Loeb, Catherine. 1980. "La Chicana: A Bibliographic Survey." *Frontiers* 5:59–74.

Longeaux y Vasquez, Enriqueta. 1969a. "The Woman of La Raza." *El Grito del Norte* 2(July):8–9.

———. 1969b. "La Chicana: Let's Build a New Life." *El Grito del Norte* 2(November):11.

———. 1970. "The Mexican-American Woman." Pp. 379–84 in *Sisterhood Is Powerful,* edited by Robin Morgan. New York: Vintage.

———. 1971. "Soy Chicana Primero." *El Grito del Norte* 4(April 26):11.

Macias, Anna. 1982. *Against All Odds.* Westport, CT: Greenwood.

Marquez, Evelina and Margarita Ramirez. 1977. "Women's Task Is to Gain Liberation." Pp. 188–94 in *Essays on La Mujer,* edited by Rosaura Sanchez and Rosa Martinez Cruz. Los Angeles: UCLA Chicano Studies Center.

Martinez, Elizabeth. 1972. "The Chicana." *Ideal* 44:1–3.

Matthiesen, Peter. 1969. *Sal Si Puedes: Cesar Chavez and the New American Revolution.* New York: Random House.

Meier, Matt and Feliciano Rivera. 1972. *The Chicanos.* New York: Hill & Wang.

Moraga, Cherrie. 1981. "La Guerra." Pp. 27–34 in *This Bridge Called My Back: Writings by Radical Women of Color.* edited by Cherrie Moraga and Gloria Anzaldua. Watertown, MA: Persephone.

———. 1983. *Loving in the War Years.* Boston: South End Press.

Moraga, Cherrie and Gloria Anzaldua. 1981. *This Bridge Called My Back: Writings by Radical Women of Color.* Watertown, MA: Persephone.

Moreno, Dorinda. 1979. "The Image of the Chicana and the La Raza Woman." *Garacol* 2:14–15.

Mujeres en Marcha. 1983. *Chicanas in the 80s: Unsettled Issues.* Berkeley, CA: Chicano Studies Publication Unit.

Muñoz, Carlos, Jr. 1974. "The Politics of Protest and Liberation: A Case Study of Repression and Cooptation." *Aztlan* 5:119–41.

Nabokov, Peter. 1969. *Tijerina and the Courthouse Raid.* Albuquerque, NM: University of New Mexico Press.

Navarro, Armando. 1974. "The Evolution of Chicano Politics." *Aztlan* 5:57–84.

Nelson, Eugene. 1966. *Huelga: The First 100 Days.* Delano, CA: Farm Workers Press.

Nieto, Consuelo. 1974. "The Chicana and the Women's Rights Movement." *La Luz* 3(September):10–11, 32.

———. 1975. "Consuelo Nieto on the Women's Movement." *Interracial Books for Children Bulletin* 5:4.

Orozco, Yolanda. 1976. "La Chicana and 'Women's Liberation.'" *Voz Fronteriza* (January 5):6, 12.

Piven, Frances Fox and Richard A. Cloward. 1979. *Poor People's Movements: Why They Succeed, How They Fail.* New York: Vintage.

Portillo, Cristina, Graciela Rios, and Martha Rodriguez. 1976. *Bibliography on Writings on La Mujer.* Berkeley, CA: University of California Chicano Studies Library.

Riddell, Adaljiza Sosa. 1974. "Chicanas en el Movimiento." *Aztlan* 5:155–65.

Rincon, Bernice. 1971. "La Chicana: Her Role in the Past and Her Search for a New Role in the Future." *Regeneracion* 1(10):15–17.

Rowbotham, Sheila. 1974. *Women, Resistance and Revolution: A History of Women and Revolution in the Modern World.* New York: Vintage.

Ruiz, Vicki I. 1987. *Cannery Women, Cannery Lives: Mexican Women, Unionization, and the California Food Processing Industry, 1930–1950.* Albuquerque: University of New Mexico Press.

Segura, Denise. 1986. "Chicanas and Triple Oppression in the Labor Force." Pp. 47–65 in *Chicana Voices: Intersections of Class, Race and Gender,* edited by Teresa Cordova et al. Austin, TX: Center for Mexican American Studies.

Shockley, John. 1974. *Chicano Revolt in a Texas Town.* South Bend, IN: University of Notre Dame Press.

Vidal, Mirta. 1971. "New Voice of La Raza: Chicanas Speak Out." *International Socialist Review* 32:31–33.

White, Frances. 1984. "Listening to the Voices of Black Feminism." *Radical America* 18:7–25.

Wong, Germaine Q. 1980. "Impediments to Asian-Pacific-American Women Organizing." Pp. 89–103 in *The Conference on the Educational and Occupational Needs of Asian Pacific Women.* Washington, DC: National Institute of Education.

Woo, Margaret. 1971. "Women + Man = Political Unity." Pp. 115–16 in *Asian Women,* edited by Editorial Staff. Berkeley, CA: University of California Press.

Towards Fortress Europe?

ELEONORE KOFMAN AND ROSEMARY SALES

CULTURAL PRACTICES

The growth of European racism has been accompanied by a rise in religious fundamentalism and the reassertion of patriarchal values, which may yield increasing control over ethnic minority women by their community leaders. At the same time, the pursuit of multicultural and integrationist policies are often based on stereotyped views of ethnic and immigrant social structures that tend to reinforce a standard image of family life and women's position and oppression within it. Such policies are nearly always mediated through male community leaders as a study of Australian multiculturalism has shown (Lepervanche, 1990).

At the same time, women's attempts to disengage themselves from unwelcome domestic situations and to seek help from outside the home may meet with incomprehension because the extended family is, in their case, supposed to offer assistance. Welfare providers often act with a stereotyped view of migrant cultures, which makes them reluctant to intervene in family matters. Asian women who report marital violence, for example, are much more likely than white women to be returned to their families and told to resolve the matter within their own communities. Following the murder of an Asian woman by her husband in London in April 1991, protesters criticised "racist and patronising attitudes from (police) officers who put violence down to cultural and religious differences . . . the problem was swept under the carpet" (*Hackney Gazette,* 1991).

Lutz (1990) argues, in her study of Turkish women in the Netherlands and West Germany, that Islamic women in these countries have tended to represent the typical migrant woman. These women are orientalised such that their oppression is considered to stem simply from the patriarchal culture paradigm ascribed to all women originating from countries with large Islamic populations. This then denies differences such as those of class, internal ethnicity (Turks, Kurds, Alevi, Arabs) religious observance and practice, and women's rights and positions in the country of origin. The geographical variety of Islam and its relationship to the construction of the nation-state are thus obliterated.

In this time of resurgence in racism and xenophobia, women are often propelled into the frontline, as symbols and bearers of ethnic values and identities and reproducers of the group (Yuval-Davis & Anthias, 1989). The affirmation of ethnic identity often focuses on traditional practices, including the most patriarchal aspects, and women's conformity to these values. Norms of sexual modesty and chastity are frequently reinforced in immigrant communities and represent the symbol of the group's integrity (Lutz, 1990). This in turn serves to confirm the image of women's subordination and backwardness in comparison to the liberated western female. The wearing of headscarves to school by Muslim girls provoked debate in Belgium, Britain, and France, and helped to fuel the idea of a rampant Islamic fundamentalism. Similarly, the battle for single-sex schools for girls, but not necessarily for boys, reveals the role of women in preserving cultural identities.

The French case illustrates many of these developments. An opinion poll in November 1989, at a time of heated discussion about the wearing of headscarves by three Muslim girls in a school in Creil (Lloyd & Waters, 1991), revealed that a large majority of French respondents saw Islam as violent, backward-looking, fanatical, and oppressive towards women (Hargreaves, 1991; for a pro-secular feminist interpretation, see Spensky, 1990). Within the Muslim population and antiracist organisations, however, attitudes towards education and the secular tradition were profoundly divided. While 30% of a group of Muslims interviewed in November 1989 were in favour of allowing headscarves to be worn in state schools, 45% were not (Hargreaves, 1991, p. 7). Religious observance, too, varied markedly, especially amongst children of North African immigrants. The two organisations set up to encourage political participation by men and women of North African background (*France Plus*) and to fight racism (*SOS-Racisme*) have pursued an integrationist stance and republican values and minimised the *droit à la différence* (the right to be different). The vice-president of *SOS-Racisme*, Hayette Boudjema, adopted a harder line on the headscarf affair than the organisation as a whole, declaring that it was a sign of oppression and constraint exercised upon Muslim women (Hargreaves & Stenhouse, 1991, p. 30). Feminist issues only formed a minor part of the public debate raised, for example, by the organisation Expressions Maghrébines au Féminin (Lloyd & Waters, 1991). In this instance women were not alone in opposing traditional values, but it is often difficult for them to adopt more distinctively feminist positions for fear of appearing to be disloyal to their group.

The emergence of feminist perspectives in such conflictual situations when the group feels itself threatened poses particular problems. The counterposing of feminist demands to antiracism by male community leaders serves to marginalise the needs of black women. Women's organisations themselves often tend to form part of a larger male-dominated organisation.

· · ·

CONCLUSION

. . . The concerns of women and of black people have tended to be seen separately both at national and EC level: *Women* are implicitly understood to be white women, and *black people* as black men. This is reflected in the lack of proposals for measures to combat racism in the Social Charter, which places considerable emphasis on equal rights between men and women, and the absence of women in the debates over migration. An example of the latter was given by Pauline Green MEP for London North at a conference held in London in March 1991 that aimed at raising the specific concerns of migrant women within Europe. She reported that the EC's Migrants' Forum had at its first meeting 87 delegates, of whom only 3 were women. Ironically, Britain, which has among the worst records on women's rights within Europe, has the strongest legislation on race. The long-established black community, most of whom have full citizenship rights, has allowed the development of a wider and stronger network of black organisations, including women's organisations, than in other European states, where migrant status has been much more fragile. Recent demonstrations and riots in Belgium and France involving black youth may well push the EC into taking issues of disadvantage and discrimination more seriously.

With increased racism and xenophobia on the one hand, and the rise of fundamentalism and reassertion of patriarchal values on the other, it is even more urgent that the specific needs of black and migrant women are not marginalised, but are placed on the agenda, both at local and national level, and within Europe-wide institutions.

References

Allen, Sheila, & Macey, Marie. (1990). Race and ethnicity in the European context. *British Journal of Sociology, 41*, 375–393.

Balibar, Etienne. (1991). Es gibt keinen staat in Europa: racism and politics in Europe today. *New Left Review, 186*, 5–19.

Beechey, Veronica. (1987). *Unequal work.* London: Verso.

Bruegel, Irene. (1989). Sex and race in the Labour market. *Feminist Review, 32*, 49–68.

Bunyan, Tony. (1991). Towards an authoritarian European state. *Race and Class, 32*(3), 19–30.

Callovi, Giuseppe. (1990). L'Europe des Douze au défi de l'immigration. *L'Evénement Européen, 11*, 27–46.

Camiller, Patrick. (1989). Beyond 1992: the Left and Europe. *New Left Review, 175*, 5–18.

Castles, Stephen, Booth, Helen, & Wallace, T. (1984). *Here for good: Western Europe's new ethnic minorities.* London: Pluto.

Collectif espagnol. (1990). Les sans-papiers en Espagne. *L'Evénement Européen, 11*, 135–154.

Commission for Racial Equality (CRE). (1986). *Race and housing in Hackney: Report of a formal investigation.* London: Author.

Edmonds, M., & Patterson, M. (1990). Slaves of the rich: report on Filipino women. *Sunday Times.*

European Commission. (1988). *The social situation and employment of migrant women.* Brussels: Author.

European Commission. (1989). *Social integration of third country migrants.* Brussels: Author.

European Parliament. (1990). *Report of expert committee on racism and xenophobia.* Submission to European Commission (July) and European Parliament (October). Brussels: Author.

Freeman, Gary. (1989). Immigrant labour and racial conflict: the role of the state. In Philip Ogden & Paul White (Eds.), *Migrants in modern France. Population mobility in the later 19th and 20th centuries* (pp. 160–1176). London: Unwin Hyman.

Goldsmith, J. (1990). *The effects on women of the creation of the European internal market in 1992 with particular reference to the problems of black and ethnic minority women in the UK.* Report prepared for Anita Pollack MEP, National Alliance of Women's Organisations.

Gordon, Paul. (1986). Racism and social security. *Critical Social Policy, 17*, 22–39.

Grahl, John, & Teague, Paul. (1989). The cost of neoliberal Europe. *New Left Review, 174*, 33–50.

Hackney Gazette. (1991, May 24). Report on demonstration at local police station. p. 2.

Hakim, Catherine. (1979). *Occupational segregation: A comparative study.* Research Paper 9. London: Department of Education and Science.

Hargreaves, Alec. (1991). Islam in France. Introduction. *Modern and Contemporary France, 45*, 3–7.

Hargreaves, Alec, & Stenhouse, Timothy. (1991). Islamic beliefs among youths of North African origin in France. *Modern and Contemporary France, 45*, 27–35.

Institut Nationale de la Statistique et des Etudes Economiques (INSEE). (1987). *Données Sociales.* Paris: Author.

Klug, Francesca. (1989). "Oh to be in England": the British case study. In Nira Yuval-Davis & Floya Anthias (Eds.), *Woman-nation-state* (pp. 16–35). London: Macmillan.

Lepervanche, Marie de. (1990). Holding it together: multiculturalism, nationalism, women and the state in Australia. Paper presented at the 12th World Congress of Sociology, Madrid.

Lloyd, Cathie. (1990). 1992 and ethnic minorities in France. Background paper for British TUC conference, 1992: Freedom of Movement and Race Equality.

Lloyd, Cathie, & Waters, Hazel. (1991). France: one culture, one people. *Race and Class, 32* (3), 49–66.

Lutz, Helma. (1990). The myth of the "other." Western representation and images of migrant women of so-called "Islamic background." Paper presented at the 12th World Congress of Sociology, Madrid.

Mariniello. (1991). Italy: two perspectives. Racism in paradise? *Race and Class, 32*(3), 79–84.

Martin, P. (1990). *Unfinished story: Turkish migration to Western Europe.* Geneva: ILO.

Messina, Anthony. (1989). Anti-immigrant illiberalism and the "new" ethnic and racial minorities of western Europe. *Patterns of Prejudice, 23* (3), 17–31.

Organisation for Economic Cooperation and Development (OECD). (1985). *The Integration of Women into the Economy.*

Pieterse, Jan. (1991). Fictions of Europe. *Race and Class, 32* (3), 3–10.

Rathzel, Nora. (1991). Germany: one race, one nation? *Race and Class, 32*(3), 31–48.

Reed, Tanya. (1991, June 2). Wives' dilemma: be beaten or deported. *The Observer* (London).

Rose, David. (1991, June 2). Cabinet split over Baker's tough line on Refugees. *The Observer* (London), p. 00.

Saunders, O. (1990). Residence and the non-EEC spouse. *Solicitors Journal, 134,* 591–594.

Schnapper, Dominique. (1991). *La France de l'intégration. Sociologie de la nation en 1990.* Paris: Gallimard.

Social Trends. (1990). London: HMSO.

Spensky, Martine. (1990). Identités multiples: l'affaire du foulard. *Modern and Contemporary France, 42,* 48–50.

Webber, Frances. (1991). From ethnocentrism to Euro-racism. *Race and Class, 32,* 11–18.

Williams, Fiona. (1987). Race and the discipline of Social Policy. *Critical Social Policy, 20.*

Wrench, J. (1990). Employment and the labour market: reports 3 and 4. *New Community,* January and July.

Yuval-Davis, Nira, & Anthias, Flora. (1989). (Eds.). *Women-nation-state.* London: Macmillan.

Women against Fundamentalism. (1990). *Newsletter No. 1.*

FURTHER READING FOR CHAPTER 6

Bashevkin, S. (ed.). 1985. *Women and Politics in Western Europe.* London: Cass.

Boneparth, E., and E. Stoper (eds.). 1988. *Women, Power and Policy Toward the Year 2000.* Elmsford, NY: Pergamon Press.

Bystydzienski, J. M. (ed.). 1992. *Women Transforming Politics.* Bloomington: Indiana University Press.

Collins, P. Hill. 1990. *Black Feminist Thought: Knowledge, Consciousness and the Politics of Empowerment.* Boston: Unwin Hyman.

Dahlerup, D. 1986. *The New Women's Movement: Feminism and Political Power in Europe and the USA.* London: Sage.

Deckard, B. 1983. *The Women's Movement.* New York: HarperCollins.

Freeman, J. 1975. *The Politics of Women's Liberation.* New York: Longman.

Katzenstein, M. Fainsod, and C. McClurg Mueller (eds.). 1987. *The Women's Movement of the United States and Western Europe.* Philadelphia: Temple University Press.

Klein, R., and D. L. Steinberg (eds.). 1989. *Radical Voices: A Decade of Feminist Resistance*. Oxford: Pergamon Press.

Lovenduski, J. 1986. *Women and European Politics Contemporary Feminism and Public Policy*. Hempstead: Harvester Wheatsheaf.

Lovenduski, J. 1990. "Feminism and Western European Politics: An Overview." In D. W. Urwin and W. E. Paterson (eds.), *Politics in Western Europe Today*. London: Longman.

Lovenduski, J., and J. Outshoorn (eds.). 1986. *The New Politics of Abortion*. London: Sage.

MacKinnon, C. 1987. *Feminism: Unmodified Discourses on Life and Law*. Cambridge: Harvard University Press.

Mans Bridge, J. J. 1990. "Organizing for the ERA: Cracks in the fascade of unity" in Tilly and Gurin (eds.). *Women, Politics and Change*. New York: Russell Sage Foundation.

West, G., and R. L. Blumberg (eds.). 1990. *Women and Social Protest*. New York: Oxford University Press.

CHAPTER
7

Feminism
and Its Political Context

Feminism is defined by a common core of ideas but takes many forms. Variations in political circumstances give feminists different priorities. The context is set by the history of the countries or communities in which feminists live, work, and organize; the relative weight of religious beliefs; the kind of government, whether liberal democratic or authoritarian; whether the state is strong or weak, federal or unitary; and the role of the state in the provision of social goods. A multinational or multiracial community will generate characteristic forms of political activity and patterns of participation that will affect feminist politics, just as they affect other political activities.

Thus feminists in different countries vary in their political strategies and agendas. Not only is it important when assessing feminist politics to be aware of such factors—it is a good idea to describe the political environment of the activity we are studying. Such mapping of **institutions**, **ideas**, and **social structures** enables us to locate, and therefore to understand better, the activities of different women and helps us avoid making assumptions and drawing conclusions that deny differences between women. The awareness of multiculturalism is important for understanding differences between, and well as within, countries.

This point has been well made by Hester Eisenstein, an American feminist academic who worked as a "femocrat" in Australia between 1980 and 1986. She has written about the different impression that you get of the world when you view it from different places. Careful to detail the specificity of her experiences, she follows the feminist principle that, only when one is aware of the limitations of a particular experience is it possible to generalize from it. Although she was comparatively well-informed about feminism in other countries when she went to Australia, it was only when she began to think and learn about the nature of Australian feminism that she realized how much she overdrew intellectually on her experience in the United States.[1]

The different shapes of the women's movement in different countries has to do with the receptivity of political **institutions**, and reflects different resources, opportunities, and traditions. The greater openness of many American higher education institutions offers oppotunities that are not available in much of Europe. Exceptionally, in the Netherlands, a major reform of higher education offered the chance to establish women's studies programs during the 1980s and in France the wide remit of Yvette Roudy's Ministry of Women led to the establishment of several professorships of women's studies in the French university system. In practice, feminists will pursue the strategy that is most likely to succeed in their particular context when attempting to influence public life. This is an insight that can only come if the institutional arrangements of the countries under discussion are known.

Gisela Kaplan explores this issue when reflecting on the dominance of English speakers in feminist debate. She argues that European feminism has much to offer that has not been exported. Because knowledge about women's movements tends to be transmitted in English, it is Anglo-American, especially U.S., feminism, that is considered the norm. There are parallels between the women's movements in America and elsewhere, but the distinctive nature of American political institutions means there are also considerable contrasts. Liberal feminism has been strong in the United States, but in Europe socialist feminism has been the dominant force, a reflection of the political opportunity structures there. The similarities and differences in European women's movements, and their relationship to their domestic political institutions, are discussed in my essay on women's movements and public policy.[2]

The intellectual traditions and the role of the intelligentsia, as it is sometimes called, varies considerably between countries. For the past two decades or so, French philosophy has been enormously influential on radical thought of all kinds. French feminist thought has been widely exported, producing considerable industries of American and European scholars engaged in decoding and adapting the ideas of French feminism. Toril Moi shows how French feminist theorists, from Simone de Beauvoir to Julia Kristeva, have been influenced by the philosophical traditions of French intellectuals. Some of the implications of this are obvious; for example, literary criticism and modern psychoanalytic thought have been more important sources of ideas than political theory or social history. Moi writes that the early concern by French feminists with psychoanalysis "signals a central preoccupation in the Parisian intellectual milieux." Another preoccupation is with language, particularly with linguistic theory. Psychoanalysis and linguistic theory come together in the work of Jacques Lacan, who inspired so much French feminist writing. Moi explains Lacan's core ideas and defines the terms needed for a reading of the French feminist theorists.

Simone de Beauvoir, of course, is regarded by many as the founder of modern feminism, and her significance is undisputed. But the ideas of Cixous, Irigaray, Kristeva, and their less well-known contemporaries are politically important for several reasons. They offer a discussion of how power is embedded in the language feminists use to describe their oppression. Thus the seemingly simple act of recognizing that one is dominated and oppressed is made difficult by the lack of accurate words and ideas to describe the specific oppression of subordinate groups. The feminist literary critics of France, and their American and European followers, offer ideas about power, reflecting their intellectual and cultural origins. The ideas that have been formed in the world of literacy criticism and psychoanalytic thought have come to have increasing influence on political sociologists, political theorists, and other political commentators including political scientists.

Gemma Tang Nain illustrates the impact of social structures on feminism in her consideration of the effect of racism in Britain and the United States on the women's movements. She argues that the largely black society of her native Caribbean makes for a significantly less racist environment than is found in Britain or the United States, two mainly white countries. This means the divisions among Caribbean women reflect ideological rather than racial divisions, while in the United States and Britain feminism is plagued by racial and ideological splits. In other words, feminist movements are likely to reflect other divisions in their society. Nain then discusses the ways in which racism divides feminists. The family has been an important issue here. On the one hand the family is the location of the domestic division of labor and of considerable violence, and it therefore can be regarded as the site of much of women's oppression. On the other hand the family is, for the black communities, a crucial site of resistance to the oppression of racist society. Thus black feminists are cross-pressured. Thus feminist are cross pressured. Their racial (and/or class) and gender interests are in conflict.[3] Black feminists in the United States and Britain have been highly critical of white feminists for not recognizing this contradiction.[4] Nain concludes that the formation of black women's movements was a necessary response to the combined alienation black women experienced from male-dominated black movements and from white-dominated women's movements. Black women exposed the racism of the women's movement and the sexism of the black movement. White feminists have been made aware of their racism in the conferences, journals, and gatherings of the women's movement. Feminists have been alerted to the problem. But can we be sure that they will stay alert, that things have changed that much? And if they have, does such political work as conscious changing stay done? Or is this work that must be repeated continuously? And whatever the answer, what are the implications for the agenda and organization of the women's movement?

JONI LOVENDUSKI

Notes

1   Hester Eisenstein (1991) "Learning to speak Australian," *Gender Shock*, ch.2, London: Allen and Unwin.
2. Joni Lovenduski, "The Women's Movement and Public Policy in Western Europe," from M. Buckley and M. Anderson (eds.), *Women, Equality and Europe,* London: Macmillan, 1988.
3   An analogous argument may be made in respect of class and gender.
4   The term "woman of colour" is used in the United States, but not in Europe.

Contemporary Western European Feminism

GISELA KAPLAN

To redress the balance a little in international feminist debate, even in the late 1980s, is an urgent undertaking. That debate, up to the 1980s, has been dominated by English-speaking countries and by the English language as the international lingua franca. Not surprisingly, an English-language feminism has evolved which, over more than two decades, has become highly sophisticated. It is international in the sense that it comes from different countries and supra-national in the sense that the discourse no longer requires national identification. Judging by the great familiarity feminist writers of Canada, Australia, England and the USA have with each other, names that appear side by side in bookshops of any of these countries, it has become almost irrelevant from where the texts originated.

There is another side to this, however. English-speaking international feminism, by its own accepted standards of communication, has felt too secure in the belief that it is international when it is so only in the narrowest sense. Spivak noted in the late 1970s that 'International Feminism' in US universities spasmodically included a little French, Italian, German and Latin American feminist information (Spivak, 1981: 155), but most of it was confined to the English-language circuit. Undoubtedly though, there has been a growing interest in feminism in other parts of the world, including western Europe, and there is a growing number of people quite rightly lamenting the fact that so few publications on Europe are available in English. Indeed, few publications on European feminism pre-date 1985. Amongst them are those of French writers, and a few titles by German and Italian writers which have recently been translated into English.

There may be well over 300 million native speakers of English in the world, but just in western Europe alone there are almost as many who do not count English as their native language. Non-English-language countries have partaken in the feminist discourse largely as listeners and as recipients. This challenges the notion that all European feminism has been 'imperial' as Amos and Parmar have suggested. Mainstream feminism is undoubtedly 'white' feminism but, despite their justifiable criticism of international feminism, it has definitely never been Eurocentric (Amos & Parmar, 1984). What these writers demonstrate is that they too have allowed themselves to believe that the English-language voices from Europe, which are almost exclusively British, somehow represent and make up Europe. The Dutch, Greek, Finnish, Portuguese, Swiss or Icelandic woman is usually not found in the English-language discourse.

The channels of written communication have been, and still are, limited by these linguistic barriers and they are not always vastly improved by the possibility of translation. First, it would be ludicrous to imagine that every text in every European language should or could be translated into every other. Second, there are delays in publications of texts that mark important stages in the women's movement of the respective country. Foreign language material must prove its worth before being taken over by a local publisher, and that may take years. Some feminist books are now beginning to cross national boundaries, but often it is five or even ten years after they have first appeared in their original language. Third, there are accidental criteria for a publication of a text, governed by such factors as whether someone happens to have seen and read a title in another language and is willing to promote it and find a suitable publisher. Although these conditions apply to any non-feminist text as well, it must be remembered that the publishing houses which are heavily involved in the publication of feminist texts are usually feminist publishing ventures operating on shoestring budgets and are therefore not in a position to take risks.

How unpredictable and haphazard the communication of feminist ideas via the written text is across western European countries can be gauged by an examination of book titles and authors in different countries. My own visits to bookshops in London, Paris and Berlin revealed that there was rarely an overlap of titles among the bookshops in these cities, apart from those stemming from English-speaking countries. A Norwegian author appeared in one, a Danish author in another, a few Italian authors in this but not that country, a Dutch author (Anja Meulenbelt) had one publication in French, another in English and yet another in German, but her complete works were not found together in one language and one place outside the Netherlands. The flow of feminist books across national borders has not been studied systematically to date but there is a good deal of evidence for the impression that this flow is rarely fast, systematic or based on reciprocity. In 1989, one was still more likely to find American and English texts (in the original or in translation) in feminist bookshops than books and journals from neighbouring countries.

The problem of dissemination of information via the written text has hardly been helped by official national attitudes, which at times almost seemed intent on suppressing feminist material. This is generally not true of English-language countries and there are other exceptions, but I have found, more often than not, that general bookshops rarely carry feminist titles. Some national and state libraries had no stock of the most representative titles; for instance, one of the large German state libraries that I visited only held a handful of feminist texts and most of these were in languages other than German, so that even these few were inaccessible to a wide circle of readers. In response to such an untenable situation, feminists have taken the matter into their own hands and have created special feminist archives: a very diffuse and almost clandestine network throughout western Europe that greets the visitor with the kind of fast, efficient, relaxed and friendly service typical of underground conspiratorial groups.

The funding of these ventures differs vastly between countries and regions but overall, with some laudable exceptions, they are noticeably skewed at the bottom end of funding and subsidy schemes for libraries and archives (Gassen, 1981:28). Most of the archives that I visited in West Germany were maintained on very small allowances or on no state budgets at all. The excellent archive in Berlin, for instance, at the time of my visit was run entirely without funding and built on strong will, long hours and idealism alone. Such archives cannot hope to build up comprehensive stocks of knowledge in one specialised area, let alone branch out and provide representative material of other countries. It has occurred to more than one devoted volunteer (feminist) archivist that the preservation of records of feminist activism, culture and thought for the future is disconcertingly insecure. In this respect, mainland European countries are at a distinct disadvantage in comparison with English-speaking, including new world, countries like the USA and Australia. In most of western Europe, the seeming resistance of some national and university libraries, and ultimately of governments, to preserve feminist knowledge can actively undermine the formulation and dissemination of western European feminist thought.

Fortunately, ideas do not only travel via the route of libraries and bookshops. European women have taken charge of their own intra-national communication via journals, conferences, meetings and intensive networking. The impetus for doing so came from the self-understanding of the movements as being intrinsically *international,* notwithstanding the fact that they were indigenous and nationally definable. In almost all movements, whether they started in the late 1960s or as recently as the 1980s, a strong sense of solidarity and sisterhood across national and European borders developed almost at once. It was partly built on the small stock of shared knowledge that almost all movements had in common. Apart from the French contribution by Simone de Beauvoir, *The Second Sex,* which preceded any other feminist book of the postwar era by over a decade, there were titles from English-speaking countries, mainly the USA, which found their way into most European countries: Betty Friedan's book *The Feminine Mystique* (1963), Germaine Greer's work *The Female Eunuch* (1970), Shulamith Firestone's *The Dialectics of Sex* (1971) and *Sexual Politics* (1972) by Kate Millet (Lovenduski, 1986: 67; Schenk, 1980: 89; De Vries, 1981: 395).

That these books became so very influential had a good deal to do with the similarity of women's experiences worldwide. Simone de Beauvoir was once asked towards the end of her life (she died in April 1986) what she had learned over the years for and about women and why she was a feminist. Her reply was: 'I have understood the unfathomable depth of women's oppression' (Schwarzer, 1983: 73). Every woman in the movement, even if she was not capable of formulating the agonising truth of women's oppression as Simone de Beauvoir had done, understood that there was oppression and that the experience of the 'second sex' was not confined geographically but was universal. The titles which did much to launch the second-wave women's movements succeeded in doing so because they reassured women that their gnawing (but often suppressed) feelings of injustice were indeed warranted, that they were not alone in thinking about their disadvantage and they were not unique in their predicament. 'Women of the world unite' was not just an empty catch-cry but arose from the firm belief that there was such a thing as a gender-based discrimination that concerned women everywhere.

Within its own national boundaries, each western European country has produced feminists right across the ideological spectrum. Each country has its share of liberal, socialist or radical feminists and a share in public protest actions on such issues as rape, abortion or employment. The price for diversity is often fragmentation, which indeed some second-wave movements in western Europe have experienced. The disadvantages of local fragmentation have often been blurred, however, by participation in intra-national and international forums. If the forum was capable of remaining international, it did so by entering already existing communication channels and networks of English-speaking overseas countries, by supplying arguments, news and general information to international feminist journals, news networks and organisations. A second venue of internationalism was assured for those feminists who joined forces with other international movements of the postwar era, such as international socialism, the peace movement and the gay liberation movement. The feminist and gay movements, as well as the peace movement and international socialism, have a well-established international forum for generalist and scholarly conferences with extraordinarily high participation rates of delegates from all over the world. All these activities ensure a level of continuity of thought and provide a basis for shared knowledge and spontaneous communication, superseding even the efforts of women in the 1920s.

Western European feminists of the second wave have developed unusual strengths all their own. Although each country has produced proponents of every political shade and for any issue dubbed 'women's issue', the European strength lies in what appears to be national specialisations and emphases. As if a division of labour had been planned, western European countries complement each other by difference. French feminism, while it can boast many very important groups, has made its best known contributions in highly abstract philosophical debates. Italian feminism is much more readily identifiable with political activism and political theory of the left than it is with other areas. German feminism is chiefly pragmatic or historical in orientation but has excelled also in film-making. Dutch feminism relies heavily on consciousness raising. Greek feminism, however embryonic, is revolutionary in fervour. Swedish and Finnish feminism is much more a mainstream political reformism than elsewhere, while Norway, Denmark and Portugal have made outstanding contributions to literary feminism. Most countries have produced a wealth of new literature of astounding variety and excellence. Whatever the predominant paradigm of a country may be, together, western European countries offer a very original tapestry, rich in colour and surprising in design and texture, which has helped shape the face of culture, of political debate, of literature and of everyday life.

References

Amos, V. and Parmar, P. (1984) 'Challenging Imperial Feminism', *Feminist Review* 17, Autumn, 3–19.

De Vries, Petra (1981) 'Feminism in the Netherlands', *Women's Studies International Quarterly*, vol. 4, no. 4, 389–407.

Gassen, Gisela (ed.) (1981) *Wohin gent die frauen bewegung? 22 Proto kolle*, Frankfurt/M.: Fischer Verlag.

Lovenduski, Joni (1986) *Women and European Politics*, Brighton: Harvester.

Schenk, Herrad (1980) Die feministische Herausforderung: 150 Jahre Frauenbewegung in Deutschland, Munchen: C.H. Beck.

Schwartzer, Alice (1983) *Simone Debeauvoir*, Reinbeck/Hamburg: Rowohlt.

Spivak Gayarti Chakravorty (1981) 'French Feminism in an International Frame', *Yale French Studies*, no. 62, 154–184.

From Simone de Beauvoir to Jacques Lacan

TORIL MOI

SIMONE DE BEAUVOIR AND MARXIST FEMINISM

Simone de Beauvoir is surely the greatest feminist theorist of our time. Yet in 1949, when she published *The Second Sex*, she was convinced that the advent of socialism alone would put an end to the oppression of women and consequently considered herself a socialist, not a feminist. Today her position is somewhat different. In 1972 she joined the MLF (Women's Liberation Movement) and publicly declared herself a feminist for the first time. She explained this belated recognition of feminism by pointing to the new radicalism of the women's movement: 'The women's groups which existed in France before the MLF was founded in 1970 were generally reformist and legalistic. I had no desire to associate myself with them. The new feminism is radical, by contrast' (*Simone de Beauvoir Today*, 29). This change of emphasis has not however led her to repudiate socialism:

> At the end of *The Second Sex* I said that I was not a feminist because I believed that the problems of women would resolve themselves automatically in the context of socialist development. By feminist, I meant fighting on specifically feminine issues independently of the class struggle. I still hold the same view today. In my definition, feminists are women—or even men, too—who are fighting to change women's condition, in association with the class struggle, but independently of it as well, without making the changes they strive for totally dependent on changing society as a whole. I would say that, in that sense, I am a feminist today, because I realised that we must fight for the situation of women, here and now, before our dreams of socialism come true.

> (*Simone de Beauvoir Today*, 32)

In spite of its commitment to socialism, *The Second Sex* is based not on traditional Marxist theory, but on Sartre's existentialist philosophy. Beauvoir's main thesis in this epochal work is simple: throughout history, women have been reduced to objects for men: 'woman' has been constructed as man's Other, denied the right to her own subjectivity and to responsibility for her own actions. Or, in more existentialist terms: patriarchal ideology presents woman as immanence, man as transcendence. Beauvoir shows how these fundamental assumptions dominate all aspects of social, political and cultural life and, equally important, how women themselves internalize this objectified vision, thus living in a constant state of 'inauthenticity' or 'bad faith', as Sartre might have put it. The fact that women often enact the roles patriarchy has prescribed for them does not prove that the patriarchal analysis is right: Beauvoir's uncompromising refusal of any notion of a female nature or essence is succinctly summed up in her famous statement 'One is not born a woman; one becomes one'.[1]

Though most feminist theorists and critics of the 1980s acknowledge their debt to Simone de Beauvoir, relatively few of them seem to approve of her espousal of socialism as the necessary context for feminism. In this respect it would seem that her most faithful followers are to be found in Scandinavia and in Britain. In the Scandinavian social democracies the debate within the women's movement has never explicitly pitted non-socialist against socialist feminists, whereas considerable energy has been spent arguing over the kind of socialism feminists ought to adopt. Thus in the early 1970s in Norway there was a considerable degree of hostility between the centralized Maoist 'Women's Front' and the more anti-hierarchical 'Neo-feminists' whose adherents represented everything from right-wing social democracy to more radical, left-wing forms of socialism and Marxism.[2] Scandinavian feminist criticism reflects this emphasis on socialism, particularly in its tendency to situate the textual analysis within a thoroughly researched account of class structures and class struggle at the time of the literary text's production.[3] The recent rise to power of conservative political parties in many of the Scandinavian countries has only superficially modified this picture: in spite of the emergence of some 'light-blue' Establishment feminists, the overwhelming majority of Scandinavian feminists still feel at home somewhere on the political Left.

Traditionally, British feminism has been more open to socialist ideas than has its American counterpart. Most Marxist-feminist work in Britain, however, is not carried out within the specific field of literary theory and criticism. In the 1980s it is women working within the recently developed areas of cultural studies, film studies and media studies, or in sociology or history, who are producing the most interesting political and theoretical analyses. . . .

FRENCH FEMINISM AFTER 1968

The new French feminism is the child of the student revolt of May 1968 in Paris, which almost toppled one of the more repressive of the so-called Western democracies. For a while, the realization that 'May '68' had almost managed the apparently impossible inspired an exuberant political optimism among left-wing intellectuals in France. 'Les événements' enabled them to believe both that change was at hand and that intellectuals had a real political role to play within it. At the end of the 1960s and in the early 1970s, political activism and intervention thus seemed meaningful and relevant to students and intellectuals on the Left Bank.

It was in this politicized intellectual climate, dominated by various shades of Marxism, particularly Maoism, that the first French feminist groups were formed. In many ways, the direct experience that led to the formation of the first French women's groups in the summer of 1968 was strikingly similar to that of the American women's movement.[4] In May, women had fought alongside men on the barricades only to find that they were still expected to furnish their male comrades with sexual, secretarial and culinary services as well. Predictably enough, they took their cue from American women and started to form their own women-only groups. One of the very first of these groups chose to call itself 'Psychanalyse et Politique'. Later, when the politics of feminism had reached a more advanced stage, this group, which in the meantime had founded the influential publishing house *des femmes* ('women'), renamed itself 'politique et psychanalyse', reversing the priorities of politics and psychoanalysis and dropping the hierarchical capitals once and for all. The concern with psychoanalysis signals a central preoccupation in the Parisian intellectual *milieux*. Whereas the American feminists of the 1960s had started by vigorously denouncing Freud, the French took it for granted that psychoanalysis could provide an emancipatory theory of the personal and a path to the exploration of the unconscious, both of vital importance to the analysis of the oppression of women in patriarchal society. In the English-speaking world, the feminist arguments in favour of Freud were not heard until Juliet Mitchell published her influential book *Psychoanalysis and Feminism* in 1974, which was translated and published in France by *des femmes*.

Though French feminist theory was already flourishing by 1974, it has taken a considerable period to reach women outside France. One of the reasons for the relatively limited influence of French theory on Anglo-American feminists is the 'heavy' intellectual profile of the former. Steeped as they are in European philosophy (particularly Marx, Nietzsche and Heidegger), Derridean deconstruction and Lacanian psychoanalysis, French feminist theorists apparently take for granted an audience as Parisian as they are. Though rarely wilfully obscure, the fact that few pedagogical concessions are made to the reader without the 'correct' intellectual co-ordinates smacks of elitism to the outsider. This holds for Hélène Cixous's intricate puns and Luce Irigaray's infuriating passion for the Greek alphabet, as well as for Julia Kristeva's unsettling habit of referring to everyone from St Bernard to Fichte or Artaud in the same sentence. That the exasperated reader sometimes feels alienated by such uncompromising intellectualism is hardly surprising. Once the Anglo-American reader has overcome the effects of this initial culture-shock, however, it doesn't take long to discover that French theory has contributed powerfully to the feminist debate about the nature of women's oppression, the construction of sexual difference and the specificity of women's relations to language and writing.

One problem for the English-speaking reader, however, is caused by the French word 'féminin'. In French there is only one adjective to 'femme', and that is 'féminin',[5] whereas English has two adjectives to 'woman': 'female' and 'feminine'. It has long been recognized usage among many English-speaking feminists to use 'feminine' (and 'masculine') to represent social constructs (gender) and to reserve 'female' (and 'male') for purely biological aspects (sex). The problem is that this fundamental political distinction is lost in French. Does *écriture féminine*, for instance, mean 'female' or 'feminine' writing? How can we know whether this or any other such expression refers to sex or to gender? There is of course no standard answer. . . .

. . . With a few exceptions, such as Claudine Herrmann and Anne-Marie Dardigna,[6] French feminist critics have preferred to work on problems of textual, linguistic, semiotic or psychoanalytic theory, or to produce texts where poetry and theory intermingle in a challenge to established demarcations of genre. Despite their political commitment, such theorists have been curiously willing to accept the established patriarchal canon of 'great' literature, particularly the exclusively male pantheon of French modernism from Lautréamont to Artaud or Bataille. There can be no doubt that the Anglo-American feminist tradition has been much more successful in its challenge to the oppressive social and political strategies of the literary institution.

. . .

It has often been claimed that the new generation of French feminist theorists have rejected Simone de Beauvoir's existentialist feminism entirely. Turning away from Beauvoir's liberal desire for equality with men, the argument goes, these feminists have emphasized difference. Extolling women's right to cherish their specifically female values, they reject 'equality' as a covert attempt to force women to become like men.[7] The picture, however, is somewhat more complex than this. For all h er existentialism, Simone de Beauvoir remains the great mother-figure for French feminists, and the symbolic value of her public support for the new women's movement was enormous. Nor is it true to say that her brand of socialist feminism remains without followers in France. In 1977 Beauvoir and other women founded the journal *Questions féministes,* which aims to provide a forum precisely for various socialist and anti-essentialist forms of feminism.[8] The Marxist-feminist sociologist Christine Delphy, who holds that women constitute a class, was, for example, one of its founding members.

In spite of her very different theoretical orientation, many of Julia Kristeva's central preoccupations (her desire to theorize a social revolution based on class as well as gender, her emphasis on the construction of femininity) have much more in common with Beauvoir's views than with Hélène Cixous's romanticized vision of the female body as the site of women's writing. Similarly, Luce Irigaray's impressive critique of the repression of woman in patriarchal discourse reads at times like a post-structuralist rewriting of Beauvoir's analysis of woman as man's Other. (Given that Heidegger seems to be the common source of both Lacan's psychoanalytic 'Other', which influenced Irigaray's study, and Beauvoir's existentialist 'Other', this is hardly surprising.) Though existentialism in general was marginalized by the shift to structuralism and post-structuralism in the 1960s, it would seem that nothing dates *The Second Sex* more, in relation to the new women's movement in France, than Beauvoir's rejection of psychoanalysis. Cixous, Irigaray and Kristeva are all heavily indebted to Lacan's (post-) structuralist reading of Freud, and any further investigation of their work therefore requires some knowledge of the most central Lacanian ideas.[9]

JACQUES LACAN

The Imaginary and the Symbolic Order constitute one of the most fundamental sets of related terms in Lacanian theory and are best explained in relation to each other. The Imaginary corresponds to the pre-Oedipal period when the child believes itself to be a part of the mother, and perceives no separation between itself and the world. In the Imaginary there is no difference and no absence, only identity and presence. The Oedipal crisis represents the entry into the Symbolic Order. This entry is also linked to the acquisition of language. In the Oedipal crisis the father splits up the dyadic unity between mother and child and forbids the child further access to the mother and the mother's body. The phallus, representing the Law of the Father (or the threat of castration), thus comes to signify separation and loss to the child. The loss or lack suffered is the loss of the maternal body, and from now on the desire for the mother or the imaginary unity with her must be repressed. This first repression is what Lacan calls the primary repression and it is this primary repression that opens up the unconscious. In the Imaginary there is no unconscious since there is no lack.

The function of this primary repression becomes particularly evident in the child's use of the newly acquired language. When the child learns to say 'I am' and to distinguish this from 'you are' or 'he is', this is equivalent to admitting that it has taken up its allotted place in the Symbolic Order and given up the claim to imaginary identity with all other possible positions. The speaking subject that says 'I am' is in fact saying 'I am he (she) who has lost something'—and the loss suffered is the loss of the imaginary identity with the mother and with the world. The sentence 'I am' could therefore best be translated as 'I am that which I am not', according to Lacan. This re-writing emphasizes the fact that the speaking subject only comes into existence because of the repression of the desire for the lost mother. To speak as a subject is therefore the same as to represent the existence of repressed desire: the speaking subject *is* lack, and this is how Lacan can say that the subject is that which it is not.

To enter into the Symbolic Order means to accept the phallus as the representation of the Law of the Father. All human culture and all life in society is dominated by the Symbolic Order, and thus by the phallus as the sign of lack. The subject may or may not like this order of things, but it has no choice: to remain in the Imaginary is equivalent to becoming psychotic and incapable of living in human society. In some ways it may be useful to see the Imaginary as linked to Freud's pleasure principle and the Symbolic Order to his reality principle.

This exposition of the transition from the Imaginary to the Symbolic Order requires some further comments. The Imaginary is, for Lacan, inaugurated by the child's entry into the Mirror Stage. Lacan seems to follow Melanie Klein's views of child development in so far as he postulates that the child's earliest experience of itself is one of fragmentation. One might have said that at first the baby feels that its body is in pieces, if this wouldn't give the mistaken impression that the baby *has* a sense of 'its' body at this early stage. Between the ages of 6 to 8 months the baby enters the Mirror Stage. The principal function of the Mirror Stage is to endow the baby with a unitary body image. This 'body ego', however, is a profoundly alienated entity. The child, when looking at itself in the mirror—or at itself on its mother's arm, or simply at another child—only perceives another human being with whom it merges and identifies. In the Imaginary there is, then, no sense of a separate self, since the 'self' is always alienated in the Other. The Mirror Stage thus only allows for *dual* relationships. It is only through the triangulation of this structure, which, as we have seen, occurs when the father intervenes to break up the dyadic unity between mother and child, that the child can take up its place in the Symbolic Order, and thus come to define itself as separate from the other.

Lacan distinguishes between the Other (Autre) with a capital 'O' and the other with a small 'o'. For our purposes it is useful to look at a few of the many different significations these concepts take on in Lacan's texts. The most important usages of the Other are those in which the Other represents language, the site of the signifier, the Symbolic Order or any third party in a triangular structure. Another, slightly different way of putting this is to say that the Other is the locus of the constitution of the subject or the structure that produces the subject. In yet another formulation, the Other is the differential structure of language and of social relations that constitute the subject in the first place and in which it (the subject) must take up its place.

If, for Lacan, it is the entry into the Symbolic Order that opens up the unconscious, this means that it is the primary repression of the desire for symbiotic unity with the mother that *creates* the unconscious. In other words: the unconscious emerges as the result of the repression of desire. In one sense the unconscious *is* desire. Lacan's famous statement 'The unconscious is structured like a language' contains an important insight into the nature of desire: for Lacan, desire 'behaves' in precisely the same way as language: it moves ceaselessly on from object to object or from signifier to signifier, and will never find full and present satisfaction just as meaning can never be seized as full presence. Lacan calls the various objects we invest with our desire (in the symbolic order) *objet a* ('objet petit a'—'a' here standing for the other (autre) with a small 'a'). There can be no final satisfaction of our desire since there is no final signifier or object that can *be* that which has been lost forever (the imaginary harmony with the mother and the world). If we accept that the end of desire is the logical consequence of satisfaction (if we are satisfied, we are in a position where we desire no more), we can see why Freud, in *Beyond the Pleasure Principle,* posits death as the ultimate object of desire—as Nirvana or the recapturing of the lost unity, the final healing of the split subject.

Notes

1. The politics of *The Second Sex* has been the object of much debate. For an introduction to some of the issues raised see the articles by Felstiner, Le Doeuff, Dijkstra and Fuchs in *Feminist Studies,* 6, 2, Summer 1980.
2. For an account of this and other developments in the new women's movement in Norway see Haukaa.
3. In Denmark Jette Lundboe Levy has furnished a superbly researched study of the historical context of the great Swedish novelist Victoria Benedictsson. In Norway Irene Engelstad and Janneken

Øverland have explored the representation of class and sexuality in the works of Amalie Skram and Cora Sandel respectively (see the articles in their joint collection *Frihet til å skrive*).

4. See pp. 21–4.
5. The French 'femelle', denoting a female animal, is only used pejoratively about women.
6. The pioneering work was Herrmann's *Les Voleuses de langue*. Due to the fact that the author teaches in the US, it is more 'American' than 'French' in its outlook.
7. This development parallels the American move towards a 'woman-centred' analysis. For a full account of the politics of woman-centred feminism see Eisenstein.
8. *Questions féministes* also runs an American edition entitled *Feminist Issues*. Their manifesto is reprinted under the title 'Variations on common themes' in Marks and Courtivron (eds), 212–30.
9. Other short introductions to Lacan are provided in Wright and in Eagleton (1983). For a fuller presentation see Lemaire.

Black Women, Sexism and Racism

Black or Antiracist Feminism?

GEMMA TANG NAIN

INTRODUCTION

As a black woman and a feminist from the Caribbean—Trinidad and Tobago to be exact—I am concerned about the apparent polarization of feminism into 'black' and 'white' in both Britain and the USA, given that, as an ideology and a political practice concerned with the oppression of women, feminism still has to struggle to achieve and maintain legitimacy. It has been argued that racism in these societies, including its existence within the women's movement itself, is responsible for this polarization.

We in the Caribbean are no strangers to racism, having experienced some of its most extreme manifestations during slavery and for some time after its abolition. However, given the numerical advantage of persons of African descent in the region, it has been possible since the end of colonial rule, and particularly since the 1970s, to weaken the force of racism. White men (both local and foreign) may still control the economies of the region but black men have achieved political power and do exercise considerable control over the public sector. To the extent, then, that power changed hands, it went from white men to black men; women did not feature in the equation. Caribbean women, therefore, have not found it necessary to differentiate feminism into 'black' and 'white', and the five-year old Caribbean Association for Feminist Research and Action (CAFRA) does in fact attest to this. The women's movement in the region thus comprises women of different 'races' and backgrounds, with divisions, where these exist, emanating from ideological differences rather than racial antagonisms.

I can well appreciate that racism must be a potent force for black people in both Britain and the USA where, numerically speaking, they constitute a minority. I can empathize, too, with the plight of black women in these societies, caught as they are between racism on the one hand and sexism on the other. What I cannot understand is the tendency, on the part of black women, to allow the force of racism to overshadow that of sexism, which in turn has implications for strategizing. It leads to ambivalence towards, if not total rejection of, feminism on the part of some black women.

In the case of Britain, for example, the relevance of feminism to black women became a contentious issue within the Organization of Women of Asian and African Descent (OWAAD). While it was acknowledged that some of the issues being addressed were of relevance to black women, given that we 'do have to deal with things like rape and domestic violence, and Black men are as sexist as the next man' (Bryan, Dadzie and Scafe, 1985: 174), the point was also made that 'if you're a Black woman, you've got to begin with racism. It's not a choice, it's a necessity' (Bryan *et al.*, 1985: 174). In reference to the USA, Joseph noted that both the black movement and the women's movement are crucial to the black woman's life, 'for to choose one and omit the other is detrimental to her well-being' (Joseph and Lewis, 1981:38). Having said that, however, Joseph concluded that 'given the nature of racism in this country, it should be obvious that the *Black Liberation struggle claims first priority*' (Joseph and Lewis, 1981:39, my emphasis).

It would seem, then, that the relationship to feminism of black women in Britain and the USA is aptly summed up by Lauretta Ngcobo when, in reference to black women in Britain, she noted that:

It is . . . true that few of us are feminists in the sense understood by white middle-class women. Ours is an ambivalent position where we may be strongly critical of our men's assertive sexism . . . yet we are protective of them, not wanting them attacked . . . or even grouped with other men for their sexism. (1988:31).

From the writings of several black women (see for example Amos and Parmar, 1984; Bryan *et al.*, 1985; Hooks, 1982; Joseph and Lewis, 1981; Ngcobo, 1988) it is evident that this ambivalence derives from: an assessment of feminism as a white ideology and practice which is antimen; a sense that it is incompatible with the black struggle against racism and that attention to it will detract from and divide that struggle; a belief that it does not address issues of relevance to black women; disenchantment over the experience of racism (and/or indifference to it) by black women who were involved in the movement. But more fundamental, perhaps, has been the claim of black feminists that:

1. some of the concepts of mainstream feminism do not take into account the experiences of black women. They are thus race-blind and as such lack applicability and relevance to black women (Amos and Parmar, 1984; Carby, 1982; Joseph and Lewis, 1981);
2. some of the practices of mainstream feminism demonstrate insensitivity to the experiences of black women and the entire black population (Amos and Parmar, 1984; Bryan *et al.*, 1985).

The concepts of reproduction, patriarchy and the family were singled out as problematic in their application to black women, as were activities surrounding the issues of abortion and male violence, including rape. Part of the problem, however, lies in confusing different levels of analysis (Chhachhi, 1986). For example, the concepts of reproduction and patriarchy are at different levels of abstraction from that of the family, given that the latter, unlike the former, can be viewed as 'a concrete social phenomenon . . . ' (Chhachhi, 1986: 3). . . .

CONTROVERSY OVER POLITICAL PRACTICE

As with the concepts discussed above, black feminists have criticized mainstream feminism for aspects of its political practice. In this section, I will discuss the critique of the family, the demand for abortion and the issue of male violence.

The Feminist Critique of the Family

Given that a number of feminist concepts point to the family as a crucial site of women's oppression, it was logical for it to be targeted for criticism. But this feminist critique, like the Marxist critique before it, has met with little popularity, and at times open hostility and counter-attack (Barrett and McIntosh, 1982). But before moving into a discussion of this counter-attack, exactly what is meant by 'the family' should be clarified. Part of the ambiguity results from a failure to distinguish between 'an aggregation of kinsfolk or a household of co-residents' (Barrett, 1980:201). Thus, for Barrett, it is more useful to speak of the household rather than the family, and of a familial ideology. Barrett does, however, make use of the combination term 'family-household', and this is the usage which will be followed here to refer to both kinsfolk and co-residents, since the two need not be mutually exclusive, and often are not.

A key source of counter-attack to the feminist critique of the family has come from black feminists who have vocalized their defence of the black family-household as an arena of solidarity and resistance against racism in both Britain and the USA (see for example Amos and Parmar, 1984; Carby, 1982). This view of the black family-household is supported by other writers (Flax, 1982; Lees, 1986), who also point to a similar function on the part of the white working-class family in these societies, against the vicissitudes of capitalism.

However, one should not allow this reality—the family-household as a source of resistance to other forms of oppression—to disguise or distort the oppressive elements to women within that very institution. And the black feminists cited above do acknowledge the possibility of such family-based oppression. In adding their support to the view of the family-household as oppressive to women, Arthur Brittan and Mary Maynard point to the mothering, domestic, sexual and emotional services performed by women within the family-household: 'We regard such activities as oppressive . . . because they are expected of women, but not of males' (Brittan and Maynard, 1984: 145). And while women may not perform these tasks to the same degree, given variations in family-household organization in contemporary Britain and the USA, it is arguable that they do perform more of them than men do. But an even more telling point is the ideological expectation that these activities will be performed by women, which means that 'no woman, adolescent, unmarried, lesbian or whatever her status can escape the oppression built into her real or imputed family position' (Brittan and Maynard, 1984: 146). Additionally, there is the issue of violence against women in the family-household, and this will be discussed under a subsequent heading. Thus it is obvious that the family-household embodies the contradictions of oppression which are characteristic of the wider society.

A further point which needs to be made is that even the white, middle-class, nuclear family which has been the prime focus of the feminist attack, is not without its merits. As Coote and Campbell (cited in Rowland, 1984: 16) note: 'Of course, it would be easier to develop a clear political analysis of family life if it were altogether a bad thing . . . but . . . there are ways in which the family can be a source of care, affection, strength and security.' And this is particularly so given the ideological justification of the family as 'the "haven in a heartless world" of capitalism' (Barrett, 1980: 212).

It is apparent, therefore, that a certain degree of ambivalence has characterized feminism's critique of the family, an ambivalence which has not been acknowledged by black feminists, and hence feminism's consensus on this issue tends to be exaggerated (Barrett and McIntosh, 1982). Further, it is, perhaps, the ambivalent nature of the feminist critique, and its general unpopularity, which at least partly explains why revisionist/pro-family feminists, as well as antifeminists, have launched their counter-attack in this area, in an attempt to discredit feminism. (See Eisenstein, 1984, and Stacey, 1986, for a discussion of revisionist/pro-family feminism.) Elshtain and Friedan, both writing in the early 1980s in defence of the family and in celebration of motherhood, are viewed as the key architects of this revisionist/pro-family backlash within feminism (Eisenstein, 1984; Stacey, 1986). It is regrettable that the black feminists, in their counter-attack, did not address this alternative trend, either to support it or to distance themselves from it.

It can be suggested, then, that feminism's critique of the family has been, and remains, a contentious issue, antagonizing and alienating women of different races, classes and political persuasions. Undoubtedly, it is necessary for feminism to develop a knowledge base about different family-household forms (Barrett and McIntosh, 1985), in order to analyse the power relationships within them which in turn can inform appropriate action.

The Demand for Abortion

The issue of abortion represents another area of controversy between feminist action and black women in Britain and the USA. The claim of black feminists that the issue must be that of a woman's right to choose rather than simply limited to abortion *per se* is indeed valid. In fact, the struggle must be for women to control their sexuality and fertility through access to safe contraception and abortion, and to decide if and when they want children. But did the broadening of the demand necessarily have to involve an attack on the original demand for abortion? Let us examine this matter further in the context of Britain.

It has been argued by black feminists that doctors were all too willing to administer abortion to black women, at times against their will and even to sterilize them without their knowledge. Given this reality, then, abortion was dismissed in almost flippant fashion in the 1970s by members of the BBWG. They stated that 'abortion wasn't something we had any problems getting as black women—it was the very reverse for us!' (Bryan *et al.*, 1985: 149). But by the early 1980s, under the threat of the Corrie Abortion Amendment Bill, both the BBWG and OWAAD were articulating their support for the right to abortion, since its removal as a legal right would mean a return to the 'back street' abortionist and, perhaps, a greater risk of being given the dangerous drug, depo provera. This serves to highlight the fragile nature of any rights won by women, and the need for co-operation among feminists even where disagreement may occur.

In fact, the 1980s has witnessed the emergence of strong antiabortionist lobbies in both Britain and the USA, and hence the right to state-funded abortion is now under attack for all women, both black and white. This antiabortionist position has gained ground even among so-called progressive elements in the USA, 'to the point . . . of denying the right to abortion to women who are the victims of rape or incest' (Barrett and McIntosh, 1982: 14).

With reference to the antiabortionist groups in the USA, *Women's International Network News (WIN News)* notes that these groups 'have resorted to an incredible range of tactics, from blatant propaganda and harassment to personal intimidation and legal action' (*WIN News* 14, 1, 1988: 35). It is important to note, too, that antiabortionists are not limited to individuals and voluntary groups, as the state is also involved. In July 1989, the Supreme Court in the USA just fell short of reversing the 1973 Roe v. Wade ruling which had granted women the right to decide whether to have an abortion. The 1989 ruling, in Webster v. Reproductive Health Services, now permits individual states to make the decision for the woman (*WIN News*, 16, 1, 1990). In Britain, successive attempts to reduce the time limit within which abortions can be performed have failed, but as the antiabortionist lobby grows, with active support and assistance from US groups, the need to be vigilant cannot be overemphasized (*WIN News* 15, 4, 1989).

Male Violence Against Women

Although one may assume that women of different races and classes can unite over the issue of male violence, here again conflict has emerged. Under this heading I will discuss two manifestations of male violence: domestic violence and rape.

Domestic Violence

Women suffer from an inordinate amount of violence within their homes, usually perpetrated against them by their husbands or other males with whom they are sexually involved. But it is a crime which is grossly under-acknowledged and under-reported, and even where it is reported it tends to be dismissed or not taken seriously by the police. Feminism has drawn attention to this issue, and has achieved some success in having it put on the agenda as a problem which needs to be addressed.

But for black women in Britain and the USA (who suffer this fate at the hands of their black men), their situation is compounded by two additional factors: the fact that the 'white' police service is likely to be even less sympathetic, if not downright hostile (Mama, 1989, provides some examples of white police hostility towards black women in Britain who reported such crimes); and their own ambivalence towards reporting their men to agencies which have shown themselves to be racist. Some have gone further and have argued: 'What's the point of taking on male violence if you haven't dealt with State violence?' (Bryan *et al.*, 1985: 175) Thus black women are truly caught in a 'no-win' situation, and at times are further abused by black men, secure in the knowledge that they would not be turned over to the police. However, within recent times, black women in Britain have been refusing to remain silent victims of this abuse, and have been seeking shelter within women's refuges which have been in operation in Britain since the middle-to-late 1970s. (See Mama, 1989, for a full discussion of this issue).

Rape

Another crime which affects women and which continues to take place at a staggering rate is that of rape. It is a crime which, given the mere possibility of its occurrence, has served to severely limit the mobility of all women. Feminism has been active in focusing attention on this manifestation of violence against women, and some feminists have organized 'reclaim the night' marches. Centres for rape victims are also in operation. There have, however, been problems with 'reclaim the night' marches in Britain, for example, when some white feminists marched in areas of black concentration. This had the effect of suggesting a link between black people and violence and was justly criticized. However, it ought to be mentioned that while women's mobility is affected by the fear of rape and other attacks on the streets, this has not attracted anything near the level of concern and outrage which the fear of racial attacks has produced.

This crime of rape, as well, has produced ambivalence among black women in Britain and the USA with black feminists contending that rape cannot be addressed without at the same time mentioning the lynching of black men (Amos and Parmar, 1984; Davis, 1981). It has been pointed out that in the USA, for example, several black men in the post-emancipation period were lynched for raping, or suspicion of raping, white women. This so overshadowed the rape of black women, however, that when Brownmiller asked a black male librarian for information about rape, she was told that for 'black people, rape has meant the lynching of the black man' (cited in Wallace, 1979: 119). It is important to recognize, therefore, that while there was a link between the raping of women and the lynching of black men at certain historical periods and in specific socio-economic environments, what is involved are two separate and distinct social problems. In fact, if the mass media is to be believed, it would seem that the crime of lynching is now a relic of the past or, at any rate, is now quite rare. On the other hand, the raping of women in contemporary Britain and the USA continues unabated, thus constituting justifiable grounds for treating the two issues separately.

With regard to the rape of black women, in both Britain and the USA, once again, as in the case of domestic violence, they face additional difficulties. If a black woman is raped by a white man, no one is likely to take her seriously, and even if he is arrested he is unlikely to be convicted. (Information from the USA confirms that few white men have been convicted of rape. Davis, 1981) If she is raped by a black man, she faces the dilemma of reporting it and being ignored or further abused by the police, in addition to having feelings of disloyalty to black people (Omolade, 1985), or of suffering in silence. Either way, she is the loser.

What is not easily understandable is why black women should feel a sense of disloyalty to, or betrayal of, the black population in reporting acts of violence against them by black men, while the black men seem not to harbour any such sentiments by abusing them in the first place. This undoubtedly amounts to an asymmetry of loyalty. Further, given the frequent references in black writings to the 'black community', should this 'community' not have acted to protect its women from, and to condemn its men for such acts of abuse in the light of the racism of the state and its agencies? Or is the reference to a black community simply a façade, intended to disguise deep internal divisions and a lack of consensus? These issues should provide fertile ground for investigation by black feminists.

Having discussed the areas of controversy (conceptual and practical) between mainstream feminism and black women in Britain and the USA, we must now turn our attention to the viability of black feminism in addressing the issue of women's oppression.

THE VIABILITY OF BLACK FEMINISM

What Does the 'Black' in Black Feminism Stand For?

Despite differences within radical feminism and socialist feminism, it has been suggested that one can attribute to these groupings certain core tenets. Radical feminism, for instance, asserts the primacy of sexual exploitation over all other forms of oppression while socialist feminists assert that an integrated understanding of sexual oppression and class exploitation is necessary. Therefore, the describing adjectives of 'radical' and 'socialist' are associated with specific political/ideological meanings. With regard to black feminism, while it is postulated that it is oppression based on race, sex and class which must be addressed, it has to be acknowledged that some ambiguity is associated with the adjective 'black'. Is it intended to be political, racial, or both? There is thus an on-going debate as to who is black (Murphy and Livingstone, 1985), which in turn has implications for the boundaries of black feminism. Let us first examine the situation in Britain.

If 'black' in Britain is not about skin colour, as has been argued by Bryan *et al.* (1985) and Sivanandan (1985), then on what basis are persons included or excluded? If it is a political term, as suggested by Bryan *et al.*, to refer to people who have suffered colonial and imperialist domination, then can Irish women, who are considered 'white', be included? If not, why not? Amina Mama's attempts at clarifying the issue are far from satisfactory, since she takes the position that the term should not be extended to encompass all those who have suffered from imperialism: 'In Britain it is clear that Black refers to Africans (continental and of the diaspora), and Asians (primarily of Indian subcontinent descent). All have a shared history of oppression by British colonialism and racism.' (Mama, 1984:23). But a similar argument about colonial domination and racism can be put forward in the case of the Irish at the hands of the British. According to Husband (1982) and Miles (1982) the Irish, in an earlier period of British history, had also been racialized, although skin colour did not constitute the difference. It was felt that their 'Celtic Blood' was different from that of the British (Husband, 1982). Mama's definition of black also confirms the view of Anthias and Yuval-Davis (1983) that Greek Cypriots and Jews are not black.

In order to limit the term 'black' to Africans and Asians, one would have to confirm its reference to skin colour. This is, perhaps, quite legitimate in the British context, given that the survey referred to by Daniel (1968) showed that Africans (primarily from the Caribbean at that time) and Asians (primarily from the Indian subcontinent) were subjected to more severe racial discrimination than other immigrants who were considered 'white' (e.g. Hungarians). But, then, one would have to be honest and state that it does in fact refer to skin colour as well as being political. However, this raises another issue—whether Asians (from India, Pakistan, etc.) will accept the label of black if skin colour is what is intended, since they have angrily objected to being called black in Trinidad and Tobago, insisting that they are *brown*. And while it can be argued that their experience of racism in Britain may have served to foster an acceptance of blackness, none the less it means that their relationship to the term is qualitatively different from that of persons of African descent. For example, while it is true that colour variations were acknowledged by Afro-Caribbeans before their arrival in Britain, blackness as part of their identity was never fully disallowed.

In the USA the term 'black' has been less ambiguous, referring primarily to people of African descent. Among some non-white women the term 'women of colour' has been used, at times to refer to all who are not white, including those of African descent (Murphy and Livingstone, 1985), and at times to refer to non-whites other than Africans, thus reserving the term 'black' only for those of African descent (Mama, 1984).

It seems apparent, then, that since the term 'black' is so closely linked historically to people from Africa and of African descent, encompassing both a racial and political definition, it becomes problematic to attempt to transform this into a purely political term to refer to other non-white peoples. It is an issue, therefore, which should be addressed by black feminists.

Is Black Feminism an Alternative Movement?

The ambiguity surrounding the question of who is 'black' is replicated in black feminism's location and constituency. Can black feminism be viewed as part of feminism and hence the women's movement in the West, as part of the black movement (encompassing both black women and black men in the struggle against racism), or as part of both movements? Relatedly, is it functioning on behalf of all women, only non-white women or, more narrowly still, only black women?

If we assume, for a moment, that it is part of feminism, here again a comparison with the other strands within feminism is useful. Radical feminism asserts that it is for all women, regardless of class, race, sexual orientation, or whatever other differences may exist among women. Socialist feminism also claims that it is for all women, but recognizes class as a major factor dividing women. Logically, then, black feminism, too, should be for all women, while recognizing race and class as significant dividers among women. But the reality has been that while radical and socialist feminism have been seen as open to all women, though in fact they have been dominated by white, middle-class women, black feminism has been perceived as restricted to black women.

In order to try to unravel some of these inconsistencies, we will look at the situation of black feminism in Britain. Let us address, first, the focus of black feminism, i.e., try to ascertain the constituency on whose behalf it functions.

Most, if not all, black feminist writings have stressed the need to address sex, class and race oppression, which theoretically means that black feminism as an ideology and a movement is open to all women who support such claims. However, some of the writings within black feminism have also encouraged the perception that it is only applicable to black women. Claudette Williams, for example, points to black feminism as 'an important and valid dimension of the struggle of black people for their total liberation' (Williams, forthcoming). A similar position is alluded to by the BBWG although some ambiguity is apparent. The group states that it adheres to socialist feminism, while also adhering to black feminism. Further, the latter at times seems to refer to part of a total struggle for liberation of all oppressed people, while at other times it seems to refer specifically to part of the black struggle (see *Speak Out* No. 4). And this brings us back to the ambiguity associated with the word 'black'. For, if only certain women are black, as suggested by Mama (1984), then how can black feminism be applicable to women who are not black? It is probably this lack of clarity which motivated Anthias and Yuval-Davis to question, within the context of Britain, the polarization of feminism into mainstream (white) and black. 'The notion of "black women" as delineating the boundaries of the alternative feminist movement to white feminism leaves non-British non-black women ... unaccounted for politically' (Anthias and Yuval-Davis, 1983: 63). This reference to an alternative movement thus leads to a discussion of black feminism's location.

Although Williams (forthcoming) indicates that the black women's movement did not emerge as an alternative to the (mainstream) women's movement in Britain, and Mama (1984) questions the reference to it as such by Anthias and Yuval-Davis (1983), the writings of Amos and Parmar (1984) do in fact lay claim to the status of black feminism as an alternative movement. They specifically make mention of what 'true' feminism ought to be, and of black feminism 'as a distinct body of theory and practice' (Amos and Parmar, 1984: 18). On the other hand, the BBWG acknowledges that it holds a socialist-feminist viewpoint, while advocating black feminism (*Speak Out* No. 4). Thus, there seems to be some ambivalence as to precisely where black feminism stands in relation to mainstream feminism in Britain. With regard to its relationship to the black movement, Williams's comment that it is part of the black struggle seems to indicate a positive relationship.

As mentioned earlier, in the USA the term 'women of colour' is sometimes used to refer to all non-white women or, at times, to refer only to those who are not of African descent. Hence when the term 'black' is used, it usually refers specifically to women of African descent, and this is borne out by writings of black women in the USA (Davis, 1981; Hooks, 1982; Joseph, 1981). However, regarding the location of black feminism in the USA, here, too, some ambiguity exists. In terms of its constituency, it is possible to suggest, again from writings of black women (for example, Hooks, 1982), that it, caters only for black women. When it is acknowledged, then, that the black population in the USA, as in Britain, constitutes a minority (although in the former they are a larger minority than the latter), it can be contended that without co-operation with mainstream feminism, the viability of black feminism in both Britain and the USA is rather limited.

It is understandable that black feminism may have been important and in fact necessary to black women in both Britain and the USA at a particular historical juncture. It was, perhaps, a strategic political choice, given the alienation felt by black women in both the male-dominated black movement and the white-dominated women's movement. It must also be acknowledged that black feminism did play a vital role in exposing racism within the women's movement, and in having oppression based on race accepted as a valid and legitimate issue for the feminist agenda. But it would seem that black feminists in both countries now need to decide whether they want to retain this narrow focus, i.e., catering specifically for black women, or whether they want to broaden their constituency. If the latter choice is made, it may entail a change of name, given the ambiguity surrounding the term 'black'. A possibility could be Antiracist/Socialist feminism (despite it being such a mouthful), to reflect its concern with sex, race and class oppression, and to allow all women who adhere to this viewpoint—black, other non-white, and white—to be involved. This is perhaps the kind of alternative being alluded to by Hooks (1982). For, although hooks is a black woman and a feminist, and believes that feminism should deal with sex, class and race oppression, in her writings there is some ambiguity as to whether one can classify her as a black feminist in the sense of advocating a feminism specifically for black women. In fact, while she acknowledges the support and solidarity enjoyed by black women in black women's groups, she is critical of a separate black feminism: 'Rather than black women attacking the white female attempt to present them as an Other, . . . they acted as if they were an Other' (Hooks, 1982: 151).

CONCLUSION

In this article I have examined the claims of black feminists, regarding the inapplicability to black women of some key feminist concepts, and the adverse consequences for black women of some aspects of feminist political practice.

Although black feminists have identified the concepts of reproduction, patriarchy and the family as problematic, I contend that reproduction and patriarchy constitute different levels of analysis from that of the family. Therefore, while reproduction and patriarchy have been discussed under the rubric of conceptual issues, the feminist critique of the family, the demand for abortion, and male violence against women are treated as areas of political practice.

Through an examination of the concepts of reproduction and patriarchy within the context of Britain and the USA, I conclude that these concepts do have relevance for black women in these societies. Regarding feminist action connected with the family-household, abortion and male violence against women, I acknowledge that some of the claims of black feminists are valid, although areas of common concern and interest to both black and white women are clearly evident.

In my assessment of black feminism's viability, I have drawn attention to the ambiguity surrounding the term 'black', as well as to black feminism's location (in which movement or struggle is it located), and to its constituency (on whose behalf is it functioning). The conclusion I have reached is that black women represent its constituency, although I have not made a conclusive decision on its location. I have conceded that black feminism may have been necessary at a particular historical moment, given black women's experience of multiple oppression, but ask whether it should now seek to expand its constituency. I have suggested that this may involve a change of name, perhaps to Antiracist/Socialist feminism, to reflect concern with the triple oppression of sex, race and class, and to allow all those who adhere to this viewpoint to participate.

As argued in this article, then, feminism is an ideology and practice which acknowledges the oppression of women and which seeks to transform this situation. It does not follow from this that it is anti-men, as perceived by some black women, though aspects of early second-wave feminism may have been anti-men, for example SCUM (Society for Cutting Up Men). However, one should not generalize from that faction to feminism as a whole. Within the Western world feminism consists of various strands—liberal, radical, socialist and black feminism—and while liberal feminism is not necessarily interested in transformatory change, it is the view of this writer that the different strands do have their place within contemporary feminism in Britain and the USA, and that ideology should inform political organization and practice.

The assertion that political organization and practice should flow from ideology is made to encourage a shift away from the polarization in Britain and the USA between black feminism and the other feminisms which are considered 'white'. The experience of feminism in Britain, where the mainstream 'white' movement collapsed due to conflict between radical and socialist feminists, and the subsequent demise of the black women's movement, should have served to highlight the fragility of race as a unifying factor for organization and practice within feminism. And this point is made all the more cogent when it is acknowledged that those women considered 'black' in Britain are as divided among themselves as they are from 'white' British women (James, 1986, makes mention of the antagonisms between Afro-Caribbeans and Asians in Britain and urges that it should not be ignored). Parmar, in a somewhat reflective mood following her scathing attack on 'white' feminism (along with Amos in 1984), wrote in a 1988 article that 'Racial identity alone cannot be a basis for collective organising as the black communities are as beset with divisions around culture, sexuality and class as any other community' (Parmar, 1989: 59).

If black feminism is converted, then, into Antiracist/Socialist feminism, it will thus constitute an ideological position to which women, of whatever race, can subscribe. But precisely because this aspect of feminism is likely to be dominated by black women and hence by issues connected with racism, it is important for feminism to retain its other dimensions. Socialist feminism will ensure that class exploitation is not marginalized but since it, too, runs the risk of being dominated by class issues, radical feminism needs to be retained in order to stress the issue of sexual oppression. Liberal feminism will continue to work for reforms within the present system and that, too, is desirable. These four emphases within a broad-based feminism should co-operate with each other and take part in collaborative action wherever possible.

It is, of course, not at all certain that women in general, and black women in particular, will accept this four-pronged approach of feminism. Several black writers (Amos and Parmar, 1984; Davis, 1981; as well as Bhavnani and Coulson, 1986) have contended that racism should be elevated to the same level of primacy as sexism within feminism. Assuming, then, that this is undertaken, and disregarding for a moment that it will shift the focus of the feminist project, what role will be left for the black/antiracist movement to play and, perhaps more importantly, what role is envisaged for black (including, here, other non-white) men? Will black men join with women, black and white, in such an antiracist feminism which will entail struggling against both racism and sexism? Since this eventuality seems unlikely, it is, perhaps, more realistic to have a component of feminism concentrate on issues of racism, in keeping with my suggestion. We should all be wary of 'proxy fights for freedom' (Stimpson, 1971: 474).

By way of a final comment, it should be noted that some congruence exists between the view of Iris Young (1981) and the views of black feminists. Young insists that the struggle against patriarchy and capitalism is a struggle against one system, that of capitalist patriarchy. Black feminists, too, insist that it is one struggle against racism, sexism, and capitalism. King (1988), for example, asserts that one-dimensional struggles, emphasizing sex, class or race oppression, respectively, ignore the reality of black women's lives. What Young and the black feminists seem to be suggesting, then, is one mass movement against the various sources of oppression, given that these sources are an integral part of one system. While this sounds reasonable and, perhaps, represents an ideal solution, the implications of such a mass movement for organization, focus and political practice would seem to make this ideal unrealistic, at least at the present time. Therefore while, at the level of theorizing, work should continue regarding the interrelatedness of these various forms of oppression, at the practical level it would seem more feasible for the movements—feminism, black/antiracist, and socialist—to retain their autonomy, while ensuring mutual collaboration and co-operation. Some women may decide to remain within the black/antiracist movement, or the socialist movement, where it is hoped that feminist issues will form part of the agenda. This is quite legitimate, perhaps even desirable, for as noted by Lees (1986), paraphrasing Audre Lorde, each woman must decide for herself whether it is oppression based on race, class or gender that is the most crucial for her.

The twenty-year history of second-wave feminism has been marked by fragmentation and internal contradictions, serving to highlight the differences between women. But, as stated by Bulbeck (1988:146): 'Accepting then our differences, must these become divisions?' I sincerely hope not, and I trust that we women, from our various viewpoints and within various movements, will seek to support each other as we struggle to achieve our liberation.

References

Amos, Valerie and Parmar, Pratibha (1984) 'Challenging Imperialist Feminism' *Feminist Review* No. 17, 'Many Voices, One Chant: Black Feminist Perspectives.'

Anthias, Floya and Yuval-Davis, Nira (1983) 'Contextualizing Feminism—Gender, Ethnic and Class Divisions' *Feminist Review* No. 15.

Barrett, Michèle (1980) *Women's Oppression Today* London: Verso.

Barrett, Michèle and McIntosh, Mary (1982) *The Anti-social Family* London: Verso.

Barrett, Michèle and McIntosh, Mary (1985) 'Ethnocentrism and Socialist Feminist Theory' *Feminist Review* No. 20.

Bhavnani, Kum-Kum and Coulson, Margaret (1986) 'Transforming Socialist-feminism: The Challenge of Racism' *Feminist Review* No. 23.

Brittan, Arthur and Maynard, Mary (1984) *Sexism, Racism and Oppression* Oxford: Blackwell.

Brixton Black Women's Group (1984) 'Black Women Organising' *Feminist Review* No. 17, 'Many Voices, One Chant: Black Feminist Perspectives'.

Bruegel, Irene (1989) 'Sex and Race in the Labour Market' *Feminist Review* No. 32.

Bryan, Beverly; Dadzie, Stella and Scafe, Suzanne (1985) *The Heart of the Race: Black Women's Lives in Britain* London: Virago Press.

Bulbeck, C. (1988) *One World Women's Movement* London: Pluto Press.

Carby, Hazel (1982) 'White Woman Listen! Black Feminism and the Boundaries of Sisterhood' in Centre for Contemporary Cultural Studies (1982).

Cashmore, E. and Troyna, B. (1982) editors. *Black Youth in Crisis* Herts: Allen & Unwin.

Centre for Contemporary Cultural Studies (1982) *The Empire Strikes Back: Race and Racism in 70s Britain* London: Hutchinson.

Chhachhi, Amrita (1986) 'Concepts in Feminist Theory—Consensus and Controversy', Paper presented at the Inaugural Seminar: Gender in Caribbean Development, The University of the West Indies, St Augustine, Trinidad and Tobago.

Crompton, R. and Mann, M. (1986) editors, *Gender and Stratification* Cambridge: Polity Press.

Daniel, W. W. (1968) *Racial Discrimination in England* Middlesex: Penguin Books.

Davis, Angela (1981) *Women, Race and Class* London: The Women's Press.

Edholm, F; Harris, O. and Young, K. (1977) 'Conceptualising Women' *Critique of Anthropology*, Vol. 3, Nos. 9/10.

Eisenstein, Zillah (1984) *Feminism and Sexual Equality* New York: Monthly Review Press.

Eisenstein, H. and Jardine, A. (1985) editors, *The Future of Difference* New Jersey: Rutgers University Press.

Elshtain, J. B. (1982) editor, *The Family in Political Thought* Sussex: Harvester Press.

Flax, Jane (1982) 'The Family in Contemporary Feminist Thought: A Critical Review' in Elshtain (1982).

Fowaad (1979a) Newsletter of the Organization of Women of Asian and African Descent, July 1979.

———(1979b) September 1979.

———(1980a) February 1980.

———(1980b) July 1980.

Fuller, Mary (1982) 'Young, Female and Black' in Cashmore and Troyna (1982).

Gornick, V. and Moran, B.K. (1971) editors, *Woman in Sexist Society: Studies in Power and Powerlessness* New York: Basic Books.

Haralambos, Michael (with Robin Heald) (1980) *Sociology: Themes and Perspectives* Slough: University Tutorial Press.

Harding, Sandra (1981) 'What is the Real Material Base of Patriarchy and Capital?' in Sargent (1981).

Hartmann, Heidi (1981) 'The Unhappy Marriage of Marxism and Feminism: Towards a More Progressive Union' in Sargent (1981).

Hooks, Bell (1982) *Ain't I A Woman! Black Women and Feminism* London: Pluto Press.

Husband, Charles (1982) editor, *'Race' in Britain: Continuity and Change* London: Hutchinson.

James, W. (1986) 'A Long Way From Home: On Black Identity in Britain' *Immigrants and Minorities* Vol. 5, No. 3.

Joseph, Gloria (1981) 'The Incompatible Ménage à Trois: Marxism, Feminism and Racism' in Sargent (1981).

Joseph, Gloria I. and Lewis, Jill (1981) *Common Differences: Conflicts in Black and White Feminist Perspectives* New York: Anchor Press/Doubleday.

King, Deborah, K. (1988) 'Multiple Jeopardy, Multiple Consciousness: The context of a Black Feminist Ideology' *SIGNS* Vol. 14, No. 1.

Lees, Sue (1986) 'Sex, Race and Culture: Feminism and the Limits of Cultural Pluralism' *Feminist Review* No. 22.

Lewis, Diane K. (1977) 'A Response to Inequality: Black Women, Racism, and Sexism' *SIGNS* Vol. 3, No. 2.

MacEwen Scott, Alison (1986) 'Industrialization, Gender Segregation and Stratification Theory' in Crompton and Mann (1986).

Mama, Amina (1984) 'Black Women, the Economic Crisis and the British State' *Feminist Review* No. 17, 'Many Voices, One Chant: Black Feminist Perspectives'.

Mama, Amina (1989) 'Violence Against Black Women: Gender, Race and State Responses' *Feminist Review* No. 32.

Miles, Robert (1982) *Racism and Migrant Labour* London: Routledge & Kegan Paul.

Mitchell, J. and Oakley, A. (1986) editors, *What is Feminism?* Oxford: Blackwell.

Murphy, Lindsay and Livingstone, Jonathan (1985) 'Racism and the Limits of Radical Feminism' *Race and Class* Vol. 26, No. 4.

Murray, Pauli (1970) 'The Liberation of Black Women' in Thompson (1970).

Ngcobo, Lauretta (1988) editor, *Let It Be Told: Essays by Black Women in Britain* London: Virago Press.

Oakley, Ann (1976) *Woman's Work: The Housewife, Past and Present* New York: Vintage Books.

Omolade, Barbara (1985) 'Black Women and Feminism' in Eisenstein and Jardine (1985).

Parmar, Pratibha (1989) 'Other Kinds of Dreams' *Feminist Review* No. 31.

Rowland, Robyn (1984) editor, *Women Who Do and Women Who Don't, Join the Women's Movement* London: Routledge & Kegan Paul.

Sargent, Linda (1981) editor, *Women and Revolution* London: Pluto Press.

Sivanandan, A. (1981) 'From Resistance to Rebellion: Asian and Afro-Caribbean Struggles in Britain' *Race and Class* Vol. 23, Nos. 2/3.

Sivanandan, A. (1985) 'RAT and the Degradation of Black Struggle' *Race and Class* Vol. 26, No. 4.

Speak Out (undated) Newsletter of the Brixton Black Women's Group, Issues 2, 3 and 4.

Stacey, Judith (1986) 'Are Feminists Afraid to Leave Home? The Challenge of Conservative Pro-family Feminism' in Mitchell and Oakley (1986).

Stimpson, Catherine (1971) '"Thy Neighbour's Wife, Thy Neighbour's Servants": Women's Liberation and Black Civil Rights' in Gornick and Moran (1971).

Thompson, Mary Lou (1970) editor, *Voices of the New Feminism* Boston: Beacon Press.

Wallace, Michele (1979) *Black Macho and the Myth of the Superwoman* London: Calder.

Women's International Network News (1988) Vol. 14, No. 1.

———(1989) Vol. 15, No. 4.

———(1990) Vol. 16, No. 1.

Williams, Claudette (forthcoming) 'We Are a Natural Part of Many Different Struggles: Black Women Organising'.

Young, Iris (1981) 'Beyond the Unhappy Marriage: A Critique of the Dual Systems Theory' in Sargent (1981).

FURTHER READING FOR CHAPTER 7

Anthias, F., and N. Yuval-Davis. 1992. *Radicalized Boundaries: Race, Gender, Colour and Class and the Anti-racist Struggle.* London: Routledge.

Beauvoir, S. de. 1953. *The Second Sex.* Harmondsworth: Penguin Books.

Bono, P., et al. 1991. *Italian Feminist Thought.* Oxford: Blackwell.

Buckley, M., and M. Anderson (eds.). 1988. *Women, Equality and Europe.* London: Macmillan.

Cixous, H. 1981. "The Laugh of the Medusa." In E. Marks and I. de Courtivron (eds.), *New French Feminisms.* Hempstead: Harvester Wheatsheaf.

Dahlerup, D. (ed.). 1986. *The New Women's Movement.* London: Sage.

Eduards, M.L. 1991. "The Swedish Gender Model: Productivity, Pragmatism and Paternalism." *West European Politics.*

Eisenstein, H. 1991. *Gender Shock.* London: Allen and Unwin.

Feminist Review Collective (eds.). 1991. "Shifting Territories: Feminism and Europe." *Feminist Review* special issue, no. 39.

Irigaray, L. 1980. "When Our Two Lips Speak Together." *Signs* 6, pp. 69–79.

———. 1985. *Speculum of the Other Woman.* Ithaca: Cornell University Press.

Kaplan, G. 1992. *Contemporary Western European Feminism.* London: UCL Press.

Katzenstein, M. Fainsod, and C. McClurg Mueller. 1987. *The Women's Movements of the United States and Western Europe.* Philadelphia: Temple University Press.

Lovell, T. (ed.). 1900. *British Feminist Thought.* Oxford: Blackwell.

Lovenduski, J. 1986. *Women and European Politics.* Hempstead: Harvester Wheatsheaf.

Lovenduski, J., and V. Randall. 1993. *Contemporary Feminist Politics.* Oxford: Oxford University Press.

Mani, L. 1990. "Multiple Mediations: Feminist Scholarship in the Age of Multi-national Reception." *Feminist Review* 35.

Moi, T. 1985. *Sexual/Textual Politics.* London: Routledge (1988 reprint).

Nain, G. Tang. 1991. "Black Women, Sexism and Racism." *Feminist Review* 37 (Spring).

Norris, P. 1987. *The Politics of Sexual Equality.* Hempstead: Harvester Wheatsheaf.

Skjeie, H. 1991. "The Uneven Advance of Norwegian Women." *New Left Review* 187.

CHAPTER
8

Feminist Political Ideas

Feminist thinking is wide-ranging and diverse, but it is possible to identify five political ideas at the heart of contemporary feminism:

1. Women and men are entitled to equal rights.
2. The personal is political.
3. Gender is a hierarchy of power.
4. Sisterhood is a basis for political organization.
5. The social contract on which modern liberal democracies are based is a fraternal contract.

Feminists have organized to gain equality of citizenship for women. They argue that women's citizenship has been constrained in two main ways. First, women have historically been excluded from a civil society in which citizens were **heads** of households and women could be only **members** of households. Heads of households spoke politically (for example, they voted) on behalf of all household members, including women, children, servants, and sometimes slaves. Second, women's citizenship has been constrained by their economic exclusion. Women tended to be poor because they were not in paid employment, hence had no independent income, or because they had low-paid jobs in the labor market. Poverty may prevent citizens from participating fully in democratic politics.

Feminists question the basis of traditional definitions of politics when they assert, "The personal is political." By this they mean that power relationships are part of family and personal life as well as the public world of institutions. Indeed, many feminists go further than this and argue that it is only because of power relationships in private life that public life, as we experience and define it, is possible.

Political scientists have had difficulty accepting the feminist view that personal life is political and that therefore gender hierarchies are an appropriate object of study. But they have little trouble with the notion of sisterhood, because during the last century there have been widespread and visible feminist movements in support of political objectives. Such instances of solidarity among women are evidence that sisterhood is a basis for political organization, and women's movements are often studied under the rubric of social movements. Nevertheless, feminist ideas about politics challenge the conventions of the discipline. Often that challenge is explicit, as feminists ask questions about what politics is and criticize the inadequacies of considerations of gender from the viewpoint of traditional theories of power.[1] The way feminists understand power is an implicit challenge to the discipline. The preoccupation of political scientists with a limited range of political acts and actors—politicians, office holding, voting, lobbying, policy-making—contrasts sharply with the feminist quest to understand how power is generated and used in everyday life. Feminism is a theory about power relations between men and women that has their change as its goal. At a minimum, feminism is politics because it engages power which it locates in domestic life, the state, and in knowledge itself. The argument here is that BY THE VERY ACT OF SAYING IT WAS SO, feminism exposed male power in different spheres. But feminists disagree about how to treat male power. These differences reflect liberal, socialist, and radical sources of feminist thought. Put very simply, liberal feminists believe that democratic political structures may be reformed to accommodate women's equality; socialist feminists believe that such structures must be transformed; and radical feminists believe that they should be boycotted. Thus liberals pursue strategies of altering and adjusting laws that discriminate against women, socialist feminists work to restructure institutions, largely to make them more participatory, and radical feminists operate strategies of separatism, avoiding as far as possible any contact with existing political institutions. In practice there are often alliances between the three tendencies and there is a considerable overlap between liberal and socialist feminism. But European feminists are generally more skeptical than American women about the usefulness of liberal feminism which they think does not seriously challenge non-feminist understandings of inequalities between the sexes. But, to borrow a point from Caroline Ramazanoglu, most of the people who will read this book owe their capability of doing so to the education that was won for them by liberal feminist struggles.[2]

Ways of classifying feminism reflect the different intellectual and cultural backgrounds of writers. In the first of our extracts, Jean Bethke Elshtain addresses the different strands of feminism. She identifies a fourth feminism, eco-feminism and she shows significantly more sympathy for liberal feminism than many European writers. These differences may be because Elshtain is an American who writes from the perspective of the history of political thought. Both her intellectual and national backgrounds predispose her to value liberalism. In keeping with the conventions of political theory, Elshtain draws out several of the ideas that are in play in contemporary feminist politics and relates them to traditions of political thinking. In keeping with the conventions of political theory, Elshtain draws out several of the ideas in contemporary feminist politics. In the course of doing this, she summarizes brilliantly a central underlying idea of feminist politics: the political individual is not an abstract, independent pursuer of a discoverable, interested, rational strategy in a world of known rules and predictable outcomes, but an encumbered, embodied, familial, and social being. And, of course, the encumbrances are significantly influenced by gender. By raising the possibility of alternative gender relations, Elshtain addresses the issue of feminist goals and considers the form of political citizenship that will be necessary to embrace feminism. This, Elshtain believes, will involve a high valuation of mutuality and familial ties.

Feminist discourses of citizenship alert us to the dangers of traditional contract-based concepts of citizenship, notably, to requirements that all other particular loyalties be suspended in an overly abstract view of citizen equality. No one has contributed more to exposing the way male interests are embedded in modern ideas of citizenship than Carole Pateman. Citizenship in contemporary democracies is normally understood in terms of social contract. The idea of the social contract was used by liberals in historic struggles against autocratic rulers. The central idea of contract theory is that government rules by the consent of the governed. On the face of it, there is no reason why the contract should not include women. But everything depends on who made the contract. Pateman argues that women were not included—the contract was fraternal. Moreover, the social contract cannot simply be amended to add women because it presupposes a sexual contract that subordinates women. The contract that underpins civil society was made by male heads of households. Men were the consenting citizens; women were members of the households represented by the contracting men. Thus women were outside civil society.[3]

In the second extract, Carole Pateman is replying to a long essay about sex, democracy, and political thought written by Anna Jonasdottir.[4] Pateman takes issue with Jonasdottir's account of how classic political texts did, and did not, deal with women's subordination. Pateman offers a concise statement of the fraternal assumptions of social contract theory. She also deals with the implications of gender differences for women's citizen equality. She argues that the problem of motherhood must be treated as a problem of democracy if the contradictions and ambiguities in women's political position are to be recognised.

We can conclude that getting citizenship for women is not just a matter of making laws granting women the same rights as men, as some modern liberals (including liberal feminists) would argue. Public institutions, organizations, and laws—the key arenas of citizenship—were established in the absence of women and for the convenience of the men who created them. Even where women's formal legal position as citizens has become equal to men's, they remain at a disadvantage when they try to function in male institutions. Parenthood has different implications for men and women; it constrains women from adapting to the norms of political institutions. So do conventions about appropriate masculine and feminine behavior. The logic of such arguments is that women will have a full place as citizens only when the nature of citizenship is changed.

JONI LOVENDUSKI

Notes

1. See especially S.C. Bourque and J. Grossholtz (1974) "Politics an Unnatural Practice: Political Science Looks at Female Participation," *Politics and Society,* Winter; M. Goot and E. Reid (1975)

Women and Voting Studies: Mindless Matrons or Sexist Scientism, Sage Professional Papers in Comparative Political Sociology; J. Lovenduski (1981) "Toward the Emasculation of Political Science" in D. Spender (ed.) *Men's Studies Modified,* Oxford: Pergamon Press; K.B. Jones (1988) "Towards the Revision of Politics" in K.B. Jones and A.G. Jonasdottir (eds.) *The Political Interests of Gender,* London: SAGE.

2. See Caroline Ramazanoglu (1989) *Feminism and the Contradictions of Oppression,* London: Routledge for a good discussion of these points from a European perspective.

3. Carole Pateman (1989) "The Fraternal Social Contract" in *The Disorder of Women,* Cambridge: Polity Press; and (1989) *The Sexual Contract,* Cambridge: Polity Press.

4. Anna Jonasdottir (1988) "Does Sex Matter to Democracy," *Scandinavian Political Studies,* Vol. 11, No. 4.

Ethics in the Women's Movement

JEAN BETHKE ELSHTAIN

ETHICS IN THE WOMEN'S MOVEMENT

Contemporary American society is marked by moral conflict. This conflict has deep historical roots and is reflected in our institutions, practices, laws, and norms. The women's movement is not only not exempt from such conflict, but it reflects, deepens, and extends it. Thus there is no single ethics or moral theory of feminism; rather, one finds contrasting, overlapping feminisms. The politics and ethics of the women's movement, however, cannot be understood simply as the terrain occupied by the small number of feminist philosophers located in the academy whose task it is to engage in explicit and more or less systematic theorizing. Rather, feminism from its inception has assumed or exuded an ethic, or several competing ethics, having to do with questions of justice, equality, freedom, and virtue.

Liberalism has been attractive to feminist thinkers. The language of rights is a potent weapon against traditional obligations, particularly those of family duty or any social status declared natural on the basis of ascriptive characteristics. To be free and equal to men became a central aim of feminist reform. The political strategy that followed from this dominant feminism was one of inclusion: women, as well as men, are rational beings. It followed that women as well as men are bearers of inalienable rights. It followed further that there was no valid ground for discrimination against women qua women. Leading proponents of women's suffrage in Britain and the United States undermined arguments that justified legal inequality on the basis of sex differences. Such feminists claimed that denying a group of persons basic rights on the grounds of difference could not be justified unless it could be shown that the difference was relevant to the distinction being made. Whatever differences might exist between the sexes, none, in this view, justified legal inequality and denial of the rights and privileges of citizenship.

Few early feminists pushed liberal universalism to its most radical conclusion by arguing that there were no justifiable bases for exclusion of adult human beings from legal equality and citizenship. Proponents of women's suffrage were also heirs to a tradition that stressed the need for social order and shared values, emphasized civic education, and pressed the importance of having a propertied stake

233

in society. Demands for the inclusion of women often did not extend to all women. Some women, and men, would be excluded by criteria of literacy, property ownership, disability or, in the United States, race.

At times, feminist discourse turned liberal egalitarianism on its head by arguing in favor of women's civic equality on grounds of difference. One finds the case for greater female political participation argued in terms of women's moral supremacy or characteristic forms of virtue. These appeals, strategic though they have been, were never merely strategic. They spoke to and from women's social location as mothers, using motherhood as a claim to citizenship and public identity. From the vantage point of rights-based feminism, the emphasis on motherhood was a trap. But the historical discourse that evoked images of maternal virtue was one feminist response to a complex, rapidly changing political culture. That political culture, in the Western democracies, was committed to liberalism but included as well civic republican themes of social solidarity and national identity.

Feminists also turned variously to socialism, in its utopian and scientific aspects, and to romanticism. Finding in notions of class oppression an analogue to woman's social position vis-à-vis men, socialist feminists promoted notions of sex-class struggle and revolt. Feminists indebted to romanticism embraced a robust notion of a passionate, feeling self breaking the encrustations of social custom. Pressing a notion that women suffered as much from repression, or internalized notions of their own incapacities, as from oppression, or systematically imposed rules and customs that guaranteed sex inequality, feminist romantics stressed women's "especial genius," in the words of the American transcendentalist Margaret Fuller, and hoped to see a social transformation that would free women's "difference" and allow it to flourish, even to dominate.

The diverse history of feminisms forms the basis for current feminist discourse and debate. These debates secrete ethical imperatives and trail in their wake moral implications whether the thinkers involved articulate fully such imperatives or implications or not. Varieties of liberal, socialist, Marxist, and utopian feminism abound. Sexuality and sexual identity have become highly charged arenas of political redefinition. Some feminists see women as universal victims; others as a trans-historical sex-class; others as oppressed nature. A minority of feminists urge women to separate entirely from male-dominated society. Some want full integration into that society, hence its transformation toward liberal equality. Others insist that the feminist agenda will not be completed until so-called women's values, correctly understood, triumph. There are feminists who embrace a strong notion of women's difference and others who reject any such idea as itself sexist. Feminism remains an essentially contested concept. What follows is an attempt to explicate the defining features of contemporary American feminism in its major theoretical and political constructions.

FEMINIST POLITICS: THEORY, RHETORIC, AND ETHICS

All feminisms share an explicit political urge—to reform or to remake the world in line with a deeply held conviction that women have been the victims of faulty and exploitative social institutions. One cannot separate feminist politics from ethics; they are entangled at each and every point, from the assumptions that undergird alternative feminist theories to the explicit projects that feminists endorse. This holds whether one is addressing radical, liberal, Marxist or socialist, or what is now called ecofeminism.

Radical Feminism

Each of these feminisms emerges in a variety of forms or modes of discourse. Take, for example, radical feminism. Radical feminist views on male and female natures and their account of the history of human social relations are inseparable and necessary to one another.[1] Radical feminists in their dominant forms of contemporary expression tend to present an essentially dualistic political rhetoric that divides the sexes into something akin to separate species. For sex polarists, the root of the matter is sexuality. This view of male and female natures forms the core of radical feminist thought. It follows that the problem historically has been, from this point of view, that the male has dominated, oppressed, exploited, and victimized the female. An unmediated conduit is presupposed between the so-called normal violence of the heterosexual male and the patriarchal, repressive family, up to and including militarism, wars, nuclear technology, despoliation of nature, advertising, and pornography: all are construed as the outgrowths of unchained masculinism.[2]

The literature amplifying and reencoding an ethic of sex polarity is massive. There is little room for moral ambiguity in this highly charged discourse. The picture of woman as universal victim is, needless to say, troubling, for it suggests that radical doctrines of sex polarity require a collective victim—all women—in order to hold themselves intact. Thus evidence of victimization is good, not bad, news, proof that the theory is correct.

Patricia Meyer Spacks has warned that "the discovery of victimization can have disastrous intellectual consequences. It produces ... one note criticism. Readers newly aware of injustices perpetrated on one sex find evidence of such injustice everywhere—and, sometimes, *only* evidence of this sort. They discover over and over again, in language, structure, and theme, testimony to women's victimization." The upshot, Spacks concludes, is almost invariably a monotonous rhetoric caught in the self-confirming cycle of its own story.[3] The "disastrous intellectual consequences" of which Spacks warns hold for ethical life as well. For radical feminism inverts the misogynistic picture of women by sketching a vision of the male that is unrelenting and unforgiving in its harshness.

Liberal Feminism

Very different indeed are liberal feminist assumptions. Modern liberal feminists also embrace, whether explicitly or tacitly, a particular notion of the self, of human nature. There is no single, shared understanding of the self that grounds all forms of liberal theorizing, including its feminist variants. Nonetheless, in general, liberalism's vision stems from seventeenth-century discourse in which the self is posited as a bearer of rights, a chooser in whose choices lie his—and initially this character was male—freedom and autonomy. Affirming the primacy of rights, liberalism in its contemporary, American form denies the same status to any principle of belonging or obligation.

Closely linked to the primacy of rights is the central importance that liberalism attaches to freedom understood as freedom to choose one's own mode of life, to constitute and choose values for oneself. In making freedom of choice an absolute, what might be called ultraliberalism "exalts choices as a human capacity. It carries with it the demand that we become beings capable of choice, that we rise to the level of self-consciousness and autonomy where we can exercise choice, that we not remain mired through fear, sloth, ignorance, or superstition in some mode imposed by tradition, society, or fate which tells us how we should dispose of what belongs to us."[4] Solidified by market images of the sovereign consumer, this atomist self was pitted with great success against the self of older constraints.

Liberal feminists make their indebtedness to these assumptions powerfully manifest when they proclaim choice an absolute. This means that important questions that arise as one evaluates the tension between individual right and social obligation are blithely ignored if one simply gives everything over to the individualist pole in advance. Thus ultra-liberal feminist ethics becomes an ethics that combines a strong quest for control—over one's body, over social circumstances, over socialization of children so that they are not imprinted with strong gender codes.

Marxist and Socialist Feminism

Marxist and socialist feminism, on the other hand, stresses a different view of the self and of what the completion of the feminist project would entail. Women are construed in their discourse as a sex-class. Their feminist narrative holds that males constituted women as the first oppressed class. All subsequent oppression—class, race, Third World—is modeled on this original historic fall. But women's oppression alone is pan-cultural and universal, coterminous with history itself. Women are prisoners of a systemic sex-gender system that dictates social roles, purposes, and norms.

All sex-gender systems, the argument continues, are dominated by the male sex-class. Women are consigned to the sphere of reproduction, or unfree nature; men are assigned to the world of production, a world of artifice, of at least potential freedom. The broad historicizing sweep of this perspective gathers all differences of cultures, past and present, into a single bin. The implicit theory of human nature is familiar: tabula rasa. We are raw material who come out as gendered "social products."[5] This means that a system of controls and reinforcements can, on this theory, consistently produce conventional results. We perforce require a new sex-gender system to create androgynous or symmetrical human beings.

Going in as generic human, no longer assigned more or less arbitrarily to a gender category, human beings in the ideal future society would come out stamped with the imprint of sexual neutrality and infused with a combination of the positive qualities of each gender but without the destructive extremes gendered identity now requires. By resocializing away from sexed identities, we can erase men and women, eliminate any biological need for sex to be associated with procreation, eradicate all sex-based role differentiation, and, at last, transcend sexual gender. The drive of such a perspective is to forestall ethical questions until such a time as the new social being creates a wholly new world with an ethics appropriate to it.

Ecofeminism

Finally, we find a feminism indebted to the romantic revolt against the Enlightenment, stressing women's nature and experience as involving and exuding values and virtues that the patriarchal world sorely needs if it is, first, to survive and, second, to evolve toward an authentic enlivening humanism. Some thinkers within ecofeminism hold to a strong normative cleavage between male and female natures. Others stress that cleavage but hold that men can be pushed toward a more nature-friendly perspective under the tutelage of women, who historically never strayed so far as men have from the natural in part because their bodies are less susceptible than those of males to radical severance from the imperatives of nature. The indictment by ecofeminists of current social arrangements is strong, filled with the rhetoric of prophetic warnings. More green than red, ecofeminists find liberal feminist tinkering with reform woefully inadequate; Marxist feminism's teleology suspect, permeated through and through with the destructive imperatives of a culture of productivity; and radical feminist obsessions with female victimization too negative. As an ethics, ecofeminism calls for us to embrace rather than war on nature, and nature, as this feminism symbolizes it, is a benign, feminized figure. What is more natural is, by definition, to be preferred. Thus the stage is set for exploring how radical, liberal, and Marxist or socialist feminists and ecofeminists respond to two concrete political and ethical concerns—war and the new reproductive engineering.[6]

FROM TEXT TO CONTEXT: FEMINIST RESPONSES TO WAR

As I have already indicated, feminists have debated from the beginning whether the feminist project requires fighting men or joining them, whether sex differences are to be deplored or celebrated. If the question at hand is war and peace, feminists uniformly support peace or some future authentic peace in contrast to the oppressive and violent present.[7] Yet wars are an endemic feature of human history. War, or collective violence, presents ethical and moral challenges of the most solemn nature. How do feminists respond?

Contemporary liberal feminists are caught up in a serious quandary. In 1981, the National Organization for Women, which has from its inception championed an integrationist perspective holding that women have the right to do or be anything that men have done or been, filed a legal brief as part of a challenge to all-male military registration. Beginning with the claim that compulsory, universal military service is central to the concept of citizenship in a democracy, the organization insisted that if women are to gain "first-class citizenship," they, too, must have the right to fight. Laws excluding women from draft registration and combat duty perpetuate "archaic notions" of women's capabilities based on unacceptable assumptions of sex difference; moreover, "devastating long-term psychological and political repercussions" are visited upon women given their exclusion from the military of their country.[8] No doubt this position is not a particularly happy one for many liberal feminists, but it is consistent with the assumption with which liberal feminism is entangled.

To prevent wars from occurring, liberal feminists repair to a perspective that condemns wars not so much because they are immoral as because they are irrational throwbacks to more barbaric eras. They trust that war will one day be rendered obsolete, given the rising interdependence of nations and the spread of uniform liberal laws throughout the globe. Though pretty thoroughly contradicted by events, this trust in the teleology of progress continues to simmer just beneath the surface of liberal argumentation. It also requires that civic loyalty to one's own country should take a back seat to some sort of internationalist identity or connection. The ethic is one of liberal universalism.

This is pretty prosaic when it is compared with other feminist alternatives, those flowing from the radical, Marxist, or ecofeminist perspectives. Radical feminism itself is aptly termed a war discourse that depicts all of social life as battleground, reversing the Clausewitzian dictum by viewing politics as war by other means. Military metaphors are generously sprinkled about in the discourse. Politics is a case of oppressor and oppressed, and power is a force to be deployed, for or against. The argument is that human beings will never know peace until men are defeated. Matriarchal society, defined as a society in which all relationships are modeled on the nurturant relationship between a mother and child, is celebrated as the healing vision that will one day triumph. Several ethical positions are here embedded: a provisional, instrumental ethic that allows or requires the most drastic means, such as reducing the proportion of men in the human race, in order to arrive at a utopian moment that will, once achieved, sustain itself. Then and only then will peace prevail. In the meantime, there is the bad violence of patriarchal society, and no distinction is made between, on one hand, individual acts or state actions, and, on the other, the good actions of feminists in combatting that violence even if those actions themselves are harsh. Dozens of essays and books have pushed arguments along this line from the late 1960s to the present moment.

Ecofeminists rush in a pacifist direction. They seek not confrontation with men but redemption for men and masculinist society, away from its current warmaking ways. Tactics include mass demonstrations and encampments, such as Greenham Common in England and heavy use of dramatic symbolism identifying women with assaulted nature and stressing maternal imperatives as a counter to militaristic affronts. Because they hold that the human race is currently in a condition of war, the actual outbreak of hostilities seems, to ecofeminists, not so much a rupture in the social fabric as an extension of it. Pacifism, in this scheme of things, is something that comes more naturally to women than it does to men, but male pacifism is accepted and welcomed even if women choose to remain in separate organizations to fight, militantly but nonviolently, against war. Ecofeminists share with liberal feminists a suspicion of patriotism, or any strong tie to one's nation or people, fearing that it must inevitably erode into nationalist excess. They are citizens of the world. Theirs is an ethic of diffuse universalism that yields general condemnations of nation-states' formations and politics as practiced, past and present. Women are required to locate themselves as far as possible outside of, or in opposition to, the power structures of their own societies in favor of connecting themselves to women everywhere who are struggling to give birth to new social forms.

Marxist feminists, on the other hand, offer provisional acceptance, at times enthusiastic endorsement, of collective violence if it is the right sort—revolutionary violence against an oppressor. They see in much liberal feminism queasiness about violence, or in pacifist feminism, rejection of it, bourgeois niceties unsuited to the harsh realities of power struggles. Their rhetoric is aimed at mobilization for the struggle, and the form that struggle takes is determined by whatever the historical matrix offers up. To reject violent struggle is a strategic, not an ethical, question. Using whatever is required to do the job is the rule of thumb. Wars pursued by established Western powers are, by definition, unjust wars for imperialistic aims. Wars of revolutionary liberation, however, can and must be fought by all, men and women, in behalf of all. Those who oppose such struggles must themselves be opposed. The yardstick for the evaluation of violence, then, is a political one itself determined by the predeterminations of an ideology that locates good in history.

What is missing from all these formulations, and underdeveloped inside feminist theorizing, is something like a just-war perspective, an ethical stance that puts the burden of proof on those who would resort to violence but makes room for the prohibition against violence to be overridden if particular conditions are met. Most important for these considerations is the fact that just-war thinking is complex, requiring of citizens, male and female, that they reflect on what their governments are up to in a way attuned to moral reasoning and capable of and bounded by a sense of responsibility and accountability. Men and women are constituted alike as citizens and moral agents who must reflect rather than react with absolutist responses to situations in which collective violence is anticipated or actually taking place. Perhaps because just-war thinking is not geared toward ultimate outcomes but, instead, works to limit the damage that is being done here and now, it is less attractive to those for whom a specific political mission is first and foremost and whose task would be made far more difficult were they to adhere to a moral perspective that does not lend itself to easy moralizing or to simplistic condemnations.

FROM TEXT TO CONTEXT: FEMINIST RESPONSES TO REPRODUCTIVE TECHNOLOGY

Although war is a perennial vexation, contemporary society also faces new and daunting challenges, among them a panoply of real or potential techniques for manipulating, redirecting, controlling, and altering human reproduction that some have called the new eugenics. In vitro fertilization, artificial insemination by donor, embryo flushing, surrogate embryo transfer, surrogate motherhood, sex preselection—what was once science fiction is now social fact. As one explores various feminist positions, one discovers that there are often ways in which an explicit stance—say, opposition to surrogacy—is undermined by a tacit commitment to a framework embedded in presumptions that erode such opposition. Needless to say, this needs explaining, and I will do so by referring the reader back to the distinctions between various feminisms.

Although contemporary feminist discourse, in all its major variants, is dedicated to the notion of reproductive freedom, few feminist thinkers paid much attention to newer technologies for controlling human reproduction other than to issue manifestos in behalf of a 100 percent safe and effective contraception and in behalf of abortion on demand. The voices within the feminist camp that questioned arguments for abortion couched exclusively in the language of absolute freedom of choice, or rights, did not prevail in the debates. These voices now seem prescient given the runaway developments of the past decade.

For one group, the radical pro-interventionists, the new eugenics presents no problem so long as it can be wrested from male control.[9] Radical feminists and many, though by no means all, Marxist feminists belong in the pro-interventionist camp. Radical interventionists express their indebtedness both to a Marxist teleology of history and to celebrations of choice by construing technology as an instrument that will usher in a new social order so long as feminists control it.

The only possible opposition to the new eugenics that might emerge from the pro-interventionist camp takes the form of warning that evil forces—masculinists, antifeminists—are controlling the means of control. Therefore an ongoing political struggle is required to be sure patriarchalists do not succeed in this effort. But pro-interventionist caveats have been compromised by the fact that they share rather than oppose the assumptions of their masculinist counterparts: that nature must be overcome; that, where human beings find the will to indulge acts of overcoming, they must find a way; that only the fearful and the backward will cavil at these inexorable developments—again, with feminist interventionists of the radical and Marxist varieties insisting that if women are in charge, the outcomes will be beneficent.

Radical interventionism goes so far as to envisage forms of biological engineering that would create such possibilities as the following:

> for instance, one woman could inseminate another, so that men and nonparturitive women could lactate and so that fertilized ova could be transplanted into women's or even into men's bodies. These developments may seem far-fetched, but in fact they are already on the technological horizon; however, what is needed much more immediately than technological development is a substantial reduction in the social domination of women by men. Only such a reduction can ensure that these or alternative technological possibilities are used to increase women's control over their bodies and thus over their lives.[10]

The standard of evaluation here is control: what abets it is good, what mutes it is bad. Thus the way is paved for supporting invasive techniques in and upon human bodies as a form of biosocial engineering. Seeing in women's links to biology, birth, and nurturance the vestiges of our animal origins and patriarchal control, anything that breaks those links is, by definition, to be applauded.

Opposed to the radical pro-interventionist stance is the radical noninterventionist voice associated with ecofeminism. Continuing to sustain the right to choose, the noninterventionists ponder the nature of the many choices that the new reproductive technology throws up. Is amniocentesis really a free choice, or is it all too often a coercive procedure with only one correct outcome, to abort if the fetus is defective? What about the right to a child pandered to by the new technologies—is this yet another imposition of patriarchal society upon women who see themselves as failures if they cannot become pregnant? As well, the values identified with mothering are reassessed as anti-interventionist feminists encourage nonexploitative maternity. For separatists this means only within lesbian relationships. Others allow that male-female relationships may be acceptable so long as so-called female values prevail in the relationship.

What is curious about much of the anti-interventionist argument is that many of its most radical proponents share the same assumptions as pro-interventionists about the nature of human social life and all of history: it is patriarchal, with women cast either as universal victims or an oppressed sex-class. The difference is that anti-interventionists hold that all modern technology is designed explicitly to deepen and extend patriarchal control and masculinist patterns of thought. They are deeply skeptical that this technology can be turned to good purposes. Thus the new forms of reproductive engineering cannot be reconfigured to meet feminist and women's needs. Working from the analogy of prostitution, radical noninterventionists insist that just as males moved successfully to control female sex parts through various forms of prostitution, including marriage, so they seek a new reality: the reproductive brothel. Writes Andrea Dworkin, " 'Women can sell reproductive capacities the same way old-time prostitutes sold sexual ones . . . while sexual prostitutes sell vagina, rectum, and mouth, reproductive-prostitutes will sell other body parts: Wombs. Ovaries. Eggs.' "[11] Needless to say, this position is condemnatory of all men and contemptuous of many women.

Liberal feminists are more vexed by these issues than are feminists whose positions are more absolutist, and the same holds for the new eugenics. Liberal feminists face a series of dilemmas when confronted with transformations in human reproduction, and their quandary is crystallized in the Baby M. case. Here was a situation in which biological motherhood and social parenting were severed—as feminists, including liberal feminists, had long claimed they could or should be. Here was a case in which everyone presumably freely agreed to a contract, and liberal feminism emphasizes contractarian imperatives. Yet many liberal feminists, including Betty Friedan, saw in the initial denial of any claim by Mary Beth Whitehead, as natural mother, to her child, " 'an utter denial of the personhood of women—the complete dehumanization of women. It is an important human rights case. To put it at the level of contract law is to dehumanize woman and the human bond between mother and child.' "[12] Friedan here implies, though she does not spell out, an ethical limitation to freedom of choice and contract.

In the meantime, feminist quandaries concerning the new eugenics inexorably pitch feminists back into discussions of men, women, children, families, the wider community. To insist, as all radical—and many equal-rights and Marxist—feminists have done, that we must refuse to privilege any norm of the family as consisting of men, women, and offspring and must, instead, either remain neutral or privilege nonpatriarchal familial forms may, paradoxically, have opened up women's lives to more potential forms of control. If the female body is an entity over which more and more control must be exercised, with no limits save those of the sovereign choice of the individual on what can or should be manipulated or altered, the moral barriers to radical interventionism are erased. The political point—that if a woman chooses it, it is correct—is insufficient to block the dubious advance of the new eugenics; for in this matter as in all others of importance, ways can be devised to manipulate permission. What this question, together with the uncertainties and inadequacies of feminist political responses to war, points to is the need for more subtle and sophisticated feminist ethical theorizing.

MOVING AWAY FROM DOGMA: TOWARD THE ARTICULATION OF A FEMINIST ETHIC OF LIMITS

The editors of a recent volume, *Women and Moral Theory,* find two main perspectives at work in current, explicit moral theorizing by women, with women in mind. They tag these the justice versus care perspectives.[13] The justice perspective posits an autonomous moral agent who discovers and applies fundamental rules through the use of universal and abstract reason. The care perspective emphasizes personal responsibility and connectedness to others. Within justice, rights are reaffirmed. The care outlook, however, is more aptly seen as a form of virtue theory, Aristotelian as opposed to Kantian. Justice stresses the abstract individual; care, the encumbered familial and social being.

Although I am troubled by construing justice in opposition to care, this formulation is helpful in sorting out the ethical implications of contrasting feminist perspectives. It requires of theorizers that they pay sensitive attention to just what the world would be like for ordinary men, women, and children were it to be refashioned in line with their directives. A subtle theory attuned to the justice-care dialectic, if I may use an overused word, opens up our inquiry and deepens our ethical capacities by refusing the bargain-basement salvation of original positions, clearly identified enemies, ahistoricizing sweeps, and predetermined end points. One presumes instead that all points of view are partial and incomplete and that hermeneutical and ethical dilemmas cannot be evaded.

Unlike the abstract, overdetermined subjects of sex-neutralists and polarists, those abstract subjects who populate the worlds of their texts, the human beings I here envisage are engaged in social relations in diverse settings. Although gender may be determinative to some ends and purposes, it also matters whether one is American or Russian, an urban Catholic or a rural Baptist. One cannot explore these other features of identity, or describe them adequately, if one begins by presuming that a person's ethnic heritage, religion, community ties, favorite books, or political candidates are trivial icing on the real cake of gender.

Within this world of ethical feminism, the possibility is present, and sought, for citizens, male and female, to act together toward ends they debate and articulate in public. A feminist politics that does not allow for the possibility of transformation of men as well as of women, in ways over which no ideology has or should have control, is deeply nihilistic; it does not truly believe in human possibility or the ideal of mutuality. How to go about articulating the ethics intimated in these general comments? The most effective way is through storytelling, narratives of human tragedy and achievement, of perseverance and failure. One poses certain questions: how can or might we relocate ourselves in order to create space for a less rigid play of individual and civic virtues than those we have known? what alternative images of citizenship can we draw upon? what perspectives currently within our reach offer hope for sustaining an ethos, stripped of utopian pretensions, that extends the prospect of limiting force and the threat of force?

Who should be our moral teachers? I suggest that we look not toward the fabricators of abstract systems but toward the livers of concrete lives. The best current women's studies scholarship helps us to do just that by apprising us that the world is untidy and complex. For example, Natalie Zemon Davis, in an essay on men, women, and the problem of collective violence, argues that the opposition presumed by sex-polarists between "life-givers" and "life-takers" is not so clear-cut if one looks at "the historical record of the late Middle Ages and the early modern period."[14] She sketches the numerous competing and compelling notions of manhood available in early modern Europe, from warrior to pacifist, with reflections about male violence carried out in "a nuanced fashion" in contrast to the "simplistic terms" that tended to dominate discourse on women and violence. The distinguishing characteristics of Davis's discussion are its desimplifying quality and the ways in which she alerts us to the fact that each historical epoch defined and set limits to acceptable human conduct.

A lesson about human love and protest, about pain and moral triumph, can be gleaned from the words and deeds of the Mothers of the Plaza de Mayo, of Buenos Aires, Argentina. The Mothers illustrate a moral perspective that challenges violations of moral limits yet sets limits to their own response. Their morality is one that does not set justice and care at odds but fuses them into a discourse that is double: speaking the language of the anguish of a mother's loss and the language of human rights.[15] The Mothers, by their public presence and courageous action, shattered the systematic deceit that had shrouded the disappearances of their children; they transgressed official orders in marching in the Plaza de Mayo. "*Las locas*" ("the madwomen") they were called—beyond the pale, outside the boundaries of legitimate politics. They reversed the strategy of their detractors and fashioned it into a political weapon. Their aim was to refuse to sacralize any new victims and to refuse to cast themselves as victims. The victims were those who had been abducted, tortured, killed. The truth that the Mothers offer is not a big, booming teleological truth, but a truth that disallows him or her who has grasped it to serve as judge and executioner. Their openness to beginnings, even under conditions of terror and torture, renewed the world, making possible future beginnings and sustaining the hope that human beings might one day be delivered from revenge.

Notes

1. I draw upon my book *Public Man, Private Woman: Women in Social and Political Thought* (Princeton, NJ: Princeton University Press, 1981) as well as several previous essays for this discussion.

2. For one of the liveliest examples of this genre by one of its best-known spokeswomen, see Mary Daly, *Pure Lust* (Boston: Beacon Press, 1984).

3. Spacks's essay appears in E. Langland and W. Gove, eds., *A Feminist Perspective in the Academy: The Difference It Makes* (Chicago: University of Chicago Press, 1981), pp. 7–24.

4. Charles Taylor, "Atomism," in *Power, Possessions and Freedom: Essays in Honor of C. B. McPherson,* ed. Alkis Kontos (Toronto: University of Toronto Press, 1979), p. 48.

5. See, for example, Gayle Rubin, "The Traffic in Women: Notes on a 'Political Economy' of Sex," in *Toward an Anthropology of Women,* ed. Rayna R. Reiter (New York: Monthly Review Press, 1975), p. 165.

6. See, for example, Ann Ferguson, "Androgyny as an Ideal for Human Development," in *Feminism and Philosophy,* ed. M. Vetterling-Braggin, F. Elliston, and J. English (Totowa, NJ: Rowman & Allanheld, 1977), pp. 62–63.

7. I draw freely upon my book *Women and War* (New York: Basic Books, 1987) for these reflections on feminism and war.

8. The brief is available from the NOW Legal Defense and Education Fund, 132 West 42d Street, New York, NY 10036.

9. See Anne Donchin, "The Future of Mothering: Reproductive Technology and Feminist Theory," *Hypatia,* 2(2):121–37 (Fall 1986). Donchin divides feminist positions into noninterventionist, moderate interventionist, and radical interventionist.

10. Alison M. Jagger, *Feminist Politics and Human Nature* (Totowa, NJ: Rowman & Allanheld, 1983), p. 132.

11. Cited in Genoveffa Corea, "How the New Reproductive Technologies Could Be Used to Apply the Brothel Model of Social Control over Women," *Women's Studies International Forum,* 8(4):299 (1985).

12. Cited in James Barron, "Views on Surrogacy Harden after Baby M. Ruling," *New York Times,* 2 Apr. 1987.

13. Eva Feder Kittay and Diana T. Meyers, eds., *Women and Moral Theory* (Totowa, NJ: Rowman & Littlefield, 1987).

14. Natalie Zemon Davis, "Men, Women and Violence: Some Reflections on Equality," *Smith Alumnae Quarterly,* Apr. 1972, pp. 12–15.

15. For those readers not familiar with the political events that gave birth to the Mothers, suffice it to say that between 1976 and 1979 at least 10,000 Argentine citizens were abducted and murdered by their government. Many of them were young people, the sons and daughters of the Mothers of the Plaza.

"Does Sex Matter to Democracy?" —A Comment

CAROLE PATEMAN

Two aspects of the relation between sexual difference and democracy are discussed: (i) the construction in classic contract theory of the 'natural' difference between the sexes as a relation of superiority and subordination: (ii) the peculiarities and paradoxes of women's standing as citizens as the 'different' sex. This is illustrated by the examples of motherhood—women have been seen as having a distinctive political duty as mothers, but motherhood is also seen as the antithesis of citizenship—by the difficulties surrounding women and consent, and by the questions raised by contemporary feminists about the meaning of ('normal') 'sex'.

· · ·

Political theorists still tend to ignore three hundred years of feminist argument and the fact that the problem of the relation between the sexes was central to the political theories of the seventeenth and eighteenth centuries.

CONTRACT THEORIES

Theories about the state of nature and the original contract are important precisely because the classic contract theorists held that the natural difference between the sexes was the political difference between freedom (for men) and subjection (for women).[1] Only men 'by nature' possessed the capacities of 'individuals' that enabled them to make the original contract and then participate as equal citizens in the free civil society they had created through their agreement. Contract doctrine has had a new lease of life since the publication of Rawls's *A Theory of Justice* (1971). We are told that the idea of an original contract is the appropriate way in which we can understand the character of our political institutions, and that contract doctrine provides the appropriate metaphors, images, models and analogies through which we can represent our political life to ourselves. Contemporary contract theorists, however, do not tell the whole story. They merely discuss the social contract, which justifies the government of the

state. But the social contract is only half of the original contract. The sexual contract, which justifies the government of men over women, is always missing. The
original contract is an agreement which creates modern *patriarchal* civil society.
(The details of this interpretation can be found in Pateman 1988.)

The classic contract theorists' appeal to nature enabled them to exclude sexual relations from the revolutionary implications of their own premise of individual (natural) freedom and equality. The same brilliant theoretical manoeuvre enabled them to place sexual difference at the centre of their political theories and
to justify patriarchal rule and yet, at the same time, to exclude the ('natural') relations between the sexes from the scrutiny and criticism to which other forms of
government were subjected. 'Nature' (in other words, womanhood and manhood
or sexual difference) and convention or 'politics' were brought into opposition
with each other. The exclusion of sexual difference, women and the relation between the sexes from 'the political' began as an explicitly political strategy, but is
now accepted as a valid limitation on the scope of political enquiry by most contemporary students of politics. They accept that the public world of politics can be
understood, investigated and theorized in isolation from relations between men
and women and the private world, and thus they fail to ask how this isolation of
the public and political was established. That is to say, they fail to explore the interdependence between the meaning of the political, the public, manhood, equality, freedom and citizenship, and the meaning of the natural, the private, womanhood, difference, subordination and sex and love.

WOMEN AS WOMEN

The construction of politics and citizenship in exclusion from, and in opposition
to, sexual difference is central to the second issue on which I wish to comment:
namely, women's standing as citizens, and what Jónasdóttir calls 'the struggle over
the creation and confirmation of a self-evident authority of women' (p. 313). The
difficulty for women is that citizenship as an equal political status is seen as anti-
thetical to sexual difference. 'Equality' requires a standard of measurement, and
the present standard is the masculine construction of what it means to be an 'individual' and citizen; women are always 'different'. Thus, on the one hand, to demand that women must be equal to men in all respects as citizens is to demand
that women must be like men; on the other hand, the demand that has long been
heard from feminists, that women's 'different' capacities and tasks should be recognized as relevant for citizenship or become part of citizenship, is to try to attain
something that at present is out of reach, because citizenship is held to transcend
such differences between the sexes. So the question, as Jónasdóttir emphasizes, is
how women are to be citizens 'as women'.

. . . When I refer to 'women as women . . . I am referring to the curious manner of women's incorporation into political life. Women's political standing is so
peculiar and complex because our political exclusion and political inclusion are
both based on our difference from men; women have been excluded and included
'as women'. In the past, women have been excluded as women, as men's natural

subordinates, and also included as women, as beings who have a different political contribution to make from men whether or not they are citizens. In the future, feminists hope, women will be included 'as women', that is as autonomous, full members of the citizen body, who have 'self-evident authority'—but who are not the same as men. The crucial point is that it has not been, and is not, a matter of whether women will be excluded/included as women (i.e. whether sexual difference is politically relevant) but always of how sexual difference will be given political expression and how women will be incorporated into politics. Is the patriarchal expression of sexual difference as the difference between freedom and subordination to continue?

. . . There cannot be a genuinely democratic theory and practice unless the problem of motherhood is treated as a problem of democracy. Most democratic theorists see no special problem about women and citizenship, and tacitly assume that motherhood stands outside politics. The contradictions and ambiguities in women's political position thus remain unrecognized and the antagonism between motherhood and citizenship appears irresolvable.

. . . [There is a] connection between my interest in women and consent and the figure of the mother: women usually only become pregnant as a result of sexual intercourse, and 'consent' determines whether pregnancy and motherhood have been undertaken freely or are a result of coercion or violence. . . . Feminists have raised two fundamentally important and related questions: firstly, to what extent 'consent' in any genuine sense can be said to exist for women in democracies given the present structure of sexual relations: and secondly, what exactly is the meaning of 'sex'?

Women's relation to the practice of consent is very peculiar. 'Consent' has meaning if and only if withdrawal of consent and refusal of consent are actually possible. Yet women's moral and sexual characters are seen to be such that, simultaneously, women are held to lack the capacities required to enter the practice of consent, yet always consent, and can always have their refusals of consent reinterpreted. Both the texts of political theory and empirical evidence about contemporary sexual relations raise disquieting questions about the comfortable assumption that 'sex' is consensual, constituted by the freely given consent of the two partners, and thus is decisively separated from coercion and violence. Popular belief and legal and social practice mean that enforced submission is often taken to be 'consent'. Empirical evidence about rape and sexual harassment, the fact that in many jurisdictions husbands still have the legal right of sexual access to their wife's body irrespective of her consent and the fact that the sex industry is now a world-wide branch of capitalism, mean that there are some very severe, and barely recognized, obstacles to women's 'self-evident authority' and, hence, to their citizenship (Pateman 1989b).

Political theorists emphasize the fundamental importance of public speech, debate and deliberation to the practice of consent and democracy. But they rarely take account of the problems that stand in the way of the creation of 'democracy' when 'everyone knows' that women always say 'no' when they mean 'yes', and women's speech is thus systematically invalidated every day in their sexual relations with men. Nor do they ponder on the meaning of 'sex' and its significance for democracy in the light of the problems about women and consent. In my investigation of the texts of classic contract theory and the contemporary marriage contract and prostitution industry in *The Sexual Contract* (Pateman 1988), I came to the conclusion that 'sex' means men's mastery, their demand to have right of sexual access to women's bodies. This is not to say that it is impossible for (heterosexual) sex to be consensual. But any such relationship has to be created in the face of the constraints imposed by the present patriarchal structure of meaning of 'masculinity', 'femininity', 'husband' and 'wife' (whether *de jure* or *de facto*).

The questions that feminists have raised about . . . 'ordinary' sexuality also pose problems. . . . From ancient times philosophers have insisted that love is possible only between equals—and so the argument comes back to the problem of creating the conditions for women's citizenship and the political recognition of our 'self-evident authority'. Sex matters to democracy because the construction of sexual difference and sexual relations is part of the construction of political life. Women will not be citizens of a democracy *as women* until sexual difference is given expression in a manner that acknowledges and maintains, instead of denying, women's freedom.

Note

1. Hobbes is an exception; he argued that men and women were natural equals and both free by nature. Political theorists typically ignore the significance of this difference between Hobbes's theory and the other contract theorists. On Hobbes see Pateman (1989a).

References

Firestone, S. 1970. *The Dialectic of Sex*. New York: W. Morrow.
Foucault, M. 1980. *The History of Sexuality*. Vol. 1. New York: Vintage Books.
Gilligan, C. 1982. *In A Different Voice: Psychological Theory and Women's Development*. Cambridge MA: Harvard University Press.
Greer, G. 1970. *The Female Eunuch*. London: MacGibbon & Kee.
Kerber, L. K. 1986. *Women of the Republic: Intellect and Ideology in Revolutionary America*. New York: W. W. Norton & Co. Inc.
Pateman, C. 1988. *The Sexual Contract*. Cambridge: Polity Press.
Pateman, C. 1989a. ' "God Hath Ordained to Man a Helper": Hobbes, Patriarchy and Conjugal Right'. *British Journal of Political Science*, 19, 445–464.
Pateman, C. 1989b. 'Women and Consent', in Pateman, C. *The Disorder of Women: Democracy, Feminism and Political Theory*. Cambridge: Polity Press.
Ruddick, S. 1980. 'Maternal Thinking', *Feminist Studies* 6(2), 342–367.

FURTHER READING FOR CHAPTER 8

Bourque, S., and J. Grossholtz. 1974. "Politics as an Unnatural Practice:PoliticalScience Looks at Female Participation." *Politics and Society* 4:4.
Bryson, V. 1992. *Feminist Political Theory*. London: Macmillan.
Coole, D. H. 1988. *Women in Political Theory: From Ancient Misogyny to Contemporary Feminism*. Hempstead: Harvester Wheatsheaf.

Diamond, I., and N. Hartsock. 1981. "Beyond Interests in Politics: A Comment on Virginia Sapiro's 'When Are Interests Interesting?' " *American Political Science Review* 75(3):717–726.

Elshtain, J. Bethke. 1981. *Public Man, Private Woman: Women in Social and Political Thought.* Princeton: Princeton University Press.

Eisenstein, H. 1984. *Contemporary Feminist Thought.* London: Allen and Unwin.

Evans, J., et al. 1986. *Feminism and Political Theory.* London: Sage.

Jones, K. B. 1990. "Citizenship in a Woman-Friendly Polity." *Signs* 13(4):779–810.

Jones, K. B., and A. Jonasdottir (eds.). 1988. *The Political Interests of Gender.* London: Sage.

Okin, S. Moller. 1979. *Women in Western Political Thought.* London: Virago.

Pateman, C. 1988. *The Sexual Contract.* Cambridge: Polity Press.

———. 1989. *The Disorder of Women.* Cambridge: Polity Press.

Phillips, A. 1991. *Engendering Democracy.* Cambridge: Polity Press.

Ramazongolu, C. 1989. *Feminism and the Contradictions of Oppression.* London: Routledge.

Sapiro, V. 1981. "When Are Interests Interesting? The Problem of Political Representation of Women." *American Political Science Review* 75(3): 701–716.

CHAPTER
9

Difference and Feminist Politics

Gender politics are greatly influenced by class, race, ethnicity, sexuality, and other differences between women. Perhaps the most disappointing development in the women's movement of the 1960s and 1970s was the fragmentation that resulted from these divisions. No sooner had the slogan "Sisterhood is powerful" become established in feminist rhetoric than bitter arguments in the movement made sisterhood seem impossible. Such divisions afflicted feminist movements everywhere, although the relative influence of class, race, and sexual preference varied considerably.

The issues dividing feminists are referred to in this chapter as difference issues. There is an irony here because difference is the starting point of feminist politics and coupled with demands for equality for women, generated the women's movement of the 1960s. But the movement soon began to fragment, as feminists became aware of what divided them.

The debates centered on this issue may be described as discourses of difference, by which we mean the way we think, talk, and argue about differences. A significant feature of this debate is the realization that women have many competing identities. Explorations of the meaning of class, race, ethnicity, sexuality, physical disability, and the continuing feminist exploration of the nature of masculinity and femininity, turn on the recognition that identity is central to difference. Some feminists demand equality with men. Others argue that to be equal to men means being like men, thereby giving up what is good and valuable about being women, so it would be better for feminists to identify and stress women's identity as women.

Class, race, sexuality, and gender interact in numerous ways and produce hierarchies of power that mean different women experience gender relations differently. Socioeconomic class is probably the main determinant of access to resources in society. We have already mentioned that the poverty many women experience impedes their full participation as citizens. The socioeconomic positions of women and men differ in all modern societies. Men tend to be located in more privileged, better-paid positions in the occupational hierarchy as a whole; to be in the higher grades within each occupational category; and to be wealthier than women. Nevertheless, there are class differences between women, and this has significant effects on women's resources. In addition, within traditional households, women's life-styles are strongly influenced by the socioeconomic status of their male partners. Finally, through the labor movement and left-wing parties, social class underpins the party system in most liberal democracies; hence, women's socioeconomic position has direct political consequences.

Equally critical are race and ethnicity, which interact with gender and class in numerous ways. While black women and women of color are aware of their race, white women have been less conscious of theirs, even though it is crucial to their identity.

Sexual preference is also a source of identity and therefore difference. By the early 1990s feminist attempts to understand and to theorize sexuality had become a major preoccupation. In this endeavor feminists draw on a growing interest in the subject by academic sociologists, philosophers, and psychoanalytic theorists. Feminists contest the popular view that sexuality is "natural." In so doing they raise the political question of whose interests are served by the assumption that heterosexuality is natural. Feminists are also concerned about the way sexuality is represented in popular images and advertising, and women have shown that pornography strongly influences the way relations between men and women are understood and idealized. These projects are not exclusive to feminists, of course, but they are central to their concerns and have resulted in a significant feminist contribution to the analysis of sexuality.

Finally, feminists have explored how individuals come to acquire masculine and feminine identities. The political object of these studies is to discover whether masculinity and femininity are fixed or the result of social conditioning. If masculinity and femininity are socially constructed, then they may be amenable to change.

In the extracts that follow, each of these issues is considered. In the first extract, Anne Phillips describes what class means to British women. Next, Pratibha Parmar reviews the emergence of black feminism in Britain and the problems of fragmentation that plague "identity politics." Identity politics plays a vital part in the creation of liberation movements. As Parmar's interview with the American feminist June Jordan indicates, the assertion of an identity may be liberating, but it is only the first step in political activism. If liberation stops with the assertion of identity and does not proceed to the formation of alliances and coalitions, the problem will never be solved.

Carole Vance addresses the social construction of sexuality. She utilizes, and implicitly criticizes, the ideas of Freud and his successors on the significance of sex to the making of an individual personality. For Freudians, sexuality is a manifestation of the embodied self in which the unconscious mind carries the experience of the infant, and in which biological needs may also be working. But, as Vance indicates with her explanation of how different social groups have defined and constructed categories of sexuality, the development of sexuality is also a social process. Vance shows how ideas about sexual practice are used to marginalize lesbians, gays, and bisexuals. If we accept that sexuality is socially constructed, we must also accept that it is a political process with political consequences. Feminists have shown how the dominance of heterosexuality is imposed and maintained in contemporary society. There is a hierarchy of power that relates to sexuality, and the social penalties for adopting a homosexual identity may be severe.

Recent feminist studies of gender and power emphasize that the acquisition of gender identity is also a social process. Masculinity has become a major preoccupation for feminists who have reasoned that only by exploring masculinity will it be possible to learn the nature of femininity. In the last extract Robert Connell has used the analytical techniques of social construction to show the great variety of competing masculinities in contemporary society. He argues that the way one particular masculinity has come to be dominant illustrates how power operates in gender relations.

JONI LOVENDUSKI

Class Matters

ANNE PHILLIPS

One problem in identifying the differences between women is that we are both so vague and yet so confident over what we mean by class. Just a few moment's acquaintance, and most of us will happily volunteer an opinion on another woman's class, for it is a label we employ all the time to place ourselves and those we meet. Sometimes it is ambiguous, sometimes we have our doubts, but rather than admit to no opinion at all, most of us will then resort to the qualifying adjectives of 'upper' and 'lower': 'upper working class', 'lower middle class', 'upper middle class'. If we cannot place someone immediately as either working or middle class, we try out our finer distinctions.

Class is deeply engraved in our culture, yet what it stands for can be surprisingly hard to define, and when we turn to our own biographies we are often at a loss to say just what we are. For myself as a schoolgirl, I was thoroughly convinced that I must be working class, for my parents were short of money, my uncles worked in manual trades—and what seemed most important of all in my adolescence, I said dinner instead of lunch. In the claustrophic environment of a middle-class girls' school, I felt simultaneously proud and ashamed of the fact, embarrassed by what I feared was my cultural poverty yet inclined to despise what I saw as the privileges of those around me. In my progress through university to the relative securities of an academic job I then found myself occupying an uncomfortable middle ground, quick to assume the trappings of a new lifestyle yet reluctant to abandon my claims as a member of the working class. The credentials became more and more shaky—they were never that strong!—but it was a long time before I could admit that I might be middle class, and indeed in retrospect that I had probably always been so.

From a different background a friend once described her own initiation into these mysteries, which in her case entailed a journey in the opposite direction. A teacher in secondary school had asked each girl to say which class she came from, and in a response which would have gratified 1950s students of social mobility, many replied that they must be middle class for their parents had a colour TV. Only as the teacher went on to talk of the workers as those who produced the wealth of society—introducing for perhaps the first time the notion that being working class was something to be proud of—did the girls come to perceive that their objective status might in fact be working class.

Accounts like these are just the tip of the iceberg and they hint at major discrepancies in our perceptions of class. At one time we operated with what seemed a straightforward distinction between manual and non-manual workers, taking this as the chasm that marked our differential access to income, security and power. The 'never-had-it-so-good' post-war boom jarred this convention, for it brought unprecedented improvements in average living standards and promised new opportunities for social mobility via the free system of public education. Our understanding of class was inevitably disturbed. Average incomes soared; luxury commodities like that colour TV were made widely available through the cheapening techniques of mass production; the income gap between at least the skilled manual workers and those in non-manual jobs began to close, as did the gap in terms of working hours, holidays and pension rights. The 1950s was the age of the 'affluent worker', when a generation of sociologists proclaimed the end of class society, and went out, questionnaires in hand, to investigate the 'embourgeoisement' of the working class. And if their findings rarely confirmed the initial pronouncements, this did not dissolve the problem: the boundary between manual and non-manual workers had undoubtedly shifted, and what class meant was less than sure.

Official statistics, and accompanying them much of academic sociology, have tackled the question in a way that mirrors our commonsense evasions. But instead of those sub-sets of upper and lower working class, upper, lower and even 'middle' middle class, the categories of the Registrar-General have divided us into six distinct social classes, relying on occupational criteria. Depending on whether our work is manual or non-manual, but also whether it is professional, skilled, semi- or unskilled, we are allocated to one of the 'classes' A, B, C1, C2, D and E that figure in reports of surveys and opinion polls. Not so much classes as occupational groups, these get round the ambiguities in our usage of middle and working class, but at the expense of abandoning much of what we mean by these notions.

Traditional marxism veers in the opposite direction, though it too disdains the mystifications of a middle and working divide. In the tradition of Marx and Engels, this distinction is necessarily suspect, for it raises to undue prominence what marxism sees as relatively insubstantial demarcations *between* workers, glossing over the more basic power relations between capital and labour. Class, from the marxist perspective, is about the relations of production; it rests on that decisive gulf between those who own capital and those who do not, between those who employ and those who must work for a living. The kind of job you do is then of secondary significance: you may be a teacher, a cleaner, an engineer or an assembly worker; if you have to work for your living (and it hardly matters whether your employer is the state or a private firm) you belong to the working class. The workers are those who work, a conception embedded even in the non-marxist practices of the British Labour Party, whose famous Clause Four calls on the 'workers by hand or by brain' to secure the full fruits of their industry, and makes no distinction between manual and non-manual workers. These workers are of course divided by history and status and income, and when we talk so obsessively of 'middle' and 'working-class' we are referring to what *can* be major divisions. But when it comes down to the real questions of class power, we are all in much the same boat.[1]

The commonsense distinctions between middle and working class; the more purist marxist emphasis on the relationship between capital and labour; the multiple categories of the Registrar-General: all these have entered in some way into feminist debates on class. The result is that like everyone else, the women's movement has used class to mean different things at different times. Imagine a meeting advertised on the topic of 'women and class': you would be hard put to it to guess what that meeting might cover, and only when you learn the context will you decide whether you want to attend. If it heralds a meeting organised by the Revolutionary Communist Party, you could expect a discussion of the bourgeois deviations of feminist politics, an assertion that it is capitalism and class that determines our lives. If it announces a seminar of the British Sociological Association, you might anticipate a critique of academic conceptions of class, a discussion of how these have reflected the positions of male heads of households, defining women by their marital role. If it refers instead to a meeting of non-academic feminists, it is much more likely to cover tensions between middle-class and working-class activists, to explore the ways in which middle-class concerns have come to dominate the movement's campaigns. And if it refers to a meeting with a Women Against Pit Closures group, it will probably focus attention on the experiences and activities of working-class women, in the context of that paradigm of class action—a miners' strike. All these and others are aspects of 'women and class', and none has the monopoly on definition.

CLASS AS CAUSE OF WOMEN'S OPPRESSION

Much of the discussion within the contemporary Women's Liberation Movement has in fact hinged around the marxist conception of class, for it has focussed on the prime *causes* of women's oppression, trying to tease out the relative weight of gender and of class. 'Class' in this context has operated as shorthand for the forces of capital: is it capitalism or is it patriarchy that marks down our lives? capital or men that make up our problem? Take just one element in women's experience— the marked sexual segregation of the workforce which keeps women concentrated in lower paid, less skilled jobs. Sexual segregation at work has increased rather than diminished in the course of this century,[2] and it clearly accounts for much of women workers' low status and low pay. But what accounts in turn for sexual segregation? Do we put it down to capitalism or to patriarchy? to the divisive structures of capitalist production? or the exclusionary activities of unionised men? or to a combination of the two?

Pursuing the first line of argument, you might point to the way that capitalism's search for profits creates (at a minimum) two kinds of workers: those with skills and training who will be paid a higher rate in order to keep them with the firm; those who are so easily replaced that their wages can be criminally low. If the former group of workers are predominantly men, while the latter are mainly women, capitalism can keep the two groups apart, thereby blocking any potential 'wage drift' from the higher earners to the lower. The advantages of the former will not then spill over to the latter: to put it more starkly, a strategy of divide and rule can secure capital's future.[3] Or you might point out that it is part of the nature of capitalism that it goes through cycles of boom and collapse, and argue that to smooth out its path it draws on women as a 'reserve army of labour'—workers who can be taken into employment at times of expansion, but shunted back into the privacy of their homes at times of recession.[4] You might note further that capitalism has organised work as an activity separate from the home, for instead of the household being the place where production occurs—as it was for example, for the self-employed weavers and spinners before the industrial revolution—wage-earners for capital go *out* to their job. Men have become the breadwinners, women the home-bound dependants, and when they nonetheless do take up jobs they are paid by pin-money's pitiful standards.[5] And while such arguments have been pursued from a variety of theoretical persuasions, what binds them together is that all in principle search out a root cause in the nature of capitalist production. In this sense they identify 'class' as the major determinant of the oppression in women's lives.

One of the criticisms of such approaches from within the women's movement has been that they do not adequately explain why *women* end up at the bottom of the scale, for if all that matters is that there have to be two types of workers, or that some group or other must act as a reserve army of labour, why is it women who fall into these traps? After all, capitalism *has* sought female employment, not just in the lower reaches of unskilled or part-time or casualised work, but in the areas that men had considered their own. The history of class struggle has been punctuated by attempts to replace expensive men by cheaper women, for if the labour is forthcoming, employers do not concern themselves about who looks after the baby. The crucial occasions may have been changes in skill: as new technology has altered the basis of previous production, employers have tried to introduce semi-skilled women into what were once skilled men's jobs. For feminists the key point is this: in virtually every trade to which this process has applied, male workers have fought to keep out the women—journeymen tailors in the 1820s and '30s; skilled engineers in the First World War; compositors; transport workers; post office clerks.[6] 'The men are as bad as their masters', a woman worker complained to an Owenite paper in the 1830s,[7] and generations of women have repeated her cry. Each change in the labour process gave employers their chance, and wielding women as their weapon they leapt to the fray. The men fought back with all at their disposal: excluded women from their unions; campaigned against the use of (usually female) homeworkers; made sure that women when employed were kept in different grades. There were worthy exceptions, like the London dockers in the 1880s and '90s who gave considerable support to the struggles of women workers,[8] or the National Union of Clerks who in the early 1890s saw that equal pay for equal work could solve the problem at a stroke.[9] But on the whole it was a shoddy affair in which few people shone. Employers took on women, not because they favoured equal opportunity but because women were cheap; trade unionists fought gamely against the intrusions of their masters, and in the process secured their privileges as men.

In her influential article on 'The Unhappy Marriage of Marxism and Feminism', Heidi Hartmann argued that marxism as a theory and capitalism as a social force are both sex-blind.[10] Capitalism takes no interest in the sex of the people it employs—it does not concern itself with who goes down the mine or who looks after the babies—for what it cares about is how to make most profits. Marxism, in similar vein, can explain why capitalism creates certain 'places'—more skilled, less skilled, high paid, low paid—but it cannot explain the pattern which has so universally condemned women to the worst of these roles. To account for women's position in a sexually segregated workforce we must then call on the alternative theory of patriarchy: those processes through which men have established control over the labour of women, developing and securing a vested interest in female subordination. It is men who benefit from the domestic service women provide in the home, not capital; it is men who reap the reward of keeping women out of higher paid jobs. If capital then joins in their game, it is largely following their lead.

The notion that capitalism is sex-blind has considerable plausibility—I can well imagine a capitalism which makes no difference between its workers. But it would be one squeezed by labour shortage, forced to extract its workers from every nook and cranny, pressed to eliminate the wastage of women at home. In the wartime emergencies that provide us our best example, nurseries and creches sprang up overnight, and women workers did the jobs assumed to be peculiarly male. Reconstruction after the Second World War made similar demands on labour, but by then there were alternatives: Britain drew on labour reserves in its colonies and ex-colonies; Germany on 'guest-workers' from Turkey and parts of Eastern Europe; France on the small farmers expelled from a declining peasant economy. Women played their part, but in Britain in particular, this was to be as part-time workers; labour shortages were not acute enough to sustain the wartime conditions. And today, when unemployment on world scale is such a massive problem, capitalism is hardly short of labour; why should it bother to rock the male boat?

The arguments have gone backwards and forwards, and most contemporary feminist writing on women and work has converged on the notion that class and gender intertwine: in the spectrum of opinions between 'capital versus men' those who identify with either of the extremes are now in a minority. But still where you place yourself within that continuum has its significance, for the analysis of causes is not academic and implies very different courses of action. In a recent article on 'The British Women's Movement' Angela Weir and Elizabeth Wilson have challenged what they see as the women's movement's retreat from an emphasis on class, arguing among other things that the pauperisation that faces women today stems most directly from capitalist crisis. 'The *key* (my emphasis) issue for women is an expansion of the economy, and the creation of secure full time jobs for women'.[11] Whatever the forces of discrimination (and the authors do not deny its power), the situation of women cannot improve in the context of economic depression: for this moment at least, the over-riding priority is for men and women alike to mobilise around campaigns for an alternative, non-capitalist, economic strategy. Those who in the name of feminism have turned their arguments *against* the labour movement, focussing on its record of denying the women, thus do us a disservice. However divisive male practices have been, it is now *capitalism* not the unions that must be targeted for change.

It is not (I am glad to say!) part of my self-imposed task to resolve these disputes, though it should be clear from my analysis that I do not accept any universal priority, that I see the 'key issues' shifting through context and time. As our male-structured capitalism runs through its course it poses different sets of problems to different groups of women, and what is interesting about the whole capitalism versus patriarchy' debate is that it connects only tangentially with the question of divisions between women. There is a half link: those who view capitalism as the major source of our problems may see a feminism that downplays this as too 'middle class'. But it is worth noting that the preferred term of criticism will probably be 'bourgeois', for in the marxist categories that inform the arguments the term middle class must be suspect.

There is in other words no neat overlay between those who argue the centrality of the marxist conception of class and those who stress the importance of class divides between women. Both groups are saying that class matters. But in the former it is a shorthand for capital and its powers, while in the latter it refers to a more conventional divide.

Notes

1. Contemporary marxism is more wary of such a solution, and for recent attempts to engage with the categories of middle and working class see N. Abercrombie and J. Urry, *Capital, Labour and the Middle Classes*, Allen and Unwin, London, 1983, or John Westergaard, 'The Once and Future Class', in James Curran (ed) *The Future of the Left*, Polity Press, Oxford, 1984.
2. Catherine Hakim, 'Sexual Division within the Labour Force: Occupational Segregation' *Employment Gazette*, November 1978; 'Job Segregation: Trends in the 1970s', *Employment Gazette*, December 1981.
3. In the literature this is known as the dual labour market theory, and a key article is R.D. Barron & G.M. Norris, 'Sexual Divisions and the Dual Labour Market' in Diana Leonard Barker and Sheiler Allen (eds) *Dependence and Exploitation in Work and Marriage*, Longman, London, 1976. For a critical discussion see Veronica Beechey, 'Women and Production: a Critical Analysis of some Sociological Theories of Women's Work', in Annette Kuhn and AnnMarie Wolpe (eds) *Feminism and Materialism*, Routledge and Kegan Paul, London, 1978.
4. For a discussion of this theory see for example Irene Bruegel, 'Women as a Reserve Army of Labour: a Note on Recent British Experience', *Feminist Review*, no.3, 1979.
5. The implications of the resulting 'family wage' are discussed (though not from a perspective that relies exclusively on the effects of capital) in Michele Barrett and Mary McIntosh, 'The "Family Wage": Some Problems for Socialists and Feminists', *Capital and Class*, no. 11, 1980.
6. See for example: Barbara Taylor, " 'The Men are as Bad as Their Masters . . . " Socialism, Feminism and Sexual Antagonism in the London Tailoring Trade in the Early 1830s', *Feminist Studies*, 5, no. 1, 1979; Heidi Hartmann, 'Capitalism, Patriarchy and Job Segregation by Sex', in Zillah Eisenstein (ed) *Capitalist Patriarchy and the Case for Socialist Feminism*, Monthly Review, New York, 1979; Sarah Boston, *Women Workers and the Trade Unions*, Davis-Poynter, London, 1980; Cynthia Cockburn, *Brothers: Male Dominance and Technological Change*, Pluto Press, London, 1983.
7. Quoted in Taylor, op.cit.
8. Boston, op.cit., p. 54.
9. ibid., p. 79.
10. Heidi Hartmann, 'The Unhappy Marriage of Marxism and Feminism: Towards a More Progressive Union', *Capital and Class*, no. 8, 1979.
11. Elizabeth Wilson and Angela Weir, 'The British Women's Movement', pp. 102–103, *New Left Review*, no. 148, 1984.

Other Kinds of Dreams

PRATIBHA PARMAR

In 1984 a group of us who guest edited a special issue of *Feminist Review* entitled 'Many Voices, One Chant: Black Feminist Perspectives' stated in our editorial: 'We have attempted to provide a collection of perspectives which are in the process of continual development, refinement and growth. It [the issue] also indicated some of the diversities within Black feminism, a diversity from which we draw strength.' (Amos *et al.*, 1984:2).

Rereading that issue now, it seems difficult to fathom where the optimism and stridency which many of us had who were active in the black women's movement has gone, and why. Where are the diverse black feminist perspectives which we felt were in the process of growth? And where indeed is the movement itself? In moments of despair one wonders if those years were merely imagined. Four years is not a long time, but it is obviously long enough to see the disintegration of what was once an energetic and active black women's movement. The history of OWAAD [the Organization of Women of African and Asian Descent] and its subsequent demise has been well documented and discussed, for instance by the Brixton Black Women's Group in their article 'Black Women Organizing' (Amos *et al.*, 1984:84–9) but suffice it to say here that there were some very real grounds for the optimism that many of us felt as we witnessed and became part of the growth of black women's groups around the country; groups that initiated campaigns around education, housing, immigration, health and policing.

• • •

RACIAL IDENTITIES

Another problem that has been more specific to black women and the black communities is that of shifting definitions of black identity. In a[n] article that I wrote on the politics of representation and the work of black women photographers, I argued thus:

> The idea of blackness which in the past has enabled different cultural and racial communities to form alliances and engage in collective political struggle seems to be foregrounded in recent times as an arena for contestation. For some of us there has always been a vigilance against the entrapment of cryptic nationalistic sentiments which rely on biologistic definitions of race. Yet it is once again becoming increasingly important to restate certain basic first principles which have been assumed to be the modus operandi for many black activists in the past: race is a social and political construction and racial identities are created in and through particular historical moments. If the unifying strength of 'blackness' is diminishing because it has become an organising category of a nationalist discourse and is responsible for wasted energies and political

259

> fragmentation then the time is ripe for a radical reassessment. Racial identity alone cannot be a basis for collective organising as the black communities are as beset with divisions around culture, sexuality and class as any other community. . . . The black communities of Britain have discontinuous histories and have been culturally and socially displaced through migration, slavery, indentured labour systems and as political refugees and exiles. The concept of diaspora which embraces the plurality of these different histories and cultural forms is one which allows access into the diversity of articulations around identity and cultural expressions. It is also a way out of the essentialism of certain notions of blackness which refuse to acknowledge or understand the transitory nature of historical and political moments. (Parmar, 1988:9)

While I do want to point here to some of the problems and consequences of identity politics I would not want to conclude that any analysis of the political and cultural articulations around identity should be abandoned. Rather, as Stuart Hall has argued:

> It seems to me that it is possible to think about the nature of new political identities, which isn't founded on the notion of some absolute, integral self and which clearly can't arise from some fully closed narrative of the self. A politics which accepts the 'no necessary or essential correspondence' of anything with anything, and there has to be a *politics of articulation*—politics as a hegemonic project. (Hall, 1987:45)

In trying to find my way towards such a politics I myself have turned to the writings of June Jordan, a black American poet and essayist whose work has clarified many of my doubts and confusions and helped to clear the cobwebs of despair and anger. Val Amos and I found her book *Civil Wars* invaluable when we taught an adult education class on 'Women and Racism' at London University in 1984. At a time when many contemporary movements need to reassess the method and basis of their organizing, June Jordan's moral and political vision offers an inspiration. Her commitment to internationalism and her ability to articulate the complex links and contradictions between the deeply personal and the deeply political in a clear and passionate way is rare. Her writings are a timely reminder that identity politics 'may be enough to get started on but not enough to get anything finished'. She visited Britain for the first time in September 1987 when I talked to her about some of the problems I have outlined above. Below are extracts from this interview by way of a conclusion. (Parmar, 1987)

> PRATIBHA: One of the most interesting and challenging things I have found in your writings is the way in which your radicalism refuses to suppress the complexity of our identities as women and as black people. In Britain there has been a tendency in the women's movement, both black and white, to organise around the assumptions of our shared identities but in the process of political organising many of these assumptions have fallen apart. Can you talk about some of the issues raised around identity politics and what you think it means to define oneself as a political person.
>
> JUNE JORDAN: We have been organising on the basis of identity, around immutable attributes of gender, race and class for a long time and it doesn't seem to have worked. There are obvious reasons for getting together with other people because someone else is black or she is a woman but I think we

have to try to develop habits of evaluation in whatever we attempt politically. People get set into certain ways of doing things and they don't evaluate whether it's working or not. Or if they do evaluate then it's to say it's not working but it's not our fault, there couldn't possibly be anything wrong with our thinking on this subject or this issue. The problem invariably is that the enemy is simply inflexible or impregnable. This is a doomed modus operandi. We have to find out what works and some things may work to a certain extent and not beyond that.

I don't think that gender politics or that race politics per se are isolated from other ways of organising for change, whether reformist change or revolutionary change. I don't think that they will take us where we want to go. I think that's abundantly clear if we look at our history as black people. We as black people have enormous problems everywhere in the world and we women have colossal problems everywhere in the world. I think there is something deficient in the thinking on the part of anybody who proposes either gender identity politics or race identity politics as sufficient, because every single one of us is more than whatever race we represent or embody and more than whatever gender category we fall into. We have other kinds of allegiances, other kinds of dreams that have nothing to do with whether we are white or not white.

A lot of awareness of ourselves as women, as black people and third world people really comes out of our involuntary forced relationships with people who despise us on the basis of what we are rather than what we do. In other words our political awareness of ourselves derives more often than not from a necessity to find out why it is that this particular kind of persecution continues either for my people, or myself or my kind. Once you try to answer that question you find yourself in the territory of people who despise you, people who are responsible for the invention of the term racism or sexism. I think it's important to understand that each one of us is more than what cannot be changed about us. That seems self-evident and accordingly our politics should reflect that understanding.

This is not at all to disparage or dismiss the necessity for what I would call issue oriented unity among different kinds of people, women, black people, or black women. I am not dismissing it but just saying that it's probably not enough. It may be enough to get started on something but I doubt very much whether it's enough to get anything finished.

PRATIBHA: So you are saying that in order to move forward, a crucial part of the political process is to go beyond the personal and experiential ways of organising. You have written, 'It occurs to me that much organisational grief could be avoided if people understood that partnership in misery does not necessarily provide for partnership for change: *when we get the monsters off our backs all of us may want to run in very different directions.*'

JUNE JORDAN: Yes, for example, I think that for any woman who has ever been raped, the existence of feminist or all female rape counselling centres is absolutely necessary, the recourse to a refuge where a woman can retire to repair herself without fear. But the problem is more than an individual problem. She didn't rape herself. In order to eliminate the possibility of rape or even the likelihood of rape for women generally we have to go beyond ourselves. We have to sit down with and/or stand up to and finally in some way impact upon men. I don't think it's ever enough on your own. And I would say the same thing about race identity politics. I didn't, nor did my people or my parents, invent the problems that we as black people have to solve. We black people, the victims of racism are not the ones that have to learn new ways of thinking about things so that we can stop racist habits of thought. Neither do we have the power to be placed in appropriate situations to abolish the social and economic arrangements that have assured the continuity of racism in our lives. That's for white people. What we really need to do is pass the taking of succour from each other, so to speak and build on our collective confidence and pride. Some people who I have met since I have been in London have been saying, it's terrible because nothing is going on politically. But that's not the point. I don't mean to knock that at all, but okay, now you know and I know that something is terrible, what are you going to do about it. Let's not sit inside our sorrows, let's not describe things to death. My orientation is activism. Other than that it's like a kind of vanity or a decadence. I will tell you how I suffer and you tell me how you suffer . . . it's bad enough to suffer but to talk about it endlessly . . . I say to them stop it . . . stop it . . .

PRATIBHA: Many movements such as the women's movement, the black movement and black women's groups have been organising for a number of years around their shared oppressions. But it seems to me that many of these movements are stagnating because there is a refusal to acknowledge the need to move away from modes of being, that is accumulating all the isms of race, sex, class, disability etc, to modes of doing. What do you think are the dangers of this? How do you think we can move forward from this paralysis.

JUNE JORDAN: I am sure there is a danger. The first part of the political process is to recognise that there is a political problem and then to find people who agree with you. But the last part of the political process which is to get rid of it is necessary and something too many of us forget. I am not interested in struggle, I am interested in victory. Let's get rid of the problems, let's not just sit around and talk about it and hold each other's hands. That's where you make the evaluation: is it getting us there, if it's not, then let's have other kinds of meetings with other kinds of people. I think people can get stuck absolutely. What is the purpose of your identity? That is the question. So what? is the way I would put it in my abrupt American way. What do you want to do on the basis of that? You just think that if you fill a room by putting out flyers, with 50 women of the same colour as you, somehow you have accomplished everything you set out to accomplish. I don't think so. Not at all, why are you meeting.

Almost every year black students at Stonybrook where I teach, come around to say to me that they want to hold a meeting and I say, yes and I ask what's it about. They say unity and I say unity for what? I am already black and you are black so we unify okay but I don't need to meet with you about that. When we get together, what's the purpose of that, what do you want to do? I don't need to sit in a room with other people who are black to know that I am black—that's not unity. Unity has to have some purpose to it otherwise we are not talking politics. I don't know what we are talking, maybe a mode of social life. That's okay, but beyond that people have to begin to understand that just because somebody is a woman or somebody is black does not mean that he or she and I should have the same politics. I don't think that's necessarily the case.

We should try to measure each other on the basis of what we do for each other rather than on the basis of who we are.

PRATIBHA: There has been a strong tendency in the women's movement to create hierarchies of oppression. What is your experience of this?

JUNE: I have a tremendous instinctive aversion to the idea of ranking oppression. In other words for nobody to try and corner misery. I think it's dangerous. It seems to me to be an immoral way of going about things. The difficulty here is the sloppiness of language. We call everything an oppression, going to the dentist is an oppression, then the word does not mean anything. Revisions in our language might help and it might also steer us clear from saying something as useless as, but mine is this and yours is that. If I, a black woman poet and writer, a professor of English at state university, if I am oppressed then we need another word to describe a woman in a refugee camp in Palestine or the mother of six in a rural village in Nicaragua or any counterpart inside South Africa.

PRATIBHA: In the last few years there has been much talk about the need for coalitions and alliances between different groups of women not only nationally but internationally. What is your assessment of this form of political organising?

JUNE: I would say about coalitions what I said about unity, which is what for? The issue should determine the social configuration of politics. I am not going to sit in a room with other people just to demonstrate black unity, we have got to have some reason for unity. Why should I coalesce with you and why do you coalesce with me, there has to be a reason why we need each other. It seems to me that an awareness of the necessity for international coalition should not be hard to come by in many spheres of feminist discourse because so many of our problems, apparently have universal currency. I think that never having been to London, for example, I can still be quite sure that most women here, whatever class or colour, are going to feel shy about walking out at night just as I do. I just assume that. That's about safety in the street. There is a universal experience for women, which is that physical mobility is circumscribed by our gender and by the enemies of our gender. This is one of the ways they seek to make us know their hatred and respect it. This holds throughout the world for women and literally we are not to move about in the world freely. If we do then we have to understand that we may have to pay for it with our bodies. That is the threat. They don't ask you what you are doing on the street, they rape you and mutilate you bodily to let you remember your place. You have no rightful place in public.

Everywhere in the world we have the least amount of income, every- where in the world the intensity of the bond between women is seen to be subversive and it seems to me there would be good reasons to attempt international work against some of these common conditions. We cannot eliminate the problems unless we see them in their global dimensions. We should not fear the enlargement of our deliberate connections in this way. We should understand that this is a source of strength. It also makes it more difficult for anyone to destroy our movement. Okay, they can do whatever they want to in London, but there is Bangladesh, it's hydra headed, it's happening everywhere, you can't destroy it. That's not to negate the necessity or obviate the need to work where you live but this is only part of a greater environment. I am talking against short sightedness.

I also think it's a good idea not to have any fixed notions in one's head. I don't want any one to tell me where I should put my attention first. If down the line we can try to respect each other according to the principle of self determination then we can begin to move forward. There are enough of us to go around and you don't have to do what I do and vice versa. I do this and you do that, there is plenty of room.

References

Amos, Val, Lewis, Gail, Mama, Amina and Parmar, Pratibha (1984) editors 'Many Voices, One Chant: Black Feminist Perspectives' *Feminist Review* No. 17.
Barrett, Michele and Mcintosh, Mary (1985) 'Ethnocentrism and Socialist-Feminist Theory' *Feminist Review* No. 20.
Bhavnani, Kum-Kum and Coulson, Margaret (1986) 'Transforming Socialist-Feminism: The Challenge of Racism' *Feminist Review* No. 23.
Carby, Hazel (1982) 'White Women Listen! Black Feminism and the Boundaries of Sisterhood' in Centre for Contemporary Cultural Studies (1982).
Centre for Contemporary Cultural Studies (Race and Politics Group) (1982) *The Empire Strikes Back: Race and Racism in 70s Britain* London: Hutchinson.
Grewal, S., Kay, J., Landor, L., Lewis, G. and Parmar, P. (1988) *Charting the Journey: Writings by Black and Third World Women* London: Sheba.
Hall, Stuart (1987) 'Minimal Selves' in *ICA Documents* 6.
Lewis, Gail and Parmar, Pratibha (1983) 'Black Feminism: Shared Oppression, New Expression' *City Limits* 4–10 March 1983.
Parmar, Pratibha (1987) 'Other Kinds of Dreams: An Interview with June Jordan' *Spare Rib* October 1987.
Parmar, Pratibha (1988) 'Transitory Movements?' *Spectrum Women's Photography Festival Catalogue*.
Ramazongolu, Kazi, Lees and Mirza (1986) 'Feedback: Feminism and Racism' *Feminist Review* No. 22, pp. 82–105.
Segal, Lynne (1987) *Is the Future Female? Troubled Thoughts on Contemporary Feminism* London: Virago Press.

Social Construction Theory: Problems in the History of Sexuality

CAROLE S. VANCE

Social construction theory in the field of sexuality proposed an extremely outrageous idea. It suggested that one of the last remaining outposts of the 'natural' in our thinking was fluid and changeable, the product of human action and history rather than the invariant result of the body, biology, or an innate sex drive.

Empirical and theoretical work on the history of sexuality has grown dramatically in the last twenty years, for which social construction approaches plus the invigorating questions raised by social movements like feminism and lesbian and gay liberation are largely responsible. Indeed, the links between social construction theory and gay activism run very deep. Efforts to transform society inevitably raised questions about the past and the future, as they also called into question prevailing ideological frameworks for examining the 'facts' about sex and gender.

. . . To suggest that any feature of human life, for example, national or ethnic identity, is socially constructed is not to say that it is trivial. Nor is it to say that entire cultures can transform themselves overnight, or that individuals socialized in one cultural tradition can acculturate at whim to another.

. . .

The openness to recognizing difference in behavior and subjective meaning, however, in no way commits the researcher to always finding it, nor does it rule out the discovery of similarity. The very nature of historical and cultural change makes it likely that peoples closely related by time and space will show many continuities.

. . .

THE SEXUAL SUBJECT'S DESIRE FOR HISTORY

A common motivation for fans of lesbian and gay history was a desire to reclaim the past and to insist on lesbian and gay visibility in every place and at every time. But the discoveries of the new sex historians have sometimes proved disturbing, as researchers gave up their initial certainty about the existence of 'gay people' and embarked on a more complicated discussion about the origins of gay identity in the 17th to 19th centuries. In these discussions, sexual acts could not be read as unproblematic indicators of homosexuality; and rather than an unchanging essence which defied legal and religious prohibitions, homosexuality increasingly came to be seen as a variable experience whose boundaries and subjectivity were shaped through complex negotiations between state institutions, individuals, and subcultures.

Variability, subjectivity, negotiation and change often violated the wish for a continuous history. If the point of gay history was to document an ancestry, a gay *Roots*, then for many activists this kind of gay history was frustrating, even a failure. The disappointment and anger at not being able to see oneself reflected in the mirror of history has fueled some of the criticism of social construction theory in the belief that a more essentialist perspective would permit the development of group history and solidarity.

In addition, it is common for mainstream lesbian and gay political and lobbying groups in the United States to use essentialist argument and rhetoric in advancing their case. Lesbians and gays are deserving of civil rights, they say, much like women, ethnic, and racial groups. This argument derives less from a self-conscious theoretical commitment to essentialism and more from the pervasiveness of essentialist frames in American culture, particularly in regard to race and ethnicity. In an ideological system that defines these groups as natural, real, and organized according to relatively unchanging biological features, one obvious and powerful symbolic strategy is to claim an equal status for lesbians and gays. In this ideological and political context, it is to the advantage of all groups struggling for resources to stress not only group unity and historical privilege (buttressed by and documented through histories of the ancestors), but their status as an essential group to which members have no choice in belonging. Fundamentalists and conservatives are fond of ridiculing the analogy between gay rights and minority rights: minorities are 'real' groups to which members can't help but belong through their racial features, whereas no one has to be gay, if he or she simply refrains from sin and lust. Gays and lesbians do not constitute a natural group, rightwingers insist; they are just a bunch of perverts.

In such an arena, gay politicos and lobbyists find it helpful in the short run to respond with assertions about gays through the ages, to assert a claim to a natural group status, and to insist that being gay is an essential, inborn trait about which there is no choice. And, indeed, essentialist arguments about sexual identity can be extended to heterosexuals and used to good advantage: if sexual identity is inborn, or at least fixed by age three, then lesbian or gay schoolteachers pose no threat to students in terms of influencing their identity or development (in an undesirable way, the argument would seem to concede). By dint of repetition, ideas about gay essentialism were reinforced in the contemporary gay movement (though they were hardly unknown in American culture) and, more importantly, linked to group advancement, success, and self-affirmation. Therefore, arguments which opposed or undercut essentialist rhetoric about gay identity were increasingly unfamiliar and heretical, even perceived as damaging to gay interests. Within the lesbian and gay community's internal discussions and self-education, the failure to make a distinction between politically expedient ways of framing an argument and more complex descriptions of social relations promoted an increasingly rigid adherence to essentialism as an effective weapon against persecution.

THE RELATIONSHIP OF MARGINAL GROUPS TO DECONSTRUCTION

In a similar vein, it is ironic to note that in the war of ideas against heterosexual hegemony social construction theory has become most influential only in the intellectual circles of oppositional groups. Social construction theory may be the new orthodoxy in feminist, progressive, and lesbian and gay history circles, but it has made a minimal impact on mainstream authorities and literatures in sexology and biomedicine. These groups continue their investigation and theorizing from the assumption that sexuality is essential. At most, the deviant status of homosexuality calls for inquiry into its etiology (whether hormonal, psychological, or sociological), but the causes of heterosexuality have attracted little interest. In traditional sexual science, heterosexuality remains an unexamined and naturalized category, and little in popular culture causes heterosexuals to consider their sexual identity or its origins and history.

In contrast, the social constructionist framework common in lesbian and gay history has become disseminated to a larger lesbian and gay public. Some wonder whether this constructionist perspective is helpful. What are its implications? Why should lesbians and gays have a developed consciousness that their sexual identities have been 'constructed', when heterosexuals do not? Does this intellectual sophistication lead to a sense of group frailty instead of robustness? And does any history of construction inevitably pose the theoretical possibility of a future deconstruction, even disappearance, which is alarming and uncomfortable? The retorts of Dorothy Allison and Esther Newton at recent conferences—'deconstruct heterosexuality first!' and 'I'll deconstruct when they deconstruct'—reflect in their immediacy and robustness both anxiety about group dissolution and the improbability of such a development.

The tension here is identical to a tension felt within feminism, which simultaneously holds two somewhat contradictory goals. One goal is to attack the gender system and its primacy in organizing social life, but the second goal is to defend women as a group. Defending women or advancing their interest (in equal pay, abortion rights, or child care, for example) emphasizes their status as a special group with a unique collective interest, distinct from men, thus replaying and perhaps reinforcing the very gender dichotomy crucial to the system of gender oppression.

The same irresolvable tension exists within the lesbian and gay movement, which on the one hand attacks a naturalized system of sexual hierarchy which categorizes and stabilizes desires and privileges some over others, and on the other hand defends the interest of 'lesbian and gay people', which tends to reify identity and essential nature in a political process I've described. There is no solution here, since to abandon either goal for the other would be foolish. Real, live lesbians and gays need to be defended in an oppressive system, and the sexual hierarchy which underlies that oppression, needs to be attacked on every level, particularly on the intellectual and conceptual levels where naturalized systems of domination draw so much of their energy. There is no easy solution here, but even an awareness of this tension can be helpful, since it powerfully contributes to the larger political and emotional climate in which social construction theory is received, and rightly so.

Gender and Power

Society, the Person and Sexual Politics

R. W. CONNELL

HEGEMONIC MASCULINITY AND EMPHASIZED FEMININITY

The central argument can be put in a few paragraphs. There is an ordering of versions of femininity and masculinity at the level of the whole society, in some ways analogous to the patterns of face-to-face relationship within institutions. The possibilities of variation, of course, are vastly greater. The sheer complexity of relationships involving millions of people guarantees that ethnic differences and generational differences as well as class patterns come into play. But in key respects the organization of gender on the very large scale must be more skeletal and simplified than the human relationships in face-to-face milieux. The forms of femininity and masculinity constituted at this level are stylized and impoverished. Their interrelation is centred on a single structural fact, the global dominance of men over women.

This structural fact provides the main basis for relationships among men that define a hegemonic form of masculinity in the society as a whole. 'Hegemonic masculinity' is always constructed in relation to various subordinated masculinities as well as in relation to women. The interplay between different forms of masculinity is an important part of how a patriarchal social order works.

There is no femininity that is hegemonic in the sense that the dominant form of masculinity is hegemonic among men. This is not a new observation. Viola Klein's historical study of conceptions of 'the feminine character' noted wryly how little the leading theorists could agree on what it was: 'we find not only contradiction on particular points but a bewildering variety of traits considered characteristic of women by the various authorities'. More recently the French analyst Luce

Irigaray, in a celebrated essay 'This Sex Which Is Not One', has emphasized the absence of any clear-cut definition for women's eroticism and imagination in a patriarchal society.

At the level of mass social relations, however, forms of femininity are defined clearly enough. It is the global subordination of women to men that provides an essential basis for differentiation. One form is defined around compliance with this subordination and is oriented to accommodating the interests and desires of men. I will call this 'emphasized femininity'. Others are defined centrally by strategies of resistance or forms of non-compliance. Others again are defined by complex strategic combinations of compliance, resistance and co-operation. The interplay among them is a major part of the dynamics of change in the gender order as a whole.

The rest of this section will examine more closely the cases of hegemonic masculinity and emphasized femininity, making brief comments on subordinated and marginalized forms. . . .

In the concept of hegemonic masculinity, 'hegemony' means (as in Gramsci's analyses of class relations in Italy from which the term is borrowed) a social ascendancy achieved in a play of social forces that extends beyond contests of brute power into the organization of private life and cultural processes. Ascendancy of one group of men over another achieved at the point of a gun, or by the threat of unemployment, is not hegemony. Ascendancy which is embedded in religious doctrine and practice, mass media content, wage structures, the design of housing, welfare/taxation policies and so forth, is.

Two common misunderstandings of the concept should be cleared up immediately. First, though 'hegemony' does not refer to ascendancy based on force, it is not incompatible with ascendancy based on force. Indeed it is common for the two to go together. Physical or economic violence backs up a dominant cultural pattern (for example beating up 'perverts'), or ideologies justify the holders of physical power ('law and order'). The connection between hegemonic masculinity and patriarchal violence is close, though not simple.

Second, 'hegemony' does not mean total cultural dominance, the obliteration of alternatives. It means ascendancy achieved within a balance of forces, that is, a state of play. Other patterns and groups are subordinated rather than eliminated. If we do not recognize this it would be impossible to account for the everyday contestation that actually occurs in social life, let alone for historical changes in definitions of gender patterns on the grand scale.

Hegemonic masculinity, then, is very different from the notion of a general 'male sex role', though the concept allows us to formulate more precisely some of the sound points made in the sex-role literature. First, the cultural ideal (or ideals) of masculinity need not correspond at all closely to the actual personalities of the majority of men. Indeed the winning of hegemony often involves the creation of models of masculinity which are quite specifically fantasy figures, such as the film characters played by Humphrey Bogart, John Wayne and Sylvester Stallone. Or real models may be publicized who are so remote from everyday achievement that they have the effect of an unattainable ideal, like the Australian Rules footballer Ron Barassi or the boxer Muhammed Ali.

As we move from face-to-face settings to structures involving millions of people, the easily symbolized aspects of interaction become more prominent. Hegemonic masculinity is very public. In a society of mass communications it is tempting to think that it exists only as publicity. Hence the focus on media images and media discussions of masculinity in the 'Books About Men' of the 1970s and 1980s, from Warren Farrell's *The Liberated Man* to Barbara Ehrenreich's *The Hearts of Men.*

To focus on the media images alone would be a mistake. They need not correspond to the actual characters of the men who hold most social power—in contemporary societies the corporate and state elites. Indeed a ruling class may allow a good deal of sexual dissent. A minor but dramatic instance is the tolerance for homosexuality that the British diplomat Guy Burgess could assume from other men of his class during his career as a Soviet spy. The public face of hegemonic masculinity is not necessarily what powerful men are, but what sustains their power and what large numbers of men are motivated to support. The notion of 'hegemony' generally implies a large measure of consent. Few men are Bogarts or Stallones, many collaborate in sustaining those images.

There are various reasons for complicity, and a thorough study of them would go far to illuminate the whole system of sexual politics. Fantasy gratification is one—nicely satirized in Woody Allen's Bogart take-off, *Play it Again, Sam.* Displaced aggression might be another—and the popularity of very violent movies from *Dirty Harry* to *Rambo* suggest that a great deal of this is floating around. But it seems likely that the major reason is that most men benefit from the subordination of women, and hegemonic masculinity is the cultural expression of this ascendancy.

This needs careful formulation. It does not imply that hegemonic masculinity means being particularly nasty to women. Women may feel as oppressed by non-hegemonic masculinities, may even find the hegemonic pattern more familiar and manageable. There is likely to be a kind of 'fit' between hegemonic masculinity and emphasized femininity. What it does imply is the maintenance of practices that institutionalize men's dominance over women. In this sense hegemonic masculinity must embody a successful collective strategy in relation to women. Given the complexity of gender relations no simple or uniform strategy is possible: a 'mix' is necessary. So hegemonic masculinity can contain at the same time, quite consistently, openings towards domesticity and openings towards violence, towards misogyny and towards heterosexual attraction.

Hegemonic masculinity is constructed in relation to women and to subordinated masculinities. These other masculinities need not be as clearly defined—indeed, achieving hegemony may consist precisely in preventing alternatives gaining cultural definition and recognition as alternatives, confining them to ghettos, to privacy, to unconsciousness.

The most important feature of contemporary hegemonic masculinity is that it is heterosexual, being closely connected to the institution of marriage; and a key form of subordinated masculinity is homosexual. This subordination involves both direct interactions and a kind of ideological warfare. Some of the interactions were . . . police and legal harassment, street violence, economic discrimination.

These transactions are tied together by the contempt for homosexuality and homosexual men that is part of the ideological package of hegemonic masculinity. The AIDS scare has been marked less by sympathy for gays as its main victims than by hostility to them as the bearers of a new threat. The key point of media concern is whether the 'gay plague' will spread to 'innocent', i.e., straight, victims.

In other cases of subordinated masculinity the condition is temporary. Cynthia Cockburn's splendid study of printing workers in London portrays a version of hegemonic masculinity that involved ascendancy over young men as well as over women. The workers recalled their apprenticeships in terms of drudgery and humiliation, a ritual of induction into trade and masculinity at the same time. But once they were in, they were 'brothers'.

Several general points about masculinity also apply to the analysis of femininity at the mass level. These patterns too are historical: relationships change, new forms of femininity emerge and others disappear. The ideological representations of femininity draw on, but do not necessarily correspond to, actual femininities as they are lived. What most women support is not necessarily what they are.

There is however a fundamental difference. All forms of femininity in this society are constructed in the context of the overall subordination of women to men. For this reason there is no femininity that holds among women the position held by hegemonic masculinity among men.

This fundamental asymmetry has two main aspects. First, the concentration of social power in the hands of men leaves limited scope for women to construct institutionalized power relationships over other women. It does happen on a face-to-face basis, notably in mother–daughter relationships. Institutionalized power hierarchies have also existed in contexts like the girls' schools pictured in *Mädchen in Uniform* and *Frost in May*. But the note of domination that is so important in relations between kinds of masculinity is muted. The much lower level of violence between women than violence between men is a fair indication of this. Second, the organization of a hegemonic form around dominance over the other sex is absent from the social construction of femininity. Power, authority, aggression, technology are not thematized in femininity at large as they are in masculinity. Equally important, no pressure is set up to negate or subordinate other forms of femininity in the way hegemonic masculinity must negate other masculinities. It is likely therefore that actual femininities in our society are more diverse than actual masculinities.

The dominance structure which the construction of femininity cannot avoid is the global dominance of heterosexual men. The process is likely to polarize around compliance or resistance to this dominance.

The option of compliance is central to the pattern of femininity which is given most cultural and ideological support at present, called here 'emphasized femininity'. This is the translation to the large scale of patterns already discussed in particular institutions and milieux, such as the display of sociability rather than technical competence, fragility in mating scenes, compliance with men's desire for titillation and ego-stroking in office relationships, acceptance of marriage and childcare as a response to labour-market discrimination against women. At the mass level these are organized around themes of sexual receptivity in relation to younger women and motherhood in relation to older women.

Like hegemonic masculinity, emphasized femininity as a cultural construction is very public, though its content is specifically linked with the private realm of the home and the bedroom. Indeed it is promoted in mass media and marketing with an insistence and on a scale far beyond that found for any form of masculinity. The articles and advertisements in mass-circulation women's magazines, the 'women's pages' of mass-circulation newspapers and the soap operas and 'games' of daytime television, are familiar cases. Most of this promotion, it might be noted, is organized, financed and supervised by men.

To call this pattern 'emphasized femininity' is also to make a point about how the cultural package is used in interpersonal relationships. This kind of femininity is performed, and performed especially to men. There is a great deal of folklore about how to sustain the performance. It is a major concern of women's magazines from *Women's Weekly* to *Vogue*. It is even taken up and turned into highly ambivalent comedy by Hollywood (*How to Marry a Millionaire; Tootsie*). Marilyn Monroe was both archetype and satirist of emphasized femininity. Marabel Morgan's 'total woman', an image that somehow mixes sexpot and Jesus Christ, uses the same tactics and has the same ambivalences.

Femininity organized as an adaptation to men's power, and emphasizing compliance, nurturance and empathy as womanly virtues, is not in much of a state to establish hegemony over other kinds of femininity. There is a familiar paradox about antifeminist women's groups like 'Women Who Want to be Women' who exalt the *Kinder, Kirche und Küche* version of femininity: they can only become politically active by subverting their own prescriptions. They must rely heavily on religious ideology and on political backing from conservative men. The relations they establish with other kinds of femininity are not so much domination as attempted marginalization.

Central to the maintenance of emphasized femininity is practice that prevents other models of femininity gaining cultural articulation. When feminist historiography describes women's experience as 'hidden from history', in Sheila Rowbotham's phrase, it is responding partly to this fact. Conventional historiography recognizes, indeed presupposes, conventional femininity. What is hidden from it is the experience of spinsters, lesbians, unionists, prostitutes, madwomen, rebels and maiden aunts, manual workers, midwives and witches. And what is involved in radical sexual politics, in one of its dimensions, is precisely a reassertion and recovery of marginalized forms of femininity in the experience of groups like these.

FURTHER READING FOR CHAPTER 9

Anthias, F., and N. Yuval-Davis. 1983. "Contextualizing Feminism: Gender, Ethnic and Class Divisions." *Feminist Review* 15.

Barrett, M. 1988. *Women's Oppression Today: The Marxist/Feminist Encounter*, rev. ed. London: Verso

Barrett, M., and M. McIntosh. 1985. "Ethnocentrism and Socialist Feminist Theory." *Feminist Review* 20: 23–47.

Beechey, V. 1987. *Unequal Work*. London: Verso.

Bruegel, I. 1989. "Sex and Race in the Labour Market." *Feminist Review*, 1989.

Campbell, B. 1980. "Feminist Sexual Politics." *Feminist Review* 5: 1–18.

Collins, X. 1989. "The Social Construction of Black Feminist Thought." *Signs*.

Crowley, H., and Susan Himmelweit (eds.). 1992. *Knowing Women*. Cambridge: Polity Press.

Connell, R. W. 1987. *Gender and Power*, chap. 8, pp. 183–188. Cambridge: Polity Press.

Hooks, B. 1984. *Ain't I a Woman? Black Women and Feminism*. London: Pluto Press.

McDowell, L., and R. Pringle (eds.). 1992. *Defining Women*. Cambridge: Polity Press.

Parmar, P. 1989. "Other Kinds of Dreams." *Feminist Review* 31: 55–65.

Phillips, A. (ed.). 1986. *Feminism and Equality*. Oxford: Blackwell.

———. 1987. "Class Matters." In *Divided Loyalties*, chap. 2, pp. 15–21. London: Virago.

Rich, C. 1980. "Compulsory Heterosexuality and Lesbian Existence." *Signs* 5 (Summer): 631–660.

Rutherford, J. (eds.). 1990. *Identity, Community, Cultural Difference*. London: Lawrence and Wishart.

Segal, L. 1987. *Is the Future Female*. London: Virago.

———. 1990. *Slow Motion: Changing Masculinities, Changing Men*, chap. 10, pp. 279–294. London: Virago.

Credits

Chapter 1

Vicky Randall. "Feminism and Political Analysis," *Political Studies, 39,* 1991.

Sandra Harding. "The Instability of Analytical Categories of Feminist Theory," *Signs, 11,* 1986, p. 4.

Chapter 2

Carol Christy. "Trends in Sex Differences in Political Participation: A Comparative Perspective." (Unpublished paper)

Jewel L. Prestage. "In Quest of the African American Political Woman," *Annals of the American Academy of Political and Social Sciences, 515,* May 1992, pp. 88-103.

Chapter 3

Pamela Johnston Conover. "Feminists and the Gender Gap," *Journal of Politics, 50* (4), November 1988, pp. 985-1010.

Nancy J. Walker. "What We Know About Women Voters in Britain, France, and West Germany," *Public Opinion,* May/June 1988, pp. 49-55.

Jo Freeman. "Feminism vs. Family Values: Women at the 1992 Democratic and Republican Conventions," *PS,* March 1993, pp. 21-28.

Chapter 4

R. Darcy, Susan Welch, and Janet Clark. "Women as Congressional Candidates." *Women, Elections and Representation* (New York: Longman, 1987).

Eliza Newlin Carney. "Weighing In," *National Journal,* June 13, 1992, pp. 1399-1403.

Janet Clark. "Getting There: Women in Political Office," *Annals of the American Academy of Political and Social Science, 515,* May 1991, pp. 62-76.

Marjorie Randon Hershey. "The Year of the Woman?" In Gerald Pomper (ed.), *The Election of 1992: Reports and Interpretations* (Chatham, N.J.: Chatham House, 1993), pp. 177-180.

Pippa Norris. *The Impact of Electoral Systems on Women in Politics.* (Unpublished paper)

Chapter 5

Diane Sainsbury. *Gender and Comparative Analysis: Welfare States, State Theories and Social Policies.* (Unpublished paper)

Gertrude Schaffner Goldberg and Eleanor Kremen (eds.). *The Feminization of Poverty: Not Only in America?* (New York: Praeger, 1990), pp. 201-217.

Joni Lovenduski and Joyce Outshoorn. "Introduction." *The New Politics of Abortion* (London: Sage, 1986).

Dorothy McBride Stetson. *Abortion Rights in Russia, the United States, and France.* (Unpublished paper)

Carole Goldberg-Ambrose. "Unfinished Business in Rape Reform," *Journal of Social Issues, 48* (1), 1992, pp. 173-185.

R. Amy Elman and Maud L. Edwards. "Unprotected by the Swedish Welfare State: A Survey of Battered Women and the Assistance They Received," *Women's Studies International Forum, 14* (5), 1991, pp. 413-421.

Chapter 6

Ethel Klein. "The Diffusion of Consciousness in the United States and Western Europe." In Marie Fainsod Katzenstein and Carol McClurg Mueller (eds.), *The Women's Movement of the United States and Western Europe: Consciousness, Political Opportunity and Public Policy* (Philadelphia: Temple University Press, 1987).

Robyn Rowland. "Women Who Do and Women Who Don't, Join the Women's Movement: Issues for Conflict and Collaboration," *Sex Roles, 14* (11/12), 1986.

Alma Garcia. "The Development of Chicana Feminist Discourse 1970-1980," *Gender and Society, 2* (2), 1989.

Eleanore Kofman and Rosemary Sales. "Towards Fortress Europe?" *Women's Studies International Forum,* (1) 1992.

Chapter 7

Gisela Kaplan. *Contemporary Western European Feminism* (UCL Press Ltd, 1992), xxii-xxv.

Toril Moi. "From Simone de Beauvoir to Jacques Lacan." Chapter 5 of *Sexual/Textual Politics* (London: Routledge, 1985). (1988 reprint)

Gemma Tang Nain. "Black Women, Sexism and Racism," *Feminist Review*, 37, Spring 1991.

Chapter 8

J. B. Elshtain. "Ethics in the Women's Movement," *Annals of the American Academy of Political and Social Sciences, 515*, May 1991, pp. 126-139.

Carole Pateman. "Does Sex Matter to Democracy?—A Comment," *Scandinavian Political Studies, 13* (1), 1990, pp.57-63.

Chapter 9

Anne Phillips. "Class Matters." Chapter 2 of *Divided Loyalties* (London: Virago, 1987), pp. 15-21.

Pratibha Parmar. "Other Kinds of Dreams," *Feminist Review, 13*, 1989, pp. 55-65.

Carole S. Vance. "Social Construction Theory: Problems in the History of Sexuality." In D. Altman et al. (eds.), *Homosexuality, Which Homosexuality: Essays from the International Scientific Conference on Gay and Lesbian Studies* (Amsterdam/Schorer/London: GMP Publishers, 1989), pp. 13-34.

R. W. Connell. *Gender and Power* (Cambridge: Polity, 1987), pp. 183-188.